The Rise of Mike Tyson,
Heavyweight

ALSO BY WILLIAM F. MCNEIL
AND FROM MCFARLAND

*Black Baseball Out of Season: Pay for Play Outside
of the Negro Leagues* (2007; paperback 2012)

Red Sox Roll Call: 200 Memorable Players, 1901–2011 (2012)

*All-Stars for All Time: A Sabermetric Ranking of the
Major League Best, 1876–2007* (2009)

*The California Winter League: America's First Integrated
Professional Baseball League* (2002; paperback 2008)

Miracle in Chavez Ravine: The Los Angeles Dodgers in 1988 (2008)

*Backstop: A History of the Catcher and a Sabermetric
Ranking of 50 All-Time Greats* (2006)

The Evolution of Pitching in Major League Baseball (2006)

*Cool Papas and Double Duties: The All-Time Greats of the
Negro Leagues* (2001; paperback 2005)

*Visitors to Ancient America: The Evidence for European and
Asian Presence in America Prior to Columbus* (2005)

Gabby Hartnett: The Life and Times of the Cubs' Greatest Catcher (2004)

*The Single-Season Home Run Kings: Ruth, Maris,
McGwire, Sosa, and Bonds, 2d ed.* (2003)

*Baseball's Other All-Stars: The Greatest Players from the Negro Leagues,
the Japanese Leagues, the Mexican League, and the Pre–1960 Winter
Leagues in Cuba, Puerto Rico and the Dominican Republic* (2000)

*Ruth, Maris, McGwire and Sosa: Baseball's Single
Season Home Run Champions* (1999)

*The King of Swat: An Analysis of Baseball's Home Run Hitters from the
Major, Minor, Negro and Japanese Leagues* (1997)

The Rise of Mike Tyson, Heavyweight

William F. McNeil

McFarland & Company, Inc., Publishers
Jefferson, North Carolina

LIBRARY OF CONGRESS CATALOGUING-IN-PUBLICATION DATA

McNeil, William.
The rise of Mike Tyson, heavyweight / William F. McNeil.
p. cm.
Includes bibliographical references and index.

ISBN 978-0-7864-9648-8 (softcover : acid free paper) ∞
ISBN 978-1-4766-1802-9 (ebook)

1. Tyson, Mike, 1966– 2. Boxers (Sports)—United States—Biography.
3. African American boxers—Biography. I. Title.
GV1132.T97M37 2014   796.83092—dc23   [B]   2014029922

BRITISH LIBRARY CATALOGUING DATA ARE AVAILABLE

© 2014 William F. McNeil. All rights reserved

*No part of this book may be reproduced or transmitted in any form
or by any means, electronic or mechanical, including photocopying
or recording, or by any information storage and retrieval system,
without permission in writing from the publisher.*

On the cover: Mike Tyson before his match with Steve Zouski
on March 10, 1986, at Nassau Coliseum in Uniondale, New York (Paul Post)

Printed in the United States of America

*McFarland & Company, Inc., Publishers
Box 611, Jefferson, North Carolina 28640
www.mcfarlandpub.com*

To my wife Janet
who was always there to provide me with
support and encouragement and, along the way,
gave me 64 years of beautiful memories.

Acknowledgments

I wish to thank all those people who generously contributed to the production of this book.

In particular I wish to thank Michael Marton, producer of the timeless and historic television documentary *Watch Me Now*, the story of Cus D'Amato and the Catskill Boxing Club. With Mr. Marton's permission, I have drawn freely from his material to produce the flavor of Mike Tyson's early days in Catskill.

Roger Sala, former business executive and boxing manager, captured Cus D'Amato's philosophy of life on an audiocassette, which he graciously allowed me to utilize.

Gunther Hafner, former publisher of the *Catskill Daily Mail*, permitted me to draw freely from information on the career of Mike Tyson that appeared in the *Daily Mail*.

Many other individuals and organizations also permitted me to draw from their knowledge of Mike Tyson and the boxing game, including the *Albany Times Union*, United Press International, the *Berkshire Eagle*, the *Times Herald-Record* of Middletown, New York, Dardis McNamee, editor of *Capital Region Magazine*, *People Weekly* magazine, and Home Box Office, Inc.

Other sources consulted during the research for this book included the *Springfield Republican*, the *Boston Globe*, the *New York Post*, the *New York Daily News*, *Sports Illustrated*, *Ring Magazine*, *KO Magazine*, *World Boxing*, *Boxing Scene*, WNYT Channel 13 (Albany, N.Y.), WTEN Channel 10 (Albany, N.Y.), ABC-TV Sports, ESPN, WNYW Channel 5 (New York), the *Philadelphia Inquirer*, *The Atlantic City Press*, *Vanity Fair*, *Time*, *GQ*, *Boxing Illustrated*, and *The Greene County News*.

In addition, I interviewed numerous people who knew Mike Tyson—childhood friends from Brooklyn, friends from Catskill, boxing associates, trainers, teachers, and neighbors.

Paul Post, Paul Antonelli, and Teddy Atlas generously provided me with photographs to enhance the manuscript.

And a special thanks to Sally Talay, formerly of the *Catskill Daily Mail*, for her cooperation during my research.

Table of Contents

Acknowledgments vi
Prologue 1

1. From Brownsville to Johnstown 3
2. The Man—Cus D'Amato 12
3. The Birth of a Boxer—1980–1981 25
4. The Quest Begins—1982 47
5. A Taste of Glory—1983 64
6. The Fall and Rise of Mike Tyson—1984 77
7. Assault on the Professional Ranks—1985 99
8. The Road to the Championship—1986 129
9. Everest Conquered—November 22, 1986 157
10. The Unification and Beyond—1987 183
11. The People's Champion—June 27, 1988 214

Epilogue 230
Appendix: The Complete Amateur and Professional Boxing Record to June 27, 1988 231
Chapter Notes 235
Bibliography 238
Index 239

Prologue

"Hey, little fairy boy, you should wear a dress like your sister."

"Ladies and gentlemen, I give you the 1986 Boxer of the Year, the new WBC heavyweight champion of the world, and the youngest man ever to wear the crown."

The little fairy boy and the heavyweight champion of the world have a lot in common. They are the same person. His name is Mike Tyson.

This is his story.

1

From Brownsville to Johnstown

The Mike Tyson story began in the Fort Green section of Brooklyn on a hot muggy day in the summer of 1966. An eight-pound baby named Michael Gerard Tyson was born on June 30 in Cumberland Hospital, the third child of Lorna Tyson and Jimmy Kirkpatrick. Lorna Tyson, born Lorna Smith somewhere in the South in 1930, relocated to Brooklyn after World War II. She married Percel Tyson when she was very young, but they were subsequently divorced. Lorna never remarried but she always needed a man, earning her a reputation for being promiscuous as well as for being alcohol dependent. She met and moved in with a big, boisterous laborer named Jimmy Kirkpatrick who, according to her son Mike, may have been a drug dealer and a pimp. Kirkpatrick reportedly had fathered 16 children with various women, three of them with Lorna: Rodney, five years older than Mike, Denise, one year older than Mike, and Mike. She took the Kirkpatrick name even though she never married Jimmy, and after Jimmy was hospitalized with a heart condition and subsequently deserted her and the children before Mike was born, she brought home a new boyfriend, Edward Gillison. As Tyson would note in later years, it was a dysfunctional family. One of her boyfriends beat her up one day but was soon forgiven when he returned to the apartment with liquor and cigarettes. Another boyfriend was thrown out of the apartment after he tried to molest Denise.

Lorna Tyson deserved better than life in the ghetto. The 36-year-old single mother had her problems but she combed her Brooklyn neighborhoods in search of opportunity, only to find, like thousands before her, nothing but poverty and misery in the segregated sewers of the great northern city. With no man to bring home a regular paycheck, she was forced to subsist as best she could on public assistance. Still, in spite of the poverty and violence that dominated her world, she was able to provide the strong mother image that seemed to be the nucleus of so many black urban families in the 1960s and 1970s. One of Tyson's friends said Lorna was a tough lady, given to violent outbursts, and he kept his distance from her. Be that as it may, Lorna Tyson made a superhuman effort to shield her children from the evil outside influences that pervaded the crime-ridden New York City suburb. But her efforts on behalf of her children were only partially successful. Rodney and Denise survived the violence and degradation that was part of their life in Brownsville, but young Mike was not as fortunate. Rodney, a good student, enlisted in the United States Navy after graduation from high school and continued his education following his discharge, eventually becoming a physician's assistant in a Los Angeles trauma center. Mike would admit in later years to a love-hate relationship with his brother. "I was really envious of Rodney. I hated my brother.

Everybody loved my brother and sister. They always had more dignity and pride. I was always jealous of them because they had nothing but everybody in the neighborhood loved them. My brother was always something and I was nothing."[1] Denise married Roger Anderson, moved to Queens, and had two children before succumbing to a heart attack in 1991.

Lorna Tyson kept her children by her side as long as possible, and during their formative years she tried to teach them right from wrong along with respect for people and for people's property. Shortly after Mike was born, his brother Rodney began his association with the hostile outside world, leaving the family cocoon daily to attend the nearby public school. Mike was left at home with his mother and his sister Denise, Nisee to her friends, and that situation created serious problems for Mike when it was his turn to leave the cocoon. He spent hours playing with his sister in the apartment, and Mike's gentle nature and quiet personality were developed during these sessions. Combined with a soft, high-pitched voice and a lisp, it left him with some effeminate characteristics that went unmentioned at home but became a source of great embarrassment to Mike once he came in contact with children outside the home.

When he passed his fifth birthday, the youngest member of the Tyson clan was cut loose from his mother's apron strings and cast adrift on the sea of life. The first few years were a painful and humiliating journey for the youngster. Every morning he kissed his mother goodbye and set out with his brother Rodney, books in hand, for school. The classroom instruction was strange and frightening to young Mike, but he eagerly tried to adapt to the new environment and social structure. He struggled with reading, writing and the rudiments of mathematics, leaving him frustrated and bewildered. School was a definite learning experience, but it was outside school, in the schoolyards and the streets, where Mike's real education began.

Mike Tyson's early school years in Bedford-Stuyvesant were unhappy. He was a timid, chubby little kid with eyeglasses, who spoke softly and lisped. He was one of the poorest kids in a poor neighborhood. His clothes were always ragged and dirty, and his shoes bore holes worn through by previous owners. His small size and sensitive nature made him the perfect target for the self-appointed school toughs, particularly the fifth- and sixth-graders who were grooming themselves for membership in the neighborhood street gangs. It was during this period that Mike first heard the taunts of "little fairy boy" along the school corridors and on the sidewalks of Brooklyn. He was also called "Bummy Mike" by the arrogant Brooklyn bullies. Many days, after school, the beleaguered six-year-old would run back to the safety of his apartment with tears streaming down his face, and would cower in a corner until his mother came home to comfort him. One time, a boy took his milk and his glasses, drank the milk and dropped the glasses into the gas tank of a parked truck.[2]

In 1976, the Tyson family moved "cross-town," four blocks to be exact, to the Brownsville section of Brooklyn. Brownsville was the stereotypical slum, a barren, battered, battle zone of abandoned cars, junk-filled fields, and garbage-strewn streets. Desolate tenements stood like toy soldiers, cold and forlorn, their plastic-covered windows and boarded-up doors casting a pall over the inner city. Periodically, the silence was broken by the piercing wail of a siren. Here, a police cruiser responded to an armed robbery in progress. There, an ambulance arrived to remove the body of a dead prostitute from Lincoln Terrace Park. Brownsville became Mike Tyson's hometown. His first home, on Howard Street, was a squalid, rat-infested hovel, without heat or running water. Obscenities decorated the walls and stairwells of the building. Garbage littered the floor. When summer came, the stench from decaying matter became almost unbearable. Lorna Tyson tried her best to preserve a semblance of dignity within the family, but the falling plaster, the broken windows, the roaches and rats, fought her every step of the way. Within months, the building was condemned. It was eventually demolished to make way for a new housing development, and the uprooted Tyson clan moved again, this time to 178 Amboy Street, Apartment 2A, nearby.

As tough as Bed-Stuy was, Brownsville was ten times worse. In fact, it was said that Brownsville made Bedford-Stuyvesant look like Beverly Hills.[3] The taunts of "little fairy boy" became louder and more frequent in Mike's new school, and the bullying and physical beatings became a daily routine. His journeys to Hopkinson Playground were often interrupted by local bullies who stole his possessions, then beat him up and chased him home, dirty, crying, and bleeding. It was about this time that Mike developed an interest in pigeons, commonly known as "street rats," as an escape from the squalid world that awaited him in the streets below. Many of the city kids took up the hobby of raising pigeons on the rooftops of Brooklyn, to take them away from the dirt and clamor of the city sidewalks, and free them from the dangers that lurked in every alleyway and around every corner. Mike captured some pigeons in the city park, stole money from someone's house to buy other pigeons, and built a wooden coop atop the old Vanderbilt Hotel to house them. In time, he assembled a family of almost 100 of the loving birds. When he was with his pigeons, Mike's innate gentle nature surfaced and he was at peace with the world. He would sit with his pigeons for hours, talking to them and sending them skyward to fly in peace over the squalor of the city. When they were sick he would nurse them, and when it was cold he would move them inside. Unfortunately, the interludes with his feathered friends were much too short, and the time spent on the sidewalks of Brooklyn was much too long. The quagmire of the ghetto dragged him inexorably downward to a life of violence and petty crime.

The Rattleys were neighbors of the Tysons in Brownsville, and Mike Tyson stayed with them overnight when he visited Brooklyn years later. Michelle Rattley remembered that the Tysons were poor, that nine-year-old Mike was big for his age, and that his clothes were always dirty. Michelle said the quiet youngster didn't go to school much. He spent his time mostly "sloppin' pigeons." Michelle's older sister, Dolores, said that Tyson was always a bad kid. There was a rumor that Tyson and a friend got caught stealing a pigeon. The friend was hanged off a fire escape and Tyson was almost hanged before help arrived, but Dolores said nobody got hanged. That was a lie. She said Mike did a lot of bad things but he was never involved in a murder. Grace Rattley added that you might not like Mike's mother Lorna because she was an alcoholic and she was not a good housekeeper, but she was always good to the kids and stuck up for Mike. The apartment, however, was cluttered and dirty, and the kids were never clean. They had to look out for themselves.[4]

Young Mike Tyson was not yet 11 years old when his life changed abruptly, thrusting him into the depraved world of the inner city. By this time he had filled out physically and was bigger than most boys his age. He was short, but stocky, with a thick neck and broad shoulders. But he still had a gentle and passive nature, and an inferiority complex to match. That changed quickly when two of the neighborhood bullies invaded his rooftop domain and stole one of his street rats. Mike yelled for help. "I said, 'Mommy, please. They're taking my birds.' I called my mom to help me. One guy took the bird and he just ripped open the neck, and he just put the bird in my face. Somebody said, 'Mike, fight him.' And I just fought him."[5]

For the first time in his life, he attacked someone with his fists. The violent force of clenched fist against bare skin and bone felt good, and it started the adrenaline flowing. His body exploded with a burst of energy and he hit the boy again—and again—and again— releasing years of pent-up frustration. The older boy backed off, not knowing what to make of this little monster he had set loose. Mike struck again. His fist crashed against the bigger boy's face. Blood spurted from the boy's mouth. Another punch smashed the boy's nose, breaking it. The boy tried to fight back. He flailed away at the half-crazed boy, but Mike walked right through his punches and continued to batter him with both hands. Finally the thief had enough and fled, leaving young Tyson bloody and breathing hard but fully satisfied.[6]

Mike Tyson had discovered the love of fighting, and things would never be the same for him. He enjoyed the physical contact and the one-on-one confrontation. Daily fights became second nature to him—fights with fists, sticks, bricks, or knives. It didn't make any difference to him. Physical encounters became part of Mike's new world. He himself estimated that he had as many as seven fights a day.[7] As Nisee admitted, "Mike loved beating people up." One morning Mike woke up to find that his favorite pigeon, Julius, had died. He planned to bury Julius but when he went inside to get something, a sanitation worker took the crate containing the pigeon and put it in the crusher in the garbage truck. An enraged Tyson raced to the scene too late to recover Julius, so he took his frustration out on the sanitation worker, knocking him cold with one punch.[8]

Mike's stature in the neighborhood grew with each fight. His talent for brawling eventually brought him to the attention of one of the local street gangs, a group of fuzzy-cheeked thieves his own age, who got their kicks out of vandalism and petty crime. Mike and his new buddies entertained themselves in the evenings by terrorizing late-night pedestrians along Rockaway Avenue and Sutter Avenue. They also ran roughshod through the subway trains, snatching jewelry and purses from frightened old ladies as they went. Most inhabitants of Brownsville dreaded the night. With darkness came the street gangs, and with the street gangs came the muggings, the rapes, and the murders. The streets of Brownsville were not safe to walk once the sun went down, so most people stayed inside their apartments, bolted their doors, lowered the shades, and waited for morning. Better to battle the four-legged rodents inside the building than to challenge the two-legged variety that roamed Rockaway Avenue. At least the rats wouldn't slit your throat for a buck. But even the apartment was no guarantee of safety. The street gangs also specialized in nighttime burglaries, an activity that almost cost the 11-year-old Tyson his life. He and his gang concentrated on empty apartments. Whenever they located a vacant one, they would break in and ransack the place. On one occasion, however, Mike Tyson entered an apartment only to find the occupant still inside. The enraged man was waiting for him, pistol in hand. Mike bolted like a young colt and, as he raced for freedom, a shot rang out and a .22 slug whistled past his head, narrowly missing him. Mike felt a sense of relief and elation as he flirted with death and came away unscathed. The following night found him back on the streets again, in search of more excitement.

The young hoodlum's minor league activities soon came to the attention of the "big boys." He was invited to join the neighborhood street gang, the "Jolly Stompers," an organized group of young thugs, 15 and 16 years old, who satisfied their lust for power and recognition by committing an assortment of vicious crimes throughout Brooklyn. Mike was honored to be offered membership in such a notorious group and jumped at the opportunity even though he was four or five years younger than most other gang members. Overnight he became a celebrity at school, but one to be feared rather than admired, a member of a brutal street gang at the tender age of 12. As Mike admitted later, he entered into this lifestyle with his eyes wide open. He knew the sad consequences of his actions, but his sensitive nature and lack of self-esteem left him yearning for recognition by his peers, and he was willing to pay the price for that recognition, no matter how steep.

Mike's education immediately took a new turn. Instead of math, he learned the art of picking pockets from the experts. He learned to size up a prospective victim to determine where his valuables were hidden. He became adept at selecting an optimum location to commit the act, a location that was crowded and noisy so the victim wouldn't notice the delicate feel of his wallet leaving his pocket. Nisee once boasted that her brother was the best thief in New York. Rodney tried to qualify that statement. He said that Mike had been volatile since his encounter with the pigeon thief, but that as long as he was doing something with his hands besides putting them in other people's pockets, his family was happy. Unfortunately, Mike was headed down a different path. When he decided on a criminal career, he dedicated himself completely to learning his trade. This ability to make a commitment to a goal and follow it through to completion would be a key ingredient in Mike's quest for boxing's heavyweight championship years later. But for now, he mastered the art of mugging from a professional standpoint, learning to rob people at knifepoint and vanish from the scene almost instantly.

He learned all the ins and outs of planning and carrying out an armed robbery, from selecting a prosperous establishment like a check cashing store or a drug house, to determining when the establishment would have the most money and when police units normally patrolled the area. Each member of the gang had a specific job to do, and since Mike was the baby of the group at 12, he was generally given the job of bagman, holding the sack open while the gang members filled it with loot, or cleaning out the cash register while the older members held the victims at gunpoint. Some gangs became skilled at breaking into parked automobiles and stripping them clean in a matter of minutes. The precision and coordination with which these local gangs worked would make Tony Kanaan's Indianapolis pit crew blush with envy.

These were special years in the life of Mike Tyson. They were years filled with pain and violence, but they were also years of happiness and satisfaction. As Mike Tyson grew in size, he became a leader in the neighborhood. He was no longer the victim. Now he was the aggressor. He wasn't called "little fairy boy" or "Bummy Mike" anymore. Now he was addressed as Mr. Mike Tyson. He no longer wandered helplessly through his environment. Now he controlled it. At 12 years old, Mike Tyson "owned" Rockaway Avenue and nearby Bristol Park. He ran with a tough crowd, and he was the meanest of the lot. In his few short years as a juvenile delinquent, he developed an all-consuming attraction to danger, a fascination with living on the edge. He enjoyed fighting, and he thrilled to the excitement of armed robberies and police chases. Now that he was king of Brownsville, he felt like a true warrior, wild and free at last.

Although he had become highly respected and feared in this jungle that was Brownsville, the rest of his world was collapsing around his ears. His newfound prosperity, the compensation for his clandestine activities, was immediately evident to his mother. Loose money, new clothes, and gaudy jewelry were obvious signs that all was not well in the Tyson household. Mike's mother couldn't understand her son's newfound way of life. She tried everything she could to dissuade him from his criminal pursuits. She cried whenever he came home with some ill-gotten gain from his evening's enterprise. She begged him to get away from the gang that was corrupting his life. "How can you steal? I never stole anything in my life." Lorna was afraid that some night Mike would either kill someone or be killed. She also warned him of the inevitable consequences of his actions, and threatened him with the juvenile authorities if he didn't reform. But all her attempts to reach her son fell on deaf ears. Mike was determined to keep the respect and friendship of the gang members, even if he had to sacrifice his family to do it. He became more distant from his mother as time passed, withdrawing into a shell and displaying a sullen and hostile façade to the outside world. Lorna Tyson had lost her son, at least temporarily. Years later, after his mother died, Mike remembered with regret his failure as a son. "I never saw my mother happy with me and proud of me for doing something. She only knew me as being a wild kid running the streets, coming home with new clothes she knew I didn't pay for. I never had a chance to talk to her about it. It's crushing, emotionally and personally."[9]

Mike's schoolwork was going downhill rapidly. His reading skills hovered around the third grade level and did not improve. He became defensive about his limitations in that area, and the feeling of inferiority carried over into all his subjects. He dreaded going to school now, and his absenteeism began to increase. His truancy brought him to the attention of the local authorities, and eventually a social worker visited the Tyson apartment to make his mother aware of the problem. Mrs. Tyson, distraught, assured the officer that her son would attend classes regularly. Her promise was a hollow one, of course. She no longer had any control over her son or his actions. His truancy continued, his absences eventually reaching epidemic proportions. His nighttime activities became more time-consuming now, and there were nights when he didn't come home at all. After a particularly late-night caper, Mike would sleep wherever he could find a comfortable corner, usually in one of the deserted, rat-infested tenements in the neighborhood.

Young Tyson's world had become a sordid excursion into the seamy side of life. As a frequent late night habitué of the neighborhood's parks and playgrounds, the young thug witnessed stabbings, beatings, and rapes, things that most American youngsters can't even relate to. While the majority of teenagers around the country were fascinated by the violent police shows on television, Mike Tyson was witnessing the gore and bloodshed first-hand. Violence and death became a way of life for him before he even reached puberty. As the months passed, the Tyson name began to appear on the local police blotter. The desk sergeant at the 73rd precinct knew him well, as did the cops at the "Alamo," or 77th precinct. He was arrested for the first time when he was 12 years old, for stealing purses on Pitkin Avenue. After a short period of confinement, he was remanded into the custody of his mother. But Mike Tyson's police record continued to grow. Assault with a deadly weapon, mugging, burglary, resisting arrest—Mike's name was becoming familiar to all the law enforcement agencies around Brooklyn. He was frequently detained in local juvenile detention centers for short periods of time in an attempt to make him see the error of his ways. Then he was returned to his mother.

Finally, after one particularly violent crime, he was sent uptown to Spofford Juvenile Center in the Bronx. It was there that Mike branded himself with the mark of the joint, a homemade tattoo. Armed with a do-it-yourself knife, the young hoodlum carved the name "Mike" into the skin on his right biceps, then rubbed pigment into the open wound, mixing it with his blood to give it consistency. The kid from Brownsville also met Muhammad Ali at Spofford, and he noticed the way people looked up to Ali and how happy they were to see him. That was the first time Mike thought about becoming a boxer. He later said he thought to himself, "That's what I wanna be. I wanna be champ of the world."[10]

Mike's eight-month stay at Spofford did nothing to rehabilitate him, and he returned home as hostile as ever. Within weeks the terror of Brownsville was arrested for armed robbery and was sent back to juvenile court for the last time. The judge, eyeing the Brooklyn thug's arrest record that had more than 40 entries, had seen enough of him by this time and decided to teach him a painful lesson, one that hopefully would shock him into turning his life around. Mike Tyson was permanently removed from the custody of his mother and was handed over to the Tryon Division for Youth in Johnstown, New York, a school for juvenile delinquents. Mike's life had reached the bottom rung of the ladder. There was nowhere else to go but up. It was either that or complete self-destruction. The year was 1979, and Mike was now 13 years old.

Johnstown is located in upstate New York, near Albany, almost 200 miles from the violence and turbulence of Tyson's Brooklyn home. Mike entered the facility with an enormous chip on his shoulder, his new tattoo prominently displayed on his muscular right arm, and an intense hatred for any kind of authority. His relationship with the other inmates was hostile and violent. He came to Johnstown with the reputation as a brawler and a hoodlum, an uncontrollable thug. Even so, he preferred solitude to confrontation, and he kept pretty much to himself. Before long, however, that small flame of pent-up hostility burst into a conflagration. Tyson and another inmate went at each other with fists blazing in a knockdown, drag-out brawl in the quadrangle one day, a confrontation brought on apparently by the other prisoner's refusal to accept Tyson's authority. It took two large penal officers to separate the burly Tyson, now 5'8' tall and 208 pounds, from his battered opponent. Standing before the director of the facility, still unrepentant, Tyson heard the ultimate punishment meted out, transfer to the Elmwood Cottage.

The Elmwood Cottage was the pits, the building where the incorrigibles in the institution were confined. It was popularly referred to as "The Bad Boys Cottage." Here fate entered the picture, took young Tyson by the hand, and offered to remove him from the snake pit of despair and set him on the road to a useful life. The hand of fate was assisted by a former professional boxer named Bobby Stewart. Stewart was a counselor at the Elmwood Cottage, and his first glimpse of Tyson sent shivers up his spine. Two of the biggest guards at Tryon were escorting Tyson over to the Cottage. One of the guards told Stewart, "Be careful of this kid. He beats the kids up. He'll attack anybody."[11] Mike Tyson arrived at the Elmwood Cottage sullen and silent. He wouldn't associate with any of the other inmates, still preferring to remain alone. In fact, he never spoke to anyone. If he was instructed to do something by one of the counselors, he would grunt a reply, but that was all. Some of the counselors were convinced that Mike was mentally retarded. Others felt he had brain damage. Certainly, he didn't give any indication that he could relate to the real world. The sweet little five-year-old boy who sang songs with his mother and who played "house" with his sister had become almost autistic in a period of three short years.

Mike Tyson was an accomplished street fighter, however, and he was fascinated and impressed by Bobby Stewart's professional ring credentials. Back in Brownsville, fighting was a way of life for the youthful Tyson. He loved to fight. Everyone on his block loved to fight. They idolized the professional boxers who could earn thousands of dollars beating people up legally. The professionals were very visible in Brooklyn, flaunting their new-found wealth and driving their big, fancy cars around the neighborhood, sporting expensive clothes and gold jewelry, and escorting two or three beautiful women at a time. Mike's favorite boxer was Sugar Ray Leonard, a flashy knockout artist who made everything look easy. Mike thought Ray was a bad dude. Bobby Stewart also looked like a bad dude to the Brooklyn native.

After a long period of contemplation, Mike approached Stewart with a petition. "Mr. Stewart, I wanna be a fighter." Taken aback by this unusual request from the Cottage's problem child, the counselor regained his composure. "No. I'm sorry. I don't have the time right now." But Tyson wouldn't take no for an answer. He kept after Stewart, slowly wearing the older man down. Stewart finally realized that this might be a way to reach Tyson, to reclaim him from the refuse pile of society, and to return him to the world as a useful citizen. He formulated a plan that he subsequently proposed to the 13-year-old inmate. "Okay, Mike. I'll teach you to box on one condition. First, you've got to work harder in school. I don't care what marks you get. But if you work as hard as you can, and if you pay attention in class, I'll work with you in the gym."[12] Tyson agreed, and the sudden change that came over him puzzled his fellow inmates and astounded his teachers. The teachers remarked about his new positive attitude and his new-found interest in education. Bobby Stewart just stood by as an observer and shook his head in disbelief. He was somewhat amused by what he had brought about.

After keeping his end of the bargain, Tyson challenged Stewart to a real boxing match inside the ring. Stewart weighed about 180 pounds at the time, almost 30 pounds less than the rugged Tyson, and about eight or ten pounds above his professional fighting weight. Bobby Stewart had been a light heavyweight fighter, his primary claim to fame being a victory over the future WBA heavyweight champion of the world, Michael Dokes, en route to winning the National Golden Gloves championship in 1974. By now, however, Stewart was overweight and out of condition, and he was being challenged by the meanest inmate in the Cottage, a young thug looking for blood. Mike Tyson was barely a teenager, and his prodigious talent was still raw and undeveloped. Stewart felt confident that he could outthink and outbox Tyson in the ring, offsetting Mike's greater strength. Tyson did not want to be embarrassed in front of his peers, but Bobby Stewart knew that he had to humble Mike if he expected to exert any influence over him in the gym. Mike's fellow prisoners surrounded the ring on the day of the fight with mixed emotions. Half the inmates were rooting for Tyson to whip the counselor, while the other half wanted to see the Brooklyn punk get his head knocked off. Mike himself approached the fight with typical street mentality. "I thought he was a small, white guy. I was gonna kill him."[13]

As the fight progressed, Tyson's persistent charges were deftly avoided by Stewart's dancing feet. Bobby jabbed and moved, jabbed and moved, and when Mike cornered him, Bobby tied Mike up so he was unable to get his hands free to unleash a punch. Mike became frustrated at his inability to hit Stewart with a solid punch, but he remained determined. He moved in again on Stewart. Stewart responded with a crushing left to the midsection, causing Tyson to gasp and sending him to the canvas. As Tyson later recalled, "He hit me in the body and I went down. My air stopped. I thought I was dead."[14] The fight was over. Mike, humiliated in front of his friends, had received his first instruction in a boxing ring, and a painful one at that.

Mike developed a new respect for his instructor as a result of the fight, and the agreement between the two paid immediate dividends. In the classroom, Mike kept his nose to the grindstone as he had promised, and his reading level soon improved significantly. Stewart, for his part, received permission from the Division for Youth to work with Tyson in the gym three nights a week. Tyson was an avid student in the ring and absorbed his lessons quickly and proficiently. Before long, he was breaking through Stewart's guard and causing considerable discomfort to his trainer and mentor. Bobby Stewart realized that he was in a lot of trouble. "I had to go back into training myself. It was either that or get killed." Even that didn't help for long. Tyson progressed at an amazing rate and soon outgrew his teacher's capabilities to advance his pugilistic talents. He achieved his high level of skill through sheer determination and dedication to the sport. Stewart fondly remembered Tyson's almost fanatical approach to boxing. "I'd show him something at eight o'clock right before I went home and someone on the night shift would come back and tell me the next day that they'd have to put him to bed at 3 a.m. He was practicing in the dark. Lights go off at 10 or 11 p.m. That's how dedicated he was."[15]

Another change came over Tyson at Tryon School. He began to take stock of himself and to evaluate his prospects in life. He knew that the first 13 years of his life had been a complete waste. And he knew where that road would lead him if he didn't change. "Whenever I went home to visit all my friends—they were 15 or 16 years old—they were either dead or in jail for the rest of their lives. Either one and nothing less. And I was younger than them. It could've happened to me. It made me realize that life isn't a game. It's survival. It's no fun at all, especially when you're on the losing end. And I wasn't winning."[16] Mike was determined, however, that he would win the battle and not follow the road travelled by his Brooklyn cohorts. Deep down inside, he knew he was destined for something good. He didn't know what it was, but he always knew he would be successful in life. In spite of all his adversity he still had confidence in himself, and at Tryon he found that vehicle for survival. The prize ring would be his ticket out of the ghetto, his means of personal salvation

Bobby Stewart looked around for help in developing Mike Tyson's great boxing potential. He immediately thought of Cus D'Amato, an old friend and one of the world's outstanding trainers. D'Amato had a gym in Catskill, New York, 80 miles southeast of Johnstown, where he operated the Catskill Boxing Club while quietly searching for a new world champion. "Cus, this is Bobby Stewart. I've got a thirteen-year-old here at Johnstown I'd like you to see. I think he has the talent to be a great fighter." "Okay, Bobby, bring him down. I'd be glad to take a look at him."

It was mid–1980 when Stewart and Tyson arrived at D'Amato's dingy gym on the third floor of the Village Building, just over the police station, on Main Street. When 52-year-old Don Shanagher, an associate of D'Amato's, first caught sight of the 200-pound teenager, he winked at Cus and whispered, "If this kid is thirteen years old then I'm only twelve. The kid's gotta be at least seventeen. I know how these guys are. They say they're younger than they are so they can be treated like juveniles. You can't believe what they say. Look at him. No way he's thirteen."[17] Stewart and Tyson sparred for three impressive rounds that day, with Tyson always on the offensive and Stewart fending off his furious rushes. Mike kept the pressure on for three minutes every round, and Stewart had to fight like hell to survive. In the second round, a Stewart right hand smashed flush against Tyson's nose, splattering blood all over the ring. D'Amato's assistant, Matt Baranski, suggested the fight be stopped at the end of the round, but Tyson would have none of that. He insisted on finishing out the scheduled three.[18]

When it was over, D'Amato eyed the young gladiator for a minute, then glanced at Bobby Stewart and smiled. "That's the heavyweight champion of the world. If he wants it, it's his."[19]

2

The Man—Cus D'Amato

Constantine "Cus" D'Amato was the reigning guru of the boxing profession for more than five decades prior to his death from pneumonia on November 4, 1985. D'Amato taught his fighters the principles of living, not just the rules of boxing. He considered boxing to be a part of life, and the attributes it took to be successful in the boxing ring were also required in order to be successful in life. Cus tried to prepare his students for life after boxing as well as for a career in the ring. His philosophy was developed and honed at the grass roots level, beginning with his childhood in the tough Frog Hollow section of the Bronx, New York.

His father, Damiano D'Amato, was an immigrant who arrived in New York City from Italy around the turn of the twentieth century. Once the young man had established himself in business, he married his sweetheart Elizabeth, and settled down in the Italian section of the Bronx to raise a family. Damiano was a typical, hard-working Italian businessman who believed in frugal living and strict family discipline. He made his living by delivering ice to the apartment dwellers of Frog Hollow. His horse-drawn wagon could be heard clattering through the streets of the Bronx every day of the year, except Christmas. On hot summer days, a crowd of kids would follow his wagon up and down the searing city thoroughfares. Occasionally a ragged street urchin would jump up on the rear step of the wagon to steal a small sliver of ice to soothe his parched throat. Damiano's rasping curses and bodily threats brought only jeers from the youngsters who would thumb their noses at him and run away, to return again the next day for another refreshing sliver of ice.

Life was tough but also good in the New York of the early 1900s. It was a time of pride, hard work, and close family and neighborhood ties. As the years passed, the D'Amato family grew one by one, and by 1908, when little Constantine was born, four older brothers were waiting to welcome him. Sadly, three other siblings had died before Constantine was born. When Cus was four years old, tragedy struck the D'Amato family again. His mother Elizabeth passed away, and the boys were left under the sole authority of their tough disciplinarian father. Damiano D'Amato was a stern taskmaster who insisted on a full daily work schedule for his offspring. After school there were chores to be done. In the evening, after dinner, there was homework. Idle hands meant trouble, and Papa D'Amato was determined that his boys would grow up to be honest, hard-working citizens, not juvenile delinquents and petty criminals like Dutch Schultz, Frankie Carbo, and the other thugs who called Frog Hollow their home. The elder D'Amato assigned the boys specific responsibilities, both at home and at the family business. These tasks included cleaning out the rented stable, grooming and feeding the horse, accompanying their father to the Knickerbocker Brewery to pick up ice cakes, and delivering ice around the neighborhood. And woe to the boy who didn't complete his daily chores—punishment was swift and severe.

Cus enjoyed grammar school, his favorite subject being reading. He developed a voracious appetite for books, particularly those about great achievers. The youngest of the D'Amato clan was a quiet, introspective boy, and very religious. He spent hours contemplating the complexities of life and the meaning of existence. He wondered what God was like, and pondered over his relationship with God. During his early years, until he was 15 or 16 years old, Cus considered becoming a priest.[1] Somehow it never happened. Perhaps God had ordained that Cus would spread His good news elsewhere, outside the walls of the seminary and away from the sanctuary of the church, in the streets and in the gymnasiums of the inner city, and in the violent arena of blood and gore called the boxing ring where, strangely enough, useful citizens can be developed, and tormented lives can be healed.

Cus's happiest childhood memories revolved around the warm summer months of July and August when the sun was high and the grass was cool. He liked nothing better than to stretch out on a lush green knoll and study the bright blue sky overhead. His thoughts invariably drifted to the people who populated his world, why they did what they did, and what made one person different from another. Young Cus also spent considerable time on the more practical aspects of life, like how to survive in a world of violence, corruption, and moral degradation. William Plummer noted that the young man read constantly. "Mark Twain was an early favorite. Cus later dipped into Clarence Darrow, Bertrand Russell—even Einstein—to see what all the fuss was about." But survival was the ultimate name of the game, and Cus had learned to be a survivor through his many painful childhood experiences. As a youngster, he too was a victim, not only in the streets, but at home was well.

When Cus reached his teenage years, he developed the bad habit of coming home late at night. Despite his father's stern warnings, Cus continued his nocturnal practices. Finally, in frustration, "Damiano used a bullwhip on his seventh son, crashed it down on the boy's bare shoulders even as he lay shuddering unrepentant beside his bed," according to Plummer. The beating didn't dissuade Cus from his activities however, nor did they alienate him from his father. He understood the reason for his father's actions and he admired his father's determination and strong character, but he felt the need to be out on the streets after dark where he could study people and learn what made them tick.

As hard as life was at home for Cus, it was much more difficult on the streets of the Bronx. Cus was taunted and threatened by local bullies who tried to intimidate him almost daily. On one occasion, when he was only 12 years old, he was forced into a street fight with an older man. He was badly beaten, and his left eye was so severely damaged that it left him almost completely blind.[2] But Cus wouldn't knuckle under to the intimidation of the street thugs. He concentrated instead on developing intestinal fortitude and willpower as a means of combating the threats of physical violence that surrounded him. It was the beginning of his life-long philosophy, his credo. Thousands of promising young fighters would hear the same philosophy over the next 50 years. "In the final analysis, mind triumphs over matter. Fear is natural. Everyone is afraid. The secret is to control your fear."[3] Cus set about strengthening his will and disciplining his body to withstand any degree of physical pain and suffering. He learned to absorb the pain of beatings without cowering and without letting it influence his actions. As he got older, he drove himself harder, determined to mold his mind into an impervious steel wall. William Plummer reported that "at 16, D'Amato went four days without eating—this he says, so no one could ever intimidate him with threats of starvation. Later, drafted into the Army during World War II, he would shave only with cold water, stand at attention for hours on end, sleep on the barracks floor."

In his sophomore year of high school, much to the chagrin of his father, Cus terminated his formal education and pursued what he saw as the more valuable education of the streets, hanging out with his best friend, Danny Tosto, selling costume jewelry in the Bronx, and observing street life and human behavior. He continued to read anything he could get his hands on. During this period, Cus also became Frog Hollow's "lawyer in residence," helping neighbors find solutions to their problems. Gradually young D'Amato gravitated more and more toward the world of boxing. He often followed his brothers to the local gym to watch them train. It was his first indoctrination into the fight game, and it stirred an interest in him that eventually developed into a life-long career. He himself never boxed because of the injury to his left eye, but he realized the therapeutic value of the sport. To him, boxing was an ideal way to mold street kids into worthwhile citizens, and to experiment with and fine-tune his own personal philosophy of life.

Late in 1939, the 31-year-old D'Amato bought the old Grammercy Gym on 14th Street, a second floor walkup over a dance hall. He converted it into his own little world—his business, his laboratory, and his home. During the day, he taught boxing and philosophy in the gym. Only at night, when darkness blanketed the city, did Cus retreat across the street to sleep alone in his small apartment. By day, he perfected his boxing philosophies and his method of teaching.

> When I first opened my gymnasium, it was in a pretty tough neighborhood down in the 14th Street section of New York. I opened it on the basis of rentals and so forth. One day I had a committee of women come up and ask if I could help them out. The neighborhood kids were getting into trouble on the streets and they wanted a place for the kids to go. So I said "All right, I would do so." So they sent them up and they had no money. I didn't have any money either. It was during the depression. Anyway, if the kids came in alone, I knew they would be easy to work with because they wanted to be a fighter. Now, if someone brought them in, I knew I had my work cut out for me because they didn't have the discipline to come up by themselves. If you have to be brought up, you have a problem that has to be overcome.[4]

> People, especially if they come up in a tough area, have to go through a number of experiences in life that are intimidating and embarrassing. These experiences form layer upon layer over their capabilities and talents. So my job as a teacher was to peel off these layers. When the kids first come up, I sit them down and talk to them, and the subject of my first talk is something that everyone is familiar with—fear. Fear is the greatest obstacle to learning and accomplishment. Fear is an embarrassing, emotional experience. Everyone is embarrassed to say they're afraid so they do every damn thing in the world to prove that they're not. I tell them that fear is a normal feeling. I tell them how I felt when I was growing up. I was scared all the time, but nobody ever knew about it. If you let fear get the better of you, you can't succeed. Now in explaining this to the boys, it helps them to understand that everyone has the same feelings. They're not different than everyone else because they're afraid. Now I've been in many situations during the course of my career where I thought my life was at stake. I didn't know if the next minute was gonna be my last. I knew that my ability to face up to all the eventualities would help me do what I had to do.

> In the gymnasium, I first make my kids eliminate two words from their language; impossible and can't. When a person says that a thing is impossible, what he's sayin' is that it's impossible for him. It's not impossible. Nothing is impossible. We all set our own limitations on what we can do. When a boy comes to me they are really greenhorns. Half of them don't know they're alive so to speak. But you have to educate them, to prepare them for what they're gonna hafta do. Many things I do and say to a boy to motivate them. We don't use that term in boxing. But you have to speak the language they understand. You can't talk down to them. Can't talk up to them. You have to talk to them. Next you have to eliminate the word can't. If there's a situation you can't cope with at the time, you say, "I am unable to do it at this time." Never say the word can't because that implies you'll never be able to do it. You're unable to do it because of the fact that circumstances don't allow it at that particular time or moment.[5]

Cus continued to refine his boxing theories over the next two decades, working with dozens of fighters, always searching for but never finding that world-class boxer that he could direct to the championship of the world. In the course of his search however, Cus developed the distinctive boxing style that became the trademark of his fighters, a style that was sarcastically referred to as the peek-a-boo style by his later adversaries in the IBC (International Boxing Council). The peek-a-boo style was designed to give the fighter maximum protection while allowing him to be aggressive and entertaining at the same time. The gloves were held high against the cheekbones with the fighter peeking between them at his opponent, the elbows tucked in close to the body, protecting the rib cage. Cus kept hammering away with his philosophy during this growing period and it became a major part of every fighter's indoctrination. The control of fear and the belief that willpower could overcome skill were the dominating principles in the D'Amato theology. He repeated the same speeches to his fighters every day until they believed the philosophy as strongly as Cus did.

His physical training theories were sometimes discovered by accident. In the mid-1940s, a friend of Cus's wanted to patent a technique for improving the typing speed of office secretaries. The technique involved playing a recording that dictated sentences to a typist. The record started out slowly at first, then increased in speed until the secretary improved her basic typing speed. Cus recognized this as a technique for increasing a boxer's hand speed, rather than a secretary's typing speed. He didn't want to see it patented for training typists, he wanted to keep it a secret so he could perfect it on his fighters. He began letting his friend hang around the gym after that, and the friend helped him to apply the theory to boxing. His friend never did patent the method, but Cus D'Amato developed a new and successful technique for increasing hand speed. Over the years, Cus's boxers were noted for having the fastest hands in the business. Cus's method involved marking numbers on the heavy body bag—odd numbers to the left, even numbers to the right.

```
**************************
*     1         2        *
*     3         4        *
*     5         6        *
*     7         8        *
**************************
```

He started fighters out on the heavy bag with number drills on a 78 rpm record—1-1-1, 2-2-2, 3-3-3, etc.—slowly at first, then gradually faster as the boxer's hand speed increased.[6]

Cus added to his gym equipment over the years, expanding on his basic drills. Another bag that became standard in the D'Amato training arsenal was a small, weighted sand bag called a slip bag. The slip bag was put in a swinging motion like a pendulum, front to back. The boxer had to move his head to the side to avoid the bag as it approached him, then had to move his head again to avoid the bag as it moved from back to front. This helped perfect bobbing and weaving technique. Another of Cus's drills utilized a clothesline hung up between two walls. The fighter had to bob and weave, up and down, back and forth, crouching low to get underneath the clothesline without touching it.[7]

Frankie Carbo, one of D'Amato's boyhood acquaintances from Frog Hollow, infiltrated the boxing scene in 1949. Cus knew Carbo:

> He was a professional killer. I knew the man when he was a young fella. I remember the first man he killed. Came from my neighborhood. Know how he did it. Know how cold blooded it was. It was

up in the poolroom. He was about 18. He had a piece in his belt, and he was playin' with a hat, the type the real tough guys wore in those days. So a fella says, "What the hell are ya carryin' that for? You haven't got the guts to use it."

"I don't?"

"No."

Bam! Shot him just like that. That was the beginning of his career. God knows how many guys he killed.[8]

After that he became a professional killer. He became a killer for Murder Incorporated, an organization that did the killings for all the mob guys around the country. That was their business, killings. And so this fella was a killer for that organization. He was one of the fellas involved with these wealthy businessmen. Now how James D. Norris, Jr. [millionaire Chicago businessman] got involved with this kind of people is very simple. His father [James D. Norris, Sr.], was known as the grain king. He controlled the grain market in Chicago. And God knows all the businesses he was in. He was a very powerful man, political and every other way, as well as financial. And when those big people come and visit him, he would sit at his desk. His son, Jim Norris, Jr., was there you know, probably 15, 16 years of age. He'd see these important people come up, his father would sit there. They'd come over to him. But when a tough guy came in, his father would get up and walk over to him like that, you know. That made a big impression on him, see. So later, when Jim Norris, Jr. became active in boxing—they owned arenas all over the country, these mobsters—when he became active in boxing, he catered to these people. He got this fella, Frankie Carbo, involved, and with himself and the reputation he had, he had no trouble organizing the fight business.[9]

Frankie Carbo subsequently became known in boxing circles as the underworld's "overlord of boxing."

This unholy alliance was formalized in 1949, when Carbo and Norris joined forces under the auspices of the IBC, with the express purpose of establishing a boxing monopoly in the United States. Their plan was simple: put the top rated boxers in all the weight divisions under contract to managers who were paid by or owed allegiance to the IBC. The heavyweight title was the most lucrative title in the boxing world and the first one they attacked. Since they did not control the champion, Joe Louis, they did the next best thing. They paid him $150,000 to retire from the ring. Having thus eliminated Louis from the division, the IBC could then match its own fighters in a tournament to select Louis' successor. The same format was followed down the line in all divisions, light heavyweight, middleweight, welterweight, lightweight, featherweight, etc. Within a short time, it became virtually impossible to establish a ranking in the boxing world without doing business with the Carbo-Norris group. The IBC hovered over the fight game like a giant octopus, its tentacles reaching the very bottom of the sport, to every club fight and every "smoker" in the country. Almost every promoter, every manager, every fighter, came under the influence of the IBC. Boxers were like thousands of puppets dancing to the tune of the giant syndicate.

Cus D'Amato however was one who was not dancing. He was known as a maverick in the boxing world, and he was thirsting for a fight with the IBC. He remembered his quixotic quest:

> You gotta overcome fear. That's how I fought the IBC. The Norris family was worth maybe 50 to 500 million dollars in those days. They had power—tremendous power. Now I was considered crazy to even dream I could oppose 'em. But I had one advantage. I knew I had the experience and the knowledge and the desire. That's the most important thing. Without desire, you're nothing. People are under the impression you have to be intelligent, but the most important thing is the motivation, the drive, that's what's important. Now, getting back to my fight with the IBC, by the early '50s, Norris had it so completely organized that if you didn't get work from him you didn't get any work. Today there are three or four promoters and anyone with any capability at all can play one against

the other some way or other. So just trying to buck people like Norris was considered impossible. That is why I have no respect for the word impossible. That's why nobody should ever think of a thing as being impossible. You must know your mind well enough to know that given a set of circumstances that are threatening, your mind will find excuses to avoid and evade, not to accept a confrontation of any kind. See, but I always say it's like crossing a bridge, a suspension bridge going from one side to the other. Now when you cross to the other side knowing what you have to cope with, and knowing all that could be dangerous to you, you chop the bridge down so you can't retreat. Now you can only think in terms of accomplishment. So when you take one step forward, two steps forward, make sure you chop that back so you constantly have a chasm there where you can't retreat. Then whatever you have to do, you can only think of one thing, accomplishment. Don't be afraid to put yourself in that position. You'll be amazed at the things you can do when you're forced to. Nobody really knows his capabilities until he tries. That's how I beat that organization, believe it or not. I never let myself think in terms of defeat. Whatever it was I had to do, I figured there must be a way to do it, and there always was.[10]

For Cus to achieve his objective it was necessary to find a fighter who had the talent and the desire to be the champion of the world and, in addition, who was 100 percent loyal to him and his cause. Cus found his man in young Floyd Patterson. Patterson, Brooklyn born, had a very troubled childhood, including numerous incidences of truancy from school, and running away from home. When he was 12 years old, he was sent to the Wiltwyck School for Boys in Esopus, New York, by the Family Court. Wiltwyck was a school for emotionally disturbed children, and it was hoped that the environment and the instruction at the school would settle Floyd down. The Brooklyn truant did respond to the professional treatment at Wiltwyck, and eventually he was released back to the custody of his family. The 14-year-old Patterson immediately began to trail after his older brothers, Frank and Bill, when they made their daily trips to the Grammercy Gym to work out. Both boys had brief boxing careers, and Floyd used to carry their equipment bags around for them. Soon Floyd took an interest in boxing himself, and within a few months his determination had impressed Cus D'Amato so much that the veteran trainer agreed to take young Patterson under his wing.

Floyd was painfully shy at the time, so much so that D'Amato often refrained from speaking to him directly. "When I was teaching people, I always expected to teach direct, you see. He was the type of guy I couldn't teach direct." Many times when Cus wanted to get a point across to young Patterson, he would enter into a conversation with a third party, but always within earshot of Floyd. Cus had to teach Patterson by example.

> I was always careful about the way I dressed, not like now. I always wore a homburg and a coat, so I used to look like a dignified kind of guy. I wasn't, but I used to look it. Patterson would study everything I did. When I spoke in his presence, I was always very careful what I said and how I said it. My appearance was always, you know, what a person in my position should have been. One day he was being interviewed, and I was over on the side, and this fella said to him, "You know, you dress very well for a boy your age." Patterson said, "Oh, I watch my manager. I always watch my manager." See, which confirms what I thought at the time I did it. You have to set examples for fighters.[11]

Patterson observed and he learned.

By 1952, Floyd Patterson had developed into an outstanding amateur boxer, and he was selected by the United States Olympic Committee to represent his country at the Summer Olympic Games in Helsinki, Finland. Floyd breezed through the middleweight competition in Helsinki, winning four straight fights to the delight of the Scandinavian crowds who were thrilled by his two-fisted attacks. In the finals, he met Romanian champion, Vasile Tita. Floyd took charge from the outset, stalking his man with deadly purpose. A tremendous uppercut dropped Vasile to the canvas for the full ten count, giving Patterson the championship and the coveted gold medal. It took him only 74 seconds to dispatch the Romanian.

Cus was now ready to move against the IBC. He had the plan, and he had the weapon.

> Now in preparing to fight the IBC, I had this young fighter, Patterson, who had come back from Europe having won the Olympic Games. When his ship docked, there was a big crowd of newspapermen waiting to greet him. I spoke to them and I told them, "This young man is going to be the champion of the world, and go down in history as the youngest heavyweight champion that ever lived. And, in addition, he will be the most promising fighter of this era." Now why did I do this? Well, first of all, I had to let them know that I had a very loyal person here, because the practice in those days was for the IBC to get the boxers, financially, physically, or some other way, see. But if he was loyal, they couldn't steal him. Now I learned about the loyalty of Floyd Patterson through one of his teachers at Wiltwyck, Miss Vivien Costen. She said to me, "You know, I always liked Floyd, and I always knew he had something in him." And then she told me a story that revealed him to me. It was her practice to give a bag of candy to the most deserving student every week. And Floyd, you see, was absolutely crazy about candy. Well, this one week Miss Costen wanted to give Floyd the candy, but he wouldn't take it. He had an agreement with another boy whereby he had to share it, see. Whatever they got, they would share, candy, whatever it was. And when she tried to give him the candy, he refused to accept it, and the reason he refused to accept it was because she said it could be only his. He couldn't share it with anybody. Under those conditions, he refused to accept it. Well, she kept pressing, pressing, to find out why. When she found out that he had this agreement, of course she let him have it, but it told me something about the boy. It told me that, at the age of 16, or at a very young age, at that time when the incident happened, he had the character to stand up and do what he thought was right. Now this is a very important thing because character is what makes a man predictable. Character is what tells you that he can do this, and he will do this because he has character. It's very easy to fold up like an accordion. Anybody can do that. But a man who has character will stick with it and go along to what he has to accomplish. And this is what this boy had. And I said, "With this boy I'm going to make a fight." And I did, successfully.
>
> Now at the time I made my plans, I knew the people I was going to cope with. I knew they were tough guys and all that. I made my plans knowing at some point the pressure was gonna build up, and when it built up, and the threats were there, my reaction would be, Let me get the hell outa here, you know, because nobody likes to get hurt or get dumped somewhere. That's the way it is. Nobody likes that. It's a weakness. A man's gonna give himself an excuse to run, like I told you. I didn't give myself that chance, see. I said to myself, "When I get to that point when the threats have built up, I must remember, I made my plan when I was cool, calm, and collected, when there were no threats. So therefore I must never change my plan unless some factor comes to my attention that I didn't consider in making the plan." See, in that case, and only then, would I change it. Otherwise I'd stick to it, and to make a long story short, I succeeded.[12]

As soon as Patterson returned home from the Olympics, D'Amato signed him to a professional contract. In a prepared statement to the press, D'Amato announced that Floyd Patterson was immediately entering the professional boxing ranks in the middleweight division, and that within four years he would be the heavyweight champion of the world. Right from the outset, D'Amato avoided all connections with the IBC. Floyd fought only independent boxers and fought only for independent promoters. D'Amato's strategy was calculated to bring Patterson to the threshold of the title before confronting the IBC directly. Patterson won his first 13 fights impressively—eight by KO—before losing a close decision to former light heavyweight champion, Joey Maxim. Eleven of 12 sports columnists at ringside had Floyd in the lead at the end of the Maxim fight but the official verdict went the other way. That was just a temporary setback, however, and Floyd's career continued to blossom with another string of consecutive victories. By 1956, Floyd had compiled a record of 27 victories against the lone defeat to Maxim, and he had disposed of 19 of his victims by knockout.

D'Amato was now ready to make his move against the IBC, a move that would bring the heavyweight championship of the world to the Patterson-D'Amato camp.

Floyd had achieved a number three rating in the heavyweight division, and the time was ripe for a title shot. Like all D'Amato manipulations, this one had to be carried out with the utmost discretion so as not to put Frankie Carbo in a bad light. As Cus recalled,

> Carbo called me the crazy man, because nobody would ever do what I did. But you see everything I did was calculated. I knew the type of people. I grew up in the street. I knew the type of thinking they lived by. So I knew exactly how far to go. But you had to be very careful. It was like walking a tightrope. Just a little bit off and you'd be shot. I could never let what I was doing challenge them, because if I challenged them, they were the kind of people who never dropped a challenge. Because anything that was a threat to their reputation or whatever they were going to do, they couldn't afford to have anybody challenge them. They had to just get 'em out of the way. It had to be such that anybody who dealt with them would know the consequences of threatening them. So I did everything to accomplish what I was gonna accomplish just short of a challenge. And while I irritated and aggravated them, I never let it get to the point where they were gonna do something about it.[13]

Cus put his plan into action.

> Rocky Marciano was about to retire but nobody knew about it. And Al Weill, his manager, was swindled out of $90,000 by Jim Norris, so when he discovered it, he tried to get the money back and he couldn't get it. So he turned against Norris. Now Weill and Carbo were partners so Carbo gave him privileges that nobody else had. He could make his own decisions, believe it or not. But when I learned there was trouble, I went into the place where the mobsters were hanging out. They all said to me, "Look, why don't you make up with the IBC? You can get a million bucks under the table. You're better off. You can't trust fighters." So I said, "What the hell is Norris gonna do? Let me tell you. In order to defeat me, he needs a better fighter. He can't beat me with hundred dollar bills. He needs a better fighter. Since, he hasn't got one, he can't beat me. Furthermore, unless he makes the match that I want, which is a match he don't wanna give, and pay the money I want, unless he pays me the money I'm afta, I'm gonna fight Rocky Marciano for another promoter." See I gambled on the fact that this guy Weill, being angry with Mr. Norris and his people, wouldn't open his mouth to them if I said I wanted to fight Marciano. So, when I said this, they laughed. They said it's under Carbo's control, but I also knew that Weill had the privilege of doin' his own business. So the moment I left, one guy ran across the street to the Garden and said to Norris, "You know what's happenin' to Cus D'Amato and Weill?" He, knowin' it was the result of his quarrel, immediately made arrangements to meet with me to prevent me from fightin' Marciano, which is all I wanted. If I fought his fighter, the number two contender, I knew who was gonna win, see, and that's how I got the championship.[14]

Norris and D'Amato agreed to stage a heavyweight elimination fight in Madison Square Garden between Patterson and the number two contender, Tommy "Hurricane" Jackson. The winner would then be matched against the number one contender, the current light heavyweight champion, Archie Moore. The elimination bout took place on June 8, 1956. Patterson was expected to knock Jackson out, but broke his hand early in the fight and had to be content with a unanimous 12-round decision. Still, it was enough to bring him a title shot. D'Amato recalled:

> So when Floyd boxed Archie Moore, Moore had developed a style of defense that wouldn't allow you to get to his body. Someone said, "How you gonna overcome that defense?" So I said to him, "Sometimes a man's greatest strength becomes his weakness though he may not be aware of it." Now Moore's defense appeared to be impregnable, but it was very, very vulnerable. So when the time come to fight, the night before the fight we had a big press conference, maybe 150 newspapermen and radio and television, and when I spoke, I said to them "Tonight you fellas have picked Archie Moore to win, and most of you have picked him to win by a knockout. However, tomorrow night, after Floyd

Patterson knocks out Archie Moore, all of you people are gonna say he beat an old man." Because what I had on my mind was gonna make him look like an old man. Now at the fight, I only spoke to Patterson once. I just told him one thing, "Get close to this guy, and in order to punch he has to pull his hand back first. As he pulls his hand back, you hit him on the side of the head. Automatically, his head'll go here. When he moves his hand up, you hit him in the ribs. His head'll go here. You'll have him like this all night long." That's what happened. After the first round, I never spoke anymore. Anyhow, Patterson knocked him out in the fifth round. Now these people all thought the defense was impregnable, and if we get ourselves to say a thing often enough, everybody believes it. And that becomes an advantage to the person who is determined and aggressive and doesn't believe in the word impossible, and doesn't believe in the word can't, see.[15]

After Patterson won the title, the pressure on the IBC mounted. They were cut out of all heavyweight title fights by the crafty D'Amato. Even Madison Square Garden was on Cus's hit list. The IBC, in retaliation, tried to coerce D'Amato into a cooperative effort. The coercion included threatening telephone calls in the middle of the night, but nothing worked. Cus couldn't be intimidated. He continued to avoid the IBC like the plague, and in fact held numerous secret fights—22 by one count—just to keep his fighter active and in condition between title defenses. The gamble paid off for D'Amato and Patterson, as the IBC empire finally collapsed under the weight of its own shady dealings in 1959. New York County District Attorney Frank Hogan obtained an indictment against Frankie Carbo for being an undercover boxing manager. Carbo was found guilty and was sentenced to two years on Riker's Island. Less than a year later, Carbo was indicted again, this time by a federal grand jury in Los Angeles. He was charged with conspiracy in an attempt to extort money from the manager of lightweight champion Don Jordan. Frankie Carbo got 18 years on that charge and disappeared from the boxing game for good. Jim Norris did not fare much better. In 1959, the United States Supreme Court ruled the International Boxing Club to be a monopoly in the restraint of trade. Norris was ordered to divest himself of all his stock in Madison Square Garden and to dissolve the IBC. He immediately sold his interest in the Garden for four million dollars and dissolved the IBC as ordered. But he didn't leave boxing altogether. He continued to promote fights in Chicago for several years thereafter, televising the "Wednesday Night Fights" from his Chicago Stadium, in direct competition with Madison Square Garden's more popular "Friday Night Fights."

Floyd Patterson's skills reached their peak in the years following his ascendancy to the throne. He successfully defended his title four times between 1957 and 1959, knocking out in order, Tommy "Hurricane" Jackson, Olympic champion Pete Rademacher, Roy "Cut and Shoot" Harris, and European champion Brian London. After a shocking third round knockout loss to Sweden's Ingemar Johansson in 1959, Patterson bounced back with a fury in 1960 to destroy Johansson in the fifth round of the return bout. He thus became the first man in history to recapture the heavyweight title, succeeding where boxing legends like Joe Louis and Jack Dempsey had failed. But all was not well in Patterson's camp. Friction had developed between Floyd and his mentor, Cus D'Amato. Unscrupulous individuals had gotten Patterson's ear, and they worked hard to alienate him from his manager. Patterson claimed that a lawyer brainwashed him and poisoned his mind against Cus. He was told that Cus really didn't have any interest in him and that he had been used by Cus to get revenge on the IBC. "In fact," the source said, "Cus associates with known mafia henchmen." That was the last straw. Floyd, a moral and righteous individual, couldn't accept the possibility that D'Amato associated with criminals.

Floyd broke his agreement with D'Amato, dissociated himself from his manager and went his way. The separation proved disastrous for Patterson, both professionally and personally. Not only did he miss Cus's careful selection of opponents, but Cus was no longer around to provide the psychological support he required in order to concentrate on his professional objectives. Patterson's new advisor immediately maneuvered him into a title fight with a mean-looking ex-con named Sonny Liston. It was good guy versus bad guy and the press played it to the hilt. Everybody from his sparring partner to President John F. Kennedy reminded Floyd that he had to win this fight in order to protect the children of America from Liston's evil influence. He had to uphold the honor of the heavyweight division. He was King George and Liston was the dragon. Floyd desperately needed Cus's guidance at this critical juncture, but Cus was not around, and Floyd did not have the emotional strength to isolate himself from all the media hype surrounding the big event. As fight time approached, the psychological warfare heated up, leaving Patterson only a shell of his former self, weighed down by oppressive responsibilities. Floyd found himself unable to cope with the tremendous pressure he felt was placed on him by the American public.

He answered the bell in the first round like a man in a daze, a sleepwalker, and Liston gladly obliged him by putting him to sleep in a little over two minutes. Floyd was so humiliated by his inept performance that he donned a false mustache and sneaked out of Las Vegas in disguise. Several years later, Patterson and D'Amato were reconciled, but Floyd always regretted the fact that he ever doubted Cus's intentions. As Floyd freely admitted, Cus was like a father to him. And had he not severed relations with D'Amato at a critical point in his career, he probably would have enjoyed a much longer reign as heavyweight champion of the world, and his 64–8–1 ring record would have been even more impressive.

As Patterson's career was blossoming, D'Amato discovered yet another fighter of championship caliber. Jose Torres from Ponce, Puerto Rico, was a highly intelligent kid who learned to fight in the Army. He turned pro in 1958, joining Patterson in the D'Amato stable. The early days were particularly rough for Torres who struggled to make ends meet while living in a dingy Brooklyn tenement with his wife and children. Being a D'Amato fighter meant being managed very carefully. It also meant bucking the IBC octopus. This, in turn, meant meager fights in small, smoke-filled arenas before sparse crowds for minuscule purses. Torres never earned as much as $15,000 for a single fight until after he had won the title. It was expensive for fighters to be associated with Cus D'Amato during the days of the big IBC feud. In addition to earning a scant income, Torres's abilities were constantly questioned. In spite of an impressive record of 35 wins against a single loss, Torres was not even rated by the World Boxing Association. He was accused of fighting has-beens and pushovers, and his record was considered a mockery.

Torres split with D'Amato in 1963 and immediately moved up to the light heavyweight division with an impressive first round knockout of former middleweight king, Carl "Bobo" Olson, a fight for which Torres received the princely sum of $2,000. The stunning victory catapulted him into the light heavyweight picture, and put him in line for a title fight with the champion, Willie Pastrano. Torres quickly sought out D'Amato and convinced his old friend to join his camp as the number one trainer. D'Amato immediately took his young fighter into seclusion. He wanted to be sure that Torres would be in the best shape of his career for his golden moment. The big night was March 30, 1965, and the site was New York's Madison Square Garden, no longer a mob-controlled operation. Eighteen thousand fans poured through the turnstiles to witness the extravaganza, and Torres did not disappoint. This was the opportunity of a lifetime for Torres, a chance to give his family some of the better things in life, and he was determined not to be stopped. On this night, he was a tiger, an invincible, destructive force. He tore into Pastrano from the opening bell and completely dominated the fight. It was impossible to tell which fighter was the champion and which one was the challenger. In the sixth round, a left hook to the midsection sent Pastrano hurtling to the canvas gasping for air, the first time in his 14-year career he had been knocked off his feet. Willie gamely picked himself up off the floor and survived the round. He survived two more rounds before referee Johnny Lobianco mercifully stepped between the two fighters, stopping the carnage, and saving the valiant Pastrano from further punishment.

Jose Torres was a gracious and dignified champion. He held the title for 20 months, making three successful defenses of his crown before Dick Tiger dethroned him on December 16, 1966, and then thwarted his attempt to regain the crown with a decisive 15-round decision four months later. After two more winning efforts in the ring, the Puerto Rico native hung up his gloves for good, leaving an enviable record of 41–3–1 behind him. Torres went on to hold a number of professional positions after his retirement, including a two-year stint as chairman of the New York State Boxing Commission. In that capacity, he worked to protect the rights of boxers, the men who put their health and even their lives on the line every time they climb between the ropes. Torres always held Cus D'Amato in high esteem.

> Cus D'Amato was the greatest man boxing ever produced. He understood fighters, and he taught them how to think, not just what to think in boxing. Cus believed that a good manager was there to protect his fighter, to get the most money for the least possible risk. If his fighter lost, after giving his best, Cus always blamed himself. It was his bad judgement to match him with a guy that was better than him at the time.[16]

After Torres's retirement from the ring, D'Amato's fortunes took a turn for the worse. Never one to concern himself with money, Cus went bankrupt in the late '60s. At the time, he was living in Catskill, New York, with Camille Ewald, the sister of his brother Rocco's wife, Anna. Mrs. Ewald owned a large 14-room Victorian mansion on nine and a half acres overlooking the majestic Hudson River. She intended to sell the house in 1969 but, at D'Amato's request, she took it off the market. Thanks to financial support from former protégé Jim Jacobs, Cus was able to rent the house from Camille and turn it into a year-round boxing camp. Camille stayed on as "house mother" and resident cook.

The reigning guru of boxing for five decades, Cus D'Amato trained three world champions: Floyd Patterson, José Torres and Mike Tyson (courtesy Paul V. Post).

Catskill, New York—which would replace Easton, Pennsylvania, as the boxing mecca of the United States—was an unlikely site. The area is Washington Irving country, a peaceful land of gently rolling hills and fertile valleys, a land of farmers and ranchers, of haunting legends and ghostly tales. Today little changed from 300 years ago, Catskill was still a small town of 5,000 in 1980, nestled on the eastern extremity of the Catskill Mountains. It could have been the setting of a modern-day Irving tale itself, a village that—like Rip Van Winkle—time forgot. It was a sleepy community, whose buildings hadn't felt the touch of a paintbrush for decades. Irving described the houses in Van Winkle's village as "sadly time worn and weather-beaten." He might well have been talking about Catskill. It was apparent from the rundown condition of the buildings, and from the poverty that pervaded the area, that the 20th century had not been kind to this peaceful community. Conveniently located near the New York State Thruway about 135 miles north of New York City, Catskill was once a favorite summer resort for New Yorkers attempting to escape the heat and humidity of the metropolitan area. But with the dawning of improved air travel and modern highway systems, the town was soon forgotten.

It didn't stay forgotten, however. Cus D'Amato brought boxing to Catskill, and with it a world champion—all the ingredients that were necessary to bring about a resurgence to the village's economy. When Cus moved into town, he rented a large auditorium on the third floor of the Village Building in the center of town, and converted it into a bustling gymnasium. The Police Department was located on the first floor, as was Hose Company #5 of the Citizen's Fire Department. Large double doors located between the two municipal departments opened onto a stairway leading to the second floor. The Town Clerk and the Water Department had offices on the second floor overlooking Main Street, but the rest of the offices were empty and desolate. A dingy hallway, devoid of decoration or furniture, ended at another stairway that led to another austere town office. On the left were two large oak doors, one near the stairs and one at the far end of the hall. Both doors opened into Redman's Hall, the gymnasium that would house Cus D'Amato's newly formed Catskill Boxing Club.

The 35 by 100 foot room looked like a boxing gym should look, stark and well lived-in. The hardwood floors bore the scars of decades of scuffling feet. The white tin ceiling was decorated with the ornate beam design typical of 19th-century American architecture. Pale yellow walls, grimy with age, completed the effect. One look verified that this was the training ground for the modern-day gladiators whose field of battle was the boxing ring. Directly in front of each door was a heavy cylindrical body bag suspended from the ceiling by a long chain. On the left wall was a large mirror where the fighters could study their form while shadow boxing. Next to the mirror, in the center of the wall, was a stage originally built when the room was probably used as a municipal auditorium, now it was equipped with the accouterments of the fight game—a large body bag, a small speed bag, and an even smaller teardrop-shaped slip bag. Beyond the stage, the wall was covered with dozens of faded newspaper clippings, announcing the glorious victories of various members of the boxing club. The wall at the far end of the auditorium contained yet another stage. At one time it may well have been the scene of a local minstrel show, or perhaps a rollicking Gilbert and Sullivan musical. But now it served as an exercise area, equipped with an inclined exercise table, used by local athletes for their daily stomach-tightening sit-ups. The rear wall of the stage was a giant billboard where numerous posters advertised the upcoming fights of such illustrious ring legends as Muhammad Ali and Floyd Patterson. The wall on the right side of the gymnasium was, like its counterpart across the room, covered with splashy newspaper clippings proclaiming the superiority of Catskill fighters over less worthy opponents. Next to the clippings, a large, ancient, cast iron radiator, covered with cheap silver paint, hissed its mournful tune in cadence with the rat-a-tat-tat of the speed bag.

A regulation size boxing ring, 20 feet square, stood at the far end of the gym near the stage. The 15-year-old relic, a veteran of countless ring wars, had been purchased by D'Amato for $2,000. The white canvas mat had long since turned a dirty gray. Dark crimson spots stained the canvas, somber reminders of the violence inherent in this strange occupation where men beat one another senseless with their fists. Faded red, white and blue ropes enclosed the ring, in turn supported by equally dingy red, white and blue ring posts. The entire scene was suitably illuminated by an X-shaped assembly of fluorescent lights hanging from the ceiling, emitting an eerie yellow glow that flickered from time to time. On any given day, a dozen or more fighters could be seen busily engaged in the normal activities of the facility. The heavy bag near the door received a constant thump, thump, from heavy-set boxers in gray cotton sweat suits. Featherweights practiced their footwork in front of the mirror, spitting out jabs and ducking imaginary punches from imaginary opponents. "Hot dogs" impressed naïve visitors with fancy rope skipping routines in the center of the room, while other fighters were busily engaged doing sit-ups on the inclined bench, or beating out a rapid rat-a-tat-tat on the speed bag. All the while the ring echoed with the pop-pop-pop of leather gloves striking bare skin as modern gladiators went through their regular sparring sessions under the watchful eye of a professional trainer.

It was a gym bustling with activity and purpose. The fighters—mostly black, Hispanic, and Irish—ranged in age from about 10 to 30. Some worked out just to keep in good physical condition. Others were trying to prevent the final curtain from falling on a mediocre pugilistic career. Still others, in the infancy of their fighting lives, dreamed of that day to come, when they would stand in a brightly lit ring in some exotic locale, receiving the adulation of thousands of screaming fight fans as the referee raised their hand in victory and proclaimed them champion of the world. Gymnasiums such as this are microcosms of life. Dreams are born here, dreams are realized here, dreams also die here. And Constantine "Cus" D'Amato, graduate of the school of the streets, conqueror of the IBC, and manager of two world champions, was the dreammaker.

3

The Birth of a Boxer—1980–1981

"I think you have the talent to be the heavyweight champion of the world some day. But you've got to really want it." It was Cus talking. "If you wanna, you can stay with me for a couple weeks and make up your own mind. Then, afta you get outta Johnstown, you can come here to live, and I'll teach you how to be a champion. It's up to you." Tyson pawed the floor nervously, never raising his eyes off the ground. "Um, ah, I guess so."[1] So it was that Mike Tyson came to live at the Ewald house. He spent two weeks there during the summer of 1980, getting the feel of the house and the surroundings, getting to know Cus and Camille, and meeting the other fighters who lived in the big house on the river. He also spent a couple of hours a day at the gym working out with trainer Teddy Atlas, another D'Amato reclamation project.

It was a lonely two weeks for the 13-year-old Tyson. He didn't mix easily and he didn't trust anybody. He spent most of the time by himself, walking around the large yard or staring out at the scenic Hudson River as it wound its way past the old house, then flowed under the Rip Van Winkle Bridge on its way to New York harbor and the Atlantic Ocean. Mike didn't know what to make of Cus, Camille, and Teddy. They were, after all, white folks, and Mike came from an all-black environment. He studied them very carefully, but from a distance, and decided he would never trust them too much. But he did like the countryside around Catskill. It was quiet and peaceful, and the hours spent in the gym were exhilarating and rewarding. Mike knew he couldn't go back to Brooklyn when he got out of Johnstown. That would be a ticket to certain oblivion. Mike Tyson wanted most of all to be a boxer, and the opportunity appeared to be in Catskill, New York, with Cus D'Amato. That one fact made Mike's final decision easy. Even though he thought Cus was a "crazy old white dude," he decided to give the old man and Catskill a chance. Maybe things would turn out for the best and, after all, anything was better than Brownsville. Mike Tyson walked through the gates of the Tryon School for Boys one last time in September of 1980. He was released into the custody of Cus D'Amato, who would, a year later, become Tyson's legal guardian. Cus was confident that his protégé would one day wear the crown of the heavyweight boxing champion of the world.

The old station wagon wheezed and coughed as it made its way down the New York Thruway, covering the eighty miles from Johnstown to Catskill in a little less than two hours. Teddy Atlas departed from the Thruway at exit 21, followed routes 23 and 385 to Thorpe Road near the village of Athens, and came to a stop in front of a large white Victorian mansion. After being welcomed to his new home by Camille Ewald, Mike took his duffel bag and made his way up the narrow stairway to the third-floor attic bedroom where he would share living quarters with other boxing hopefuls, Kevin Rooney, Frankie Minicelli, Teddy Atlas, and a former boxer named Jay Bright. Jay had come to the Ewald house almost 13 years before, his ten-year-old heart set on becoming a fighter, but Cus quickly discovered that Jay couldn't move fast enough in the ring, couldn't avoid enough punches, and couldn't hit hard enough to offset those weaknesses. Jay subsequently retired from the ring to pursue other interests, including acting and teaching. Through Cus, however, he was able to fulfill one of his boyhood dreams. One dreary September afternoon, as the world outside busied itself with the day's activities, Jay Bright climbed through the ropes of a boxing ring for the last time. There, in a small, nondescript gymnasium, before a sparse gathering of boxers and stragglers, Jay Bright traded punches with his idol, Muhammad Ali.

The third-floor bedroom at Ewald House was a large, austere room with several compact beds strategically located around the perimeter. A regulation size pool table dominated the center of the room, and a Tiffany-style lamp hanging from the ceiling provided adequate lighting for the local hustlers. Large windows, set into three of the walls, let in golden streams of sunlight during most of the daylight hours, making the room bright and cheery. A large movie screen blocked one of the windows, and directly across the room from it a 16mm projector stood at the ready. Dozens of large, 16mm film cans were stored haphazardly in a nearby bookcase, fight films from the private collection of Jim Jacobs showing most of the famous professional fighters of the past 80 years in action. From "Gentleman Jim" Corbett to Muhammad Ali, Jacobs had them all. Fight movies were not specifically a mode of entertainment in the Ewald household. They were primarily an educational tool. Almost every night, boxing movies were reviewed in the upstairs bedroom. Many young boxers, not only the residents but also visiting locals, sat huddled around the room, studying the great legends of the sport while Cus D'Amato pointed out the little nuances that go unnoticed by the general viewing public. They scrutinized each fighter in minute detail, to learn how the great champions fought, what style they used, what strategies they utilized, and how they avoided and escaped from physical difficulties.[2]

Mike spent his first day of freedom in Catskill strolling around the grounds and generally familiarizing himself with the territory. He did not spend much time with the other fighters, choosing instead the privacy of his thoughts. In the evening he puttered around the pool table, playing several games of rotation, trying to adjust to his new surroundings. It was the first day of his new life, and he needed time to think and to organize himself. Acceptance, however, would be a long time coming. Tyson's mind was contaminated with the mentality of the streets, built up over a harrowing 13-year period. During that time, he had developed a prisoner's attitude toward life—sullen, suspicious, and hostile. It was a poison that blanketed his mind like a dark cloud, and it would take a long time to remove, if it could ever be removed. As Cus said many times, a person's bitter and unhappy experiences have to be eliminated layer by layer before the inner person can be revealed. To do that requires the utmost patience. Fortunately for Tyson, Cus was up to the task.

Tyson spent weeks observing his "white family," always wondering what they were after. He was convinced they would take advantage of him sooner or later if he let his guard down. And he waited for them to make their move. He knew from experience that no one was ever kind to another person without a selfish reason. Everyone had an angle. Throughout the long, lonely days at home and in the gym, the Brooklyn teenager wondered what Cus's angle was. Practically every white person that Mike had ever come in contact with in Brooklyn and in Johnstown was an adversary. That included truant officers, social workers, police officers, lawyers, judges, prison officials, counselors, and guards. They were all out to get him. It seemed obvious that Cus and Camille were adversaries too. But they wouldn't outwit him, he told himself. He would always be on his guard. His negative attitude resulted in numerous confrontations during his first months in Catskill. He was stubborn and rebellious, and he had to be forced to carry his share of the workload around the house. Camille had to tell him repeatedly to stop eating food with his fingers, and to clean his place at the dinner table when he was finished eating. His sloppy living habits, such as leaving his bed unmade in the morning and dropping his dirty clothes on the bedroom floor, brought frequent rebukes from both Cus and Camille. And it was impossible to get Mike to cooperate with the other fighters in sharing the dishwashing responsibilities.

It was a critical time in Tyson's life. He could be rescued from his self-imposed emotional prison, or he could plunge deeper and deeper into the abyss of anti-social behavior. It all depended on how he was handled. D'Amato understood the situation perfectly, having grown up on the streets himself. He had also been through the same situation with Floyd Patterson, as well as with many other fighters whose names have long since been forgotten. Early morning was Mike's favorite time of the day. He was up and out of bed at 5:30 a.m. and, by six o'clock, he and Teddy Atlas were doing their roadwork. The morning air was crisp in the fall of the year, and it was invigorating to get out of the house and to inhale the fresh scents of the river and the countryside. It presented a stark contrast to Mike's boyhood days in Brooklyn where municipal and industrial pollution hung heavy over the city. A light fog covered the Hudson as the sun came up, and the dew hugged the grass like thousands of tiny crystal beads. At times like these, Mike felt all alone in the world and completely at peace with himself.

He liked to run, and the quiet surroundings had a calming influence on him. He thought how nice it would be if he could run forever, and no one could ever bother him again. The dirt road leading away from the Ewald house was desolate at dawn, and the only sounds that broke the silence were the rhythmic breathing of the two runners and the melodious refrains of the cardinals and robins. Mike normally jogged two or three miles each morning, just enough to get the adrenaline flowing. The morning run was not a major part of his conditioning program. Its real value was in the discipline required to get out of bed at 5:30 a.m. sometimes in the dark, and long before most people rose to greet the day. After jogging, it was back to the house for a refreshing shower, then a nutritious breakfast of ham and eggs, or pancakes, or hot cereal, often prepared by Cus himself.

Tyson's emotional education started early in the day. Cus's lectures began while breakfast was cooking, continued through the meal, and lasted right up to the time that Mike left to catch the bus for school. Mike attended the Catskill public school system and was enrolled in the eighth grade at the Catskill Middle School. He did not particularly enjoy school but Cus insisted that he get an education. "Someday," Cus told him, "you're gonna be famous and on television, and it's important for you to know how to speak properly. School is important."[3] Despite a major effort on Mike's part to concentrate in school, he still could not wait for the end of the day. As soon as the 2:30 bell rang, Mike was out the door like a shot, racing the two miles to Main Street in nothing flat. He spent most of his afternoons at the Catskill Boys Club sharpening his skills at basketball, ping pong, and pool. Then at 5:30, it was off to Redman's Hall and his two-hour conditioning program in the gym. Mike was placed under the tutelage of Teddy Atlas, who was to be his trainer and confidant during his formative years at the Catskill Boxing Club. D'Amato had the utmost confidence in Teddy's ability to train young fighters in the physical and scientific aspects of the sport, and also to nursemaid them, so to speak, on an emotional level.

Teddy was able to relate to boys like Tyson because he too had been an orphan of the streets. Although born into a wealthy physician's family in Staten Island, Teddy nonetheless gravitated toward the smoldering social structures of the gutters and alleyways. A jagged four-inch scar running the length of Teddy's face, just behind his left eye, was a stark reminder of a juvenile knife fight. Teddy originally came to Catskill in 1976 at the age of 19 to study boxing under the watchful eye of the old master. He was recommended to D'Amato by his boyhood chum, Kevin Rooney. Before Cus could begin his rehabilitation program, however, he first had to rescue young Atlas from a Staten Island courtroom where the judge was ready to lock him up and throw the key away. Teddy boxed for Cus for two years, went home to Staten Island in 1978, then returned to Catskill two years later, more determined than ever to become a professional fighter. Teddy lived at the Ewald house for several years, and Camille noticed a drastic change in his personality during that time.

> Teddy was a rough guy, a guy that you can't fool around with. You just look at him cross-eyed, he was gonna hit you. That's the kind of boy Teddy was. And I would say now he's changed. He has more love, more understanding, and he also sees differently. That's why he's so good to the boys now, because he sees what he was. He'd pick up the kids from the street and he's so good to them, buys them this, buys them that. I feel that's the way he is.[4]

Mike Tyson loved the gym work and the physical effort involved in developing his body. He was naturally endowed with a magnificent physique, squat but rippling with muscles, and he took pride in the way he looked. He was built like a weightlifter, with a normal-size lower body and an immense upper torso, carrying 208 pounds on a 5'10' frame. His thick 19¾-inch neck was perched atop mammoth shoulders and chest, the whole being supported by relatively spindly legs. The Brooklyn native had ruggedly handsome features,

His career in the ring cut short by a back injury, Teddy Atlas learned his trade as a trainer under D'Amato (courtesy Teddy Atlas).

3. The Birth of a Boxer—1980–1981

his innocent smile set off by two gold-capped front teeth that glistened in the yellow glare of fluorescent lights. A wide gap between the front teeth created a noticeable lisp when he talked. For several months, Teddy's program concentrated on only two things: building up Mike's stamina and his strength. Cus did not get involved in the regimen, and he wouldn't get involved until Mike Tyson became receptive to his instructions, which wouldn't happen until Cus was able to strip off all the inhibitions that had accumulated on Mike's psyche during his years in Brooklyn.

Teddy worked with Mike on the basics: the speed bag to develop his hand speed and tone up his shoulder muscles, the body bag to strengthen his arms and increase his punching power, the small slip bag to improve his upper body dexterity, and the jump rope to strengthen his leg muscles and increase his stamina. A full regimen of gym exercises and calisthenics was also utilized to build up the strategic areas of Mike's body. These exercises included sit-ups to tighten his stomach muscles, and the wrestler's bridge to toughen his already powerful neck muscles. Mike was allowed to spar in the ring, but only on the rudiments of the sport; no fancy strategy and no boxing psychology, only straightforward boxing fundamentals. Mike's bag work included several drills on the "Willie," the name given to the numbered body bag that Cus had designed many years before, in the old Grammercy days. The bag was dubbed the Willie after it was used extensively by Jose Torres during training for the light heavyweight title fight with the champion, Willie Pastrano. Cus provided a tape recording to be used in conjunction with the Willie, and every day Mike toiled under the invisible direction of the wily old trainer as the recorder blared its repetitive instructions—1-1-1, 2-2-2, 3-3-3. Faster. Faster. Combinations—7-2, 7-2, then 8-2, 8-2, 8-2. The tape was timed to three-minute rounds, and Mike got in a full five rounds before he moved on to the next drill.

When the gym work ended, Mike headed back to the Ewald house and Cus D'Amato's other classroom. The rest of the day and the evening were spent in sessions with Cus, with Cus doing most of the talking and Mike doing most of the listening. At first Mike was a poor student. He resisted Cus's teachings completely, still very suspicious of the "crazy old white dude." While Cus talked, Mike entertained himself with fanciful dreams. His mind frequently drifted off into space, absorbed in a fairy tale world of his own creation. But Cus kept plugging away. He had to make Mike realize that he too came from a ghetto neighborhood, from the streets of the Bronx, and that he too went through years of frustrating, degrading, and humiliating experiences. He tried to impress upon Mike that these early experiences could be overcome and that all people were not as bad as Tyson suspected they were. On those occasions when Mike was particularly rude or inattentive, Cus chastised him vocally, but in private. If Mike repeated the action, Cus rebuked him in public with the reminder, "You're not back in Brooklyn now. You're in Camille's house, so behave yourself." On the surface Mike appeared tough, but underneath he was strangely gentle and sensitive, and whenever he had a run-in with Cus, he would flee to the arms of Camille for comfort and sympathy.

The lessons continued. Mike still felt inadequate because of his limited reading ability, so in addition to his formal education, Cus engaged a tutor to come in several hours a week to work with Mike on his word skills. Cus also gave his student a number of books to read. Naturally they dwelt on great achievers of the past, historical figures like Alexander the Great, Napoleon, and Julius Caesar. However, Cus also included a book about a man that Mike could relate to more easily, baseball's black trailblazer, Jackie Robinson. Mike devoured every word—and came back for more. Cus inundated young Tyson with his theories of life, day after day, pounding and pounding until the teenager began to be receptive. And then the old trainer pounded some more. As with all his students, Tyson was first introduced to D'Amato's favorite subject—fear.

> Fear is the greatest obstacle to learning and achievement. But fear is normal. Everyone is afraid. I know. I grew up on the streets just like you did and I was afraid all the time, but nobody knew it. The important thing is to control fear. You have to control it or it will kill you. Do you know the difference between bein' afraid and bein' yellow? Do you know the difference between a hero and a coward? No? Well I'll tell you. There is no difference between a hero and a coward. They both feel the same. It's what they do that makes them different. Everybody is afraid. The coward is yellow. He doesn't face what he has to face. He runs away. But the hero faces what he has to face even though he's afraid. Now this is something that everybody knows, yet they don't know. They don't like to admit that. They don't like to think of themselves as being afraid. Everybody is afraid.[5]
>
> It is one of the biggest obstacles in boxing and I suppose in every field of human endeavor. Now the example I use is the same one all the time. It's about a deer crossin' a field. Comes to a forest, and at that moment his instinct tells him that danger is there. Now his instant reaction is to survive, and his adrenaline glands inject a substance into the bloodstream causin' the heart to beat faster and allowin' the deer to perform extraordinary feats of agility. Where normally the deer could jump 15 or 20 feet, the adrenaline allows him to jump 40 feet, enough to get outta the way of the immediate danger—of the mountain lion if that's what it was. Now this is nature's way of helpin' animals to survive. The same thing applies to people. Now if we allow our fear to control us, we are doomed. Fear is like fire. If we can control fire, we can use it to cook our food and heat our house. But if we don't learn how to control it, it will destroy us and everything around us. So therefore, when you deal with fear, you must never allow it to build up. If you ever have to deal with someone and you are intimidated by him, by his money or his power, or whatever, this is another form of fire. You gotta control that because he is no different than anyone else. This is important for a fighter to know. It's important to know that we all have fear. A controlled fighter, one who controls his fear, can intimidate his opponent. Fighters in the ring with Muhammad Ali were always intimidated by him. Ali's secret weapon was his fear. He was afraid to lose and he transferred that fear into a tremendous will to win, and he projected it as an irresistible force, which immediately tended to inhibit the ability of his opponent to execute what he knew. Fear can be your best friend or your worst enemy. Fear is a thing to be controlled. Make it work for you, like Ali. Don't let it control you. Control it and it makes you more alert. It gets the adrenaline goin' and helps you concentrate more.[6]

Month after month, Mike listened quietly to Cus's monologues, without any indication of whether he understood what Cus was trying to get across. As Cus stared into Tyson's vacant eyes, he often wondered, "How can I reach this kid? Does he know what I'm tryna tell him? I gotta make him realize his potential." It was very frustrating, but Cus had been through it many times before and he was prepared for the task. He knew what was required to penetrate Tyson's shell in order to expose the real boy. It would take kindness, understanding and patience. In the end, lots and lots of patience.

The discussion was ended with the call for dinner. Cus quickly made his way to the dining room to help Camille distribute the place settings. Helping with the household chores was another part of the D'Amato psychological training program. Cus placed great emphasis on teaching by example. As he carefully arranged the napkins beside each plate, his mind wandered aimlessly, reflecting on his recent domestication. "I was just thinking to myself, all my friends in my past see me doin' it and they won't believe it. But after you do it awhile, you forget about it, just like you been doin' it all your life."[7]

In addition to Cus, Mike, and Camille, dinner was usually shared with the other boxers in the house, Atlas, Rooney, Minicelli, Tom Patti, and Jay Bright. Dinner was noisy in the Ewald household with several conversations going on simultaneously, but the subject of all the conversations was the same, boxing. Some days Cus did not participate in the conversations, but instead sat back as an interested observer, and let the boys do most of the talking. Most of the boxers jabbered away incessantly about their day at the gym, but Mike rarely got involved in these dinner-time activities, preferring to study the scene from a distance, still suspicious of the entire group, still hostile. When dinner ended, Mike quietly excused himself and stole away from the group to stroll around the lawn, trying to understand his situation, trying to put his life in perspective. One thing he was sure of—he enjoyed the solitude of being alone.

When daylight disappeared, Mike quietly ascended the narrow stairway to his room to view old fight films with his new mentor, and to study the strategy of past champions. He watched so many movies over the years, and studied so many great fighters, thousands of them in fact, that he became a boxing trivia expert. In addition to learning how these legends of the ring thought and how they fought, he also knew all the vital statistics pertaining to their careers, how many fights they had, who they fought, what their won-loss record was, etc. One fight that remained embedded in Mike Tyson's memory was the spectacular battle between Battling Nelson and Ad Wolgast in 1910. As Mike told William Nack at *Sports Illustrated*, "It was 40 rounds of non-stop action. I love watching Panama Al Brown. He was 116 pounds, but nearly 5'11' tall. The things he did. A guy nearly six foot tall movin' in and out, side to side, punchin' to the body, bobbin' and weavin'." Rocky Marciano was another fighter that Mike Tyson admired. "I liked Marciano's style. He broke fighters' wills. It shows great character for a man to do that."

Cus interspersed instructive comments into the fight commentary as he and Mike watched.

> Look at Marciano. See how he finished that guy off. When you're a great finisher, you'll become popular. Joe Louis was a great finisher. So was Ray Robinson. Ray Leonard. They got a man in trouble and they threw everything they had at him. Bring him down.
>
> See how persistent [Henry] Armstrong is. He hit that guy with everything he had but the guy didn't go down. But Armstrong just kept comin'. He was a well-disciplined fighter. Without discipline, no matter how good you are, you're nothin'. You can't let yourself get discouraged. When you hit an opponent and he doesn't fall, you have to keep your composure and hit him again. You've got to maintain your discipline and your fight plan.
>
> Notice how Rocky [Marciano] attacks the body. You don't have to be a head hunter. Concentrate on the body. Be a great body puncher. You can take a man out with a well-timed shot to the liver just as easily as you can with a punch to the jaw.
>
> Concentrate on your opponent's most vulnerable targets:
>
> - The liver on the right side.
> - The floating rib on the left side.
> - The jawbone below the ear lobe.
> - The point of the chin.[8]

Tyson invariably fell asleep with boxing jargon ringing in his ears.

Despite the fact that Mike was surrounded by people in Catskill, he was still lonely, and he longed for the companionship of someone he could trust. In Brooklyn, at least he had his street rats, his loving pigeons. One day he asked Cus and Camille if he could build a pigeon coop in the back yard and stock it with a family of his feathered friends. Cus immediately vetoed the idea. He told his protégé that he would first have to earn that privilege through his actions at home and at school. This directive from the old white man caused young Tyson to brood more and to withdraw deeper into his shell of mistrust.

As fall turned to winter, the education of Mike Tyson continued unabated. Slowly the veil of mistrust and hostility began to fade from Tyson's countenance. His personal relationship with Camille grew closer, and he began to open himself up to D'Amato's philosophy. At first it was nothing more than an understanding of what Cus was saying. Little by little, however, a belief began to evolve that perhaps Cus D'Amato did hold the secret to success, not only in the boxing ring but in life in general. As Tyson's attitude changed, his ability to absorb and to comprehend increased rapidly. Cus's words from the old Grammercy Gym came to mind once again. "When he becomes receptive, I can begin teachin' him. Once he understands everything I've said, then and only then do I begin teachin'. If I tried to do it earlier, my words would fall off him like water off a window pane."[9]

Now the real ring education of Mike Tyson could begin. In the early days, ring work was designed primarily to get Tyson in the best physical condition possible and to give him a working knowledge of the ring. Now that he was receptive, Cus could zero in on the strategy of the sport and begin to develop the potential of the inner man. Tyson's ring education would now incorporate Cus's unique peek-a-boo style of defense with an aggressive offensive posture designed to entertain the fans as well as to win the fight. The new gym program also concentrated on improving Tyson's mobility and flexibility and, most important, on learning and perfecting the mental approach to the sport. Tyson arrived at the Catskill Boxing Club every day at precisely 6 p.m. following his afternoon excursions to the Boys Club. He quickly changed into his boxing gear. On entering the gym, he went through his loosening-up ritual of shadow boxing for five or ten minutes, then followed with some intricate rope skipping exercises to get the perspiration flowing freely. When he was thoroughly warmed up, Teddy Atlas set about taping his hands, lacing his gloves on securely, and tightening the protective belt over his hips, preparatory to his getting in the ring.

Cus eagerly awaited Tyson's arrival. He drilled Mike on the strategy behind the peek-a-boo style of defense, to allow a fighter to move forward aggressively, always bobbing and weaving, exploding punches in flurries without the fear of getting hit. It was important that Tyson knew the reason for using that type of defense. In order to utilize a strategy to the fullest, a fighter must first understand the reason for it and have the utmost confidence in it. Otherwise it won't work. From the beginning, Tyson was a human dynamo in the ring, a destructive force with tremendous power in either hand. He was a relentless puncher whose speed caused one expert to remark that he had "the fastest hands in heavyweight history." In the initial stages of Mike Tyson's ring education, he normally worked out with Atlas or with welterweight Kevin Rooney. He was not allowed to spar for many weeks, working instead on strategy and execution. Having once been taught a particular maneuver, Mike would be drilled repeatedly by Teddy as Cus watched. Teddy would don the big catcher's mitts and Mike would aim his punches at them as the two boxers moved around the ring. Mike concentrated on his defense, always under the careful scrutiny of D'Amato, who hung over the top rope yelling instructions to his young protégé. Three rounds on the speed bag followed Mike's ring work. Then he slowly tapered off with some sit-ups, heavy bag work, and calisthenics. Time passed quickly in the gym, as it does when you're enjoying yourself, and in a little over two hours Tyson was in and out.

Weeks passed and Tyson's progress was phenomenal, just as D'Amato had predicted.

> First I explain what it takes to be a champion. I tell 'em that these problems most everybody has, but most of them are buried under layer upon layer of life experiences, so the fella is not even aware of them himself. So one of the jobs I have is to peel off the layers until the real guy is exposed, not only

to me who knew it all the while, but to the fighter himself. And once he becomes aware that he has these potentials, now he can start learnin'. Now he can start understandin'. Now he can start makin' progress. And from that point on, progress is rapid.

Progress was rapid but it was not easy. Now that Tyson was receptive, Cus had to work on his mental attitude, his concentration, and his confidence.

Now when I tell people that boxin' is 75 percent psychological and only 25 percent physical, it's very hard to believe. But I believe it's more-so. I believe it's 85 percent psychological. And the ability to make a person see this and to make him believe and understand it are usually the things that will help to predict success.

You give me a man that believes somethin', I mean believes it, I don't mean just approves of it or agrees with it, but believes it to the exclusion of all other things, and I'll give you a champion. Now of course you gotta give him an idea of how you're gonna accomplish it. Now one of the greatest fears is of gettin' hit, because this fella has never been hit before. It's hard to make him understand, but these fellas are intimidated more easily. For these fellas you've got to develop a defense. You've gotta show them that, if they do what you say, they will develop the type of defense which makes getting hit extremely unlikely, to say the least. I've had fighters who fought for seven years, won the championship without ever takin' a hard blow. You find it hard to believe when you see all those punches flyin' around. You think they're getting' hit. They're not getting' hit. That's because they learned how to do it, and they believed in what they were doin'. They believed it enough to do it with consistency, to be relaxed, to be impersonal. To be relaxed and impersonal means your mind is clear. Now you can be watching an accident for example, and report it. And maybe there were a dozen people in the accident. You ask the dozen people who were in the accident what happened and you'll have a dozen different versions. But the one guy watchin' can tell you clearly what happened because none of his emotions were involved. He'll say just what he saw. Well, it's the same with everything else. If you're able to become relaxed, impersonal, you cannot make mistakes because the thing that causes you to make mistakes is emotion, and the highest emotion is fear, or a form of fear like ridicule or embarrassment. These kinds of things cause a fella to perform at less than his real level.

Now, first I give him this defense and, as a result of this, he gains confidence. Now for example, if a boy is boxin', I tell him when he throws a wide left hook to step inside with a right hand and the other fella's left hook will go over his head, see. Now, when he does it and doesn't move inside enough, the guy hits him on the jaw. Well, when he gets hit, he gets shook up and hurt. Now when I tell him, "move in on that left hook," he says to himself, "the hell with you." You gotta show him how to do it in such a way that when he moves in, the punch will go around his head and not hit him, or hit him on the gloves. So now when it works, he says, "Well, I didn't get hit." If he does get hit on the gloves, it didn't hurt. Now the next time you tell him to do it, he does it with more confidence. So now the point I'm bringin' out here is the effect of the mind on his learnin'. You have to teach him to do what he does in such a way that he can do it predictably and he has the confidence that comes as a result of his accomplishments. Because, unless he gets that feelin', the fear will intimidate.[10]

As Tyson's talents exploded, the time approached where he would have to be thrust into the arena to face real opponents, opponents who would be in there to take his head off. Tyson's brain trust was already hard at work mapping out the long-term strategy for his amateur and professional career. The brain trust consisted of D'Amato, Jim Jacobs, and Bill Cayton. Jacobs and Cayton owned "Big Fights, Inc.," a New York firm that produced boxing films and documentaries, films that, over the years, resulted in two Academy Award nominations. Jim Jacobs was well known in boxing circles, having been involved in the sport for over 20 years. In his younger days, Jacobs was a renowned handball player. He won the Junior National Four Wall Handball title in 1953, and between 1955–1960, advancing into the adult bracket, he captured seven more national championships, six singles and one doubles. Even today, he is frequently referred to as "The Babe Ruth of handball." At one time, Cus

D'Amato had visions of turning Jacobs into a boxing champion, being convinced that a gifted athlete could be a champion in any sport. Jacobs' boxing career never came to pass, but he did become a protégé of D'Amato's, rooming with Cus for ten years before gravitating toward a business career in boxing.

Over the years Jim Jacobs accumulated over 26,000 fight films, estimated to be about 90 percent of all the fight films ever made. These include not only the professional productions of the movie studios and television networks, but also a rare collection of amateur films taken of obscure fights by ringside patrons. The amateur films produced interesting footage of many celebrated boxers in the embryonic stages of their careers, boxers like Floyd Patterson and "Sugar Ray" Robinson fighting in the Golden Gloves. Jacobs' film collection led to one of the most popular sports television series of the 1950s. Bill Cayton, another of Tyson's managers, was weaned in the advertising business and, in the late 1940s, found himself creating television shows for NBC. In 1949, Cayton developed a show called "Greatest Fights of the Century." Each week the show would focus on the career of one of the distinguished boxers of the twentieth century, and would fascinate audiences with rare film clips from some of his legendary fights. The films were from the collection of Jim Jacobs, who also narrated the fights. In 1961, Jacobs and Cayton finally joined forces, forming a film production company called "Turn of the Century Fights, Inc." In addition to being acclaimed the world's greatest handball player, and in addition to accumulating the world's largest collection of boxing films, Jim Jacobs had one other claim to fame. He owned the world's most comprehensive comic book collection, with two Los Angeles warehouses reportedly containing a copy of every comic book ever published.

Jacobs and Cayton became boxing managers somewhere along the line. In 1977, they obtained the contract of the world's Junior Welterweight Champion, Wilfred Benitez, for a minuscule $75,000, surely one of the best bargains of the decade. Jacobs subsequently developed a reputation as a shrewd business manager. Benitez, for example, was the only man that "Sugar Ray" Leonard ever fought who got a larger percentage of the purse than Leonard did. In fact, Benitez earned $7.2 million for seven title fights over a six-year period under Jacobs' direction.

The Tyson strategy committee set about to bring Mike's career along very slowly and carefully. Time was on their side. After all, the boy was only 14 years old, and there was plenty of time to mold him into a world class boxer and eventual heavyweight champion of the world. The target date for his title shot would be sometime in 1987, when Mike Tyson would still be only 20 years old. If he were to win the title by that date, he would become the youngest heavyweight champion in boxing history, surpassing Floyd Patterson, who reached the pinnacle in 1956 at the tender age of 21 years and 11 months.

In late 1980, Mike Tyson began his climb to the top of the boxing world by fighting in "smokers," those unofficial and often poorly regulated boxing matches that are still held in every metropolitan center across the country. Mike got his baptism of fire primarily in and around the Bronx, still a hotbed of fight clubs. Teddy Atlas was training several other young boxers in addition to Tyson, and every week he piled six or seven of them into the family station wagon and hauled them to New York for matches. John Chetti, another of the promising fighters in Cus's stable, remembered the "smokers" vividly.

> We fought in the hell holes of New York City, old post offices, old churches, roach-infested buildings, mostly in the South Bronx. It was a Spanish neighborhood and Saturday night was their weekend, their night to have fun. They got all dressed up and came to the fights, and there was a lot of betting

3. The Birth of a Boxer—1980–1981

Tyson always related well to children (courtesy Paul V. Post).

on the fights—big bets. I remember Mike's first fight. It was really funny. No one in the Bronx had ever seen him before, so they all bet on the other kid, a Spanish kid from the neighborhood. Mike was really nervous before the fight and he got himself all worked up. When the fight began, Mike started hitting the other guy. He beat the kid to death on the ropes. The referee jumped in between the two of them to give the Spanish kid a standing eight count, but Mike was so excited he pushed the referee out of the way and started to pound the kid again. The crowd went wild. Half of them were standing on their seats screaming at Mike and shaking their fists at him. I thought somebody was going to get killed. The judges couldn't give a decision because of all the money that was bet on the fight so they called it no contest. The Spanish kid was crying because he got beat up so bad, and Mike was crying because he was so excited. It was really funny. The two of them were hugging each other and crying in the center of the ring.[11]

The next time around, Mike Tyson was not quite so nervous, but he was still anxious to fight. Many of the people at the fight knew who he was now, so there weren't many bets on his opponent, Jose Perez. Both boys were husky specimens, weighing about 195 pounds each, but Mike had too much talent for his older opponent and dispatched the local boy easily in the third round. He followed up his first victory with four more "smoker" KOs in quick succession to run his record to an enviable 5–0. These bouts were an important part of Tyson's development program, but they could not be included in his "official" amateur record since they were not sanctioned by the New York State Boxing Commission. The bouts did give the Catskill teenager valuable experience, however. They provided the atmosphere that is present in all sporting events, the thrill of actual competition and the excitement of fighting before a screaming crowd of spectators. Mike also learned to adapt his fight plan to combat a variety of opponents and boxing styles. He fought big men and small men, orthodox fighters and southpaws, sluggers and runners. He fought them all, and he learned how to defeat each type of fighter. He made the usual beginner's mistakes, but his skills so far outdistanced those of his opponents that he was able to overcome his mistakes and still win comfortably. And he learned not to make the same mistake twice.

Mike's early career was not all positive, however. His youth actually stifled his progress. He had matured very early and at 14 had the physique of a man several years older. Despite his enormous talent, his chronological age prevented him from competing in the Seniors competitions, such as the Empire State Games and the Golden Gloves, where the age requirement was 16. Mike had to make do, as best he could, in the Juniors, where the competition was not up to his level. The Catskill duo took advantage of this situation to concentrate on other aspects of Mike's ring education. Teacher and student worked diligently on perfecting his mental processes, a critical weapon in a boxer's arsenal. It was this segment of the sport that D'Amato focused on, first and foremost.

> When I have a kid in the gym, the first thing I do is get him in perfect condition. Then I put him in with a fighter who generally knows how to fight, but who is not gonna hurt him. That fella will keep comin'. He'll be taking punches deliberately. Suddenly this guy gets exhausted. He can't pick up his arms. Now why is he tired? I purposely got him in perfect condition so he couldn't possibly get tired, see. But yet he's exhausted. He can't pick up his arms. Well, if he were really exhausted, he couldn't come back. It's like when a car runs outta gas. You can curse it, kick it, abuse it, it's not gonna run. And in this case, if he was outta gas, he couldn't come back. But sometimes after a fella gets in a good punch, and it has an effect, suddenly he's a tiger. Sees this guy is hurt. Bang! Bang! Comes back. Well, if he was really tired, he couldn't generate that kind of energy to do that. So now he realizes it was somethin' else other than physical exhaustion that made him feel tired and wanna quit. I try to make him understand at an early age how much the mind can affect your performance. In fact, it is the mind, and it is the emotion, the ability to control your emotions, that determines whether you win or lose.[12]

That lesson was given a practical demonstration one night in a "smoker." The Catskill puncher fought a tough local kid who took his best shots and refused to quit. After seeing his courageous opponent get back on his feet time and again after seeming knockouts, the inexperienced Tyson became frustrated and discouraged. He tried to quit after the first round, claiming an injury, but trainer Teddy Atlas, realizing what was happening, pushed his fighter back out for round two. The same scenario was repeated. Tyson knocked the kid down with a devastating hook, but the youngster dragged himself upright one more time. Between rounds, a dejected Tyson told Atlas he was too tired to continue. Teddy exploded, "Get up, goddamn it!" He picked Tyson up off his stool and stood him up.[13] After struggling through the third round and winning an easy decision, a thankful Tyson recalled the words of his mentor just a few short days ago. "It's the ability to control your emotions that determines whether you win or lose." D'Amato and Tyson toiled relentlessly to refine Mike's mental and physical skills, but they were cautious and systematic in their approach. They were guided by a single goal, to win the heavyweight championship of the world in 1987, and they gauged their progress accordingly. Cus was very selective in choosing Mike's ring opponents, always looking for a man who could teach Mike something about one specific aspect of the sport, but a man who was not capable of beating him.

The strategy for each fight was reviewed in detail as soon as the opponent was known. Sparring partners were hired to simulate the opponent's style in the ring. If Mike was fighting a southpaw, then left-handed sparring partners were brought to Catskill to work with him.

Mike was taught to move to his right, away from the other man's power. If the opponent was tall, then Mike worked with tall spar mates and concentrated on working his way inside the taller man's reach, bobbing and weaving until he was in position to launch a full-scale body attack. After each fight, D'Amato and Tyson would sit down to critique the youngster's performance. It didn't matter how well Mike did in the fight, Cus would always find something wrong with his effort, some aspect of his strategy or execution that had to be improved. Cus always worked to build Mike's confidence, but tried never to let the praise reach the point where it would inflate his ego. The most dangerous thing that can happen to a fighter is for him to get cocky and overconfident. That's a sure way to bring about his downfall. Cus always had to travel the fine line between praise and criticism. Too much criticism would destroy Tyson's confidence. Too much praise, on the other hand, could result in an overconfident fighter who was in danger of taking a fall. Build the confidence but keep the fighter under control. That's what Cus worked on, and he was a master at it.

Each night, back at Ewald House, D'Amato and his protégé would sit next to the movie projector and study films of former champions. Each fighter had something to teach Mike. Initially, Cus would point out the important strategy and fight plan, why certain fighters always won and why other fighters lost. Eventually Mike learned to detect the little nuances in each fight himself, the small, often unnoticed turn of events that determined the outcome of each match. He learned how well big men could move if they were properly trained. He learned how men with great discipline could break down an opponent's will. And conversely, he learned that most fighters don't get beaten, they quit, a subject that D'Amato expounded on in great detail.

> The word quit means that you no longer want to continue even though there's nothin' serious in front of you. I know fighters who hit the guy with their best punch an' when he didn't go down, they didn't wanna fight anymore. They don't say it but they'll find a convenient blow that'll knock them down and they'll lay there until they're knocked out. Now usually when a fella quits, he quits because he wasn't properly prepared at that particular time. It's very difficult nowadays, you see. I have a friend who's a psychiatrist. His name is John Halpin, and he knows about the mind, and he says I have better results than most of the doctors he knows. That's a fact. That's what he told me. Now the reason I do have success is I'm able to do what they can't do. They have to wait for the normal development of circumstances. I create the circumstances in the gym. I can put my fella in with this fella, that fella, with their different styles, their different capabilities, their different strengths, and their different weaknesses. See, I can arrange for them to fight fellas who have weaknesses that he can meet, and the ability to beat them is the key to success. And each time he meets with success, he becomes better and stronger. Success breeds success and failure breeds failure. You always gotta give him an advantage in goals. You put him in with a guy he can't beat and it's gonna have the opposite effect. And it's hard to rebuild unless, as I do, I always leave a way out, so that if anything goes wrong, I now have this basis on which to approach him and explain to him why he failed, and it wasn't because he wasn't capable, because he failed to do one of the things he learned to do. When he recognizes that, he knows that all he needs to do is do that again and it won't happen. That's the way it works.[14]

As 1981 unfolded, winter turned to spring, the grass took on a mantle of deep green, the trees blossomed with luxuriant foliage, and Mike Tyson's scholastic career sputtered along on its turbulent course. Tyson had a deep-rooted abhorrence for authority, going back to his Brownsville days, where he had constant run-ins with both school officials and juvenile authorities. The situation was no different in Catskill, where every day was an adventure in learning for the young rebel, as well as a trial for his aged guardian. At home, Tyson was beginning to show some respect for both Camille and Cus, but at school he was in frequent trouble. One day he was involved in a loud altercation on the bus as it pulled into the schoolyard. Teacher John Turek quickly entered the bus only to find himself face to face with a hostile Mike Tyson. Although no blows were struck, Tyson refused to submit to Turek's authority and was immediately suspended from school. On another occasion, Tyson threw an eraser at a teacher whose authority he rejected in the classroom, resulting in yet another suspension. Each time Mike was suspended, Lee Bordick, the principal of the Catskill Middle School, had to entertain the recommendation that Mike be permanently expelled as a disruptive influence on the class. And each time, Cus D'Amato and Teddy Atlas would rush up to the school to plead their case. Fortunately Cus always succeeded in winning a stay of execution for Mike, permitting his formal education to continue along on the rocky road of frustration and confrontation.[15]

Mike had many problems with his new classmates, problems of both a social and educational nature. There were the daily conflicts with the school bullies who enjoyed picking on the new kid in town. Mike, who was a big kid, had above-average self-control for a boy his age and generally ignored the young punks, but occasionally the teasing got the best of him and he reacted to it violently. His relationship with the other kids was a mixed bag. He was street-wise, with well-developed innate skills, but his formal education was poor. He felt superior to his naïve classmates in day-to-day situations, but he still had deep-rooted feelings of inferiority when it came to basic reading and writing skills. He had difficulty adjusting to the study halls of Catskill Middle School after spending years on the streets of Brooklyn, but he promised Cus he would try.

Mike felt more comfortable in the gymnasium, and his attention was focused on the Junior Olympic National Championships to be held in Colorado Springs in June. His and Cus's primary goal for 1981 was winning that championship, which was open to boys from 13 to 16 years of age. Even though it was early in Mike's career, it was already becoming difficult to find satisfactory sparring partners for him, so he was forced to condition himself as best he could, keeping busy with bag work and road work, seven days a week.

On April 18, the boxing world was saddened by the passing of ring immortal Joe Louis. The "Brown Bomber" had succumbed to a heart attack after watching the Larry Holmes-Trevor Berbick title fight in Caesar's Palace in Las Vegas. He was 66 years old. Louis was considered by many boxing experts to have been the greatest heavyweight champion of all time. He successfully defended his title an unprecedented 25 times over a 13-year period, finally retiring in 1949 with his crown still intact. Mike Tyson, too, grieved over the loss of the "Brown Bomber." Joe had been one of Mike's early heroes and a man that he hoped to emulate. In spite of the Louis tragedy, May was a big month for boxing, locally as well as nationally. On May 1, Tyson's stablemate, Kevin Rooney, ran his record to 14–0 with a victory over Felix Nance. Then, on May 11, Gerry Cooney, a 6'6", heavyweight from Long Island, vaulted into the national spotlight with a devastating first-round knockout of former champ Ken Norton. Cooney destroyed Norton with a barrage of punches that left the Californian slumped in a corner, a battered hulk, at the 0:54 mark.

On Sunday afternoon, May 18, dozens of punching specialists from around the northeast descended on Saratoga, New York, to participate in the local Junior Olympic Elimination Tournament. The kids from the Catskill Boxing Club didn't disappoint their fans as they captured gold medals in four of six events. Ten-year-old Billy Ham enthralled the audience with his performance, knocking out Joe Blake in the first round. The 60-pound dynamo finished off the stubborn Blake with a right hand to the body, a trademark of D'Amato-trained fighters. Cus always drilled it into his students, "Kill the body and the head will die." Ham's brilliant performance was recognized by the local tournament committee, who selected him as the event's most outstanding boxer. Several other Catskill fighters fared nearly as well as Ham. Seventy-pound Gary Young won over Jose Ramos, and 95-pound Mane "The Flame" Moore dazzled former three-time champion Tyrone Jackson to earn a well deserved decision. Mike Tyson won his match without working up a sweat. He was awarded the gold medal in a walkover when no opponent could be found to trade punches with the 200-pound behemoth. Tyson, Moore, and Gary Young advanced to the Regionals to be held in New York from June 12 to 14. Billy Ham, the star of the tournament, was too young to compete in the tournament.[16]

The Regionals were still four weeks away so the Catskill contingent kept busy by organizing a tournament of their own. On Saturday, May 23, Cus presented a ten-bout card in Redman's Hall before an enthusiastic standing room only crowd of 400. The excitable, teenage Tyson was matched against John Shea of Beacon, and his youthful exuberance almost brought the house down, literally. Mike pummeled Shea from the start, dropping him to the canvas twice. When the referee stopped the fight without a count following a tremendous left hook to the body, the ecstatic Tyson leaped on the middle strand of ropes and held his arms aloft in a victory salute to the home crowd. The flimsy ring sagged and creaked, almost collapsing under the young heavyweight's exuberance. Frank Minicelli, working hard to keep his emotions under control, squeaked out a three-round decision over Hector Soto. Other local winners included the Young boys—Gary, Greg, Kevin, and Rodney—along with John Chetti and Pat Shanagher.

On June 1, Kevin Rooney took another step toward the welterweight title with an eight-round decision over tough Bobby Pledge. One week later, Leon Spinks stepped into the ring against champion Larry Holmes in Detroit, Michigan, but it turned out to be no contest. The 31-year-old Holmes ran his record to an impressive 38–0 and scored his 28th knockout in the process as he disposed of the overrated former champ in the fourth round. Two other heavyweight contenders on the undercard came away victorious. The talented Greg Page KO'd Alfredo Evangelista at 0:40 of round two. Page was a boxer with unlimited potential, but he was completely lacking in discipline and determination. He never displayed the inner strength required to get into top physical condition. In spite of this deficiency, his raw talent kept him in the top ten rankings for years, and even gave him a piece of the title for a short period of time. Tragically, his lack of discipline prevented him from dominating the heavyweight division. Greg Page took the easy way out. He settled for second best. The other contender, Michael Dokes, KO'd Englishman John L. Gardner at 1:51 of the fourth round. Talk around the Holmes camp after the Spinks fight was about a possible match with Gerry Cooney. The big, easygoing Irishman was the perfect opponent for Holmes. Cooney was colorful, he was powerful, he was a crowd pleaser—and he was the latest "great white hope," the type that comes along every decade or so to challenge the reigning black champion. The pre-fight bantering and racial slurs were certain to generate a multi-million dollar gate. And, not only that—Cooney was sure he could beat Holmes.

Early in the morning of Saturday, June 13, a large entourage of fighters departed from the Catskill Boxing Club and drove 130 miles to New York City where the local boxing team would do battle with fighters from eight states in the Junior Olympic Regionals. The combatants would compete for gold medals in eight different weight divisions. On the line, however, was more than just a flashy medal. The winners would also qualify for a trip to Colorado to participate in the Junior Olympic National Tournament. The two-day tournament was held in Lost Battalion Hall in Queens under sizzling hot and humid June skies. It was the kind of sticky, hot summer day that the police dread in crowded metropolitan melting pots like New York City. The oppressive temperatures made tempers short, resulting in a large increase in murders in the big city ghettos. Two of the Catskill boxers, notably Mike Tyson and Gary Young, were as hot as the weather. Mane Moore won his semi-final encounter but lost in the finals. Gary Young swept through to the gold, winning the final bout with a second-round TKO over game William Shang.

And then there was Mike Tyson. Devastating was the word for his performance. In the semi-finals, Mike made short work of Tom French, the New England representative. He knocked French down twice and, when the outclassed heavyweight struggled to his feet after the second knockdown, a thundering uppercut finished it. The finals, the following day, was not much more of a challenge. The other finalist, Ira Turner, was game and determined, but he was no match for the precocious Brownsville Bomber. Turner came out punching, but was stopped in his tracks almost immediately and sent crashing to the canvas twice in the opening round. A lightning right cross was the culprit both times. When Tyson picked up where he had left off in the second round, the referee quickly stepped in and stopped the fight to save Turner from further unnecessary punishment. Mike Tyson was king of the east.

Seven days after the Catskill teenager captured his amateur gold, stablemate Kevin Rooney made his first attempt to scale Mt. Everest. Rooney tackled the tough future Junior Middleweight Champion, Davey Moore, in Atlantic City. Rooney had taken two out of three fights from the New Yorker in the amateurs, but this time was different. Moore was at the top of his game, and he handed Rooney his first professional loss, a resounding seventh-round KO.

After a three-week sabbatical from the ring wars, Mike and trainer Teddy Atlas departed Albany on a jumbo jet and headed for the mountainous climes of Colorado. The flight to Denver was Mike's first experience with long-distance travel to a fight location. It was another aspect of boxing that the fighter had to master, how to overcome jet lag and time zone change, and how to adapt to a new locality and a new hotel in a world of strangers. The inconveniences of travelling were not difficult obstacles for the youngster, as it turned out, and his ring performance did not suffer at all. Tyson's major opponent in Colorado was his emotions. He tried hard to keep himself under control, but at 14 years of age, that task was virtually impossible. Mike was still an excitable fighter, with all the advantages and disadvantages that such a state brings. The emotional highs were sky high and the lows were depressing. Cus D'Amato and Teddy Atlas constantly worked on Tyson's state of mind, trying to teach him to remain detached during a match, to maintain a calm demeanor in all situations. It was a quality that Tyson would master by the time he turned professional, but in 1981 he was still too young and immature. He put a lot of pressure on himself early in his career by making winning a life or death struggle each time. He was always edgy before a fight, which is normal, but he carried it to extremes. At times, he almost worked himself into a frenzy by fight time, a condition that not only destroyed his concentration but sapped his energy as well. Fortunately, Mike's talent was so much greater than that of his amateur opponents, that he could overcome a multitude of mistakes and still win.

Tyson and Atlas landed at Stapleton International Airport in Denver on a bright June day and immediately took an airport limousine to the United States Air Force Academy in

Colorado Springs, some 70 miles south. Colorado was breathtaking in mid–June. Everything was green and blossoming, and the Rocky Mountains rose majestically in the distance, the snow-topped Pike's Peak glistening in the mid-day sun. The pre-fight workouts were intense but stimulating. By contrast, the evenings were relaxing in the pleasant surroundings of the Air Force Academy. Classes were out for the summer, and the Junior Olympics had the run of the entire campus. As a result, Mike and Teddy were able to enjoy the comfort of a spacious private room in one of the student dormitories. They could entertain themselves during their free time by attending the local movie theater or enjoying the extensive canteen facilities. They could stroll around the campus, enjoying the spectacular beauty of the western landscape, or they could just sit in their room and talk.

For the most part, Mike kept his mind on the upcoming fights, of which there were three beginning with the quarter-finals. On Wednesday, June 24, Mike Tyson stepped into the ring for the first time. There were three rings in the vast Academy complex, and Mike's match was the 20th match in ring number three. It began three hours after the start of the program, and for a 14-year-old, the long wait was sheer torture. The Catskill fighter spent most of the time nervously pacing the hallways and outside perimeter of the Field House like a greyhound waiting for the gates to open. His nerves were completely frazzled by the time his match was finally announced, but he took a deep breath and regained his composure before entering the arena to do battle. By the time he climbed through the ropes, he projected an air of confidence and determination to the spectators, although inside his stomach churned with terror. When the bell sounded for the start of the fight, Mike stalked his opponent, Jesse Esparza of Lindsay, California, like a starving predator, backing him immediately into the ropes. A crunching body shot to the liver dropped Esparza to the canvas for the full count. The fight was over almost before it began, leaving many patrons still searching for their seats. The official time was 30 seconds. After the fight Tyson admitted, "There was a lot of tension and I was really nervous. I really did not have that many fights behind me, and to come this far was pretty mind boggling."[17]

The next day, Mike's semi-final encounter was the 16th match in ring number two. Again, the waiting preyed on the youngster's mind and he entered the ring nervous and agitated. His adversary, a 260-pound Texan named Randy Wesley, gave his best macho performance during the referee's instructions, as he tried to stare down the New York teenager, but Tyson would have none of it. He had been trained by D'Amato to ignore such theatrics by his opponent, so he returned Wesley's stare with a menacing scowl of his own. When the fight started, Mike was ready and waiting, and Wesley fared no better than Esparza. Both fighters answered the bell quickly and met in center ring. Wesley threw several rights and lefts. Tyson slipped the punches easily, and then countered with a thundering left under the jaw, ending the contest at the 40-second mark. That same evening, 800 miles away in the Houston Astrodome, a much larger spectacle unfolded. Texas was treated to a world class doubleheader with Thomas "The Hit Man" Hearns and "Sugar Ray" Leonard fighting on the same card. Hearns had little competition in Pablo Baez as he successfully defended his WBC Welterweight title with a convincing fourth-round knockout. Leonard, on the other hand, had his hands full with tough little Ayub Kalule. The two fighters frequently stood toe to toe, whaling away at each other. Kalule took some heavy shots from the Sugar Man's flashing fists, but he never took a backward step. Leonard eventually wore him down, and the courageous African was counted out midway through the ninth round, giving Sugar Ray his second title, the WBA Super Welterweight crown.

Friday was an off-day for the Junior Olympics so many of the participants took advantage of a guided tour of the area. They visited the Pioneers Museum in Colorado Springs and the famous mineral springs in Manitou. They studied the grotesque sandstone rock formations in the Garden of the Gods, and then they motored into the mountains to obtain a better view of the 14,109-foot Pike's Peak. Others, like Tyson and Atlas, stayed at the Academy and spent a peaceful day away from the noise, the tension, and the violence of the competition, relaxing and enjoying the Academy's facilities. Saturday rolled around soon enough, and a large crowd pushed their way into the Field House as soon as the doors were opened. Most of them had come to see the new boxing sensation from the east, Mike Tyson, whose reputation as a slugger was already established in Colorado Springs, and whose early performances had made him the "hometown" favorite in the finals.

As soon as the fighters entered the ring, the bloodthirsty fans began screaming for a Tyson knockout. Mike did not disappoint them. His opponent, Joe Cortez, was not intimidated by the reception, however. He had come to fight and, when round one began, he rushed from his corner and threw two wicked hooks in Tyson's direction. Mike bobbed and weaved, slipping both punches, and then leaped in with a right hook of his own that ended the fight at the ten-second mark. Cortez's face twisted in agony as he slumped to the canvas motionless. The immense power behind the punch brought a gasp from the stunned crowd. Tyson summarized the fight pretty well at the post-fight interview. "The guy came at me really fast and tried to catch me off balance, but I slipped under his first flurry of punches and stopped him quick."[18]

Pat Napp, the United States Olympic Boxing Coach, was in the stands for the entire tournament and, like most of the other boxing experts who spent the week in Colorado, he came away very much impressed with the young heavyweight champion. "Tyson is a tremendous prospect. It's hard to believe he's only 14 years old. He has the physique and skills of a man six years older. He is fast and smart and has great power in both hands. He is a definite contender for the 1984 Olympic Team."[19]

Tyson and Atlas were on cloud nine for several days after the Junior Olympics. Euphoria set in following Mike's quick victory and turned their world into a surrealistic landscape where everything was shadowy and dreamlike. The two men were still in a daze when they deplaned in Albany, and the sight that greeted them in Catskill compounded the situation. A large banner waved in the breeze over Main Street, placed there by a grateful Board of Selectmen. It read, "Welcome home champs Teddy and Mike, Junior Olympic Champs." Although Teddy was Mike's trainer, he was not much more than a boy himself. He was only 24 years old and still very emotional. It was Cus D'Amato's job to bring Teddy and Mike down to earth and put them back on track again. "Remember," Cus said, "Control your emotions. You must not get too high or too low. You must stay detached to reach your maximum potential." Maybe it was still too early for a 14-year-old to remain detached. Maybe it was difficult for Tyson to accept his new celebrity status without suffering some minor emotional problems. Be that as it may, he was jerked back to reality in his next fight.

Mike was matched with 20-year-old Anthony Burnett from Rhode Island, an older, more experienced, more seasoned boxer than Mike had encountered in Colorado. This was Burnett's last bout before turning professional, and he made the most of it. He gave Tyson a good boxing lesson for three rounds and came away with a close decision. Mike was back in the real world once again, but he was not depressed by the setback. He realized that it was another profitable learning experience, and that it was just another step forward in his

Tyson was the world's amateur champion at age 15. With Teddy Atlas and New York social worker Ernestine Coleman (courtesy Teddy Atlas).

development process. As he told the *Daily Mail*, "Burnett was tough, smart, and fast. The lack of experience really hurt me against him, but I learned a lot from fightin' him." D'Amato put Tyson back in the ring in the blink of an eye against another experienced, older fighter. This time Mike was on track, and he won a three-round decision against Rick Melton of Albany.

Even with his ring successes, Mike Tyson was still struggling to find his identity. He was unsure of where he fit into society, and he was confused as to where his home was and where his roots were. Were they in Catskill or were they in Brooklyn? Periodically, when the doubts became too much for him to handle, Mike would disappear from Catskill without telling anyone where he was going. But Cus and Camille knew. They knew he was on his way back to Brooklyn, but also knew he would return to them once he thought things out. Mike did go to Brooklyn. He went to visit his family, and to see all his friends from the old gang, but he never stayed more than two weeks. He always found it depressing to return to the life he once knew. His mother, who had been the backbone of the family when Mike was a child, began to drink after her man deserted her. She was now a hopeless alcoholic. She was also suffering from stomach cancer and had less than 18 months to live. Brother Rodney had enlisted in the Navy by this time and was seldom home any more, and the burden of running the household had fallen on Mike's 16-year-old sister, Denise.

Mike enjoyed seeing his buddies again, and he even participated in a street holdup "for old times" sake. The thrill of living on the edge was still there, but so was the promise of punishment. Every time Mike went back to Brownsville, there were fewer and fewer friends to greet him. One by one they disappeared. One died in a knife fight. Another was in prison for armed robbery. One former Tyson associate, barely out of his teens and strung out on drugs, gave the Catskill boxer the benefit of his mistakes. "I'm dyin', man. The drugs are killin' me an' I can't stop. It's too late for me, but not for you. Stay away from drugs or you'll kill yourself."[20] Mike left town quickly, returning to the safety of upstate New York. His home was now in Catskill, but his heart would always be in Brooklyn.

On Wednesday, September 16, the attention of the boxing world focused on the Superdome in New Orleans, Louisiana, where Tommy Hearns attempted to lift the Super Welterweight crown from the head of "Sugar Ray" Leonard. In one of the classic championship battles of all time, each man's momentum and opportunities ebbed and flowed from round to round. In the sixth round, it looked like Leonard was going to finish "The Hit Man," but Hearns backpedaled and escaped Sugar Ray's coup de grace. As so often happens, the rhythm of the fight began to change almost immediately. It was imperceptible at first, but as rounds nine and ten came and went, the direction of the fight became more evident. Tommy Hearns had regained command of the action and was dominating the champion. Between rounds 12 and 13, a distraught Angelo Dundee admonished his charge with the warning, "You're blowin' it, son. You're blowin' it." That was all Leonard needed. Like the champion he was, he sucked in his gut and went back on the attack. With one eye puffed up and almost completely closed, he carried the fight to Hearns in round 13, doing considerable damage in the process. In round 14, he continued to punish the challenger until Hearns' spindly legs could no longer support the weight of his limp body, and he slumped to the canvas in defeat.

Three weeks later, Kevin Rooney got back on the victory trail with a decisive win, running his record to 16–1.

On a warm October evening, the Catskill Boxing Club journeyed to East Greenbush for another of their frequent boxing competitions. Mane "The Flame" Moore took on Tracy Harris from Floyd Patterson's New Paltz Boxing Club, and Moore ground out a three-round decision. Next on the card was likeable Frank Minicelli, who also won a three-round decision. As a matter of fact, he almost pulled off a first-round knockout, but his excitable nature betrayed him and the opportunity slipped through his fingers. Minicelli came out fast and caught Don Papenall with a left hook early in the fight, a punch that completely paralyzed the youngster. The nervous New Yorker lost his poise, however, in his anxiety to win the fight, and Papenall survived. In round two the tables were turned as the boy from New Paltz dominated and almost KO'd Minicelli in a magnificent comeback. To Frankie's credit, he withstood the onslaught and actually won round three to take a close decision.

Mike Tyson followed Frankie into the ring, fighting yet another old pro. This time the opponent was Andy Robitelli of Vermont, the country's number three ranked amateur heavyweight. Tyson was in peak condition for this fight, both mentally and physically. He moved like a lightweight and his punches were sharp and crisp, snapping Robitelli's head back every time they made contact. The Vermont fighter, realizing he had lost the first two rounds, tossed caution to the winds in round three and tried for a knockout. Tyson managed to fend off his flurries without much difficulty, and came away a decision winner to keep the Catskill Boxing Club's perfect record intact.

Mike Tyson was beginning to feel more comfortable with the other members of the gym now, and he began to enjoy the social aspect of the gym as well as the training. Over the previous 12 months, he had developed several close relationships at the Catskill Boxing Club, not only with Cus and Teddy, but with other boxers like Kevin Rooney and John

Chetti. Chetti, three years older than Mike, was something of an advisor to his younger companion. Any time Mike had a problem, particularly a problem associated with growing teenagers, girl problems, that sort of thing, he always went to Chetti for advice. If his problems were of a more serious nature, he sought out "the old folks," Teddy and Cus. Mike's circle of friends included many who were not members of the gym. In addition to John Chetti, he enjoyed the company of Teddy, Jay Bright, and Mike Murphy. Murphy's younger brother Jim, and Chetti's younger brother Chris, stayed close to the older boys, thrilled to be able to associate with their heroes.

One fall night in late 1981, the Chettis invited young Tyson to dine with them at the local Chinese restaurant. It turned out to be an embarrassing exercise in etiquette for the boy from Brooklyn, but all part of the growing process. As the meal progressed, it became apparent that Mike had never eaten in a restaurant before. He ordered spareribs and immediately tried to carve them up with a knife and fork. John Chetti told Mike it was okay to eat the spareribs with his fingers, but young Tyson frowned on that suggestion. "Oh no, I can't do that. Camille told me never to eat food with my fingers." The situation went downhill from there. After everyone had finished their meal, a Chinese waiter cleared away the plates and brought a bowl of fortune cookies to the table. Before anyone could stop him, Mike snatched one of the crisp little delicacies from the bowl, popped the whole thing into his mouth, and began to chew away. "No, no," he was told. "You don't eat the whole thing. There's a paper fortune inside the cookie. First you have to break it open and take out the fortune before you eat the cookie." An embarrassed Mike Tyson quickly removed the soggy paper and discarded it.[21]

During Tyson's early years of amateur competition, he spent most of his time in the gym perfecting his boxing style, developing new tactics, and working on the proper mental approach to the sport. Official bouts were of secondary importance to him and Cus at this stage of his development, but he still managed to fight every other month. The learning process and the drills were primary. After he turned professional, experience became primary, and his ring activity increased significantly, with a fight every two to three weeks. But for now it was school time in the gym, with Cus and Teddy giving Mike a new lesson every day, while at the same time refining and improving his basic talents. During his first year on the circuit, Mike had amassed a record of 6–0 in "smokers" with five KOs, plus an official amateur mark of 8–1 with six KOs. Cus D'Amato was satisfied with his protégé's progress as an amateur, and he told the press what they might expect from the adolescent gladiator in the future. "Mike has all the tools to reach every goal we set for him. He has drive, ambition, and skills. All he needs is time, experience, and more experience."

People in the sports world were beginning to take notice of Tyson now, and reporters occasionally stopped by Redman's Hall for an interview with the new phenom. Cus permitted interviews to some extent as long as they didn't distract Mike from his primary objective, boxing. Tyson enjoyed fighting, but his interviews showed the world that he was not one-dimensional.

> People think boxers are not human sometimes—that they just exist to fight and train, and that is simply not true. I enjoy many things. I enjoy school and gymnastics and I like to spend a lot of my spare time reading and acquiring knowledge about boxing. I really would prefer to fight regularly but I learn a lot of things in the gym and get a chance to work on new things, and good mental training is very important and makes the difference when you're in the ring. It's the mind that beats you, not the body.[22]

The boxing year ended on a sad note as two of the sport's most famous gladiators struggled to regain some of their lost glory. On December 3, "Smokin Joe" Frazier failed in a comeback bid as he was held to a draw by journeyman Floyd "Jumbo" Cummings. Frazier finally conceded victory to Father Time and hung up his gloves for good, leaving behind an enviable record of 32–4–1. One week later, Muhammad Ali also tried to fool Father Time as he fought a hungry Trevor Berbick in Nassau, the Bahamas. Ali was soundly beaten but, unlike Frazier, he would hang on for several more pitiful years.

4

The Quest Begins—1982

The gym at the Catskill Boxing Club buzzed with activity in the winter of 1982, with a dozen or more boxing hopefuls going through their conditioning exercises in and out of the ring. One of the regulars at the gym was ten-year-old Johnny Lowe, a quiet, little street urchin. Johnny adopted the gym as his second home and the residents, in turn, adopted Johnny. One day, as Johnny entered, Cus was talking to 18-year-old John Chetti, discussing his philosophy of life with the young fighter. Cus interrupted the dissertation when he caught sight of Johnny passing by. "Wait a minute. Come here. You really said hello to me." Turning to Chetti, "He did. You heard him, John. He said hello. Who's the guy on your shirt?" Cus inquired, pointing to the silk screen image of a fighter that graced the front of Johnny's t-shirt.

"You don't know him?" Johnny asked Cus incredulously.

"Who is that guy?"

"Muhammad Ali."

"Oh, Muhammad Ali. Wow. Do you know him?"

"No."

John Chetti, taking Johnny by the arm, led him over to the wall where dozens of yellowed newspaper clippings were hanging. John pointed to a photo showing Cus D'Amato playfully throwing a right-hand punch to the jaw of Muhammad Ali.

"Who's that?" Johnny asked.

"Ali."

"Who's that right there?" John pointed to the older man throwing the punch.

"That's Cus D'Amato."

"No."

"Yeah."

Johnny was impressed when he realized that Cus was a friend of Muhammad Ali's.

Trainer Teddy Atlas, wearing a red and white Coca Cola t-shirt under a blue warm-up suit, moved into the gym to work with some of the aspiring teenage fighters. Teddy was a tough-looking young guy whose protruding front teeth, big ears, and jagged scar made him appear very intimidating. The straight black hair, the mustache, and the distinctive boxer's nose added to the impression that here was a guy to be reckoned with. He seemed to have a good rapport with the teenagers in the gym, though, as he guided them through their boxing drills. "Punch inside, then get out. Good." Cus watched the proceedings with a slight smile on his face.

When Teddy first came to me, he came here with the idea of being a fighter, and I trained him as such. In fact, he was a fighter, and when I thought he was ready, I put him in a tournament, and he won every fight he had by a knockout. And it looked like he was gonna make it big someday, big. But then I caught him wincing, you know grimacing in pain. I said, "Whatsa matter?" "Oh, nothin'. Nothin'." So anyhow I pursued the point and I found out he had serious back trouble. So I began to think, maybe I can make a trainer out of him. I can train him and teach him to be a trainer just like I can train him to be a fighter. At first he wasn't so keen about it because all he wanted to do was fight, but after awhile I tried to make him see, and I think I succeeded, that even if you're not a fighter yourself, you can become the same type of success through your fighter. If you take a boy and teach him how to fight from beginning to end, part of you is in him too. So that when he fights, part of you is in the ring, and really, suddenly I discovered he had a real talent for teaching. The fella was a born teacher, and he's the type of person who wants to help people, especially kids, and they come to depend on him and rely on him a great deal. So they become very close that way.[1]

Atlas was in the corner of the ring watching his kids spar and shouting out instructions.

"Get outside his right. Keep your gloves high protecting your face. Duck under his punches. That's it."

Later Teddy held the body bag while a rambunctious youngster pounded it with murderous intentions. Suddenly he left the bag and rushed back to the ring, interrupting a sparring session that was in progress, to correct a flaw he had noticed in a fighter's movement. He put his arm around the boy, talking to him quietly, and then gave him a graphic demonstration of how to bob and weave properly in order to avoid the opponent's punches. He took the second boy aside also, and talked to him. "You know, you made up for your mistakes with courage, like a tiger, but you also gotta use your brain. You gotta be a tiger and use your brain. Come in and move your head from side to side, right?" A love tap on the cheek sent the boy back to the ring to practice his lessons.

Cus continued as he watched Teddy in action, "Teddy always comes to me when he has any doubts about something important. I let him go because I know he can do it. I wouldn't let him go if I didn't know he could do it. I'm the one that makes the final decision. But they know me, and Teddy and I are together. We're synonymous. I'm Teddy. Teddy's me." Soon it was Mike Tyson's turn in the gym and, after loosening up for 15 minutes, Mike climbed through the ropes to work out under Teddy's direction. Mike was fully covered in a white cotton sweat suit, light blue trunks, and white shoes. Teddy briefed him on the drill and then started shooting out straight rights and lefts. Mike slipped under them all easily. Cus, as usual, observed the drill, while commenting to a friend, "Mike, to look at him, he looks like a fighter. He's big. He's got the physique. He's strong. You know, he's awesome. But he's a kid in a man's body, and he's still young. He's only 15 now. He's 210 pounds and well developed."

Cus yelled a few words of encouragement out to the young Tyson as he sparred with his trainer. "You make me proud. You do this in the ring and you'll be champ of the world some day. Just keep your mind where it's supposed to be." Then to a visitor, Cus whispered,

> I'll give him a strong body and he's gonna hafta get strong in other ways on his own. He's not as tough or as hard as people think he is. When they see me, they say, "Oh boy, you got that Tyson. He just loves to fight. He just loves to hurt people. He's afraid of nothing." That's not true, but when we're done with him, he'll look like he is anyway. He comes from a tough environment. He comes from a hard upbringing. He never had nothin'. Down in that kind of environment, I know how it is. You can't trust people. You grow mistrusting, and if anybody does anything for you, there's a reason, you know. Nobody helps people. He's got the potential to go down as one of the greatest fighters ever, but he'll only reach that potential if he keeps his head screwed on straight.

4. The Quest Begins—1982

Teddy continued to prod Tyson. "Keep it goin' for awhile. Boom, boom, move and a bop, bop." Atlas demonstrated by shooting out rights and lefts in bunches, all the while bobbing and weaving. "Move, and bop, bop, bop, know what I mean? Keep it goin' like it's an exchange, and the guy's still fightin' witcha." Tyson went into his drill with the approval of his trainer. "That's it. There ya go. Again. Again. Who's the last guy to stop? Time." Tyson, dripping sweat, headed for his corner. "Very good. That's what you have to do," with a pat to Tyson's midsection. "One more round." Ten-year-old Johnny Lowe was watching the action from the apron of the ring. Atlas walked over to him. "You my friend?"

"Uh-huh."

"Gonna do good in school?"

"Uh-huh."

Teddy rubbed the top of his head and then returned to work.²

Tyson finished his workout, then slipped through the ring ropes and walked slowly over to the stage where the speed bag was hanging. A good-looking black boy moved into the ring with Teddy now, for his daily workout. Teddy had the big catcher's mitt on and was fending off Mane Moore's sharp jabs. Whomp! "That's it. Bad intentions. Don't drop it. Don't drop it even half an inch, and let it come the same height as your shoulders. Elbow, whop, straight across. Awright?" Teddy noted to a friend at ringside,

> Mane was a kid when he came here. He was without any confidence in himself. I'll give you an idea. He was what you would call yellow or somethin'. They took his lunch money at school. I try to build him up here. I tell him that what he's scared of is the feelin'. He knows how scared he feels. I said I felt the same way and the same thing happened to me as a kid. But after awhile, I said, "Hey, I'm either gonna starve to death or I'm gonna whack this guy out. I can't keep goin' this way."

Teddy took Moore aside and showed him how to hold his hands. "Straighten that wrist out. Now throw it with bad intentions. I can tell when you're throwin' it with bad intentions and when you're not. Somebody you wanna hurt." Moore threw a sharp jab that Teddy caught on the big mitt. "That's better. Throw it like you don't like somebody. Throw it harder. That's better. See the difference. It's in you all the time. It's just gotta come out. Ya gotta throw it with bad intentions. Remember, when you're in the ring, you're not playin' ping pong." Moore continued to move forward, punching, bobbing, weaving, and punching some more. "That's it. That's how you gotta slip." Then to a visitor, "He comes from a good family. You know, a tough thing because the mother raised him basically with no father. She's a religious woman. She leaned on religion. I think religion was her ace in the hole." After the workout, Moore sat down on one of the long benches, leaned back against the wall, and daydreamed, his eyes a million miles away. "I wanna be rich, and whatever I want I'll try my hardest to get it. After I take care of my mother and Teddy and Cus, I'm gonna take it and blow it. Before I blow it, I'm gonna hafta make somethin' like thirty million dollars. Naw, make it a trillion. After a trillion, I'll give up. I'm gonna take a thousand dollars with me every night and just blow it."³

Teddy promised to spend the afternoon with Johnny Lowe, so after the gym emptied out for the day, the two pals left arm in arm, jumped into the station wagon, and drove out to the Ewald house near Athens. The large Victorian mansion towered over them like the Colossus of Rhodes as they climbed out of the car. Teddy pointed up to the big, white house. "Like it?"

"Nah."

"Whatta ya mean, nah?" He playfully grabbed Johnny by the neck. After a tour of the grounds, Teddy showed Johnny around the inside of the house, then led him up the narrow staircase to the third-floor bedroom. "This is where the street rats live," referring to Tyson and the rest of his bunkmates. Johnny was impressed with the roomy sleeping quarters. "What's this screen?"

"That's for showin' fight movies. We got hundreds of fight movies over here in the bookcase."

"Got Muhammad Ali?"

"No."

"Got Sugar Ray Leonard?"

"No. How about Benny Leonard?"

"Who's he?"

Teddy laughed. "You don't know now, but when you get older, you'll appreciate him. You'll wanna see his fights then."

The bright sunlight shone through the window and fell directly on the movie screen. Johnny walked over and held his hand in front of the screen, casting a shadow of his hand. Teddy followed suit and made images of dogs and rabbits appear on the screen by manipulating his hands. They both laughed at the silly caricatures they had created.[4]

After another of Camille's famous dinners, Cus settled back in the big, overstuffed chair in the library and held court. Twenty-five hundred years ago, another philosopher by the name of Plato held court in the ancient Greek city of Athens and, like D'Amato, taught his pupils the secret of life. Plato's schoolroom was a grassy area under a large tree near the Agora or main square in Athens, while Cus taught either in the gymnasium or from the big chair in the library. On this night, Frank Minicelli and Tom Patti were the attentive students. Cus was reminiscing about Frankie's first days in Catskill. "You have to understand how bad he was when he first came here. Don Shanagher said, 'You gonna make a fighter outta him? Impossible.'" Cus looked at Frankie.

> So when you get to the point where you're not excited—see that's what you've got to tell yourself, to completely relax, to be able to see everything that's goin' on. Your sense of anticipation is sharp. And that can't happen unless you relax. A man whose thinkin' and worryin' about gettin' hit is not gonna have a good sense of anticipation. He will, in fact, get hit. And most important, when you get hit, like you get excited. When you get hit, that's when you gotta be calm. That's when you gotta be calmest, when you get hit. A professional fighter has got to learn how to hit and not get hit, and at the same time be exciting. That's what professional boxin's about. You gotta be clever. You gotta be smart and not get hit. If you're able to do this, you're a fighter.[5]

When Saturday rolled around, it was fight time again for members of the Catskill Boxing Club. Teddy Atlas and his small contingent of gladiators hit the New York Thruway and headed south for the big city. On this particular day, the fights were held at the Apollo Boxing Club in the Bronx, where a small crowd of about 100 rabid fight fans were present. Mane Moore and Frankie Minicelli were on the card, along with a large group from New Jersey. Moore was first up and he looked sharp as he danced circles around his New York opponent in the first round. Frankie Minicelli was off in a corner shadow boxing, trying to loosen up his muscles and settle his frayed nerves. Atlas was on the top step of the ring in his fighter's corner, yelling instructions to Mane Moore. "Mane, double up your jab, double up." Mane looked to be in top physical and mental condition as he moved smoothly around the ring. He completely outclassed his opponent and was awarded a unanimous three-round decision, as well as the first place ribbon. Next Frankie Minicelli climbed into the ring. Teddy queried him. "You calm? Listen to what I'm sayin'."

"Yes."

"Awright, relax and think about what you have to do now."

Teddy whispered to Don Shanagher, who had accompanied the boys to the fight, "Frankie has trouble relaxin' once the fight starts. That's what I work on with him mostly. Other people I work on mostly physical things. With Frankie, it's mostly mental." When round one ended, Frankie paced back and forth in his corner like a caged animal. "Frankie, come here. Relax. You can't throw one punch with this guy. You gotta throw two or three, you understand? Let's see you work a little more in this round. Just like it's in the gym."[6] Frankie followed Teddy's orders sufficiently well to come away with a well-earned decision.

Tyson's stablemate and friend, Kevin Rooney, was back in the news early in the year. Rooney, trying to rebound from a 1981 TKO loss to Davey Moore, was working hard for his upcoming fight with the legendary Alexis Arguello. In order to get Rooney more experience before the fight, Cus D'Amato arranged to have his fighter serve as a sparring partner for Wilfred Benitez in Las Vegas. Benitez was in training for a title fight with Roberto Duran to be held at Caesar's Palace. Rooney and his trainer, Teddy Atlas, spent two relaxing weeks in Las Vegas in late January working out with Benitez during the day, then enjoying some of the Las Vegas attractions in the evening. The workouts certainly didn't hurt Benitez. He came away from his title fight with Duran with his welterweight title intact after a tough 15-round decision on Saturday, January 30. Less than two weeks later, on February 11, Rooney flashed his wares on nationwide television, winning a ten-round decision over Marvin Jenkins on ESPN and improving his record to 18–1. He followed that up with a third-round knockout over outgunned Jackie Morrell on April 7. Things seemed to be looking up for Kevin Rooney, but it was all illusion. His star finally fell from the heavens only four months later. He was

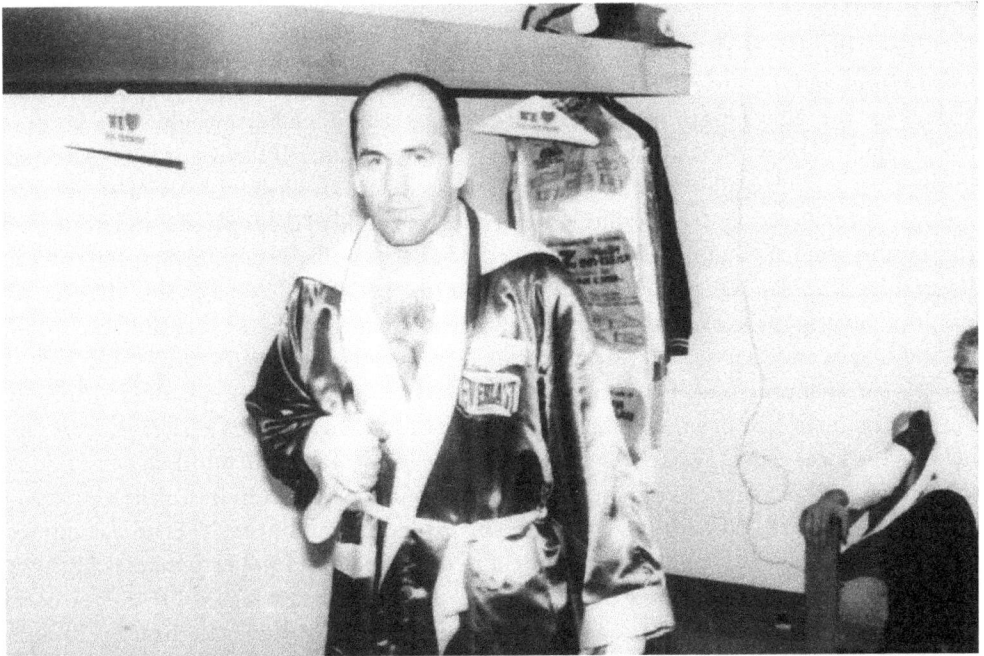

Kevin Rooney fought as a welterweight before becoming Tyson's trainer under D'Amato (courtesy Paul V. Post).

knocked cold by Alexis Arguello on July 31, although he pocketed $40,000 for his night's work. His ring record was still an impressive 20-2, but Rooney's career as a title contender was, for all intents and purposes, over. From this point on, Rooney would concentrate more on the other side of the fight game, working as an assistant trainer for Teddy Atlas and helping Teddy and Cus bring out the maximum potential in Mike Tyson.

The Catskill Boxing Club was a busy place in 1982, day in and day out, seven days a week. On Sunday, the gym was just as crowded as it was on any other day. Most, or at least, many of the young fighters were not church-goers. As John Chetti once said, "None of us had any particular religion or went to church. Everyone was too busy training on Sunday." In addition to the guys who worked out regularly in the gym, the Catskill Boxing Club also included one of the few female boxers in the northeast, a tall, sinewy blonde named Nadia Hujtyn. Nadia was a dedicated fighter who often climbed between the ropes to spar with the boys, including John Chetti. According to Chetti, she could hold her own in the ring.

When the training session ended, the gang often went out to hit the town which, in Catskill, was not a big hit. The Community Theatre on Main Street was one of the major attractions in the evening. John Chetti often served as chauffeur for his brother Chris, Mike Tyson, Teddy Atlas, and Frankie Minicelli. The five of them went to countless movies at the Community, and accumulated a thousand and one unforgettable memories over the months. There were the popcorn fights and the juvenile jokes, the times they chased each other up and down the aisles to the chagrin and discomfort of the ushers and the patrons. And, of course, there were the clumsy, adolescent attempts to pick up girls in the darkened amphitheater. Some of these attempts met with success. The necking matches that ensued were recounted in minute detail later at the local Burger King up on Maple Street. Leering Lotharios boasted of their latest conquests as they chomped away at their burgers and guzzled Cokes.

Then there were the basketball games. The crowd that Tyson hung around with all loved sports, and they attended as many of the high school athletic events as possible. Basketball was the winter sport in Catskill, and twice a week John Chetti would drive the guys to the games. Mike was already something of a celebrity in Catskill as a result of his successes in the ring, and he enjoyed the attention of the public. His sense of inferiority, weaned during 13 brutal years in Brownsville, was still deeply imbedded in his psyche, and he needed constant reassurance that he was liked. He craved affection like a starving man craves food. Invariably, when the rest of the gang got back to the car after a home game, Mike Tyson would be among the missing. No matter. They always knew where to find him. He would be standing by the door shaking everyone's hand as they were leaving.[7]

As spring approached, Tyson made preparations to defend his title in Colorado Springs. He was also interested in gaining some publicity for his hometown of Catskill, and perhaps helping the local economy. "I want to promote the town of Catskill and I want people to know that there is a fine town there."[8] The first step in Mike's return down the glory road was the Adirondack competition, which he won easily—no opponent. Next he was entered in the Regional Qualifying Tournament held in the Sheraton Hotel in Syracuse. Again he emerged victorious without ever throwing a punch. It was almost impossible to find local boxers who were willing to risk life and limb by stepping into the ring with the Catskill clubber. As a result, he won most of his qualifying matches in walkovers.

Within a few short weeks, Mike and Teddy were escorted to Albany Airport by Cus and Kevin Rooney, and they were put on a big jet for Colorado, on their way to another

4. The Quest Begins—1982

Junior Olympics. The two boys were returning to the scene of their greatest triumph, the United States Air Force Academy in Colorado Springs. But this time they were returning as the defending heavyweight champion. Mike Tyson was no longer an unknown in Colorado territory. He was a full-blown celebrity and was in demand, not only by the printed media, but by radio and television as well. Atlas had his hands full keeping Tyson isolated from the press and allowing him time to concentrate on the task at hand.

During his early sparring sessions, Tyson developed a sore shoulder, and it became a source of great concern for both him and Teddy. As fight day approached, the soreness did not get any better, so Tyson was hustled over to the Olympic medical facility for examination. The doctors found nothing seriously wrong with Mike's shoulder and gave him a clean bill of health to participate in the tournament. But the entire medical staff was amazed by his magnificent physique and by his great strength, particularly considering his age. Dick Maguire, the New York State coordinator, had encouraged similar skepticism about his age previously. And he gave the Olympic doctors the usual answer. "I have three birth certificates, school affidavits, and I even sent a telegram to God but have not received an answer yet. The kid is only 15."[9] Maguire produced photostats of the birth certificates and a copy of the Catskill High School certificate verifying his age. The doctors just shook their heads in disbelief then they proceeded to quiz Maguire and Teddy Atlas about Tyson's conditioning program. They wanted to find out as much as they could about this marvel of physical fitness, searching for a secret training method they could use in their own program with the Olympians.

Back in the gym, Mike resumed training for his first bout on Thursday, June 24, three days hence. Mike's quarter-final opponent was Jonathon Littles, a former Silver Gloves champion from Michigan. Littles proved to be no puzzle for the energetic defending title holder. The Catskill High School freshman caught Littles with several crushing body punches early in round one, and Littles got on his horse immediately, attempting to stay out of harm's way the rest of the round. But that is easier said than done when you're fighting a machine like Mike Tyson. Tyson was not to be denied. He caught Littles with an overhand right at the 1:30 mark and dropped him to the canvas for the first time. At that, it was the longest a Tyson opponent had avoided a knockout in more than two years. Tyson rocked Littles again later in the round and put him on the floor a second time. Littles miraculously survived until midway through round two, when an uppercut to the body brought the fight to a speedy conclusion. At the post-fight interview, Mike expressed disappointment at the other fighter's performance. "He didn't want to fight. He kept running."[10] Joe Louis once had an opponent who bragged he would avoid Joe's vaunted left hook by boxing him from a distance. Louis responded with his now famous remark, "He can run but he can't hide." Jonathon Littles discovered too late that he couldn't hide either.

Mike looked forward to his semi-final encounter with increased anticipation. The challenger was a curly-headed blonde thumper from California named Don Cozad. Tyson remembered Cozad well from the 1981 tournament. Although the two fighters didn't meet in the ring, Mike knew that Cozad had a punch to be respected. As a matter of fact, Don Cozad held the record for the quickest knockout in Junior Olympic history, flattening one opponent in just 11 seconds. Tyson and Teddy Atlas watched Cozad fight several times at the Air Force Academy, and they thought they spotted a weakness in Cozad's style. Every time he threw a punch, his head was up in the air. Tyson scrutinized the Cozad films in minute detail and made mental notes of Cozad's idiosyncrasies. On fight day, Mike killed time by working out in the warm Colorado sun. He spread a towel on the grass and did his back stretching exercises in cool, green comfort. Then he shadow boxed for several minutes more before meandering back to the dormitory to get dressed for the bout. Mike sat contemplatively in front of Teddy while his trainer carefully wrapped the gauze around his hand. "Make a fist. Easy. Keep it steady." Teddy methodically stripped tape from a roll and applied it to Mike's hand. "You're all set." Mike slipped into his blue satin robe with gold trim and the words "Catskill Boxing Club" emblazoned in bright gold script across the back. Teddy was adorned in a bright orange windbreaker publicizing the "Empire State Games" as the two men left the dormitory again for another breath of fresh air before the action began.

Boxing in many ways parallels war. War, they say, is weeks of boredom interspersed with seconds of sheer terror. In boxing, the weeks of boredom are followed by hours of intense tension building up to fight time. Mike nervously paced the sidewalk outside the field house as Teddy engaged two ten-year-old boys in conversation. Mike slammed one fist into the other as the boys looked on in admiration. Teddy spoke quietly to them. "This is the hardest part of boxing, you guys. The hardest part is the waitin'. Isn't that the hardest part?" The kids nodded in agreement.

"When you get in there and box, it's not as hard as the waitin', know what I mean, kid?"

One of the kids nodded. "You say 'I'm gonna get beat up.'"

"No, no, you don't say that. You hafta have confidence you're gonna win, but still your mind thinks things, but you just have to have enough discipline to go through it." Tyson had walked away from Atlas and the kids and was now 50 feet down the sidewalk, deep in thought. Teddy yelled at him, "Michael. Mike. You're so nervous, you're getting farther and farther away. Loosen up your shoulder good?"

"Yeh."

"Good. Feels looser? Now you can loosen up a little faster, shadow box a little, 'specially when you feel the tension mount. Motion relieves tension."

Teddy walked over to his young apprentice and tied the belt on Tyson's robe. "You're the champ. They're the ones that gotta worry. If you weren't nervous, there'd be something wrong with you. A nervous feelin's a sign you're gonna win. A sign you're ready. A sign you're ready to win. Just got to keep it up here," patting Tyson's head, "and go do it. Everything here is right," patting Tyson's stomach, "Just gotta keep it up here." It was nearing fight time as the defending champion and his trainer walked down the stairs to the field house. Once in the ring, Teddy adjusted Mike's protective headgear and checked his gloves. Mike was already deep in contemplation, getting himself psyched up. "They're not gonna take my title."[11]

Both fighters looked tight as they stood in their corners waiting for the start of the action. Tyson, in blue trunks with gold trim, and a white USA shirt, rushed forward at the bell and met Cozad in the center of the ring. Cozad started to throw a jab. As his left hand went out, his head came up, and Mike countered with a dynamite right that landed flush on the jaw. A glassy film suddenly covered Cozad's eyes and the young man stared out into nothingness. The Region 12 champion hesitated momentarily, then fell backward to the canvas and lay motionless as the final count was tolled. The concerned referee rushed to his side and bent over the unconscious fighter as an excited Tyson jumped up on the middle strand of rope in his corner and raised both arms in the victory salute. Atlas quickly grabbed him to calm him down. "Calm down. Hear me? Awright. Awright. Relax. Relax."[12]

After a minute or so, the Californian was helped to his feet and stumbled back to his corner. Tyson rushed right over to hug Cozad and to sympathize with him. When he returned to his own corner, Mike was greeted by one of the Olympic officials, who leaned over and whispered to him, "I'm going to have to ask you to come to a private room next to the gym. We have received a formal complaint from the other corner, and we're going to have to check your gloves for foreign substances." Tyson and Atlas were incredulous, but they dutifully followed the officials to a small room nearby. Cozad's trainers were sure that Mike's gloves contained an illegal substance that helped him to knock out their fighter so quickly. They had never seen anyone hit that hard in their lives. As the gloves came off and the wrappings were removed from Tyson's hands, it became evident that nothing except Mike Tyson himself had brought about Don Cozad's rapid demise. And Mike made sure that everyone knew that as he pointed to his glove. "There isn't anything in here except flesh and bones." Olympic officials apologized to Tyson and Atlas later for their actions, but an apology wasn't necessary. As far as the Tyson camp was concerned, it was good publicity.

On their way back to the locker room, Teddy stopped at the pay phone to call D'Amato back in Catskill. He couldn't wait to give Cus the good news. "Hey, Cus, eight second knockout of the first round. Yeah, the right hand. And he set a new record. The official came over to him and said, 'You just set a record, quickest knockout ever.' Yeah, eight seconds. Well, I rushed right over to call you, ya know. I wanted to catch you before you went to the gym. Yeah, he's fightin' a tall, thin kid. He's gonna have no problem. He's gonna hit the body. Okay, and tell her it was eight seconds. Awright. Goodbye." Mike approached the phone as Teddy hung up, and the two men embraced in celebration. "Let's go home." The newspapers and television networks had picked up on the story of Tyson's powerful hands, and they added fuel to an already blazing Tyson mystique. Suddenly he was the toast of the town, and he was sought out by dozens of media reporters prior to the finals. Teddy Atlas made sure that the victory over Cozad remained in the headlines. He wanted Mike's final opponent to read about it and dwell on it. "Mike hit Cozad so quickly, he never had a chance. He never saw the blow coming. He went down like a felled tree."[13]

By the time Saturday rolled around, Tyson's notoriety had spread far and wide. A large crowd pushed their way through the turnstiles to get a look at this brute from New York who felled opponents like so many bowling pins. The crowd wanted to see him win by a knockout in the finals so they could tell their friends that they were there when the great Mike Tyson won the championship. As fight time approached, Tyson got edgy with anticipation. He paced the locker room from one end to the other, occasionally flicking out soft rights and lefts to Teddy's midsection. Tyson was thinking out loud as he worked. "They want my title, but they're not gettin' it." Teddy countered, "Smart like a tiger, hungry tiger, but smart and confident." Both men started to pace and circle each other restlessly. Tyson's face was taut and stern. Teddy continued to counsel his fighter. "Make your arm strong with your jab—and move your head—and cover—and when you get inside, set up those body punches. Concentrate on the body."

"Yeah."

"Give him an eight, a few jabs then an eight, specially if he tries to run use the eight."

"If he keeps runnin', I'll track him down like a dog."

It was time for another fight to start, and time for another gladiator to enter the arena to test his mettle. The trainer headed for the door. "Awright Gene, let's do it." A young boxer gaily adorned in a bright yellow robe followed the older man out of the locker room and down the long corridor to the arena, hitting the air with his hands as he walked.

Teddy sat Mike down on a bench and carefully wound the gauze wrapping around Tyson's mammoth hand. "Win the title, then we'll go home to all our friends, right?"

"Yeah, right."

The conversation was slow, measured, and agitated. With the taping complete, Mike and Teddy walked outside the arena, into another bright, picturesque Colorado day. The pacing continued on the terrace. Tyson, with his hands on his hips, seemed ready to explode from the tension that was building within him. Teddy put an arm around his anxious warrior to calm him down. "C'mon. Don't worry about it. Relax. Just relax." They walked to a chain link fence at the rear of the terrace and Tyson leaned against the top rail. He put his taped hand around Teddy's shoulder and began crying softly. Teddy tried to comfort his fighter. "Relax. Just relax. Don't get tense. Relax. All it is is another boxing match. You've done it already 20 times. Against better fighters than you're ever gonna fight here."

"Yeah, I'm Mike Tyson," he sobbed. "Everybody likes me. I'm proud of myself."

"That's right. You have reason to be proud. And you're gonna continue to do it as long as you don't let anything mess you up. If you don't let yourself mess you up, you'll continue to have people like you. Just always remember, that's all."

Teddy gave Mike a reassuring pat on the back, then walked away, leaving the 15-year-old man-child alone with his thoughts. There was a minute of silence as both men composed themselves. Teddy came back and tapped Mike on the side. "Awright, let's go get ready for the fight."

Tyson moved away from the fence and walked toward the field house, throwing punches into the wind. His stride was strong now, his face determined. Mike Tyson had gotten his head together, and he was ready to go. They walked down the corridor toward the gymnasium, Tyson throwing more combinations and faster combinations. "Good. Good. Awright, that's better." Teddy put his arm around his fighter again, and Mike broke into a jog. The local TV station was reporting the fight, and the commentator could be heard in the distance. "Coming up, the fight between Mike Tyson and Kelton Brown. Both fighters have been very, very impressive. A very experienced Mike Tyson. He was the champion last year, and has been in national competition in Junior Olympics with five bouts and five knockouts." Another fighter approached Tyson in the corridor and the two men slapped hands as they passed—a message of encouragement from a fellow competitor. Kelton Brown was already in the ring with his headgear on and his mouthpiece in position, ready to go. He was tall, 6'6" to be exact, with milky white skin and curly brown hair. He was decked out in white from his jersey to his shoes. The TV commentator was still singing the praises of the Catskill boxer as Mike made his way up the steps to the ring. "Mike Tyson has not gone the distance in any of his bouts here. He's being looked at, and there's a lot of noise being made about this young man as a possible Olympic prospect, and a possible professional champion in years to come." Tyson adjusted his headgear as he listened to the referee's instructions, then headed back to his corner for last-minute advice from his trainer. "You're the champ. Fight smart. Eye like a tiger and calm." Mike slapped both of Teddy's hands with his gloves, leaned over and gave his trainer a kiss on the cheek.

At the bell, the two fighters came out quickly. Two lefts by Brown caught nothing but air. An overhand right by Tyson smashed against Brown's jaw, stunning the Texas fighter. Tyson immediately pressed his advantage, maneuvering Brown to the ropes and unloading his full arsenal of punches. Brown attempted to cover up, but a flurry of lefts and rights found his unprotected body. Brown finally succeeded in tying Tyson up, but the referee separated them immediately. The 15-year-old New Yorker came back with a hard right to the jaw, and the desperate Brown grabbed him again. The referee had to pry them apart this time, and he gave Brown a warning for excessive holding. The big heavyweight did not appear anxious to continue his struggle against the muscular knockout artist. Tyson, on the other hand, was eager to mix it up. As soon as his hands were free, he rocked the game Texan with a left to the jaw, then buckled his knees with a follow-up right. Brown's gloves dropped to his sides as the kid from Catskill pushed him to the ropes and bombarded him with both hands. The referee, seeing that Brown was defenseless against the onslaught, stepped in and declared Tyson the winner. It was officially recorded as a TKO at 42 seconds of round one. Brown, feeling he could have continued, spit his mouthpiece out in disgust and drop-kicked it out of the ring. An elated Tyson rushed to his corner and leaped up on the middle strand of rope. He was so excited he continued to bounce up and down around the ring in a frenzied victory celebration. Grabbing Teddy Atlas, he planted another big kiss on his trainer's cheek. Then he grabbed his head with his hands in disbelief and tumbled backwards to the canvas, rolling over and over across the ring. "Michael, c'mon. Come here. Come here. You gotta act with respect. Come here."

Kelton Brown, sobbing aloud with disappointment, approached Tyson, and the two gladiators embraced. Teddy tried to console the stricken fighter. "You gotta lotta guts, kid. You just stick with it and don't let this discourage you. He's a two-time national champion. You stick with it and you're gonna have your day. You have a lotta guts, a lotta guts. A lot to be proud of." He patted Brown on his headgear and sent him back to his corner. Tyson, still pumped up by the sudden end of the match, yelled to the crowd, "I don't give my title to no one." Across the ring, Brown buried his face in his hands. The referee beckoned Tyson to the center of the ring and raised his hand in the symbolic victory salute. "The winner in the red corner, in division number one, Mike Tyson. And the runner-up from Texas, Kelton Brown." Mike bent over proudly as the Olympic official placed the red, white, and blue first-place medal over his head. Mike threw kisses to the screaming crowd, thanking them for their support.[14]

The post-fight press conference was a beehive of activity as reporters clamored for attention from the dais. Teddy Atlas gave the news-starved reporters his view of the fight. "I never saw anything like it in all my boxing experience. It was just like one of the scenes from *Rocky III* where Rocky fights a professional wrestler who is over 6'7" tall. Brown tried to stare Mike down before the bout, but we have taught Mike not to be intimidated, and Mike stared right back at him and actually pushed him back with his chest before the bout started." The press wanted to know what was in store for Tyson now that the Junior Olympics were over, and Atlas obliged them with a capsule summary of Tyson's upcoming program.

> People don't realize that Mike is still just a youngster and his mental toughness still needs to mature slowly. He will be able to fight in the senior class as soon as he's 16, then we can get him experience against older and better fighters. And we will really start to work on his discipline in the ring and his mental toughness. For the rest of the year, there will be a lot of gym work and strategy sessions in the ring, and some more amateur fights around New York. The long range plan right now is to point ahead to 1983 and another defense of the Junior Olympic title, then to set our sights on the Olympic Games to be held in Los Angeles in 1984.[15]

Mike and Teddy were welcomed home by their friends in Catskill and by their "family" at Ewald House. The "Welcome Home Champ" sign was prominently displayed across Main Street again as the town fathers expressed their pride in the achievements of the two boys.

It was June 28, and the mood was festive on the banks of the Hudson. Two days later, Camille and Cus threw a house party for their "adopted son." It was a two-fold celebration: to toast Mike's achievements in Colorado Springs and to wish him health and happiness on his 16th birthday. His friends and gym associates—Teddy, Frankie, John, and Jay—were on hand, and the *Catskill Daily Mail* sent a photographer around to record the momentous event for posterity. It was a big day for Mike Tyson in more ways than one. Being 16 years old meant that he could now compete in the seniors class, something that he desperately needed. As precocious a fighter as Tyson was, there had been no challenge for him in the juniors. He needed to get in the ring with adult boxers, men who were ring-wise and could provide him with the variety of skills and styles that he needed in order to progress.

The day after the big bash, it was back to the gym for Mike and Teddy. The glory was behind them once again, and a lot of hard work lay ahead. Cus watched intently as Mike began his first workout with a rope skipping exercise. "Your mind is not on your work. Your mind is not on your work. There's something distracting you." Just then, little Johnny Lowe entered the gym and quickly made his way over to where Cus was seated. "Hi, young man. Come up." Cus beckoned to Johnny to join him. Cus loved to draw people out, to get them talking, to learn their inner secrets, to find out what made them tick. On this day, he used his psychology on ten-year-old Johnny Lowe.

"You remind me of Mike when he first came here."

"He's a good fighter, too," Johnny retorted.

"Oh, I don't think so. You think he's a good fighter? What makes you think so?"

"I don't know."

"Oh, you must have some reason for thinkin' he's a good fighter. What makes you think so?"

"He looks like he could knock out anybody."

"That's a very good reason, isn't it? A very good reason to think it anyway."

About 30 minutes later, Teddy arrived on the scene and latched onto Johnny. "How ya doin', buddy? Did you keep in shape while I was gone?"

"Yeah, but I asked Cus every day when you were coming back."

"You did, huh? That's nice. Maybe some day I'll bring you with me."

"If I'm world champ, I can box down there."

"Yeah, if you're world champ, we can box anywhere. If you wanna box in Europe, we'll box in Europe. When you're the best you can do a lot of things, remember that. But to be the best, you gotta work hard. It's a lotta work."

Back at Ewald House that evening, there was a flurry of activity as Camille arrived home with the weekly groceries. Camille, Cus, and several boys scurried around the kitchen putting everything in its proper place. Frank Minicelli grabbed the dog food and quickly disappeared outside to feed the two friendly Eskimo Huskies who were hungrily pacing the back yard.

"Whatta ya do with the sunflower seeds?" Cus inquired.

"For the birds," said Camille.

Cus shook his head. "Birds an' animals. They're better off bein' in this house than anybody."[16]

Dinner was more of a family get-together in the old mansion now. Mike Tyson was beginning to come out of his shell, and he was more open with everyone. Frank Minicelli, as usual, was always looking for fun. On this night, Mike and Frankie approached the dining room table with some light horseplay. Mike playfully grabbed Frankie from behind in a gentle bear hug. After he freed himself, Frankie spun around and faked several punches to Mike's midsection. The give and take continued as they took their seats. During the meal, Cus once again held center stage. It was always school time for Cus and his pupils. "The only guy at this table who always thinks about fightin'—he always thinks about fightin', no matter what he does—is Frankie Minicelli." "Yeah, Frankie," laughed Tyson. Frankie grinned and shook his head sheepishly. As the piping hot casserole was passed around the table, Cus went into his spiel.

> You know, a guy went into a restaurant and he took off a very expensive coat. He hung it up, and on the coat he put a card. It read, "This coat belongs to the heavyweight champion of the world." That means, don't touch it. So he went about his business, and when he came back the coat was gone. Instead, right over where the coat was, was another card. "This coat was stolen by the fastest runner in the world. Come and get me."
>
> "Is that for real?" asked a puzzled Jay Bright.
>
> Well, I don't know if it's for real, but I don't doubt that it's happened. There are very few new things in this world. Very few. That's why, when people are young, if they're smart, they try to profit by the experiences of an older guy so they won't have to go through all the pain and sufferin'. But a certain amount of pain and sufferin' is good because it makes a person think. They learn.[17]

With the approach of fall came the American rite of manhood better known as high school football. With the football games came the Friday night teen dances at the Elks Club. Mike Tyson never missed a Friday night at the Club. He loved to dance, and he was an exceptional dancer according to the local girls. Mike, who had a girlfriend named Angie, stayed on the dance floor from the time they opened the doors at 7 o'clock until the last number was played at 11 p.m. Like most small town events, the weekly dances also provided a forum for the high school jocks to show off their muscles and compete with jocks from nearby towns for boasting rights. In this locale, the guys from Catskill were always trying to outdo their next door neighbors from Cairo. Occasionally, the jousting for position approached the rumble stage. One night, Catskill kids stood toe to toe with Cairo kids, each side trying to stare down the other side. Just when it looked like the confrontation would erupt into full-scale warfare, Mike Tyson put his 210 pounds of sinew and muscle between the two factions and admonished them. "All right guys, cool off and let's dance." One glance at the Tyson physique and the kids from Cairo and the kids from Catskill quietly returned to the dance floor.[18]

October and November were busy months for the Catskill Boxing Club as a number of their fighters were engaged in tournaments around New York State. Five local boxers made the finals of the Adirondack Golden Gloves Tournament. Three came away victorious. Kevin Young, with an amateur record of 55–5, won in a walkover as his opponent was unable to compete. Greg Young (52–7) won a decision, and Frankie Minicelli (40–15) streaked to a TKO victory in the second round to win the 139-pound open classification. A left hook to the body by Frankie paralyzed his opponent late in the first round and he was unable to answer the bell for round two. Frankie moved on to the Northeast Regional Finals on Friday, November 19, and lost a heartbreaking split decision to John Powell of Boston. It was a good match. Frankie carried the fight to Powell in the opening round with a series of debilitating body punches. Powell bounced back with some good head shots in round two and, in round three, both fighters gave a good account of themselves. It was difficult to lose, but Frankie came away knowing that he fought a good fight.

Elsewhere, November was a sad month for the boxing world. On Saturday the 13th, lightweight champion Ray "Boom Boom" Mancini defended his crown in Las Vegas, Nevada, against Duk Koo Kim, a relatively unknown challenger from South Korea. From the outset it was a brutal match. Duk Koo Kim was a street fighter just like Mancini. Both fighters dished out savage punishment round after round. Early in the 14th, Mancini caught Kim on the ropes and nailed him with a vicious right hook to the side of the head. Kim pitched forward to the canvas, struggled gamely to his feet and then collapsed, unconscious. The ringside physicians were unable to revive the courageous Korean fighter, and he was finally carried from the ring on a stretcher and brought to the dressing room. Kim lapsed into a coma shortly after arrival at the hospital. His grief-stricken mother was flown in from Korea and rushed to his bedside. Her vigil was sad and lonely—and hopeless. After three days, she brought in a Chinese acupuncture team to work on her son, but they, like the American doctors, were unable to breathe life back into Kim's broken body. Finally, on Wednesday, November 18, 1982, Duk Koo Kim was declared brain-dead. His life-support system was disconnected and his mother selflessly donated his organs to medical science. It was left for the police to discover a mystical footnote to the tragic story of Duk Koo Kim. When the Korean's hotel room was examined following his death, officers found a cryptic message scrawled across the mirror in Kim's hand. It read, "Kill or be killed."[19]

Boxing promoter Bob Arum, always the opportunist, immediately called for an investigation, which was normal procedure in any case. The first thing the investigators did was clear the referee of all blame in Kim's death. There had been no opportunity for the referee to stop the fight. It had been a one-punch knockout. Ironically, if Kim had survived the final five minutes of the fight, he would have been declared the new WBA lightweight champion. He was leading on all three cards when he was struck down. As the investigation continued, there was the usual hue and cry to ban boxing, mostly from people who never liked boxing, didn't know anything about it, and didn't understand it. Some detractors asked for bigger gloves, bigger headgear, and longer rest periods. Both Kevin Rooney and Teddy Atlas had strong opinions about safety and the sport of boxing. Rooney just shook his head in disgust when he heard the latest suggestions. "If a guy gets hit right, he's goin' down, no matter how big the gloves. All these rule changes people are talking about are silly. They will just ruin boxin'." Teddy was more outspoken on the subject.

> If you switch to bigger gloves, the fighter will just take a worse beating for a longer period of time. He'll get pounded for ten rounds instead of being taken out early. I think it would make boxin' less attractive to the public, and that's the first step in abolishing the sport. If they would make fighters go through stiffer physicals, some of those guys who aren't in the right shape would be prevented from fightin'. The trainers and managers are to blame mostly. It's their job to make sure those guys are ready to fight.[20]

Kevin and Teddy both made some good points. Boxing was not banned, but tragedies such as the death of Duk Koo Kim do focus attention on the safety aspects of the sport, and do lead to legislation that will increase boxing safety without diminishing the excitement of the spectacle. Stiffer physical examinations, as advocated by Atlas, have become one of the major improvements in the sport in recent years.

On November 24, Kevin Rooney returned to the ring wars in Scranton, Pennsylvania, determined to begin a comeback after his devastating loss to Alexis Arguello. Rooney dominated the first two rounds against Terry Crawley, but in round three, the two fighters accidentally bumped heads, and Rooney suffered a deep gash just below the right eyebrow. The cut bled profusely from that point on and, although Rooney continued to lead by a wide margin on all judges' scorecards, the ring doctor decided the cut was too deep and too dangerous to allow the fight to continue. He refused to let Rooney answer the bell for round seven, awarding a TKO victory to Crawley. Rooney was bitterly disappointed and, although Crawley apologized for the accidental butt and unfortunate ending to fight, Rooney's record dropped to 19–3 and brought his career closer to the final curtain.[21]

The year 1982 was not all fun and glory for Mike Tyson either. It was the most traumatic year of his young life, a year in which two close personal relationships came to an end, scarring his psyche deeply. First, his mother succumbed to her two-year battle with cancer, a crushing blow to Mike as he stood poised on the threshold of a promising pugilistic career. Mike had wanted to earn a great reputation in boxing in order to please his mother and prove to her that he was the kind of son she could be proud of. He mourned her loss with a heavy sense of guilt. "I never made my mother happy or proud of me. She only saw me come home with clothes I never paid for. I made her cry so much. I wish she could have lived until I became champion."

Another emotional experience cast a pall over Mike Tyson's world late in the year. His trainer, Teddy Atlas, and his manager, Cus D'Amato, had a falling out, and Atlas was barred from the Catskill Boxing Club forever. The full story of the confrontation between the two men has never been satisfactorily explained. There appeared to be a real or imagined attempt by Teddy Atlas to gain full control of Mike Tyson's career from his aging manager, according to reports emanating from the D'Amato camp. There is an old adage that "familiarity breeds contempt," a phrase that contains more truth than fiction. A point is often reached in the teacher-student relationship where the student begins to feel he knows more than the teacher. From that point on, the relationship becomes strained and often ends disagreeably. The D'Amato-Atlas relationship followed such a course. Once Teddy learned his stock in trade, he became more confident in his new position, and as he became more confident, he began to develop his own ideas about how a fighter should be handled. Some of those ideas came in direct conflict with the philosophies of Cus D'Amato. This situation, coupled with Teddy's natural stubbornness, eventually resulted in an explosive confrontation between the two men.

The beginning of the end occurred in mid–1982, after Tyson had claimed his second successive National Junior Olympic title. Teddy felt that the sudden fame and media attention in Colorado had made Mike cocky and difficult to work with. Mike returned to Catskill rebellious and lazy. Some days he was late for his gym workout. Other days he didn't bother to show up at all. In his association with Teddy, he became defiant and obstinate. Teddy was determined to nip the problem in the bud and get Tyson's feet back on the ground before the situation deteriorated too far. Already, in Teddy's eyes, Mike was beginning to slack off in his school work and was beginning to hang around with an undesirable element. To combat this situation, Teddy sat Mike down and had a long talk with him, trying to make Mike see where he was going wrong. To emphasize his point, Teddy barred Mike from the gym for two weeks, a ploy he used routinely with other fighters when the situation required disciplinary action.

When Cus caught wind of this turn of events, he hit the roof. "You can't do that to Mike. He's gonna be the heavyweight champion of the world one of these days and he needs to be developed more carefully. You can't bar him from the gym. In the first place, he needs the work. He's got to work out every day. And he needs to be handled in a positive manner.

Kickin' him outta the gym will have a negative effect on him. Get him back in here. I'll talk to him."

At this point, Teddy rebelled. He had been working with Tyson for two years and the duo had been eminently successful in their boxing endeavors, two national titles and an impressive string of knockouts. The friction between Atlas and D'Amato seemed to grow almost daily, and by November, Cus D'Amato had had enough. He felt it necessary to terminate Teddy's employment before the in-fighting had a detrimental effect on Mike Tyson's career. Shortly before Thanksgiving, Cus D'Amato picked up the telephone and placed a call to his partner Jim Jacobs, to inform him that Teddy Atlas was all through as a trainer for the Catskill Boxing Club.

The final parting was bitter, at least on the part of Cus D'Amato and his associates. Cus himself had nothing to say about the matter publicly, and Kevin Rooney, a boyhood chum of Teddy's, was reputedly so full of anger for Teddy's tactics that he also refused to talk about it. The friction in the club that year was evident to all the boys. John Chetti, who had been boxing for about four years, had decided to quit the club about a week before Teddy got fired. Chetti went to Cus and informed him that he was giving up boxing so he could concentrate on his high school studies and go on to college. Cus wished him well, then inquired, "Would you be willing to help Kevin and I with Mike?" Chetti could see the handwriting on the wall as far as Teddy was concerned. He liked Teddy, but he was also fond of Cus and Mike. Not wanting to be drawn into the conflict between people who were all his friends, he declined Cus's offer and departed from the club permanently. In fairness to both parties, there was probably some guilt and some innocence on both sides. When two stubborn men collide, right and wrong often gives way to "principle." In any case, Teddy Atlas returned to the metropolitan area, where today he is a respected trainer at Gleason's Gym in New York City. He commutes to the city daily from his suburban home in Staten Island, where he lives with his wife, Elaine, his daughter, Nicole Marie, and his young son, Teddy Atlas III. Several of his fighters show considerable promise, but there's not a Mike Tyson in the bunch. A boxer of Tyson's caliber comes along only once in a lifetime.[22]

A separate incident that reportedly took place about the same time may or may not have contributed to the final confrontation. As Teddy Atlas told it, Mike Tyson groped Teddy's 11-year-old sister-in-law, Susie, causing Teddy to seek out his fighter. He put a .38 caliber pistol to Tyson's head and warned him that if he ever did anything to the Atlas family again, he would be killed.[23]

Mike's final disappointment of the year took place inside the ring on December 10. His manager, Cus D'Amato, entered him in his first "Seniors" competition, the United States Amateur Boxing Championships. Tyson drew a tough opponent in the opening round, Al "Chico" Evans of Chicago, a veteran of the ring wars. Evans, a tall, black slugger packing 210 pounds on a well-muscled, sinewy frame, had many more fights than Tyson, and against much stronger competition. Mike, still basking in the glory of his second successive Junior Olympic title, entered the ring with a feeling of invincibility. He was cocky and visibly disdainful of his opponent, just as Atlas had feared. But the good Lord has a way of bringing people back to their senses when they get too big for their britches, and this was Mike Tyson's day to taste the humble pie.

Both fighters came out punching in round one, and it wasn't long before Tyson realized he was in with a different caliber fighter than he had encountered in the Juniors. Evans took Mike's best shots and came back with some of his own. Time and again, in rounds one and two, Mike hit the Chicago fighter with his Sunday punch, but he was unable to drop the tough heavyweight. At the end of round two, the fight was dead even. Tyson, frustrated by this unexpected turn of events, lost his composure. He charged out in round three, determined to score a knockout. His fight plan was completely forgotten as he threw flurries of wild punches in Evans' direction, none coming close to making contact. The two fighters exchanged jabs in mid-ring. Then Tyson tried to surprise Evans with a haymaker right to the head. The cool Chicagoan slipped the punch easily and caught the off-balance Tyson with a counter right of his own, putting the Catskill fighter on the seat of his pants for the first time in his career. Mike jumped up quickly, more embarrassed than hurt. As soon as the referee had finished the required eight count, Mike lunged after Evans again. He pounded Evans to the body, backing the Chicago man to the ropes. During the ensuing action, Tyson slipped on the wet canvas just as Evans landed another good right hand. For a second time, Tyson fell to the floor, and this time the fight was automatically stopped because of a two-knockdown rule. Tyson was beside himself with frustration, disappointment, and anguish, but it was too late. The fight was over, and his record would forever show a third-round TKO loss to Al Evans of Chicago.

The Catskill teenager retreated to the shadows of the locker room, where he sat slumped on a bench long after the fight ended. He sobbed long and loud. The loss was a crushing blow to his ego, particularly after his glorious triumph in Colorado. Rooney too was disappointed, but he was also philosophical about the experience. "He was punchin' well to the body and wearing Evans down, but he got a little anxious. He tried to go for a knockout in the third round and it cost him. This loss could be a good thing for Mike. He'll learn some things and next time he won't make the same mistakes."[24]

On the same day as Tyson's loss, World Boxing Council President, Jose Sulaiman, announced that the WBC was shortening title fights from 15 rounds to 12 rounds in an attempt to curb late-fight fatalities. He also announced that the WBC was initiating a standing eight count for a fighter in trouble. The rule change caused considerable furor throughout the boxing world. Some fighters, like Larry Holmes, came out in favor of the rule change, while other fighters, like "Boom Boom" Mancini, called the move idiotic. For his part, Sulaiman stated that 12 rounds is the dangerous limit. Beyond 12 rounds, a fighter is in danger of being seriously hurt because he is so tired. The statistics did not seem to bear out Sulaiman's contention. Of the 439 ring deaths recorded between 1919 and 1985, only four occurred after the 12th round—less than one percent. The real need would appear to be more thorough physical examinations for the fighters, closer monitoring of their critical bodily signs, and better protective equipment. The WBA apparently did not agree with Sulaiman's assessment of the situation since they retained the 15-round limit for title fights.

5

A Taste of Glory—1983

It was dark. Mike Tyson, wearing a red warm-up suit, was alone in the bedroom. He quietly threaded the movie projector, then eased himself down into a nearby chair and flashed the light on the distant screen, adjusting the focus knob until the old black-and-white picture was sharp and clear. Jim Jacobs' articulate voice could be heard narrating the film, another in "The Greatest Fights of the Century" series. "Henry Armstrong on the left trying to win his fourth worlds championship. He's already held the featherweight, lightweight, and middleweight championships of the world. They're at Gilmore Stadium, Los Angeles, California, March 1, 1940." Tyson moved away from the projector and found a comfortable stuffed chair to view the film from. "The fight is scheduled for ten rounds. Henry Armstrong's style here is typical of him, head down on the chest of his opponent whaling away to the body and then shifting to an attack to the head." Mike was engrossed in the film, his chin cupped in his hands, his eyes glued to the screen, concentrating on every move and punch that Armstrong made. He thought to himself, "You can't stop that guy. He's got so much energy." This was Mike Tyson's classroom, and Mike was an honor student in the science of pugilism. He could identify most of the top professional boxers. He knew their styles, their strengths, and their weaknesses. He observed their styles, and he remembered. He learned what it took to become a champion, the sacrifices that had to be made, the dedication that was required. He discovered why some fighters were successful while other fighters were failures.[1]

Studying the fight films was all part of Cus D'Amato's curriculum in the school for developing world champions. Cus taught his own philosophies to his students. Then he would sit the student down and view films of the boxing masters with him, being careful to point out the significant factors in each fight and the important characteristics of each fighter. Cus would explain how his philosophy was utilized by the winning fighter in each bout. After reviewing a film with Cus, the fighter would review the film over and over by himself until he absorbed and understood what Cus was trying to teach him, just as Mike Tyson was doing on this night. Mike watched Henry Armstrong, and he silently nodded in agreement as Armstrong's tactics brought him another victory. Over the years, whether consciously or unconsciously, Mike Tyson's approach to the sport closely modeled that of Henry Armstrong—the same boundless energy, the same aggressive, pressing attack, the same head on chest, the same unrelenting body attack followed by an assault to the head. Mike Tyson could have been cloned from Henry Armstrong if he wasn't already the reincarnation of "Little Perpetual Motion." And well he should emulate Armstrong, for Henry was Cus D'Amato's all-time favorite fighter.

Outside the ring, Mike was lonely. He enjoyed the quiet moments when he could sit in his bedroom alone, viewing the fight films and meditating. He needed time to himself to recover from a traumatic 1982, a year in which he lost two of the people closest to him, his mother and Teddy Atlas. He mourned for a long time over the death of his mother, the person that he loved more than any other in the world. He felt he had let her down. He had given her numerous heartaches when he was a young street hoodlum, and he wanted so desperately to make up for all the pain he caused her that his sense of grief was even more intense than it would have been under normal circumstances. He wanted to win the heavyweight championship of the world for her, so she could see him become successful and rich, and so he could buy her a big house and lots of clothes. Now those things would never happen. It was too late to make amends. He was left alone now. With his mother gone, with no father, with his sister married and his brother in the Navy, and with many of his friends dead or in jail, his visits back to Brooklyn became fewer and fewer. Catskill, New York, became his real home now, and Cus and Camille became his real family—and his only family.

Then, suddenly, Teddy Atlas also left him. Teddy and Cus clashed violently in late 1982 and Teddy was banished from the Tyson camp forever. Mike Tyson loved Teddy Atlas but he loved Cus D'Amato even more. Cus was his new father, his family. With the death of Mike's mother, Cus became even more important in Mike's life. Cus became his adopted flesh and blood, his roots. And Mike needed roots. With time, Camille would come to be the mother he sought to please. As Cus and Teddy battled, Mike was forced to choose sides. He chose to stay close to Cus and watched Teddy leave, but he watched with a twinge of regret. Teddy was like an older brother to Mike, and to watch his "older brother" fighting with his "father" was more than he could tolerate. He watched Teddy depart with a feeling of sadness. It was the end of a cherished relationship.

The perfect cure for these crushing personal losses was work, hard work, and Mike committed himself to his training regimen with an increased intensity, as if wanting to prove Teddy Atlas wrong. Mike always enjoyed the gym work. He found it relaxing and rewarding. When he worked, Cus was always nearby, studying, scrutinizing, and instructing. He could often be seen on the apron of the ring, leaning against the top rope, a large 88 decorating the front and back of his blue football jersey. Mike Tyson was in the ring, working with Kevin Rooney. Cus often had Mike work with small, fast boxers to develop his defensive instincts. The 16-year-old slugger was not allowed to throw any punches during these sessions. He could only bob and weave and learn to be evasive. As Rooney noted, "Joe Frazier would take one or two punches in order to get in one good one. Mike doesn't take any." Mike Tyson danced around the ring, followed by Rooney. Kevin shot out a straight left and Mike easily ducked underneath it. His movement caught D'Amato's eye, and Cus was not happy with what he saw. "You're a little bit too square. Your right shoulder should be forward more. So when you're drivin' in, there's nothin' to hold that blow. You're gonna do real damage. You might drop the guy with one punch. You aim the right at his rib cage and if his guard drops you bring the same hand up to his jaw. Bang! A left hook to the head. You got a chance to get in three perfect punches, if he's still standin'."

Tyson demonstrated. Under Rooney's left. Pop. Pop. Pop. Right to the ribs. Right to the head. Left to the jaw. "That's it. See. There's no way he's gonna hit you then, right? Now remember, it's always good to throw the punch where you can hit him and he can't hit you. That's what the science of boxing is all about. Remember, from the side you can let that punch go with the worst kind of intention because you know he can't hit you back. So you can throw the bomb with all the power you can generate." Tyson continued to circle Rooney, constantly bobbing and weaving, throwing rights and lefts in clusters, always just short of

Kevin Rooney was Tyson's trainer from 1982 to 1988, during which time Tyson racked up 35 consecutive wins, 31 by KO (courtesy Paul Antonelli).

their mark. D'Amato slowly moved away, leaving Tyson and Rooney to perfect the new strategy. He quickly corralled a 12-year-old and started working with him outside the ring. Cus began throwing his left in and out continuously, teaching the youngster how to weave back and forth to avoid the punches. "No. Straight back and forth like this," motioning right and left. "Okay, good, don't stop." Next Cus began swinging both his hands back and forth, back and forth, teaching his pupil to bob and weave in perfect synchronization. The kid moved up and down, right and left, letting Cus's punches slip harmlessly past his ear or over his head. "Awright, see these are little things. But that's the difference between bein' a pro and bein' an ordinary guy." Cus whispered to a bystander, "I'm not a creator. What I do is discover and uncover. I take the flame and turn it into a roaring blaze. That's what I coach these boys. See, that's what I try to do."[2]

As February rolled around, the boxing season got under way with the Western Massachusetts Golden Gloves Tournament at the Holyoke Boys Club. Mike had been working hard in the gym, and with his two Junior Olympic titles in tow, he was already rated as the number eight amateur super heavyweight in the country. Although still only 16 years old, he tipped the scales at a solid 201 pounds. Cus arrived in Holyoke fully confident about Mike's chances, but tournament official Mike Burke was skeptical of Tyson's ability to handle the experienced fighters that were entered in the open competition. He recommended to Cus that Mike fight in the novice class. "He'll get killed in there with experienced fighters." Cus just smiled and nodded. "Yeah. Just watch him." Mike received a bye to the finals of the tourney due to a lack of willing opponents, and on Saturday, February 12, he was matched against a tough kid from South Boston, Jimmy Johnson. As with most of Tyson's amateur fights, this one ended before the crowd had settled in their seats. After a few seconds of feeling each other out, the fighters clinched. As they parted, Tyson shot out a straight right hand that landed flush on Johnson's chin, and the boy from Southie went straight down and took the full count. Trainer Kevin Rooney was more impressed with the performance than anyone else. "He went down like he was shot," Rooney exclaimed. "It was a perfect punch." Kevin, who was working in his first fight as Tyson's trainer, was happy with Mike's emotional approach to the fight. "Mike remained calm in this fight. In his past fights, he would start to get excited during the bout, but this time he was calm and cool." February 12, 1983, marked the beginning of Mike Tyson's maturing process. Mentally and emotionally Mike was breaking free of the cocoon of childhood and was moving into the adult world. The teenager was already gaining control of his inner self, a characteristic that would make him doubly dangerous in the future. Some people live their entire lives without harnessing their emotional energy. This precocious young man was on the road to achieving it while still in high school.[3]

Tyson's sudden triumph in Holyoke advanced him to the New England tournament only three days later. On Tuesday, February 15, Mike stepped into the ring in Lowell, Massachusetts, to face his semi-final opponent, Jimmy Brisson, from nearby Salem. Brisson, a husky 228-pounder, was very popular around the metropolitan area, but he had never fought a man as deadly as Mike Tyson. That Catskill Clubber, as he would come to be known to local sportswriters, was intimidating to look at, and he was perpetual motion in the ring. The upcoming encounter began to prey on Brisson's mind. Tyson and Rooney themselves were concerned about the bout. They had heard about what a rough fighter Brisson was, and they prepared themselves for a knockdown, drag-out battle. As fight time neared, both boxers worked on their mental preparation for the encounter. Mike settled down as the bell sounded for round one, but Brisson was still agitated, and he started to come unglued immediately. He retreated from Mike's initial thrust, but Mike pursued him around the ring relentlessly, finally catching him on the ropes. A hard right hand to the body followed by a left to the body and a right to the head backed the rugged New Englander into a corner. Several more body shots brought a look of anguish to Brisson's face and caused the referee to give the injured fighter a standing eight count. It wasn't enough. As soon as the final count was tolled, a towel came flying out of Brisson's corner, terminating the battle at the 42-second mark.[4]

The next day, Tyson was scheduled against Jim Rayburn of Burlington, Vermont, for the New England Five States Championship. Rayburn had impressed the Tyson camp with his semi-final performance, and Tyson and Rooney were preparing themselves for a hard match. It ended up being easier than they expected. Rayburn had sprained an ankle in the semi-final, and the tournament physician declared him unfit to fight in the finals. Tyson became the New England Golden Gloves Champion by default, a route that was not uncommon to him. Many of his opponents found various excuses to withdraw from their fights. His reputation as an executioner was growing by leaps and bounds. Another walkover in the Northeast Regionals in Ithaca, New York, automatically qualified the Catskill Clubber for the Golden Gloves National tournament in Albuquerque, New Mexico. Prior to the tournament, however, the Tyson management team met in New York City to review their fighter's performance. So far, everything looked good. His progress was on schedule. The plan was for him to win a series of national titles, including the Junior Amateur Boxing championships and the Golden Gloves, then to concentrate on making the Olympic team and winning a gold medal at the 1984 Summer Games. Assuming all went well, Mike Tyson would turn pro immediately after the Games, and would gear his timetable toward annexing the world's heavyweight championship within three-and-a-half years, making him the youngest heavyweight champion ever.

Albuquerque was a pleasant change from the cold, blustery weather that swept through the northeast in March. New Mexico was warm and sunny, with the temperature hovering around the 70-degree mark. Tyson was not on vacation, however. His week was a busy one with over 32 fighters entered in the super heavyweight division, the cream of the crop from around the country. On Tuesday, Mike faced Ron Williams of Springfield, Illinois. A Tyson left hook to the liver demolished Williams in one minute and 30 seconds. The next day, Mike was matched with Andrew Stokes of Indianapolis, Indiana. Stokes gave Tyson a battle for more than six minutes before Tyson's famous left hook sent him to Never-Never-Land in the third round. Mike Tyson was responding well to his first taste of national prominence and the pressure that accompanies it. He had the usual butterflies before a fight. After all, D'Amato preached if you don't get nervous you're one of two things, either dead or a liar. However, when the bell sounded, he was all business, moving smoothly and punching with authority.

The quarter-finals were scheduled for Thursday, March 24. Big Mike Bradwell of Jacksonville, Tennessee, again carried Tyson into the third round, but he eventually succumbed to a numbing left hook to the body. Two-time defending champion Warren Thompson was the only fighter left between Mike Tyson and a spot in the finals. To win the coveted belt, Mike had to rise to new heights to conquer this hurdle. Thompson was defiant, but Mike was more than up to the task. In the dressing room before the semi-final encounter, Kevin Rooney gave Mike his final instructions. "Get on top of this guy and stay there. He's got a good right hand and a lot of experience. If you're patient, you'll get a good shot at him and then you'll hurt him." Mike followed the fight plan that Kevin had outlined. He kept his head buried in Thompson's chest for three rounds, pummeling the former champion with rights and lefts to the body, and not giving Thompson an opportunity to unleash his vaunted right hand. Mike never found an opening to bring down the number one seed, but he did keep busy enough to win a unanimous decision and catapult himself into the finals. "It was one of his best fights," said Rooney. "He did what he had to do."

Mike had disposed of four foes in impressive fashion, including a victory over the two-time champion. Now only one obstacle separated the Catskill Clubber from the National Golden Gloves Championship, a three-round match against crafty Craig Payne. Tyson was nine minutes from glory. His strategy in the final was the same as it had been in previous matches, to stay on top of his man, to work the body incessantly with both hands and, if an opening occurred, to switch his attack to the head. From Tyson's corner, the fight seemed to go almost as planned. Mike kept on top of Payne and midway through the first round hurt his man with a thunderous right hook. The wily Payne backed off and managed to dance away from Tyson's bullish charges, giving himself time to get rid of the cobwebs. In round two, a refreshed Payne came back strong to win the round on all scorecards. Tyson appeared to dominate round three, however, and looked like a sure winner as the five judges totaled up their scores. The decision was close, and it was controversial. When their tallies were checked, Craig Payne emerged the winner by a 3–2 count. Tyson was crushed. He knew in his heart he had won the fight, and he couldn't understand how the judges could take it away from him. Kevin Rooney was more vocal than his fighter, echoing the sentiment of losers from time immemorial. "We were robbed," screamed the frustrated Rooney. "Mike beat the guy and everyone knew it." The crowd obviously agreed with Kevin because they booed loudly when the result was announced. The silver medal was small consolation for the distraught Tyson, but he had learned a valuable lesson in losing the final: Whenever you leave the decision up to a body of judges, anything can happen and usually does. In spite of the loss, Mike's reputation continued to grow in boxing circles. Tom Colter, Director of the National Ranking Committee, noted that Tyson fought five of the best super heavyweights in the country and held his own with all of them. Although failing in his bid for the national championship, Tyson achieved the number two ranking in the country, behind Craig Payne. His star was still in its ascendancy, and his hopes of making the Olympic team in 1984 were not diminished by the defeat.[5]

In the professional ranks, Larry Holmes still dominated the heavyweight division. On March 27, he defended his title in Scranton, Pennsylvania, the site of his first pro bout, against the European Champion, Lucien Rodriguez of France. Rodriguez, as it turned out, was durable but not very talented. Holmes pounded the Frenchman from pillar to post for 12 rounds en route to a unanimous decision. He floored Rodriguez in the sixth round but could not finish him off as the bell saved the European champ. Holmes did, however, manage to pile up a majority of points in successfully defending his title for the 14th time. Four days later, "Irish" Gerry Cooney announced one of his many comebacks, perhaps spurred on by Holmes' lackluster performance plus a lack of legitimate contenders for the heavyweight crown. Cooney had been KO'd by Holmes in 11 rounds in 1982 and had gone into retirement immediately after the fight.

As spring settled over the Catskills and the snow disappeared from the landscape, Cus D'Amato drove his young charge unmercifully. He continued to refine Mike's physical skills, but he spent most of his time and effort on the mental approach to the sport. As a break from these taxing training sessions, Mike liked to spend some afternoons with his friends. Now that John Chetti had dropped out of the gym, Tyson grew closer to Mike Murphy, and he began spending more and more time at the Murphy house on Spring Street. His first visit to the neatly kept red dwelling was a memorable one. Murph invited Tyson over the play hoop one afternoon after school and, while Murph went to his bedroom to change his clothes, Tyson settled comfortably into a stuffed chair in the living room to watch TV. As fate would have it, Mrs. Murphy, returning home from work, walked in on the big rugged black kid sitting in the middle of her living room. Startled by the strange sight, Mrs. Murphy unleashed a blood-curdling scream. The noise not only shocked young Tyson, but probably startled half the neighbors on Spring Street as well. A flustered Mike Tyson jumped to his feet stammering, "Oh, Mrs. Murphy, hello. I'm Mike Tyson. I didn't mean to scare you."[6]

During the rest of the year, Tyson became a regular visitor to 207 Spring Street. Mrs. Murphy liked the affable boy-giant and enjoyed having him around the house. Mike Tyson, for his part, found the Murphy house to be a comfortable place to relax, a safe haven from the pressures of the day. The Murphys had a basketball hoop in the driveway, and the boys played a lot of one-on-one there during the summer months. Jim Murphy, three years Tyson's junior, remembered Mike as a player with limited talent, but one who was intimidating. "People tended to get out of Mike's way when he drove for the basket."[7] Being a 210-pound high school sophomore might have had something to do with that. Mike Murphy was the only one of the crowd with a driver's license, so he automatically inherited the position of group chauffeur. The boys spent many pleasant summer evenings at the local baseball and softball games rooting for their favorite teams and gorging themselves on hot dogs and soda. And then there were the movies. They were still a popular form of evening entertainment. In addition to the girl-hunting trips to the Community Theater, the boys could now go to the drive-in by the carful. In spite of a full schedule of mind-boggling academic courses at Catskill High School, and in spite of the tyrannical physical and philosophical workouts under the watchful eye of Cus D'Amato, life was good for Mike Tyson in 1983. He was coming into his own emotionally. His boxing career was meeting with astounding success. He had a lot of girlfriends, a great group of guys to hang out with, and a loving family at the Ewald mansion. Mike Tyson knew it didn't get any better than this.

Cus D'Amato now considered the amateur tournaments to be of minimum value as far as Tyson's progress in the ring was concerned. Mike was physically too advanced for the young kids that he met in the junior tournaments, and his skills were rarely tested. Cus felt that Tyson could receive a better education elsewhere. In addition to developing his boxing skills in the gym, and his practical ringmanship in "smokers" and club fights, Tyson added to his experience by serving as a sparring partner for older, more mature fighters who were entering the professional ranks, or who were progressing through the higher levels of amateur ranks. On one occasion, Mike travelled to White Plains, New York, to spar three rounds with Carl "The Truth" Williams, who was beginning to make a name for himself in the professional arena. Williams needed stronger competition than the run-of-the-mill sparring partners were capable of providing, and Mike Tyson was happy to oblige. Williams' record as a pro was already 13–0, but that didn't phase the high school kid from upstate New York. Tyson put pressure on Williams from the opening bell and gave "The Truth" a sound beating to the rib cage. Tyson's chin was tested, probably for the first time, during this skirmish. Rooney remembered it clearly. "Michael was coming in and Williams hit him with a straight right hand. It was like Michael wasn't hit. He just kept coming. An ordinary person would have gone down. He's not ordinary. Needless to say, we didn't get invited back."[8]

On Saturday, May 21, Nadia Hujtyn drove half a dozen members of the Catskill Boxing Club down to the Bronx and parked the old blue Chevy station wagon next to the Apollo Boxing Club on Westchester Avenue. Several of the Catskill fighters were on the card, including Mike Tyson, who was pitted against a 22-year-old boxer from the Nassau Police Club, Bill Sammo. Tyson would always remember these "smokers" fondly in the years to come. One of the Catskill contingent claimed that most of their opponents were thugs who just wanted to see how much pain they could inflict on the other guy. Mike admitted that some of those fighters would have scared the guys from his old neighborhood in Brooklyn. Sammo had been fighting much longer than his younger opponent, compiling a 30–6 record compared to Tyson's more modest 17–3 mark. It turned out to be a good fight for Tyson because he had to work hard to maintain an advantage. Sammo was a rough guy and not the least bit impressed with Tyson's credentials. From the outset, the Sammo-Tyson bout was a war, both fighters throwing bombs with abandon. The Nassau slugger was not intimidated by Tyson's long list of first-round knockout victims in the junior tournaments. He was determined to welcome Mike to the "men's division" with a thorough beating. Tyson got in several good shots in round one, but Sammo walked right through them and kept the pressure on for a full three minutes. Round two was more of the same, busy and bloody. In round three, Tyson's jab began to take its toll on Sammo's face, which turned red and puffy. Suddenly, a Tyson right hand exploded on Sammo's face, splitting open the Nassau man's left eyebrow. Blood spurted freely from the jagged wound, covering both fighters with the sticky red fluid.

The referee jumped In immediately, wrapping his arms around Sammo to prevent further damage, and awarded a TKO victory to the ecstatic Tyson. While Tyson accepted the accolades of the crowd, Bill Sammo retreated to the confines of the dingy dressing room where a doctor took seven stitches to close the wound. Another Catskill fighter, Frankie Minicelli, also won his fight, a three-round decision over Bob Strong of Beacon.[9]

The boxing world was saddened once again on May 31 as another of its immortals, Jack Dempsey, took the full count at the age of 87. Newspapers across the country headlined the passing of the beloved "Manassa Mauler," a man who epitomized the "Golden Age of Sports" in America. Together with baseball legend Babe Ruth, football's "Galloping Ghost" from Illinois, Red Grange, tennis champion Bill Tilden, and golfer Bobby Jones, Dempsey romanticized sports in America. During the 1920s and 1930s, these heroes were larger than life, idolized by every kid from nine to 90. Dempsey, a comparatively small heavyweight at 182 pounds, captured the imagination of the American sporting public by recklessly attacking his much bigger opponents, some of whom outweighed him by 50 to 70 pounds, and battering them into submission. He was a real-life David, and he traveled the back roads of America slaying the Goliaths wherever he found them. Dempsey held the heavyweight championship for seven years before yielding the title to a former Marine, smooth-boxing Gene Tunney, in 1926.

The following year, 1927, was the year of the famous "long count" in boxing. It occurred in the return match between these two worthy adversaries. A recent change in boxing had made it mandatory for the boxer delivering a knockdown to go to the nearest neutral corner while the referee tolled the count over the fallen fighter. Prior to 1927, the standing fighter was allowed to hover over his fallen foe, waiting to knock him down again as soon as he regained his feet. On the night of September 27, Dempsey trapped Tunney in the corner in the seventh round. A vicious left hook to the chin dropped the Californian to the canvas, dazed and hurt. In a moment of excitement, Dempsey stood over his man, ignoring the new rule. The referee refused to start the count until Dempsey went to a neutral corner. The confusion gave Tunney an extra five seconds to regain his senses. It was apparent to many ringside observers that Tunney would have had considerable difficulty getting to his feet in time had it not been for the delay. As it was, Tunney was actually given a 15-second count, allowing his head to clear enough for him to get on his bicycle and avoid Dempsey's frantic rushes for the remainder of the round. By the time round eight started, Tunney was fully recovered, and he went on to defend his title with a 15-round decision. Dempsey, for his part, offered no excuses. He blamed no one but himself for the loss. "I forgot the rules. I lost my head and couldn't move as Referee Barry shouted, 'Get to a neutral corner.'"[10]

Wilfred Benitez visited the Catskill gym in early June to spar with Kevin Rooney in preparation for his July 16 title fight with Mustafa Hamsho. At 17, Benitez became the youngest professional boxing champion of all time. Turning pro at the tender age of 15, he won the World Junior Welterweight title in 1976 with a 15-round decision over Antonio Cervantes. He subsequently added the Welterweight title by beating Carlos Palomino in 1979, and the Junior Middleweight title with a convincing knockout of Maurice Hope in 1982. Another fighter of note visited upstate New York that summer. British heavyweight Frank Bruno was in training at Grossinger's for a July fight against Mike Jameson. D'Amato, never one to miss an opportunity, arranged for his young charge to spar with Bruno on several occasions, both at Grossinger's and at Catskill. It was a good experience for the up-and-coming Tyson, allowing him to get in the ring and bang away with a world-class fighter.

Bruno, a big heavyweight at 6'3½", 220 pounds, was undefeated as a professional. His record was a perfect 16–0 with 16 knockouts. Tyson worked the summer away in quiet solitude, his mind set on only one objective, winning the U.S. Amateur Boxing Championships to be held in Colorado Springs from August 17–20.

As August rolled around, D'Amato entered his boxer in the Ohio State Fair National Championships to gain additional experience prior to the trek to Colorado Springs. Tyson reached the semi-finals in Ohio with no competition. Then, on August 13, he was matched against Jerry Goff from Sainer, Mississippi. Goff must have thought he was in the ring with Hercules himself. Tyson stormed all over him from the opening bell, pounding him around the ring for the full three minutes. Goff miraculously survived the first-round onslaught, but how he did it was anyone's guess. He survived for another minute in round two before a Tyson right knocked him unconscious at the 1:12 mark. Goff was out cold for ten minutes before he could be revived, and in the process he lost two teeth. The sight of the slaughter must have had an unnerving effect on Tyson's opponent for the final. Hugh Copeland entered the ring obviously agitated and nervous the next day. When the bell sounded, he fought like a man in a trance, showing little movement and no offense. A crushing right hand counter-punch by Tyson dropped Copeland to the canvas in just 44 seconds of round one, giving Mike the Ohio State Fair National Championship.[11]

Five days later, Tyson was back at the Air Force Academy seeking the Junior Amateur Boxing Championship. Mike liked the Air Force Academy. It was filled with pleasant memories of happy days. It was the scene of his greatest amateur triumphs, his most exciting knockouts. Fighting in the Academy was like having a home court advantage for Mike Tyson. He knew that the large crowds attending the fights would be rooting for him. He was a home-town favorite in Colorado. Mike's semi-final opponent was Dave Yonko, a large hulk of a man from Long Beach, California. Yonko, at 6'4' tall and 250 pounds, towered over the muscular Tyson. He also tried to out-psyche Mike with reminders he had beaten the highly touted Henry Tillman in an earlier fight and expected to do the same thing to him. Tyson was unimpressed, to say the least. His only reaction was a shrug of the shoulders and a non-committal "we'll see." At fight time, Tyson walked his man down as he had all his other opponents, and delivered the coup de grace to Yonko at 1:38 of round one. A left hook to the body and a right to the head, the old 7–2, did the damage. The referee quickly stepped in and stopped the fight without a count after the knockdown. Trainer Kevin Rooney was thrilled at Mike's stunning victory. "Yonko was an experienced fighter, but Mike came out strong and worked the body well. He scored with a left jab and then worked the combination."[12]

Once again, Mike Tyson was thrust into a title fight, this time for the Junior Amateur Championship. The man across the ring from him in the finals was Mark Scott of Palm Bay, Florida. But Mike was not to be stopped. A left hook crashed against the side of Scott's head just 54 seconds into the fight. Scott hit the deck so hard there was no count. The referee just walked across the ring and raised Tyson's hand in victory. Not resting on his laurels, Mike Tyson was added to an International boxing card between West Germany and the United States in Lake Placid, New York, in mid–September. Mike was scheduled to meet German super heavyweight Peter Hussing at the Olympic Center on September 17. Hussing was an experienced fighter, a veteran of two Olympic Games. The 35-year-old strongman won the bronze medal at the 1972 games in Munich, and seven years later, in 1979, he won the European Amateur Heavyweight title. Rooney was slightly on edge. "This will be Mike's

5. A Taste of Glory—1983

toughest test so far. Hussing is an experienced boxer who has fought in the Olympics. I'm sure Mike will be nervous about the bout, but if he can keep calm, I think he will do OK."[13]

After the Junior Amateurs, Mike's fourth national title, more and more people began to jump on the Tyson bandwagon. The Catskill Clubber, although still only 17 years old, was ranked second nationally behind Tyrell Biggs. Tom Coulter, chief of the U.S. delegation to Lake Placid, remarked, "Mike is the best puncher in amateur boxing today. He has great natural ability and instinct, and the ability to knock out anyone. Mike's only drawback in this fight is his inexperience."[14] A couple of days before the match, Tyson, Kevin Rooney, and Cus D'Amato made the long trek from Catskill to Lake Placid, about 150 miles up the Northway. Rooney still remembered the recent sparring session between Tyson and Carl Williams. "Mike looked real good against Williams. He was quick and hard to hit. If he can keep his composure against Hussing, it could be a big win for him."

Tyson's opponent, however, turned out to be someone other than Peter Hussing, who was forced to withdraw from the competition with an injury. He was replaced by a 300-pound behemoth named Peter Geier. Tyson was not intimidated by the size of the walking mountain, even though he was outweighed by almost 100 pounds. He exploded across the ring at the opening bell as if he were fighting Willie Shoemaker. His first wild right missed its mark, but a flurry of lefts and rights left Geier stunned and glassy-eyed. A straight right hand to the jaw buckled the big German's knees. Referee Heinz Birkle gave Geier a standing eight count and then waved the fight to continue. Tyson was on top of his man immediately, backing the wobbly German into a corner. A sizzling uppercut lifted the 6'4' boxer completely off his feet, and the German's corner threw in the towel before their man suffered a serious injury. The time was 1:47, and it brought Tyson's amateur record to 23–3 with 20 knockouts. Tyson was ecstatic. "I knew I was quicker, and if I started quicker and went to the body I would do okay." Cus was equally impressed with Mike's performance. "This was important to his development. Even though the fight itself was not that hard for Mike, the pre-fight experience was helpful. He didn't know who he was fighting and he had to wait. The pressure was there, but Mike handled it well as you can see." D'Amato was also proud of the fact that his young protégé followed his instructions to the letter and didn't deviate from the battle plan as the excitement mounted. "We could see the guy was big, so we told Mike to go out quick and not let him get started." Mike did as he was told.[15]

As the year wound down, the Tyson camp pointed toward one last summit to scale, the Amateur Boxing Federation National Championships to be held in Colorado Springs in early November. "This will be the key to the Olympics for Mike," Rooney reported, "because the winner will get an automatic berth to the Olympic trials next spring. If he can impress the officials in the ABF, they will help him get the international fights he needs before the Olympics. Right now they are aware of him and they are waiting to see if he will be the Olympic heavyweight."[16] D'Amato worked feverishly to schedule some fights for his boy wonder in Catskill, but no opponent could be found. As a result, Mike had to content himself with the drudgery of gym work and some infrequent sparring sessions.

In October, the Adirondack Regional Golden Gloves Tournament was held in the IUE Hall on Erie Boulevard in Schenectady but, as usual, Mike found himself alone in the ring when the bell sounded. He won in a walkover. "Nobody wants to fight Mike," cried Kevin Rooney. "The trainers don't want their kids to get beat at the local level. But even though this might be good for Mike's ego, we wish he could've gotten a fight. It's better for him if he gets experience. We hope Mike gets a fight in the States, but we wouldn't be surprised if he didn't. Hopefully, he'll get at least one fight before the Nationals." On October 22, at Lake Placid, New York, was the New England-New York Olympic Regional Boxing Trials. And once again the lonely man of amateur boxing stood alone in the center of the ring—just him and the referee. Another walkover advanced Mike Tyson to the ABF Nationals. He would be making another long journey to the Air Force Academy, but unfortunately he wasn't getting any experience along the way. D'Amato tried to compensate for this sad state of affairs by intensifying Tyson's sparring sessions. Phil "Bazooka" Brown, a rangy black heavyweight with the build of Adonis, was brought in from California to lean on the smaller fighter and test his potential. The Louisiana slugger possessed an outstanding professional record with 21 wins and two draws in 23 bouts, 15 of the wins coming via the knockout route. He was favorably impressed by Tyson's ring savvy. "I've been a sparring partner for Ken Norton, and I've beaten Renaldo Snipes and James "Quick" Tillis in the amateurs. And I know Tyson punches harder than any of them. He's young, strong, and a comer. I don't see how anyone will beat him in the Olympic Trials." Brown's manager, Ron Iovenella, agreed. "Mike Tyson is the best amateur fighter in the United States, and will represent this country in the 1984 Olympics."

Tyson himself was confident as the ABF Tournament approached. "It doesn't matter who I have to go through, I'm gonna win this tournament." The tournament, in fact, turned out to be a star-studded event. All the top amateur heavyweights in the country were entered, including the flashy Tyrell Biggs. Also present were Craig Payne, who had decisioned Tyson in the finals of the National Golden Gloves Tournament just seven months previous, and Al Evans, the only man to knock out the Catskill Clubber. Still, Mike Tyson exuded an air of confidence when he was interviewed by the local media. "The competition doesn't matter to me because I think I'm the best super heavyweight in the country. Now I get a chance to prove it. I have just finished sparring with one of the top heavyweights in the country, Phil Brown. I haven't been hit hard in most of my fights, but Brown came right after me and landed a lot of solid body blows. I wasn't used to that."[17]

Tuesday, November 8, arrived, and Mike Tyson was in the ring again, in the opening round of the American Boxing Federation National Championships. This time an opponent stared at him from the opposite corner, a journeyman fighter named Kommel Odom. The details of the fight are hazy, but what is clear is that Mike Tyson was disqualified in the second round. His manager, Cus D'Amato, back in Catskill, was dumfounded after his telephone conversation with Kevin Rooney in Colorado. "I think they said Mike was holding, which I don't understand. This Odom is probably the weakest fighter in the class and I can't really explain it except that Mike is out of the tournament. These things happen in boxing. Now we have to go back to the gym and work." It was one of the low points in Mike Tyson's career. He was down but not out. Cus picked him up, brushed him off, and started to rebuild his confidence. Mike was showing the first signs of maturing under D'Amato's patience guidance. A setback such as he experienced in Colorado would have completely destroyed him emotionally only a short time ago. Now he was able to assess the reasons for his loss, to correct the deficiencies, and to forge ahead. Now a defeat was no longer the end of the world, but rather a temporary obstacle that had to be overcome.[18]

The days ran into weeks, and the Tyson championship express was put back on track by the deft hands of the crafty old trainer. During 1983, the relationship between Mike and his mentor had grown steadily stronger. Mike's thick shell of suspicion and mistrust was still evident in his daily relationships, but it was beginning to show some cracks in its steadfastness.

5. A Taste of Glory—1983

In the three years since Mike had moved into the big white house on the river with Cus and Camille, he had progressed to the point where he was just now beginning to feel comfortable with them. The threesome were slowly but surely becoming a family. Mike was no longer the loner he had been when he first arrived in Catskill. Gone was the sullen youth who had slinked into the Ewald house back in the late summer of 1980. In his place was a more relaxed individual, a growing boy who was outgoing and friendly. Rather than sitting quietly at the dinner table as a casual observer, Mike was now a major participant in the activities. Dinner had developed into a warm, relaxed time in the old house, and Cus felt a sense of satisfaction at the improvement in Mike's demeanor. He sensed that, at last, Mike Tyson was becoming his own man. If he continued to mature at his present rate, Cus was confident that he could handle the inevitable media pressure that would accompany his rise to stardom in the professional ranks. Tyson's self-esteem had also increased tremendously since he came under the influence of the white-haired wonder worker. The private tutor that Cus had hired had improved Mike's reading capabilities and his language skills to the point where he was on an equal level with the rest of his age group. Cus's words came back to him as he remembered the progress that he had made in the past three years. "There are no stupid people. Only disinterested people." Cus was right, and Mike smiled to himself as he thought about it.[19]

It was a cool gray winter morning as the old man and the young man emerged from the big white house on the river. They headed down the driveway as the first rays of light broke through the trees along the Hudson, walking slowly and leisurely, and talking softly to each other as they entered the old dirt road, the one dressed in baggy pants and a blue football jersey sporting a gaudy number 33, the other comfortably attired in a loose-fitting gray warm-up suit. A half-breed mutt trailed obediently behind. Their conversation touched on most of the important subjects of the day—girls, life, death, truth, belief, dedication, and boxing. In the end, the conversation always returned to boxing. Cus touched on a new lesson each day. He impressed upon Mike the importance of maintaining an honest relationship between fighter and trainer at all times. "You can't lie. You can never lie. Lying is the worst thing a fighter can do, because if you lie, I can't teach you nothin'. If I tell you to do one thing in the ring and you do somethin' else, I can't teach you." Cus's lectures were non-stop, and they dwelled on the secret to success as Cus saw it.

> In any endeavor, you have to feel that you are going to be successful, in order to be successful. Boxing is the same way. Now, if a fighter allows himself to think about losin', he can never become a success. No matter how much talent he has, he'll never realize the talent because the thing that makes you a champion is not necessarily the talent. I've known of fighters who have won championships who were crude in effect, but they had such determination and will to win, and competitive spirit, and they fought with such enthusiasm that they overcame skill. In fact, I have a sayin', and it goes somethin' like this: When you're watchin' a fight, you're watchin' more a contest of will than of skill, with the skill prevailin' only when the skill is so superior that the will is not tested. If a man fails, he only fails because he didn't believe. You gotta believe in yourself—in everything you do in life—even boxing. If a fighter goes into a fight and he believes he is gonna win, he will win. He may have other qualities to overcome the skill, but he will win. See now, there is no difference in what you do and where you do it. If you go in with the enthusiasm, the trust, the desire, you will win. The mind always wins over the body. Take knockouts, for example. Ninety percent of knockouts are not knockouts. What you witness as a knockout is a silent acknowledgment that he no longer wants to continue. That's what it means.[20]

Nationally, the high point (or low point) of the year was a middleweight match between Marvelous Marvin Hagler and Roberto Duran. The fight, held in Caesars Palace, was a boring 15-round affair that should have been staged in a funeral home. The bout was eventually won by the champion, Hagler, although he fought a surprisingly cautious fight, almost as if he were afraid of Duran. Hagler's hesitancy was Duran's good fortune, because if Hagler had been his usual aggressive self, it is doubtful that Duran would have been around to see round four. In any case, Marvelous Marvin took his $5,000,000 and ran.

6

The Fall and Rise of Mike Tyson—1984

The winter of 1984 was a time of reflection for Mike Tyson and his strategy team, coming off a busy 1983 where Mike broke into the amateur ranks under a full head of steam, compiling an impressive 12–2 record and carving out a big reputation for himself in the process. The Brooklyn teenager had acquired a considerable amount of experience over the previous 12 months, fighting a variety of opponents with different styles and physical attributes. He had advanced to the finals of the National Golden Gloves Tournament in Albuquerque, New Mexico, before losing a close decision to Craig Payne, an admirable feat for a boy of 16. His only other loss of the year came on the strange disqualification to Kommel Odom in November. Even his losses provided valuable experiences for the rapidly developing Tyson. If 1981 and 1982 were young Tyson's kindergarten years in amateur boxing, then 1983 represented his high school training, and the year ahead would be his college education preparatory to entering the professional field. Two major objectives lay ahead for the Catskill dynamo that, when achieved, would make his name a household word across America, and would vault him into the professional ranks by the end of the year, with a large asking price on his head.

The first objective was the National Golden Gloves Tournament to be held in St. Louis, Missouri, in April. Having narrowly missed winning that title in 1983, Tyson was now ready to claim the jackpot, one year older and more mature with considerably more experience. The second objective, and by far the most important, was to qualify for the Olympic Games in Los Angeles in August. With his impressive amateur record, Tyson was favored to represent the United States of America in the heavyweight division. Mike was geared for the competition. His heart was already set on winning the coveted gold medal, and he had been fantasizing about the matches for months. In the romantic eyes of a 17-year-old athlete, nothing was more important than representing his country in the world's most prestigious international sporting event, and winning impressively against all competition, including the highly respected Cuban and Soviet boxers. He dreamed about standing on the podium to accept his gold medal while the strains of the American National Anthem echoed in the background, and the Stars and Stripes rose majestically in the quiet California air to fly above all other flags in the arena. The thought of such a glorious day brought tears to the eyes of even the sensitive Tyson.

Before such things could be accomplished, however, a lot of hard work remained, including a strenuous gymnasium program complete with calisthenics, bag work, and countless hours of nerve-wracking and body-punishing ring work. The brutal regimen also included seven days a week of discipline-building road work, plus regular psychological sessions with Cus D'Amato and John Halpin. Dr. Halpin, a graduate of St. John's University, had practiced hypnosis in the city of New York for 35 years. He and Cus met for the first time in 1971, and they quickly discovered they had a common interest, a study of the subconscious mind. The two men immediately began to use Dr. Halpin's specialty to delve deep into the intellect of Cus's boxing hopefuls in an effort to make them relax more, control their natural fear, and improve their concentration. Dr. Halpin started working with Mike Tyson soon after the former juvenile delinquent was released from Tryon School. He and Cus utilized hypnosis to cleanse Mike's mind of the subconscious scars of his childhood years. Sometimes Mike and Cus would travel to New York City to Dr. Halpin's office, while on other occasions Dr. Halpin would make the two-hour drive to Catskill, combining the hypnosis sessions with a relaxing weekend in the country. Dr. Halpin started working with Mike Tyson in 1981, and their meetings continued at regular intervals for the next five years. After the good doctor put Mike under hypnosis, Cus would go to work on his psyche. "Always be relaxed when you fight—don't get personally involved, stay detached—block out everything except the fight—concentrate only on your opponent—don't allow yourself to get tired during a fight." And so it went, the duo of D'Amato and Halpin always striving to improve Mike's mental attitude and to stabilize his emotions.[1]

Other than the psychological sessions, the drudgery of gym work filled Mike Tyson's days. His trainer, Kevin Rooney, made sure that Mike kept his nose to the grindstone.

> OK, Michael, hit the jump rope, three rounds and I wanna see a hundred and fifty jumps per minute. No goofin' off. Good. Now five rounds of sparrin' and no letup. Remember, punch with bad intentions. If we need to, we'll change sparrin' partners afta the second or third round. That's good Michael, but you're not through yet. You still have some exercises to do. Situps—leg lifts—crab walk—wrestler's bridge. You gotta get those neck muscles strong. Awright. Good job Michael. Take a rest and call it a day.

Mike Tyson loved the activity of the gym, the effort, the sweat, the physical abuse. But he also enjoyed being a teenager and, after a vigorous workout, he often met his friends next door at the Village Pizza for a quick snack. He usually consumed two large slices of cheese pizza and a Sprite while the conversation turned to the usual teenage subjects of fast cars and fast girls. Mike liked both of them. He had his share of girlfriends, and he did enjoy playing the field, but he still spent most of his time with Angie. As far as Cus and Kevin were concerned, playing the field was safer for a boxer. No commitments meant no complications. When asked about his off-duty activities one day, Mike emphasized his appetite for junk food. "I'm just a normal teenager. I have friends I like to hang out with and have a good time. I like girls and junk food. But instead of drugs and booze, I get high piggin' out on pizzas, banana splits, Whoppers, and Big Macs, and I wash them down with Sprite and ginger ale." Mike Tyson was still a child. He was only 17 years old, but destiny would force him into manhood before his time. The spotlight and the pressures of being a celebrity would increase by leaps and bounds over the next two years, and Mike would lose his privacy and his childhood in his quest for the heavyweight boxing championship of the world. Would it be worth it? Only time would tell.[2]

As February rolled around, the television cameras were focused on Sarajevo, Yugoslavia, where the 17th Olympic Winter Games were in progress. The hero of the Games, as far as America was concerned, was a brash, young, downhill skier named Bill Johnson. Johnson, a cocky, blond unknown from California, burst upon the international scene like a breath of fresh air. No one outside of the international ski community had ever heard of Bill Johnson before the Olympic Games, but when he loudly proclaimed to the world that he would win the gold medal in downhill racing, everyone became aware of his existence. And they all thought he was crazy. But he was newsworthy, so his statements were carried on television and in print around the world. Johnson didn't have any kind words for the favored Austrians either. In fact, he was quoted as saying, "They ain't much." On the day of the big competition, all eyes were focused on Mount Bjelasnica to watch the bold American attempt to carry out his boast.

In far-off Catskill, New York, Mike Tyson and Cus D'Amato were glued to the TV set for the same reason. Naturally they were rooting for Johnson to succeed. Cus D'Amato made good use of events like this in his education of Mike Tyson. He would utilize Johnson's performance to impress upon the young boxer the importance of heart and courage in determining the winner of an athletic event. Johnson's boasts, as it turned out, were not just hollow bellowing without any substance. The crafty Californian had surveyed the course very meticulously, and he knew that this course could well have been designed and built specifically with him in mind. It was a perfect course for his style of skiing. The layout of the course, the surface, and the slope all pointed to one thing, a Johnson victory, so he had told everyone that, not in bragging, but simply as a matter of fact. When the starting gate opened for the first run of the day, Bill Johnson came charging out like a wild animal, confident and reckless. Flying down the hill on wings of fiberglass, he hit speeds upwards of 80 miles an hour to take an early lead in the competition. Never in the history of the sport had an American of either sex won a gold medal in an alpine event. But on this day history was being played out on a cold, snowy mountain, 6,000 miles from home. Johnson's second run turned out to be as good as his first, and he crossed the finish line triumphantly, the number one downhill skier in the world. He had said he was the best and then he went out and proved it.[3]

Another brash young man had done precisely the same thing 16 years previous, but in a different sport. Quarterback Joe Namath of the New York Jets had promised the world that his much-maligned group of American Football League misfits would emerge victorious from their Super Bowl III tussle with the powerful National Football League Baltimore Colts in 1969. And Broadway Joe backed up his boast that year by passing the Jets to a convincing 16–7 victory. D'Amato reminded Mike Tyson of these things—know what you are capable of doing, then go out and do it.

February marked the beginning of Mike Tyson's quest for the National Golden Gloves Championship. His first challenge was an easy one. On February 18, at Queensburgh High School, he won his match in another walkover when no opponent was courageous enough to trade punches with the Catskill Clubber. After the "no-fight" fight, Tyson returned home to his mentor to renew his physical training and to continue work on his mental approach to the sport. Cus and Mike took their usual early morning walks along the dusty lane that led from Ewald House to Thorpe Road. The damp mist of early March chilled their bones as they walked, the 76-year-old man and the 17-year-old boy, in perfect harmony with each other. The old man in the blue and white football jersey spoke endlessly to his charge, imbuing the boy with his philosophy of positive thinking. And the young boy listened quietly and attentively, occasionally nodding in agreement at the man's statements.

In the gym, the same scenario was evident. The teacher, in his usual pose, leaning over the top strand of ropes, carefully studied his student as the boy went through his boxing routine with trainer Kevin Rooney. Every so often something would catch the old man's eye, a weakness in the boy's execution, the beginning of a bad habit, something. As soon as he spotted an imperfection, the old man would interrupt the action, point out the mistake to his protégé, explain the consequences of making that mistake, and then instruct him in the correct way to execute the movement. Two hours of gym work did not complete the student's day. It only ended his "classroom" work. His homework continued on into the late afternoon and early evening hours until it was time to turn in. At dinner, the family discussions usually revolved around the fight game, life in general, and the close relationship between the two. The old man would regale his audience with tales from his own life, his childhood, his boxing champions, and his confrontation with the mobsters of the IBC.

After dinner, the old man would settle into a chair in the upstairs bedroom and the two of them, man and boy, would watch fight films together. The schoolwork continued as the teacher carefully dissected the strategies of each of the combatants, explaining the ebb and flow of the fight in great detail. The boy just sat on the floor, eyes fixed on the movie screen, enthralled by the boxing expertise that was hidden beneath the frail veneer of the old man. He was convinced that the old man knew more about boxing than anyone alive, so he listened intently. He absorbed the knowledge and retained it. Cus D'Amato, in turn, loved his young charge. He had seen the boy grow from a street thug to a decent young man. Once he explained the boy's development to a friend. "I believed that all the boys brought up in the environment that he did would require help, patience, and understanding. I tried to make him feel, and I hope I did, that I understand this kind of life. I grew up in a tough neighborhood myself. And having watched him come from where he was to where he is, I have a deep affection for him, I do." Cus also confided another secret to his friend.

> If he weren't here I probably wouldn't be alive today. The fact that he is here and doin' what he's doin', and doin' as well as he's doin', and improvin' as he has, gives me the motivation and interest to stay alive. I believe a person dies when they no longer want to live. Nature's a lot brighter than people think. Little by little we lose our friends that we care about, and little by little we lose our interests till finally we say, "Well, what the devil am I doin' around here?" We may have no reason to go on. I have a reason with Mike, and it gives me the motivation to stay alive, and I will watch him become a success because I will not leave until that happens.[4]

During March, the Tyson strategy committee made a momentous decision, one that would have serious ramifications before the year was out. Mike's managers decided that he would compete as a heavyweight in the upcoming Golden Gloves Tournament and the Olympic Trials. This decision meant that Mike would have to box well below his optimum fighting weight of 210 pounds. The limit for heavyweights was only 201 pounds, or nine pounds below Mike's best weight. The super heavyweight division was for a weight class above 201 pounds, and it was presently dominated by Tyrell Biggs, supposedly the preferred choice of the Olympic Boxing Committee. Biggs had been carefully groomed as America's super heavyweight challenger, competing in numerous international matches against the world's top super heavyweights, including Cuba's Teofilo Stevenson.

As Tyson warmed up in his dressing room before his final match in the New York State Golden Gloves Tournament, trainer Kevin Rooney explained their position to the press. "We didn't wanna fight the Olympic Boxing Committee. They've made up their minds they want Tyrell Biggs for the super heavyweight, so we decided to drop down and try the heavyweight class. I think we should have a good shot at that." Tyson's opponent in the final was

Mark Pettinato of Endicott, New York. The result was a knockout victory for Mike at 1:06 of the first round. "Mike came out strong and was slippin' and hittin' well," according to Rooney. "He was workin' the body and put Pettinato down for an eight count. When he got up Mike hit him with a left hook to the jaw that knocked him out. Mike looked real good. He was movin' a lot and boxin', not just throwin' wild punches." So much for the New York competition. From here on, the opposition would get tougher. Next stop, St. Louis, Missouri, and the Nationals beginning in just 13 days.[5]

Mike Tyson had many things on his mind as the tournament approached. He would have to win five tough matches within a period of five days. Not only would he have to exhibit superior skills in his matches, but he would have to be lucky as well. A cut of any kind, whether from a punch or from an accidental head butt, could end his quest prematurely. But Mike wasn't concerned about luck. Mike was thinking about making his own luck. His attention for the previous two months had been focused on only one thing, winning the tournament. Now, on April 17, he was in St. Louis and he was ready.

The 1984 Golden Gloves Tournament was held in Kiel Auditorium, and it drew one of the strongest boxing fields in history. Among the favorites was Henry Milligan, rated as the number one amateur in the country. The number two amateur heavyweight, Olin Alexander, was also entered. Tyson was oblivious to the quality of the field. Since he considered himself to be the best amateur heavyweight boxer in the world, everyone else was just an opponent to him, someone who had to be dealt with on his road to the championship. He was soft-spoken but confident in his assessment of the situation. "I'm gonna knock everyone out. I don't care who's there. It really doesn't matter to me. I'm gonna fight everyone the same way." Trainer Cus D'Amato and his assistant, Kevin Rooney, had been working Tyson mercilessly for the two weeks prior to the tournament. Cus had brought in a powerful young professional fighter named Jimmy Clark to spar three rounds with Tyson every day. Clark, from Providence, Rhode Island, stood 6'3' tall and tipped the scales at a solid 215 pounds. He had a professional record of 13–0 with 12 KO's, and he gave Mike a good workout in the gym. D'Amato was pleased with what he saw. "Mike looked real strong against Clark. He's ready for the Nationals. If he wasn't, I wouldn't put him in the tournament. His only drawback continues to be inexperience. We have a hard time gettin' anyone to spar with him, so he hasn't had the ring time he needs."[6]

On April 15, two days before the start of the tournament, the Tyson entourage, consisting of Mike, Cus, and Kevin Rooney, boarded a plane at Albany airport and set out for St. Louis. Horace Greeley, a 19th-century politician, when discussing the opportunities that existed in this land of plenty, once exhorted a fellow legislator, "Go west, young man. Go west." Over 100 years later, Mike Tyson took Horace Greeley's advice. He headed west in search of fame and fortune. After one day of leisurely gym work, Tyson began his drive to the championship. On Tuesday, April 17, he disposed of Roger Peppel in one round. The next day, the Tyson express polished off Derrick Isaman, also in the first round. And on Thursday, in a quarter-final match, Tyson met Johnny Williams of Chicago. Williams, as it turned out, was no more of a puzzle to the Catskill Clubber than his previous two opponents. Midway through round one, Mike caught Williams with a short right to the chin that stopped the Chicago boy in his tracks, causing the referee to give him a standing eight count. As soon as the action resumed, a vicious Tyson left hook found its mark on the right side of Williams' face, dropping him for the full count at the 2:15 mark. The knockout brought Tyson's tournament record to 15–3 with 11 KO's. Trainer Kevin Rooney was satisfied with

Mike's performance. "Mike is looking very strong. He's very confident and I think he'll win the tournament."

The tournament continued at a frenzied pace. Although Tyson had had three fights in three days, there was no letup. He was right back in action on Friday in a semi-final match with Richard Johnson, a scrappy Texan from Fort Worth. Johnson was getting a lot of press around St. Louis because he had eliminated the pre-tournament favorite, Henry Milligan. He was confident coming into this bout, while Tyson was a little bit apprehensive. Mike paced the locker room nervously in the minutes before the fight. He worked hard to keep his emotions under control, and tried to concentrate on nothing but his fight plan. As he climbed the steps to the ring, Mike still appeared to be agitated, but he was gradually getting himself under control, and by fight time his nervousness had been replaced by a feeling of quiet determination. When the bell rang, Mike was composed and anxious to get it on. In typical Tyson fashion, he stalked his man from the outset, trying to maneuver him back against the ropes. Mike's aggressive posture and deadly punches gave him rounds one and two on all scorecards. In round three, Tyson came out firing, looking for another knockout. He kept the pressure on constantly and eventually dropped Johnson with a sizzling left hook, flush on the button. A left-right combination put Johnson down a second time, and a crushing right hand ended the competition only 45 seconds into the round.

Tyson's opponent in the final was no other than Jonathon Littles, an old friend from the Junior Olympic days. Tyson had KO'd Littles in the second round of the 1982 tournament in Colorado Springs. As usual, Mike was fidgety before the fight, but not as bad as he had been before the Johnson fight. He knew Littles and he had no doubt he would KO his man again. But still.... "He beat Olin Alexander, one of the best heavyweights in the country, so I was a little nervous before the fight, but when I got into the ring, I said to myself, 'In the ring, I'm the king.'" And king he was. He came out winging, throwing punches in a never-ending assault on Little's body. A left-right combination early in the round put Littles down. Tyson waited patiently in a neutral corner as the referee tolled the count and then got right back on top of his man when the referee waved the fighters together. Within seconds, the ref was forced to give the helpless Littles a standing eight count. Still later in the round, Tyson had his man in trouble again. This time the referee stopped the fight. Mike Tyson was declared the winner after a hectic two-minute, four-second mauling of a greatly over-matched Jonathon Littles. The young New Yorker assessed the fight candidly for the men of the press. "He was real tough, but I hurt him the first time. He jumped right up but I knew I had him. He was tryna bluff me, but I kept throwin' punches. He wouldn't go down but he was hurt."

Not only did Tyson win the gold medal in the heavyweight division, but he also walked away with the trophy as the most outstanding boxer in the tournament, an award that caught the ecstatic Tyson by surprise. "I knew I was the best fighter there, but I wasn't really expectin' to win the 'Most Outstanding Boxer' trophy. The tournament had some of the best fighters in the world. I can't really describe how great it was when they called my name." As happy as Mike was over winning the tournament, he realized it was just one step along the path to boxing immortality—and he had a long way yet to go. "Winnin' this tournament was very satisfying, but it's only the first step. The next step is winnin' the Olympic Trials, and then I wanna win the gold medal in Los Angeles. Anything less would be a disappointment. I know I'm the best heavyweight in the world and now I want a chance to prove it." He was queried at some length by the newsmen, particularly about his probable opponents in the

Olympics, those rough, tough boxers from Russia, East Germany, and Cuba. Tyson just shrugged when he thought about it. "They're just boxers like I am. When we step into the ring it doesn't matter where we're from. Only who's the best fighter. I'm the hardest puncher in my division and I'm very confident about the future."[7]

Trainer Cus D'Amato didn't let his protégé rest on his laurels for very long. He didn't want Mike to get too used to his new-found celebrity status, a situation that could easily go to a young boy's head and upset his social values. So Tyson was whisked quickly back to Catskill, New York, and into the humdrum world of the gymnasium—the drills, the sparring sessions, and the monotonous roadwork. Only a few days removed from being the toast of amateur boxing in America, Mike Tyson was again a student, trying desperately to please his teacher. In early June the Olympic Boxing Trials would be held in Fort Worth, Texas, but a seven-week layoff was too long as far as Cus D'Amato was concerned, so he entered Tyson in the National Police Athletic League Tournament in Niagara Falls, New York, in late May. Mike's first bout, a quarter-final match, was held on May 29. His opponent, Jeff Thompson, was a perfect test for him. Thompson was an experienced fighter with over 100 fights and, to top it off, he was a southpaw, an unorthodox fighter who confused and frustrated his foes. No one liked to fight southpaws because southpaws usually made their opponents look bad. Mike Tyson was no exception. This was his first fight against a southpaw, and Mike didn't know how to maneuver against this type of fighter. As a result, he looked very clumsy in the first round as he tried to figure out a way to bypass Thompson's right jab. In round two, Mike felt a little more comfortable and started getting inside Thompson's defenses. Near the end of the round, Tyson unleashed a left-right sequence that sent Thompson sprawling. The round ended before Tyson could finish the job, but the anticipation was there. Mike knew it was just a matter of time now, and he nervously waited in his corner between rounds, pawing the canvas with his foot like a chained animal waiting to get at a piece of raw meat.

When the bell sounded for round three, Tyson bolted across the ring, throwing punches from all directions. He dug a hard left to Thompson's body and followed it up with a right to the head. Thompson went down for an eight count. As soon as he arose, Tyson was there to greet him. A left to the head and a strong combination of lefts and rights to the body took the wind out of Thompson's sails. He hit the floor again but, like a courageous gladiator, he dragged himself to his feet, barely beating the count of ten. It was bravado in the finest sense of the word, but it was also foolhardy. Thompson was standing erect on unsteady pins, and the bronze executioner stood before him, poised for the kill. It was quick but it was not painless. Tyson sent two crushing left hooks to the side of Thompson's head, causing the old warrior's eyes to roll in their sockets. Their glassy stare saw nothing but darkness as the fighter pitched forward on his face. It was 1:38 of round three and the fight was over. Tyson's tournament record now stood at 18–3 with 16 knockouts.

Tyson's semi-final opponent was scheduled to be James Thurber of Wisconsin, but Mike had developed a sore shoulder in the Thompson fight and the thought of an incapacitating injury sent shivers through the Tyson camp. D'Amato didn't want to take any chances of knocking his heavyweight contender out of the Olympic Trials. When the shoulder did not respond to heat treatment the following morning, Tyson withdrew from the competition to rest his aching muscles.[8]

Back in Catskill, Mike Tyson dropped by the Murphy home to talk with Mike and Jim. According to Jim, "He stopped over the house just to hang out. He didn't want to go out."

More than anything else, it was a sad goodbye visit to his companion of four years, Mike Murphy. Tyson and Murphy had been close for a long time, but now it was almost over. Mike Murphy was graduating from Catskill High School soon, and in September he would be starting his studies at Marist College in Poughkeepsie, New York, majoring in business with a minor in marketing. Things would never again be the same for the two Mikes. They would surely drift apart as most high school buddies do. But they would always have the memories of the good times together. And, with a bit of luck, they might meet again to renew their friendship sometime in the future.

Four days later, the New York State boxing contingent boarded a jumbo jet in Albany and flew west to Chicago, then south to Fort Worth, Texas, to keep their date with destiny. The next four weeks would determine who represented the United States in Los Angeles. It was time to separate the men from the boys. Mike Tyson's shoulder was still sore but it was healing, and it apparently wasn't a serious injury. D'Amato made sure of that. As soon as Mike withdrew from the P.A.L. Tournament, Cus rushed his valuable property to New York City to have the shoulder checked out by not one but two orthopedic specialists. Both doctors concurred in their diagnosis. After thoroughly examining the shoulder and reviewing the X-rays, they declared the problem to be nothing more than a slight muscle pull. Mike was advised to rest the shoulder for a couple of days prior to his upcoming matches.

When Tyson, Rooney, and D'Amato arrived in Fort Worth, it was Sunday afternoon. They had a day and a half to rest and get organized before the hurly-burly of the tournament began. Mike did his normal roadwork and some calisthenics on Monday, but he also took a lot of time to relax and adjust to the Texas environment. On Tuesday, the turmoil began in earnest. After the roadwork and the gym session, there was an organizational meeting conducted by the Olympic Trial Committee to familiarize all the participants with the details of the tournament and to select a draw. There were eight fighters in each weight class. Quarter-final matches were scheduled for Wednesday, Thursday, and Friday, the semis on Saturday, and the finals on Sunday. ABC television was broadcasting the big matches on Saturday and Sunday.

Mike Tyson not only had to contend with his opponents during the week, but also had to deal with heavy media pressure as well. As a two-time Junior Olympic National Champion and reigning Golden Gloves National Champion, Mike was a genuine celebrity, perhaps the most famous amateur boxer in America to the boxing community. But Tyrell Biggs was better known to Mr. And Mrs. John Q. Public. The Olympic Committee had been grooming Biggs to be the American super heavyweight representative in the Olympics for some time, and had provided him with a heavy dose of international competition plus the national television coverage that went along with it. Tyrell Biggs was an early product of the television industry, one of the so-called media darlings. Mike Tyson was a fighter and only a fighter. He fought with less fanfare than Biggs, but the men of boxing's inner circle knew him well. He was rated number one in the country, yet in spite of his stature, Mike Tyson was entered in the heavyweight division rather than the super heavyweight division so as not to confront the Olympic Committee's fair-haired boy, Tyrell Biggs. Being in the heavyweight division meant that Mike had to shed ten pounds in order to come in below the weight limit of 201 pounds. Cus D'Amato had to protect his boy from the press 24 hours a day. It was certainly necessary to grant a certain number of interviews, but the constant demands of the media could be devastating to a young fighter if they were allowed to go unchecked. Cus saw to it that it was kept to a minimum.

Mike's first match on Thursday was against Avery Rawls, and he came out like he wanted to end it quickly. He rushed his man at the bell and unleashed a solid right to the rib cage followed by a left to the head. Rawls hit the deck at the 15-second mark. With the coolness of a true professional, however, Rawls got back on his feet and survived the round. He constantly backed away from Tyson and, whenever the kid from Catskill tried to move in close, Rawls tied him up like a Christmas package. In fact, Tyson was unable to drop his man again in the fight, but he did come away with a three-round decision, advancing him to the semifinals. Tyson confessed some nervousness before the Rawls fight. "I was nervous, but I'm always nervous before a fight. When I step into the ring it all goes away. I've been working towards this for a long time now and I'm ready." Mike's confessed stage fright is a common malady affecting many professional performers. Even celebrated actors and actresses, who appear on stage six nights a week, are never completely free of the jitters. British actor Laurence Olivier once admitted that, when he was in his sixties, he developed such a bad case of stage fright he was unable to face his audience. Night after terrifying night, for a period of six months, Olivier mouthed his words with his back turned to the audience!

Cus D'Amato assessed Tyson's upcoming matches for the press.

> I'd have to say Milligan and Tillman will be the roughest opponents, Milligan because he can punch and Tillman because of his experience. You have to remember that what we're asking of Mike is almost impossible on the surface. We want a 17-year-old kid with only 20 fights to beat older men who have had hundreds of amateur bouts and have plenty of international experience. Most people would consider that an impossible task, but boxing is Mike's life. He lives, eats, and breathes the sport, and right now the only thing he cares about is winning the Olympic Trials.

On Saturday, June 9, Mike Tyson stepped into the ring to face tough Henry Milligan, as ABC cameras whirred away incessantly. Milligan, from Delaware, was a street fighter, but on this day he was no match for the excited Tyson. With all the exuberance of youth, Mike pursued his blond-headed foe from corner to corner, and he carried the first round easily with his aggressiveness. In round two, Mike dropped the Princeton University graduate for an eight count, and a few seconds later, put him down again to end the fight. The victory put the Catskill boxer into the finals against the wily veteran, Henry Tillman, six years his senior. Mike Tyson was now only nine minutes away from the Olympics. But nine minutes can be a lifetime in a boxing ring. Tillman was a classy, experienced boxer with good lateral movement and an outstanding jab. He was not about to mix it up with the New York boy wonder. He would not stand in front of Tyson and let Mike pound away at him. Tillman's strategy was to keep moving for the entire nine minutes so Mike could not draw a bead on him.

In round one, Tillman jabbed and moved, deftly avoiding Tyson's wild rushes for the first two minutes. Near the end of the round, Mike trapped Tillman on the ropes and knocked him down with a sizzling right hand to the head. The Californian was stunned by the blow, but his experience saved him from further trouble. He was fully composed as he got to his feet and danced away from his 17-year-old adversary until his head cleared. Surprisingly, Tillman won the round because he had scored the greater number of punches. Knockdowns receive no more points than a light jab in amateur boxing, and Henry Tillman had landed dozens of light jabs. In round two, Tillman managed to keep his distance and again won the round with a constant barrage of flicking jabs, punches that would almost be ignored by professional judges. But again, in the amateurs, it's not how hard you hit, but how often you hit, that counts. Cus D'Amato was openly concerned in the corner between rounds. He counseled his fighter to be aggressive in round three and go for a knockout. He knew that Tillman's jabs had piled up a lot of points for him in the first two rounds, and he didn't expect to get any favors from the Olympic judges, whom he had criticized in the past. Mike Tyson would have to win big in order to be awarded the victory. A knockout would assure it. Tyson moved out quickly in round three and put immediate pressure on his taller opponent. He chased his man around the ring for three full minutes but was unable to trap him. Henry Tillman's extensive ring savvy allowed him to escape from Tyson time after time. The difference in experience between the two men was obvious to most observers. The smooth-working Tillman made the teenage Tyson look clumsy and undisciplined, while Tillman himself appeared to be a skilled professional.

Mike Tyson had put on a strong showing, one that would have given him a victory in a professional ring. His corner was quietly confident as the fight ended. Mike had been the aggressor throughout, had landed the harder punches, and had scored the only knockdown of the fight. Tillman, on the other hand, had exhibited greater ring skills and a very effective jab. The judges had a difficult decision to make. Cus, Kevin and Mike felt they had won the fight, but victory did not come. Henry Tillman was awarded the decision while the Tyson corner fumed. True to the feelings of all losers, Rooney bellowed, "We were robbed. That's all there is to it." Perhaps he was right because the crowd loudly booed the vote of the judges. D'Amato, a controversial character for over 30 years, took the decision as a personal attack on himself. He felt it was a political decision rendered by individuals who had an axe to grind with him.

Tyson stood in his corner weeping softly, his arms hanging limply by his side, and his head on his chest, in a state of apparent shock. His dream of Olympic gold had suddenly disappeared In the hazy blue light of the Texas auditorium. In the dressing room Tyson bared his soul about the moment. "It's a disaster. What can I say? I feel terrible. I wanted so much to represent my country in the Olympics. All the kids look up to the Olympic fighters. And I wanted to set a good example for them." Kevin Rooney had the last word on the subject. "We'll be back. There's no question about it." That statement, in itself, told a lot about the philosophy of the Tyson camp. You can knock them down, but you can't beat them. They will always bounce back because they believe—they believe they are the best, and the best will always be victorious in the end. Tyson and his managers accepted the loss as an educational tool, a character builder. They lost because they did something wrong, not because they met a better boxer. They would retreat to the gym and regroup. They would study the films of the fight, see their mistakes, and correct them. The next time, Henry Tillman would not get away so lucky.[9]

Mike Tyson still had one more chance to represent the United States in the Olympics. He was scheduled to fight Olin Alexander in a heavyweight elimination bout in Colorado Springs on June 29. If he beat Alexander, he would advance to the Olympic Box-offs in Las Vegas, Nevada, on July 6. As fate would have it, he would meet Henry Tillman again. If Tyson could then defeat Tillman, the two men would have to go at it for yet a third time the following day in order to determine the American heavyweight representative. Tyson's dream could still come true, but it was a long way off, and there were a lot of mountains to climb before it could become a reality. Cus D'Amato had less than three weeks to eliminate the specter of defeat from Tyson's mind and prepare him for the new battles ahead. Cus's teachings had already laid the groundwork for this eventuality. In the D'Amato book of knowledge, Tyson did not lose to Tillman because he was an inferior fighter. He lost because he did not follow D'Amato's instructions. He made mistakes. It is easier to correct mistakes than it is to rebuild a fighter's shattered confidence. Mike Tyson was still confident that he could go all the way to the Olympics. But he had to go back to the basics in the gymnasium first. He had to work on his strategy and concentrate on Cus's instructions. He had to eliminate his mistakes.

The Tyson training camp moved to Colorado Springs three weeks before the fight to get acclimated to the Colorado environment and to fine-tune Mike's conditioning program. Mike was scheduled to spar with super heavyweight Tyrell Biggs in the three weeks prior to the Alexander match, but Biggs was a no-show. He arrived only days before the fight, forcing Mike to condition himself as best he could without any actual ring combat. He concentrated instead on the other aspects of the physical fitness program, including calisthenics, shadow boxing, and a lot of work on the bags—the heavy bag, the speed bag, and the slip bag. His ring work was restricted to light workouts with a light heavyweight fighter. But more importantly, Cus worked on Tyson's emotional state of mind and on his ring strategy. Mike had to become more proficient in cutting off the ring on his opponent. He also had to keep busier in the ring and not wait to get in one clean shot. When he trapped his man on the ropes, he had to punch more, throw lots of punches, combinations of punches, and all of them with bad intentions. Mainly he had to keep his emotions under control and not get excited. It was difficult to ask a 17-year-old boy not to get worked up in the heat of battle, but it was essential to his success. An excited fighter doesn't think clearly, doesn't stick to his fight plan, and doesn't see the opportunities when they present themselves. In short, an excited fighter is, more often than not, a losing fighter.

June 29 arrived soon enough, and Mike Tyson was ready, physically and mentally. He glared across the ring at Olin Alexander during the introductions, looking very much like a man in a trance, and determined to make the fight a short one. Mike swarmed all over the California heavyweight immediately and buried him under a deluge of punches that seemed to come from all directions. Alexander was no match for the enraged Tyson, and he meekly succumbed to the fusillade of blows at 2:06 of the first round, sending Tyson on to Las Vegas and a rematch with Henry Tillman. There would be no excuses this time. The better man would win. On July 6, Caesars Palace was all aglitter. It was a festive occasion in this city of tinsel and sequins, an Olympic Box-off, and the neon capital of the west basked in the national spotlight. Boxing fans filled the Sports Pavilion, decked out in their formal tuxedos and their finest gowns. ABC-TV was on hand to transmit the account of the fight across the country, and every celebrity in town made it a point to attend the gala event. It didn't make any difference if they knew a left hook from a right cross. Visibility was the important thing. Celebrities need to be seen.

The dressing room was buzzing with activity an hour before the big fight, and the Tyson group was brimming with confidence. "I'm gonna win the fight and that's all there is to it," remarked a solemn Tyson. "I made some mistakes down at Fort Worth, but I've learned from those mistakes. I've been workin' hard out here and I'm ready." Trainer Kevin Rooney nodded in agreement.

> We can't let up the whole nine minutes. Mike really wants to make the United States team and he's come too far to let down now. He knows what he did wrong against Tillman the first time, and we worked on it in Colorado Springs. We're ready. In order to make his punches count, Tyson must neutralize Tillman's constant movement. We have to cut the ring off. The key to stopping Tillman's movement will be the left jab. If Mike can work that jab and keep movin' to cut off the ring, I think he'll be tough to beat.

Cus D'Amato provided additional insight into their pre-fight strategy. "We had that fight videotaped and we studied it for hours. We know that Tillman is gonna try and run again, only this time Mike will be able to cut him off and land his punches."

The two fighters entered the ring amidst the bold intrusion of the television cameras and the constant babble of the ringside announcers. Both men looked ready for the battle as they bounced up and down in their corners. The perspiration covering their bodies was a telltale sign that they had warmed up vigorously in the dressing room before entering the pavilion. Perhaps Tyson left his fight in the locker room. Perhaps the gold and glitter of Las Vegas overwhelmed the young gladiator. Whatever the reason, Mike Tyson didn't follow his fight plan, while Henry Tillman did exactly as he had promised. The tall, well-built Californian kept Tyson at bay with a constant barrage of stinging left jabs. His standup style made the stylish six-footer appear to tower over his smaller, crouching foe. Henry Tillman danced and jabbed. He moved quickly side to side, ever circling, keeping away from Tyson's amateurish charges. Mike was unable to cut off the ring on the cagey veteran, and he never got close enough to his man to throw many punches. As a result, it was a dull round, and it was Tillman's round thanks to his constant, irritating jab. Round two was a carbon copy of round one. Despite the pleading of corner man Kevin Rooney, Mike was unable to execute the maneuvers he had worked on during training camp. Henry Tillman remained the elusive spirit, darting to and fro, laying occasional soft jabs on the Tyson countenance, then floating away out of danger. It was another slow round. It was also another round for Henry Tillman. As the final round began, Mike Tyson needed a knockout to win. One minute into the round, the Catskill Clubber caught Tillman with a sharp right hand, knocking the graceful boxer into the ropes. Tillman had the presence of mind to slip off the ropes, however, and escape further damage, though Tyson kept up his pursuit. Late in the round, Tyson scored with another solid right that jarred his opponent, but the bell sounded before he could press his advantage.

The controversial decision in favor of Tillman left Mike Tyson numb and distressed in his corner, and brought 3,089 catcalls from the spectators who thought Tyson had won the fight. Two judges awarded the decision to Tillman by a 60–57 count. Two other judges voted for Tillman, 58–57. A lone dissenter gave Tyson the nod, also by a 58–57 count. Tyson was dejected. "I knew I won the fight. While we were waiting in the middle of the ring, one of the judges even winked at me and said, 'Great job.' When I heard the decision, I was stunned. I just couldn't believe it." Trainer Kevin Rooney was succinct and to the point. "I'll just let the fight speak for itself. Mike was robbed. That's my official statement." Later in the dressing room, Rooney thought back on Mike's hard right hand in the third round. "It was a good punch," he said, "but it just missed the mark. If it had landed clean, the fight would have been over. When I saw Mike land that second good right hand, I thought it was over. I didn't see how they could give the fight to Tillman. But I've been around boxing too long to take anything for granted, and I had a gut feelin' Mike wouldn't get the decision." While Rooney was dealing with the press, his distraught fighter slipped out of the arena, made his way across a field and hid behind a large tree, where he screamed in anguish, venting his frustration and grief in bitter solitude.[10]

July 6, 1984, was the low point of Mike's career. He would not represent his country in the Olympics. His crusade had ended in failure. He had faced the trial and he was found wanting. It was not his skill or his courage that let him down. It was his youth and his inexperience that caused his downfall. But he would overcome those shortcomings in the months ahead. Mike Tyson did receive one measure of consolation from the competition. He was selected as an alternate on the Olympic team and, as such, he would train with the other Olympians in Colorado Springs for the next three weeks and accompany the team to Los Angeles in August. If Henry Tillman were to be injured or take ill prior to the Olympics, Mike Tyson would become the American torchbearer in the heavyweight division. And somewhere down the road, in the near future, Mike Tyson would turn professional and take aim at the Mt. Everest of boxing, the coveted heavyweight championship of the world. "I'm gonna turn pro. But I'm not sure when. I might stay around for the World Amateur Championships in November. I'd like one more chance to show everyone that I'm the best in the world. I'll have to talk to Cus of course. The final decision is up to him."

Even though Mike Tyson had lost two fights to Henry Tillman within a space of four weeks, he never doubted his superiority. He had lost because he had made mistakes, not because Tillman was the better fighter. As Rooney reminded everyone, "He's an 18-year-old kid and people forget that. He's only had 25 amateur fights and he almost made the Olympic Team. That's a commendable job any way you look at it." From another point of view, the two losses to Henry Tillman may have been more important to the advancement of Mike Tyson's career than any of his spectacular victories. Although Mike had made great strides in controlling his emotions in the ring, thanks to the guidance of Cus D'Amato, he was still unprepared for the professional ranks.

His string of easy knockouts in the amateurs made him arrogant and difficult to control. He felt invincible and viewed his opponents with utter disdain, making life difficult for D'Amato and Rooney in the gym. Tyson was often AWOL during training sessions and, as a result, he was unable to stay in peak physical condition, often coming into fights eight to ten pounds overweight. Teddy Atlas was aware of these problems, and his attempt to correct them had led to his falling-out with D'Amato. The two losses to Tillman helped snap Tyson out of his sloppy training habits. He knew now that he was not unbeatable, and he committed himself to perfecting his physical condition and his mental attitude. He listened more closely to the instructions of his trainer and his mentor. His work habits improved. He trained hard, day in and day out. Mike Tyson had finally put himself on the Yellow Brick Road that led to the Emerald City and Larry Holmes' championship belt. He would not lose another boxing match, either amateur or professional, until he had won and unified the heavyweight title.

In early August, the Olympics were in full swing and American boxers acquitted themselves admirably. They brought home an impressive nine gold medals, even without Mike Tyson. Mark Breland, the 147-pound sensation from Brooklyn who had compiled an amazing 110–1 amateur record, dazzled his Asian opponent, Young-Su, in the finals, to dance away with a 5–0 decision. Henry Tillman proved his right to be the American representative by upsetting the world amateur heavyweight champion, Willie DeWitt of Canada, thereby reversing an April decision in the World Championships. Pernell Whitaker, a 20-year-old lightweight from Norfolk, Virginia, KO'd Luis Ortiz at 2:15 of round two. Paul Gonzalez won the 106-pound title in a walkover.

Mike Tyson watched from the wings, proud of his teammates but pensive as he imagined himself standing on the podium, bending slightly from the waist as the gold medal was hung around his neck. It would have been a dream come true, but it never happened.

On Monday, August 13, Mike Tyson returned to Catskill, New York, to get on with the rest of his life. He sat in the living room of the big white house discussing his future with

Cus D'Amato and his adopted mother, Camille Ewald. The decision had been made. Mike would aim toward the National Amateur Championships in August and then would compete in the European Championships in October. Shortly thereafter, probably in late November, Mike would take the big plunge and make his professional debut in Albany, New York. The first step toward the Nationals was the Empire State Games in Syracuse. Mike hadn't done much boxing as an Olympic alternate but he did keep in shape with a lot of running and was anxious to get started again. On Friday, August 17, Mike stepped into the ring in the Carrier Dome to square off against Ian Berkley in a semi-final match. Mike was obviously ring rusty. His punches were often wild and his timing was off, but his aggressiveness carried him to a decision. The next day, in the finals, Mike was opposed by Winston Bent. During the pre-fight instructions, the two men had to be separated as open warfare almost broke out before the first bell had sounded. Cus D'Amato, of course, blamed Bent for the confrontation. "This fella began to stare at him in a very aggressive way." Once the real fight started, Mike moved forward relentlessly. His bobbing and weaving tactics caused Bent to miss numerous punches, frustrating the more experienced adversary. According to D'Amato, Bent's frustration reached the point where he actually bit Tyson in the second round. Tyson was dominating the fight midway through round three when he saw an opening and nailed Bent with a devastating right hand. Bent collapsed in a heap on the floor and took the full count as Tyson jumped with joy. It was his first knockout in almost two months. The king was back.[11]

The National Championships in Lake Placid, New York, were Mike Tyson's next stopover. "It leads to further experience," D'Amato said. "Most other fighters will have 60 to 200 fights. Tyson has about 25. Once he gets sufficient experience, he'll be turnin' pro." The Lake Placid Tournament brought together the top 120 fighters from around the country. Missing, however, would be the talented Olympic fighters, most of whom were entering the professional ranks. As the dominating force in the heavyweight division, Mike Tyson drew a bye all the way to the finals. In spite of his Olympic disappointment, Mike Tyson reached the Lake Placid event with impressive credentials. He had won the 1983 U.S. Junior Championships. He had won the 1984 National Golden Gloves Championship, and walked off with the tournament's Most Outstanding Boxer award as well. He was also the Silver Medalist in the 1984 Olympic Box-offs and served as an alternate at the Olympic Games in Los Angeles. He was definitely the force to be reckoned with in Lake Placid.

As it turned out, Tyson's opponent in the finals was a big Texan, and another adversary from the Junior Olympic days, Kelton Brown. Mike had faced Brown in the finals of the 1982 competition in Colorado Springs. In that encounter, Tyson had disposed of his adversary quickly in the first round. However, two years had passed since that bout, and Brown's progress was unknown to the Tyson crew. Obviously, Brown had more than held his own against the competition in the heavyweight ranks as evidenced by his appearance in the National finals. Kelton Brown, remember, was a big heavyweight, 6'7' tall and a bulky 300 pounds. Tyson did not spar during the week but worked out diligently in the gym, and by fight time he was raring to go. The kid from Catskill moved to the center of the ring quickly when the fight started, and scored with a left hook to the body that left the Texan gasping for air. The referee immediately made Brown take a standing eight count, while a patient Mike Tyson watched. When the action resumed, Tyson jolted Brown with a jarring right hook to the side of the head. The referee interrupted the fight to give the dazed fighter another standing eight count. Before the fight resumed, a time-out was called to repair a loose ring rope, giving an unsteady Brown an additional 20-second respite. The extra rest didn't help the young man from Dallas, however. Tyson mounted another attack as soon as the referee turned him loose, and a rapid-fire combination of punches brought an end to the fight. It had lasted only two minutes and 33 seconds.[12]

It was evident that Mike Tyson's amateur career was rapidly drawing to a close. There were very few worlds left for him to conquer in the non-professional arena. Not only did Tyson win another National Championship, but he also walked away with the outstanding boxer award again. Such things were becoming a habit with him. Mike's trainer, Cus D'Amato, was justifiably happy with his young fighter's performance in Lake Placid. "Well, I was very impressed," said Cus. "He reminded me of a modern day Jack Dempsey. He's awesome. I think Mike is ready to turn pro. He probably will enter the European Championships in Finland in October and then turn pro in December. I suspect that all the countries that didn't come to the Olympics will go to Finland. Mike will be able to get good experience fighting the fighters from the Soviet-bloc countries. They're a strong group."

After a week's vacation, Tyson was back at work In Redman's Hall, sparring and working on the bags. His last preparatory program was beginning. Soon he would be fighting for money. Cus D'Amato had the usual difficulty hiring sparring partners for his precocious destroyer of men. "Because of his punching power, it's difficult to get people to spar with him." Cus was fortunate to obtain the services of a tough heavyweight named Muhammad Hussein for a week. The 27-year-old Hussein had been in the ring with the best, including champion Larry Holmes, and his professional record totaled over 30 fights. Trainer Kevin Rooney noted, however, that the main emphasis in the training camp was not on Mike's physical condition, but rather on his mental outlook. "Mike runs about three miles every

Tyson sparring in the gym with Tom Patti and Matt Baranski observing the proceedings from a distance (courtesy Paul V. Post).

day but it doesn't mean anything. We have to prepare his mind. If he's not ready to fight mentally, he can get in there with a lesser fighter and he'll get knocked out." Mike certainly was not overwhelmed by the prospect of traveling to Helsinki to fight the capable boxers from Russia and Hungary. "I look at it as any other trip," noted Tyson, Catskill's phenomenal 18-year-old. "I look forward to any trip but I don't make one any more prestigious."

One of the physical qualities that D'Amato worked on with his fighter was Tyson's movement. He wanted Mike to move more after he punched so he wouldn't have to take a punch in return. Punch, but don't get hit yourself. That's the name of the game. D'Amato pushed his protégé to the limit, continually forcing him to stretch his horizons in order to achieve new goals. Rooney explained it this way. "Cus wants him to be perfect. Cus is a perfectionist." Kevin was right. Cus believed that everyone should strive for perfection because it's something that can never be attained and the individual will never get bored in his pursuit. Mike Tyson, as a student of the Cus D'Amato school of pugilistic excellence, pursued perfection. Like everyone before him, he would never achieve his goal, but he would come a lot closer to it than most boxers, thanks to the wisdom and dedication of his teacher.

The aging D'Amato realized that Tyson's biggest need was actual ring experience. Because of his awesome talent, Mike's 25 or so amateur fights lasted an average of only one round, hardly time enough for Mike to work up a sweat, let alone accumulate any experience. So it was that sparring became a critical part of his boxing development. The brawling Muhammad Hussein gave Mike a good workout for several days, but even the former 1980 British National Boxing Champion wilted under the relentless pressure put on by the energetic young bull. After one four-round workout, Mike offered to spar another round with the embattled Hussein, but Muhammad graciously declined the offer. Before leaving Catskill to fulfill other commitments, Hussein provided the press with his valued opinion of the New York titan. "Very strong. Very strong. He just needs experience. There's no doubt, he's excellent for his age. He could make it. At this point he's very quick. I just hope he keeps up that speed when he turns pro. Most amateurs slow down when they turn pro because the fights last longer and they have to pace themselves." D'Amato assured everyone that Tyson would not lose any of his quickness when he turned pro. "The public don't realize his accomplishments. Some day in the future, the town of Catskill will be put on the map."[13]

September passed into history. October began and the training intensified, with Tyson active in the gym six days a week. Sunday was a day of rest, relaxation, and professional football. On October 8, Mike and Cus were glued to the TV set as one of the celebrated milestones of pro football was surpassed. On this cool, crisp, autumn afternoon, a small, stocky running back for the Chicago Bears broke Jim Brown's all-time NFL career rushing record of 12, 312 yards. The ebullient Walter Payton ran over, under, and around the New Orleans Saints en route to his historic achievement. Mike envied Walter Payton his skill, his fame, and his wealth. Little did Mike know at the time, but his day would come. Some time, in the not too distant future, another youngster would watch Mike Tyson perform on television and would envy Tyson's skill, his fame, and his wealth. Life goes on relentlessly and, for a lucky few, today's dreams and fantasies become tomorrow's realities.

Monday morning, it was work as usual, but the pace was more relaxed now as the sparring sessions geared down with the departure of Hussein. Tyson did get in one last tough five-round workout in the ring with Tyrone Armstrong of Philadelphia. It was Mike's last activity before the European Championships. Armstrong, a typical tough kid from the City of Brotherly Love, was on his way to the U.S. Senior National Boxing Championships, and he needed the workout as much as Tyson did. Tyrone didn't hold out much hope for the European boxers that would be challenging Tyson's ring talents. "He's a very aggressive fighter. He has tremendous power and excellent foot movement. His speed keeps opponents off guard, especially with the many faints he throws in. When he hits them, that'll be it." Even Cus D'Amato was satisfied with his fighter's progress. He knew Mike was ready for Finland. "There's not much to do now except roadwork."

Cus's training regimen and the ring education of his protégé was essentially at an end on the amateur level. D'Amato was not accompanying Mike and trainer Kevin Rooney to Helsinki. The next time Cus would work with Tyson would be in November, and the program would be directed toward Mike's professional debut. But first things first, and before Mike could turn professional, he had to get through the tough European Championships. On October 12, a small group of Tyson supporters, including Cus D'Amato, traveled to Kennedy International Airport in New York City to see Mike off on his first international adventure. Mike and Kevin Rooney arrived in Helsinki about mid-morning on the 13th and spent the entire day relaxing around the hotel, shaking off the effects of the jet lag. There was a six-hour time difference between New York and Finland, with Helsinki being six hours later, and it usually took a day or two for a person to adjust to his new eating and sleeping schedules. It was like learning to stay up all night and going to bed at 5 a.m. rather than 11 p.m. quite a radical change for someone with a boxer's discipline and training habits.

Cus D'Amato, back in New York, was confident of Tyson's success in Europe, and he welcomed the competition. "Fighting the top Europeans, including those from the Soviet-Bloc countries, has to be a challenge." Cus had always provided suitable challenges for his fighter, even in sparring. Tyson's sparring partners were instructed to do their best against him, to force the fight, and to approach each session like a real bout. Unlike every other professional trainer, D'Amato wouldn't let his fighter wear protective headgear during the sparring sessions. "Head gear gives you a false sense of security," claimed Cus. "Whoever uses headgear gets hit far, far too often."[14]

As tournament time approached, Mike Tyson's adrenaline started pumping furiously, and he began to generate the nervous energy that was so important to his success in the ring. But Mike still had not adjusted to the time difference between the United States and Europe, to the unusual surroundings, and to the Scandinavian food. After the tournament he would confess, "I didn't fight up to par mostly because I didn't feel so well." In any case, he approached the tournament in a positive frame of mind. The participating countries included the Soviet Union, Korea, Sweden, Hungary, Finland, Denmark, Czechoslovakia, England, China, and Bulgaria. Most of the non–American fighters followed the more classical approach to boxing, being standup fighters with the predictable ring strategy of a John L. Sullivan. Tyson looked forward to the challenge of competing against these fighters and matching his style and boxing philosophy with theirs.

His first match, scheduled for Friday, October 19, was against a Finnish boxer, but as he warmed up in his dressing room prior to the fight, he was informed that his opponent was ill and had refused to fight. Mike Tyson only had to enter the ring and walk across to his opponent's corner when the bell sounded to be awarded the victory. His next fight, a semi-final encounter, took place the following day. Waiting for Mike in the ring was Istvan Szegora, a veteran Hungarian fighter who was all business. His mind was focused on only one thing, winning the match. It was obvious that Szegora would be a tough opponent. And he was tough. Tyson pursued him relentlessly for three rounds, and when he caught up with his man he was able to get in some punishing blows. He hurt Szegora on several occasions but the big Hungarian took the leather and stood his ground. He even returned some effective punches of his own. Still, Mike was awarded a lopsided three-round decision. Trainer Kevin Rooney admired the European's toughness. "Szegora was a good fighter. The guy took them like a seasoned pro. He took Michael's best shots. That was good to have a guy fight back. This guy stood there and took it, but Michael won easy." It had been a good match for Tyson. He had a vigorous workout and came away victorious and unhurt. He was ready for Sunday's final, his last step toward winning the European Championship, the 7th International Tammer Tournament as it was officially known.

On Sunday, Mike Tyson found himself in hostile territory. His opponent in the finals was a big, blond Swedish Adonis, 6'5' Hakan Brock. Brock had pulled off the upset of the tournament when he decisioned the favored Russian boxer in the semi-finals. As a fellow Scandinavian, Brock was immediately adopted by the Finnish fans as one of their own. The arena erupted in a wild display of emotion when Brock came into view and made his way down the aisle to the ring. Conversely, Tyson's arrival was greeted with a smattering of applause and a few isolated catcalls. The cool reception didn't deter the Catskill heavyweight from his self-appointed task, however. He had committed himself to bring home the title and he was emotionally prepared for any contingency. During the referee's instructions, the tall Swede towered over his diminutive foe like Goliath espying David. From the ringside seats the fight looked like a mismatch. How could the tiny American possibly stand up to the power of the Scandinavian strongman? The large crowd actually felt sorry for Mike Tyson, but the 18-year-old New Yorker had a surprise in store for them. At the bell, Tyson moved forward like a man on a mission. He quickly muscled the tall Swede back against the ropes and unleashed a torrid body attack. The crowd gasped in disbelief as the short, squat American pounded the midsection of the 6'5" Scandinavian giant with short, powerful, devastating punches. Brock winced with each thunderous shot to the rib cage. Bright red welts appeared on his milk-white skin. After what seemed an eternity, Brock managed to move off the ropes and escape his tormenter's clutches. He backpedaled out of danger, trying to catch his breath at the same time. Tyson stalked him again, but Hakan Brock had had enough of close combat with the Catskill bomber. He had met Tyson toe-to-toe and he didn't like the results. For the rest of the fight, Mike Tyson chased and Hakan Brock ran. Brock survived the fight, but lost the decision. Surviving was a hollow victory to be sure, but one that the big Swede felt was preferable to being KO'd. His performance reminded boxing scholars of another Swedish amateur boxer, Ingemar Johansson, who had humiliated his country and himself in the 1952 Olympics by being disqualified for not fighting. Kevin Rooney shook his head in disgust at Brock's effort. "The guy didn't want to fight. But again, Michael closed the show nice. All in all, it was a nice experience."[15]

Mike and Kevin relaxed in Helsinki for a couple of days to savor their satisfying victory and to recover from the mental and physical strain of the previous week. While they rested, they took a bus tour of the ancient city, founded by King Gustavus I in 1550 AD. They were fascinated by the 400-year-old buildings, the tiny winding streets, and the picturesque waterfront area. As they stared out at the cold, dark blue waters of the Gulf of Finland, they may or may not have realized that less than 50 miles away, across the vast watery wasteland, lay the country of Russia, perennial adversary of their homeland.

Mike Tyson was welcomed back to Catskill with open arms by his vast legion of friends. Foremost among the crowd was Cus D'Amato, his manager, trainer, companion, and adopted father. Cus was beaming with pride as he squeezed the boy in a giant bear hug. No words were exchanged, but the looks that passed between the two men spoke volumes. The love and respect they had for each other was evident in their eyes. Mike had a few more days of rest before he had to go back to work in the gym. He enjoyed the break from the rigors of training. And he made the most of his time off to see all his friends and have a good time.

He spent one day traveling to Brooklyn to visit some of his childhood buddies. Cus chauffeured him to the nearby town of Hudson where he boarded the Amtrak train for the "Big Apple." A short subway ride beneath the concrete facade of the city subsequently delivered him to Brownsville, where he had wasted several years of his youth in indolence. He and some of his old friends sat in one of the local fast food joints eating burgers, guzzling Cokes, and bringing each other up to date on what had transpired since their last get-together. A few hours in that depressing environment, however, was more than the Brooklyn escapee could take, and he was happy to get back to his new home in Catskill and to his new friends. For the next three days he pigged out on the good life. He and his buddies traveled to Crossgates Mall in Guilderland to see the latest Arnold Schwarzenegger movie, *The Terminator* and to frequent McDonald's, Burger Chef, Ben & Jerry's Ice Cream, and other fast food joints that operated within the shopping complex. One of their favorite pastime activities was hanging around the indoor complex and trying to pick up girls. It was a lot of fun staring at all the pretty bodies that wiggled their way through the mall, and it gave the boys a macho feeling to make sly comments as the teeny boppers passed. But it was not a good way to pick up girls. That had to be accomplished more individually and with considerably more finesse. Still it was fun, and it was a regular activity for the teenage crowd. Saturday and Sunday were usually mall days. Mike Tyson was a good-looking guy and he had his share of dates. But he was playing it cool as far as a permanent relationship was concerned, preferring, at 18, to keep things loose for the time being. He discovered that it was easy to get dates and, as his boxing success grew, he found it easier and easier. At times his extracurricular activities interfered with his training regimen. When that happened, Cus D'Amato would sit Mike down and remind him of his primary objective, winning the professional heavyweight boxing title. Mike understood his mission and he was dedicated to it, so he always followed Cus's advice. Girls and socializing would have to be secondary for the present. The title quest came first.

On October 30, the world was shocked by the news that Prime Minister Indira Gandhi of India had been assassinated. The respected leader of 500 million people had been shot eight times in the chest and stomach as she strolled in the garden of her New Delhi residence. The assassins, members of her own security guard, were apprehended immediately. Cus and Camille read the sad news over morning coffee and shook their heads in disbelief over the insanities of man. The next day was an important one for Cus D'Amato and his precocious protégé. The CBS television sports team came to town to film a special program on the Catskill Boxing Club. Television meant exposure, exposure meant more recognition, and recognition meant more money for a young, aspiring professional boxer. Cus knew all the angles, as did his partner, Jim Jacobs. Cus knew how to prepare his fighter to be successful in the ring, and Jim Jacobs knew how to get publicity and market fighters to make the most money. Cus imparted some of his philosophy to the enthralled CBS reporters. "I owned and operated a gym in New York City for many years. One day Floyd Patterson walked through my doors and I started training him. I have all my fighters right from the start. If they can fight, I keep them. If they can't, I tell them to retire. Ninety percent of juvenile problems are caused by ten percent of the people. By providing a positive occupation, I develop boxing careers as well as help to keep Catskill's youth in line."

Early in November, the Tyson strategy committee sat down to map out their future plans. Cus D'Amato traveled to New York City to meet with Jim Jacobs and Bill Cayton. It was evident that Mike Tyson would have to turn pro now. Mike had run roughshod through the amateur ranks and, except for the disappointment of the Olympic Trials, he had crushed everyone in his path. He had racked up a total of five National titles, including the 1984 National Golden Gloves Championship, and he had added the 1984 European Championship as well. In effect, Mike Tyson was the world's reigning amateur heavyweight king. Now it was time to move on to bigger and better things. Mike's overall amateur record was certainly impressive. He compiled a win-loss record of 38–6 with 31 knockouts, 21 KO's coming in the first round. The question his managers asked themselves was, "How far can Mike Tyson go in the pros?" Mike appeared to have all the talent necessary to win the heavyweight championship. He was a solidly built 215 pounds compacted onto a 5'10" frame. Of the 30 heavyweight champions, only four of them weighed more than Mike Tyson. They were Jess Willard, Primo Carnera, George Foreman, and John Tate. Mike's lack of height and reach was a subject of concern for his management team. At 5'10", he was shorter than most heavyweight champions. Only John L. Sullivan, Bob Fitzsimmons, Tommy Burns, and Rocky Marciano stood less than six feet, and only Burns at 5'7" was shorter than Mike Tyson.

Still, Mike Tyson had the talent, and he had the desire and discipline as well, qualifications far more important than the physical limitations of his height and reach. Cus D'Amato would have liked Tyson to remain an amateur for another year in order to accumulate more experience, but the well was dry. There were no amateur fighters left for him to challenge. After days of discussion, days of weighing the pros and cons of all the alternatives, it was finally decided. Mike Tyson would become a professional boxer. Cus, Jacobs, and Cayton called a press conference for November 29 to make the grand announcement. Cus explained the reason for the decision. "We're turnin' pro now because there's nowhere else to go in the amateurs. We just can't get Mike any fights. There isn't anyone around who will fight him. I've tried to get people up here and I've offered to travel, but there just aren't any opponents. It's not gonna be easy in the pros because he's had only a handful of fights and he's goin' in with boxers who have had years and years of experience."[16]

Trainer Kevin Rooney had witnessed Mike Tyson's growth first-hand. He had watched Mike spar with Carlos De Leon in Catskill the previous day and he felt confident about Mike's attack on the professional ranks. "Mike has been looking real sharp against a very talented boxer. I think he's ready for the pros. I think we'll try to get Mike about five four-rounders, and then a few six-rounders, before he moves up to the main events." Cus, although confident, was still cautious about predicting ultimate success for his charge. "It's hard to gauge how a career is gonna turn out, but Mike has all the tools to become a champion. If he fights the way he's capable of, and handles the emotional pressure of bein' a professional boxer, he will become the youngest heavyweight champion in history." The big day, Mike's professional debut, was scheduled for December 7 against John Singleton. Mike was working feverishly in the gym, determined to make his debut a speedy and successful one. Rooney liked what he saw during the workouts. "From the very first day he's been here, we've trained him as a professional. His brawlin', hard punchin' style is much more suited to the pros, and perhaps that cost him a couple of fights in the amateurs. He's excited and he's anxious to turn professional. He wants to get his career started."

6. The Fall and Rise of Mike Tyson—1984

Boxing in New York State received a welcome shot in the arm about this same time. Governor Mario Cuomo appointed former Light Heavyweight Champion, and D'Amato protégé, Jose Torres to be the new chairman of the New York State Athletic commission. The post, carrying a $49,500 salary, was responsible for overseeing all boxing and wrestling regulations within the state. D'Amato was ecstatic at the news. "Now people in boxin' will have to be qualified and toe the line. We never had a man who understands the background of the boxin' business." D'Amato's joy was short-lived, however. On Wednesday, November 29, Tyson bruised his left hand in the gym. It was the same hand he had injured during the European Championships, and the damage was apparently from the same incident. It was not a new injury. This caused some consternation in the Tyson camp and resulted in a quick appointment to see a specialist in New York City.

Cus accompanied the worried Tyson to the doctor's office. "It's only a slight bruise, but we don't want to take any chances so we're having it looked at by a specialist. I should know the test results by Thursday or Friday." The results of the examination were not as optimistic as Cus had hoped. Mike had apparently suffered a torn ligament in Helsinki and had aggravated the problem five weeks later in Catskill. Cus immediately postponed Mike's professional debut to allow the injury to heal properly. He announced his decision to a small press conference in Catskill. "Mike has a very painfully torn ligament in the knuckle of the first finger of his left hand. He has the finger in a plastic cast which he will wear for about five weeks. We're a little disappointed because the first fight is always the toughest, and for psychological reasons you want to get that first one out of the way as soon as possible."[17]

Even torn ligaments couldn't keep Mike out of the gym for long, however. He was restricted to doing only roadwork for two weeks, but as soon as he received a go-ahead from his doctor, he was right back at work in Redman's Hall. He went through all the normal routines, but as a one-armed fighter with no left hand. Soon he was even working out on the body bag with two hands, a heavy tape wrapper protecting the plastic cast. He continued to spar against top competition, using only his right hand. One of his sparring partners was undefeated heavyweight Jimmy Clark. Another, Marvin Stenison, was an outstanding prospect who had once received $5,000 a week to help train Larry Holmes. Even wounded, the precocious pugilist was progressing on schedule. Trainer-manager Cus D'Amato beamed with pride as he assessed his young fighter's capabilities. "He doesn't have the edge in one area. He has the edge in all areas."

As the year 1984 drew to a close, the eyes of the sporting world were on the hockey arenas in the United States and Canada. A young phenomenon named Wayne Gretzky was tearing the National Hockey League apart, goal by goal. On December 19, the 23-year-old superstar from Brantford, Ontario, sent two goals whistling into the strings and assisted on four other goals, shattering the magic 1000-point barrier. Gretzky, now in his sixth year in the NHL, led the league in scoring in each of the past four years and became the youngest player to score 1000 points, accomplishing the feat in just 424 games, 296 games sooner than the previous fastest player, Guy Lafleur of the Montreal Canadians.

On December 28, Mike Tyson made another visit to the orthopedic specialist in New York City. "His hand is much better," reported Rooney. "He's been workin' in the gym with his right hand." Cus D'Amato nodded in agreement. "He's always in excellent shape. He trains with a great deal of enthusiasm." The doctor asked to see Mike one more time, on January 3. Then, if all was well, the doctor promised to turn him loose to continue his pursuit of fame, fortune, and the heavyweight title.[18]

The year 1984 had been a big year for Mike Tyson, and a very successful year. Mike had compiled an enviable record of 15 wins against only two losses, and had dispatched 11 of his foes via knockout, with seven of those coming impressively within the first three minutes. In Mike's mind, however, the year had been a failure. He had failed to win a gold medal in the Olympics. In fact, he didn't even make the Olympic team, a shattering disappointment to him. But in time, the Catskill boxer would realize the year had been a success. Even the two losses to Henry Tillman were valuable learning experiences and would stand him in good stead in the years to come. Time is the great healer. It provides the salve to heal the open wounds of fractured egos and broken dreams. And Mike Tyson would recover quickly from his suffering. He was on the brink of turning professional. This was no time to dwell on the past. It was time to look ahead and to begin his assault on Mount Olympus, where the god, Larry Holmes, was comfortably ensconced.

In 1985, Mike Tyson would come face to face with his destiny.

7

Assault on the Professional Ranks—1985

New Year's Day dawned cold and raw. The sun remained hidden behind gloomy gray clouds the entire day, and the persistent early morning flurries changed to a chilling rain as the temperature slipped above the 32-degree mark. It was a good day to stay inside, and that's exactly what most members of the Ewald clan did. Many of them slept late in the morning, particularly the late-night revelers who had attended New Year's Eve celebrations in the local pubs and didn't arrive home until the sun was coming up. By noontime, however, everyone was up and around and moving freely. One by one they fixed their own breakfast and gravitated toward the library where the television was documenting the day's events. Cus and Camille were already engrossed in the spectacular Parade of the Roses from Pasadena, California, that glittery Hollywood extravaganza that precedes the prestigious Rose Bowl football game. New Year's Day was, after all, a day of parades and football games. From the first note struck by the first marching band in the first parade of the day to the final whistle blown by the referee to end the Orange Bowl in Miami late in the evening, the television set would blare its collegiate message for 14 straight hours. Strangely enough, many people across the country would sit hypnotized in front of their TV set the entire day.

Cus and Camille were joined in the library by Tom Patti, Frankie Minicelli, and Mike Tyson. The boys maneuvered for position in front of the small screen, trying to find the best vantage point without obstructing the view of the elders. Many of the boys settled in for a long day of football, but Tyson was preoccupied with other things. He seemed agitated and was unable to get interested in the festive celebrations on TV. He spent most of the afternoon wandering aimlessly from one room to another. After viewing a few minutes of the Rose Bowl parade, he ambled upstairs to his bedroom and shot pool for 15 or 20 minutes, trying to get his thoughts off his problems. He was particularly worried about his injured left hand. He detested the inactivity brought on by his injury and longed for the action of the boxing ring once again, not the monotonous non-contact sessions against smaller, faster boxers, but full-scale, no-holds-barred brawls against fighters of his own caliber. His hand felt good, and it held up well when he worked the heavy bag, but he hadn't yet put it to the ultimate test. He hadn't used his left hand in actual combat in almost six weeks, and he was apprehensive about its condition.

Cus tried to relax his wounded warrior by getting him involved in the exciting Cotton Bowl game from Dallas, Texas. Mike eased down on the floor next to his mentor as the Boston College Eagles and their miniature quarterback, Doug Flutie, took the field to face the Houston Cougars before a chilled crowd of 56,522 screaming fans. The game could not hold Mike's attention, however, and soon the youngster got up and quietly exited the room. He wandered out into the front yard, preferring to be alone with his thoughts for awhile. As he strolled the river bank in somber meditation, a familiar honking sound caught his attention. Looking up, he was fascinated by a gaggle of Canadian geese soaring high above the house in a typical V-shaped flying formation. They were obvious latecomers to the southward migration, and were heading for their winter quarters in the deep south. The sight of these innocent creatures made the sensitive Tyson yearn for his pigeons. Mike had wanted to build a pigeon coop in the front yard several years ago, but Cus nixed the idea, fearing it would distract his protégé from his primary task. Now, seeing the geese overhead, Mike was once again reminded of his "street rats" from the old tenement days. He decided to ask Cus if he could build the coop now that he was turning pro. Spring would be soon enough to broach the subject.

When he returned to the library, the Rose Bowl was just under way in Pasadena. Mike learned that Boston College had routed Houston 45–28 in the Cotton Bowl, in spite of the fact that Flutie had an off day. Now he joined the rest of the family as they watched USC battle Ohio State, but his mind was a million light years away. Dinner was catch-as-catch-can as the boys of Ewald House, still hungering for more football, protected their positions in front of the TV set to watch the third-ranked Washington Huskies edge the second-ranked Oklahoma Sooners by a 28–17 score in the Orange Bowl.

On January 3, Cus D'Amato and Mike Tyson journeyed to New York City to have Mike's huge left hand examined by several orthopedic surgeons. To everyone's relief, Mike passed the tests with flying colors. He received a clean bill of health and was given permission to resume a full training regimen. Needless to say, Mike was overjoyed at the news, as were his two trainers, and the three of them were anxious to return to Catskill to put Mike's career back on track. While they were in New York City, Cus arranged to visit his good friend, Dr. John Halpin, whose office was nearby at West 72nd Street, across from Central Park. Dr. Halpin and Cus put Mike through one of their hypnosis sessions to get him in the right mental frame of mind for his pro debut. The procedure was pretty much the same each time they sat down together. Dr. Halpin would hypnotize Mike and then Cus would take over, quickly pointing out Mike's weaknesses, and explaining to the boy how he could turn those weaknesses into strengths. Hypnosis, when used properly, can be an effective tool in helping a person overcome weaknesses and bad habits. In order for the procedure to work, however, the subject must be willing and receptive. In Mike Tyson, the doctor had an ideal subject. Mike wanted to win the heavyweight championship of the world so badly he was willing to try almost anything, even hypnosis, in order to achieve his objective.[1]

The next day at the Catskill Boxing Club, Mike Tyson was turned loose on the boxing world once again, causing the Tyson triumvirate of D'Amato, Jacobs, and Cayton to convene an emergency meeting of the management committee in New York. It was time to review the final strategy in Mike's development program, the steps that would be necessary to propel him to the world championship in the shortest possible time. The first step was to remove Mike from Catskill High School and hand him over to a personal tutor. This allowed him to schedule his training program more efficiently and conveniently. It turned out to be an easy decision. Mike had never been able to adjust completely to the small-town school environment, nor was he able to overcome his feeling of inadequacy when it came to his reading and writing skills. He was still taunted by the school bullies who took advantage of the fact that Mike was a boxer and, as such, would not fight back, even though he was twice their size.

The decision to withdraw him from school was a timely one since Mike had just been involved in another classroom disturbance. Some of the tough guys in Mike's class, the five percenters as Mr. Stickles called them, took pleasure in provoking Mike with a variety of insults, and on this day they followed him up and down the corridors verbally comparing him to "Mighty Joe Young." When Mike had taken as much abuse as he could stand, he went on the offensive, chasing one troublemaker right through the main office and into the office of the assistant principal, John Turek. Mike might have lost control of himself completely if Mr. Turek had not jumped in between the boys. As it was, Mike tripped and fell as Turek grabbed him, giving the assistant principal the distinction of being the only person in Catskill who ever knocked Tyson down. As Mike became famous, Mr. Turek not only admitted having committed the act, but also embellished the story to his own advantage. During a closed door meeting between D'Amato, Rooney, school principal Dick Stickles, and Turek, it was the unanimous opinion that Mike Tyson's interests could best be served by allowing him to leave school to pursue his pugilistic endeavors. The parting of the ways was entirely friendly, however, as Mike Tyson had a good rapport with both of the top administrators. In fact, as Mike's professional career blossomed, he returned to school regularly to visit with the teachers and to talk to the students.[2]

Mike's training was in high gear by mid-month, and Cus had his scouts beating the bushes for a new batch of sparring partners. As soon as likely candidates were found, they were herded back to Catskill en masse at a cost of $60 a day. Cus found it necessary to recruit opponents in bunches, because they seldom lasted more than two weeks with the hard-hitting Tyson. His thundering body shots quickly took their toll on his less talented opponents. January turned into February and the Tyson express moved inexorably ahead. Tyson, an intense student of the fight game, trained with complete dedication, often jogging the three miles from his home near Athens to Redman's Hall prior to his daily two-hour workout. Sparring partners came and went like a 50-cent lunch. Some of them hardly stayed long enough to earn travel money home, and none of them were able to stand up to Tyson's sledgehammer blows for long. Their names appeared like blurs in the gymnasium register—Nate Robinson, Kenny Davis, Ernie Barr, and Jimmy Young. Some of these men were very capable fighters. They were just overmatched when they stepped into the ring with the Adirondack strongman, as almost any fighter would have been. Even Jimmy Young, a former champion, was no match for the young assassin. And the aging Young cost D'Amato $600 for a week's work.

Cus did obtain the services of one world class boxer for a few days when WBC cruiserweight champion Carlos De Leon returned to Catskill. Six minutes in the ring with the classy De Leon made Mike realize what it was like to fight a real pro. De Leon took young Tyson to school so to speak, but Mike learned his lessons quickly. He marveled at De Leon's ring savvy and relished the mental exercise of trying to out-think his crafty foe. Mike made his share of amateurish mistakes, but he was never guilty of the same mistake twice. Cus D'Amato, his astute trainer, was in his usual position on the ring apron, studying his young phenom very carefully and yelling occasional instructions to him in an attempt to eliminate his bad habits. "Don't be stationary. Keep moving your head. And keep your hands up."

Another capable sparring partner followed De Leon into town. Tyrone Armstrong, the Philadelphia strongboy, returned after completing a sparring session with Pinklon Thomas. Armstrong boxed three rounds with Tyson and came away highly impressed. "The boy hits real hard, harder than Thomas. He has great balance and leverage, that's why his punches hurt so much. I haven't seen anybody in the division that can beat him." Jacobs and D'Amato continued to search for a capable opponent for Mike's professional debut, without success. They did locate a promoter, however, Tri-State Promotions, under the guidance of Lorraine Miller. Mrs. Miller immediately scheduled a press conference in Latham, New York, to introduce Mike Tyson to the Albany media representatives and announce the details of his first fight.

> We have worked hard to put on good shows in the Albany area, and we are proud to be able to promote Mike Tyson's professional debut. The fight will be held In the Albany Convention Center at 8 p.m. on the night of March 6 against an opponent to be named later. Believe it or not, it's very hard to get an opponent for Mike. Most managers have heard about Mike's success in the amateurs and they don't want any part of him. We're hopeful we can get the proper opponent, but we'll be thankful to get an opponent period.

Mike Tyson, who sat quietly during the proceedings, was matter-of-fact about his ring potential. "I have all the confidence in the world in my managers. I fight whoever they tell me. If they know I can beat the man, then I know I can beat the man too." Assistant trainer Kevin Rooney assured the press that his charge was ready for a tough struggle. "Cus D'Amato is a great manager. He wants an opponent for Mike who will come to fight. Mike needs strong opponents in order to develop. If his opponent is a bum, everyone gets cheated, and Mike gets cheated. We are looking forward to a tough match."[3]

Within a week, a suitable opponent had been signed to a contract. He was a 19-year-old Puerto Rican named Hector Mercedes, another recent entrant into the professional ranks. Mercedes, whose 0–2–1 record seemed made to order for the ambitious Tyson, had the reputation of being a tough kid. He had compiled an impressive amateur record around his hometown of Rio Piedra, but he had never fought anyone of Tyson's caliber. Cus knew the kid was a mixer, but he was bothered by Mercedes' lack of height. Although Hector weighed a solid 204 pounds, he stood only 5'7' tall, and Mike would tower over him in the ring. Cus realized that, if Mike beat Mercedes badly, the crowd would think of him as a bully picking on little guys. Cus tried to rationalize the selection of Mercedes for his own piece of mind.

> Just the fact that Art Romalla [Mercedes' manager] even lets him get into the ring with Mike shows that he isn't gonna be a pushover. I like that. It wouldn't do Mike any good to fight a bum. Newspapers make a big thing out of height and reach, but that stuff really isn't relevant. Timing is the factor. We've taught Mike from the start to get away from punches. He's quick with the fists too. Mike's elusive yet powerful. And if he delivers that exceptional punching power with either hand, he's unstoppable. In many ways, Mike reminds me of Jack Dempsey, the "tiger of the ring." He has Dempsey's ferocious attack. But he's also more of an individual with a style and punch all his own.[4]

Lorraine Miller promoted 15 Tyson fights, including his pro debut. Before the Mercedes match, Miller showed some posters to D'Amato, who growled, "Tyson's picture's too small," so Miller immediately ordered new posters and used her stack of 300 original posters to kindle firewood. In later years, she received calls from memorabilia buffs offering up to $1,000 per poster. "You live and learn," she sighed.[5]

Back in the gym again, Tyson put the finishing touches on his conditioning program. He sparred with a young fighter named Charles Thurman, an amateur who was training for the finals of the New York State Golden Gloves Tournament. Thurman caved in quickly under Tyson's constant barrage, however, calling it quits midway through the second round. Even as his career became a major focal point in his life, Mike Tyson still found time to work out with the younger members of the Catskill Boxing Club. He could often be found instructing kids like Frank Houghtaling in the proper use of the heavy bag. Houghtaling, an 11-year-old miniature bulldog, was just about ready to embark upon his own amateur adventure. He idolized Mike as did most of the other street urchins who frequented the dingy gym over the police station. Mike responded to their attention by becoming a role model for them. He wanted to give something back to the gym that spawned him and to the kids who would follow him.

Suddenly it was March 6, and the moment of truth had arrived. The final countdown began at approximately 5:30 p.m. as the light-colored station wagon pulled away from the old homestead, its headlights searching for a path through the late winter darkness. The rapid acceleration of rear wheel against gravel road sent clouds of brown dirt billowing skyward as Don Shanagher pulled out onto Route 385 with his entourage of Cus D'Amato, Mike Tyson, and Kevin Rooney. Within minutes they were on the New York Thruway headed north for Albany, for the Convention Center, and for Tyson's appointment with destiny. Mike walked through the front door of the Albany Convention Center unnoticed at about 6:30 wearing an old, beat-up brown leather jacket and carrying a cloth gym bag. He immediately headed to the locker room to get himself mentally prepared for the conflict ahead. That in itself was a major feat because the locker room in the Convention Center was also the men's lavatory. The small, cramped room had been outfitted with temporary lockers and benches to accommodate the boxers, but it was still open to the public, so the fighters constantly had to sidestep onrushing male patrons in need of the facilities.

Outside the arena, several hundred early arrivals, unaware that they were about to witness history in the making, milled about drinking beer and scarfing down hot dogs. Some of them tried to kill time by watching the inept performances in the ring. These preliminary fighters were, in general, a sad and often tragic lot. They sweated and bled and risked their health for pennies. The four-round prelim boys made about $250, out of which they had to pay their expenses, such as equipment, trainer's fees, and manager's fees. If they ended up with $50 for themselves, they were lucky. Six-round fighters pulled in $350, and eight-round boys drew the exorbitant sum of $750. Ninety-nine percent of these club fighters would wind up broke, many of them punchy. Most club fighters never even knew the names of the men who taped their hands before the fight. Fewer than one percent of them escaped from the hellholes of the small, smoke-filled arenas and went on to a successful career in the ring. Mike Tyson would be one of the lucky ones.

> The old man stood in the dressing room and watched his kid warm up, watched him wheel around the room in time with the music. *Lovergirl, Square Biz,* the pop-soul sound of Teena Marie was little more than white noise in the old man's head, which was teeming with other themes. At 6 feet and 212 pounds, the kid was an impressive physical specimen. Plus, as the veteran pugs liked to say, he carried a cure for insomnia in either hand.[6]

Cus talked to him incessantly, reminding him about the need to control his fear, remain calm, and be aggressive. "Remember what I taught you. If you do everything you learned in the gym, you will win." Mike dropped down on the hard wooden bench and began lacing up his shoes as fight time drew near. At 7:40, assistant trainer Matt Baranski came over to help Mike adjust his protective belt, and a few minutes later Cus eased down on the bench next to his edgy fighter and began wrapping his valuable hands with gauze, 18 feet of soft, white gauze. Cus then applied a few strips of tape to each hand, being careful not to let the tape get over Mike's knuckles, a practice that was frowned upon by the State Boxing Commission. When the taping process was completed, Mike clenched his hands into fists, making sure they felt comfortable and were well protected. Now the young warrior was ready to go. He rose slowly from the bench and flexed his muscles, then returned to his shadow boxing to keep warm. He was attired in white trunks and black shoes, no socks, no robe, no flashy accouterments, just the bare essentials. Tyson said it made him feel more like a gladiator to be dressed like this, remembering that the combatants in ancient Roman gladiatorial battles entered the Coliseum clothed only in loin cloths and sandals.

It was now only minutes to fight time, and the locker room reverberated with the blare of rock music as Tyson increased the intensity of his warm-up routine in an effort to get himself well loosened up before heading for the ring. He was bobbing and weaving, slipping imaginary punches, and occasionally shooting out sharp jabs with his left hand to the face of an invisible foe. Sometimes the jab was followed by more bobbing and weaving. Other times it was a prelude to a two-fisted attack. Perspiration dripped freely from the shoulders and neck of the Catskill warrior, and his bronze physique shimmered like a Greek statue in the smoky haze of the locker room/lavatory. Suddenly the door opened and a wizened head peered in, a cigarette butt protruding from between two rows of rotten teeth. "They're ready for you now." Cus cast a concerned glance at his restless fighter and gently patted him on the shoulder. "Okay, let's go, Mike." The parade left the locker room and headed for the ring, assistant trainer Matt Baranski in the lead, followed by Tyson and Cus D'Amato. Jimmy Jacobs, D'Amato's partner and co-manager, lagged behind to view the proceedings from the top of the steps, wondering what the fates had in store for his boy. Jacobs felt good about things in general. The preparation had been intense and thorough. Mike Tyson had been preparing for this night for five years, and he would be a power to be reckoned with in the heavyweight division, if Jacobs and D'Amato were any judges of people. Tyson was an impressive talent, and Jacobs was getting positive vibes about the entire venture. He was confident that the venture would be successful.

Baranski lifted the second strand of rope and Mike Tyson slipped deftly into the ring to a loud round of applause. Even though this was Mike's first pro fight, he was well known around the Albany area thanks to his exciting amateur career. His popularity was such that the Convention Center was almost filled with over 2,500 Tyson fans in attendance, all of them thirsting for blood. Hector Mercedes, attired in red trunks with a white stripe, waited in the ring. He eyed Tyson curiously, wondering why everyone was making such a fuss over a big kid with no pro fights under his belt. Mike Tyson had come a long way in the past four years, both technically and emotionally. He was no longer the excitable kid who rolled around the ring ecstatically in Colorado Springs after a winning effort. He had matured considerably, but he was, after all, still only 18 years old and just a boy, albeit a boy in a man's body. Mike could feel the butterflies squirming deep within, and his stomach muscles were knotted up with the tension of the moment. He stood in his corner anxiously waiting for the start of festivities.

As the fighters moved to the center of the ring to receive the referee's instructions, Channel 10 News in Albany, New York, was there to record the historic event. Mercedes' 5'7" stature made him seem much shorter than the solidly built Tyson. The two men shook hands and returned to their respective corners to await the bell. Tyson was edgy and impatient. At the sound of the bell, he sprang straight at Mercedes, driving the little man to the ropes. He flailed away viciously with both hands, reminiscent of his first "smoker" four years before. The unexpected activity in the ring brought oohs and aahs from the crowd. Two men who were catching a few winks in the front row suddenly bolted upright and directed their attention to the ferocity above them. Several stragglers, on their way to the concession stand, turned back to watch the action. Tyson was a good student and had mastered his lessons well. He remembered D'Amato's instructions—the floating rib on the left side and the liver on the right side. A sharp left crashed against Mercedes' liver, and two pulverizing rights found the targeted rib cage. Mercedes winced in obvious discomfort and tried to cover up. Tyson backed off momentarily and then came back with a right uppercut that straightened the Puerto Rican up like a pole. One last left hook dug deep into Mercedes' side. All the air seemed to leave his body with a hiss as he sank to one knee in the corner. The referee stopped the fight at 1:47 of round one. It was an electrifying start to Mike Tyson's career, and it brought the crowd to their feet, cheering and screaming. Mike Tyson would give them more of the same in the months to come, much more. But for now, the battle was over and the young gladiator basked in the glory of his first professional victory. When asked about his strategy for the fight, Tyson replied, "I just wanted to throw a lot of punches to confuse him." Obviously the strategy worked.

Cus was pleased with his boy's initial showing and couldn't resist gloating a little bit. "He looked good, didn't he?" The old man's eyes twinkled as he thought about it. Jim Jacobs was also impressed by what he saw in the ring. "The other fellow fought back. He threw good punches. If Mike wasn't so elusive, he would have got hit. Prior to this fight I thought Mike was a spectacular fighter. Nothing that happened tonight altered my feeling. Mike is an irresistible force." Cus nodded in agreement. "Mike was at a disadvantage in the amateurs. For example, if he knocked someone down in the amateurs, the opponent would take a nine count, then could get even in the scoring by landing a punch, though not nearly so damaging. The professional ranks are marvelous for Mike. They score for aggressiveness. I expect Mike to break Patterson's record." Tyson echoed his manager's optimism. "I fought all the best fighters in the world as an amateur. I fought the better fighters at a younger age. I have reason to be confident."[7]

Another D'Amato boxer fought on the same card. Former junior welterweight contender Kevin Rooney decisioned Garland Wright over the eight-round distance. Rooney had been a fighter on the way up until 1981, when he lost a nationally televised fight to Davey Moore. One year later, Rooney was decisively knocked out in the second round by Alexis Arguello, again on national TV. Now 29 years old, he was no longer a contender although his 20–3–1 record was still an impressive credential. If he wanted to, Rooney could probably have prolonged his pugilistic career for another half-dozen years, although he most likely would have been an "opponent," a stepping stone, rather than a contender. At Cus D'Amato's urging, Kevin Rooney chose another path to the top of the fight game. He was learning to be a boxing trainer and, with D'Amato to teach him, he had the greatest instructor in the world.

That Cus D'Amato was the ultimate trainer was no secret. His discovery of a new heavyweight sensation had been discussed in boxing circles for several years. No fighter in the country could entice 2,500 people to witness his pro debut with ringside tickets selling for $12.50 a pop. No fighter in the country could command $500 as a four-round neophyte with no pro record. Mike Tyson could. And Cus D'Amato was the reason. Even the news media was aware of the monumental story that was unfolding in the tiny hamlet of Catskill, New York. *People Weekly* magazine was the first of the popular pulps to jump on the bandwagon. They sent a reporter to D'Amato's home town to spend several days with him and his young protégé prior to the Mercedes fight, to document the resurrection of the grizzled old manager, and to introduce his new heavyweight contender to Mr. and Mrs. America. Fortunately for everyone concerned, the public's first glimpse of Mike Tyson was an awesome one. He left Hector Mercedes in a bloody heap in less than two minutes. The Ewald household celebrated Mike's victory with a lot of noise and raucous laughter into the wee hours of the morning. It was a moment to cherish and remember on the banks of the Hudson. Cus D'Amato, however, was more restrained than the rest of the family. He realized that Mike was still essentially an undeveloped raw talent. A tremendous amount of work remained if Mike Tyson was to become a world-class fighter capable of winning the championship before he was 22 years old.

The next morning at breakfast, the cagey old trainer brought his charge back to the real world. Tyson was still on cloud nine after his short and explosive night's work. His decisive victory made him feel invincible, but Cus soon made him face the reality of the situation.

> Feelin' pretty cocky, huh? Think you're tough, don't ya? Unbeatable. Well let me tell you, you're not. Oh, you did good all right, and you deserved the quick knockout, but you made a lotta mistakes too. If you had fought an experienced fighter last night, he woulda killed you. You were too excitable, too wild. You fought out of control. A good fighter would have laid back and picked you apart. You've got to stay calm so you can think out there. Champions are always calm. And that's what you've gotta learn. You did a good job in your first fight, but now we've got to go back to the gym and work on your ring discipline.

These morning-after-the-night-before discussions were to become a regular part of Mike Tyson's boxing regimen, and a part that he always dreaded. No matter how good he would do in a fight, Cus would always find some mistakes he had made. Cus wanted to drill into Mike's mind the fact that he would never be perfect, could never be perfect. He wanted Mike to realize that no one is perfect. No one should ever get cocky and think they are invincible. There is always something more that can be learned. When a person stops learning and begins to believe that he is unbeatable, that's when he becomes vulnerable. Cus wanted to perpetuate the drive and the desire in Mike Tyson. He wanted Mike to be constantly stretching for that unobtainable goal—perfection. In that way, and only in that way, could Mike maintain his equilibrium in the face of success. And only by striving for higher and higher goals could he hope to win the championship and, having won it, hope to hold it over a long period of time against younger and hungrier fighters.

After a couple of days of rest and relaxation, it was back to the gym once more, back to Cus D'Amato's school of mental alertness and pugilistic excellence. Now that Mike had one pro bout under his belt, Cus was ready to unveil his newest stratagem. He would make Mike Tyson the busiest fighter in the United States, with a scheduled match every two weeks. Cus believed that the old fighters had the right idea; you had to fight often to stay on top of your game. The more you fought, the better you got. The great fighters of yesteryear, men like "Sugar Ray" Robinson, Archie Moore, and Willie Pep, all had over 200 professional fights before they hung up the gloves for good. Cus had a dream, to make Mike Tyson the youngest heavyweight champion in history, and to accomplish that feat, he decided to spoon-feed the young lion with a non-stop diet of boxing matches in order to force his protégé to develop his almost unlimited talents faster than anyone ever had before.

Tyson acquired a new sparring partner in mid–March, Delen Parsley of New York City. Parsley was another street kid who had the heart of a lion. Tyson was a very aggressive fighter, but he found out soon enough that Parsley was also an aggressive fighter who kept coming in all the time, taking two punches and giving two in return. Or trying to. Cus emphasized defense, and he taught Mike all the cute moves. "Keep movin' all the time. Don't stand in front of him. Move to the side. You can hit him from the side but he can't hit you. It's the perfect place to be. You gotta be elusive." Cus was thrilled to have Parsley working with Mike. "He's givin' Mike exactly what he needs. He's tough. He takes a good punch and keeps comin'. I wish he had been working with us for months." Unfortunately, Parsley ran out of gas in a hurry. He had the heart, but Tyson had the ammunition. Mike was just too strong for him and, after taking a few thousand blows to the liver and kidneys, Parsley was forced to throw up the white flag and go back to the city.

Mike's second fight arrived in the blink of an eye, only 35 days after his first fight. It was once again held in the Convention Center in Albany, the second of three fights contracted for with Tri-State Promotions. The opponent was a tall black man named Trent Singleton, and if you bent down to tie your shoelace after the fight started, you might not have seen Singleton in action at all. When the bell sounded for round one, Singleton threw a feeble left in Tyson's direction, but Mike slipped it easily. That was it as far as Singleton's offense was concerned. Mike countered with a hard left that put Singleton on the seat of his pants with a surprised look on his face. A flurry of rights and lefts by the excited Catskill bomber dropped Singleton twice more in less than a whisper, automatically stopping the fight. It had lasted only 57 seconds, hardly time enough for Tyson to work up a sweat. He had a tougher workout in the locker room before coming to the ring. During the interview session after the fight, one of the reporters congratulated D'Amato. "Well Cus, you're a success." That statement caused the old trainer to deliver a little more D'Amato philosophy.

> I'm not a success yet. And neither is Mike. When these kids reach the point where they become champion, everybody thinks they're successful, they reached the top. They think I'm successful because I managed the champ. But I'm not. I don't succeed unless I make that man completely independent. How do I do that? Well, when he gets the feelin' that he doesn't need me anymore, which is terrible for fight managers, then he'll leave me. They don't need you anymore. They don't wanna pay, but you see I don't think I'm successful unless I'm able to do this. When I make him completely independent of me, then I have succeeded. Now if he succeeds before I do this, then he's successful but I'm not.[8]

Five days after Tyson's second victory, one of the great middleweight fights of all time took place in Caesars Palace in Las Vegas, Nevada, before a sellout crowd of 15,008. "Marvelous" Marvin Hagler, a future ring immortal, defended his title against Thomas "The Hit Man" Hearns, one of the hardest punchers in the game. The action was fast and furious from the outset as Hearns was determined to establish his dominance over the champion. The effort might have been successful against a lesser man, but not against a brawler of Hagler's magnitude. The two fighters stood toe to toe for three full minutes, taking turns knocking each other's head off. Hagler staggered Hearns just before the end of round one, turning "The Hit Man's" legs to jelly. The champion, in return, had received a vicious gash over his right eye, and it bled profusely for the rest of the fight. At one point in round three, it looked as if referee Richard Steele might stop the fight because of the cut and award the decision to Hearns. The fight was interrupted briefly to allow the ring doctor to examine the wound and, when he motioned the fight to continue, it spelled the beginning of the end for Hearns. Hagler attacked with a purpose, and within 45 seconds he landed a right hand that sent Hearns spinning backwards against the ropes. Hagler was on him like a big cat, and a barrage of punches sent "The Hit Man" to the floor for a full count. The battle, which will go down in history as one of the epics of the ring, lasted 8:01. Mike Tyson watched the fight on closed circuit television with considerable interest. Mike was an avid student of the sport, and he studied every match carefully, always analyzing, always learning. He learned a lot about heart during that fight, from both corners.

As Mike's professional career was launched, his personal life started to settle down and gain stability. He felt more comfortable now around Cus and Camille, and he began to consider them family rather than acquaintances. The time spent with Cus grew into a true father-son relationship instead of a trainer-fighter relationship. Camille became someone that Mike could go to with his problems and with his doubts, someone from whom he could receive the solace that he so desperately needed. Ewald House had grown into a home for Mike Tyson during the spring of 1985. It was no longer just a place to live.

The boredom and drudgery of Cus D'Amato's intense training program continued through April, and more sparring partners fell by the wayside. By the end of the year, Mike Tyson would destroy 40 sparring partners in just 52 weeks. No one could be found who could stand up to his devastating punishment for more than a week or two. Otis Bates of Denver, Colorado, was a typical Tyson opponent. Bates contracted to spar with Tyson for a week, and he arrived in Catskill in mid–April, full of determination and enthusiasm. He had sparred with the likes of Carl "The Truth" Williams and Larry Holmes, and he was looking forward to tangling with New York's bad boy. It was a mistake that he quickly paid for. Mike punished him so thoroughly in only two days that he called it quits and headed home. Cus just shrugged his shoulders in bewilderment. "Mike's opponents are not bums. He hits them quickly and they go. I can't even get him opponents for regular fights. Once a month is not enough. I'd fight him every week if I could find someone to take him on."

At one point, Tyson was forced to go five weeks without sparring due to a lack of willing volunteers. Finally, on the same day that Tyson learned the identity of his next opponent, a new sparring partner arrived on the scene. His name was Tom Sullivan, a native of Indiana and a veteran of 29 professional fights. It would be Sullivan's job to get Mike ready to mix it up with Don Halpin, a journeyman fighter from Massachusetts. Halpin, with an undistinguished record of 9–17, had the reputation of being a survivor, a gutty kid who could give an opponent a hard time and take a fight to its completion. Kevin Rooney was familiar with Halpin's record. "He's been around. He's an old war-horse. He looks to be an experienced fighter." It was obvious that Rooney was anticipating a tough struggle for his boy, one that Tyson badly needed. You don't learn much from fighting pushovers. Don Halpin had been in the ring with some proven adversaries. In 1981, he had lost an eight-round decision to Tony Tubbs, and in 1983 he was beaten by Jimmy Young. He was considered to be the type of fighter who lived by his wits and his toughness. You had to beat Halpin. He wouldn't quit on you.

As the weeks passed, Mike Tyson seemed to have taken on a new, calmer approach to the ring wars. Cus credited this change in attitude to his sparring partner, Tom Sullivan. "Sullivan fought back and didn't crumble when Mike hit him, so Mike was forced to settle down and figure out what he wanted to do. He couldn't just go in swingin' without a battle plan." Cus was so impressed with Sullivan's contribution to Tyson's preparedness that he gave the fighter a sizeable bonus, hoping to entice him back another time. May started off in grand fashion around the Catskill Boxing Club. On the tenth of the month, Cus D'Amato was honored by his peers in the boxing world. During the World Boxer Day celebration in

Madison Square Garden, Cus was presented with the Joe Louis Award for his contributions to the sport. It was only fitting that the award should be presented in the Garden, since this had been the stronghold of Cus's enemies in the infamous IBC and its mastermind, James D. Norris, Jr.

Ten days later, on May 20, heavyweight champion Larry Holmes pulled out a close decision over Carl "The Truth" Williams in Reno, Nevada, to retain his IBF crown. As it turned out, the fight was decided strictly on heart. It was a perfect demonstration of how to separate the men from the boys. After ten grueling rounds, Williams was comfortably ahead on all scorecards and was well on his way to dethroning the pride of Easton, Pennsylvania. It was obvious in the corners between rounds ten and 11 that both fighters were suffering from extreme exhaustion. Tragically, Carl Williams was not able to rise to the occasion. Even with the title in his grasp, the younger fighter could not draw on the necessary reserves to put out a maximum effort during the final five rounds. Larry Holmes, on the other hand, realizing what was required to win the fight, picked himself up by his bootstraps and outpunched his younger foe in rounds 11 through 15. On this night, Larry Holmes showed the boxing world what it takes to be a champion. His gritty performance did not go unnoticed in the Tyson camp. Mike quickly made a mental note of the achievement, particularly since it verified one of Cus's favorite doctrines: "When you're watchin' a fight, you're watchin' more a contest of will than of skill, with the skill prevailing only when the will is not tested."

The day before the Halpin fight, another local press conference was held to stimulate interest in the event. During the question and answer period, one of the Channel 10 reporters noted that Halpin hadn't fought in over 13 months, but Halpin shrugged off any inference

Tyson and Halpin with Cus D'Amato at the weigh-in for their May 5, 1985, match (courtesy Paul V. Post).

that the inactivity might affect his performance. "I haven't been the most active fighter in terms of bouts per year, but the time off has never hurt before. I've always come back strong." Tyson was more relaxed at the press conference this time, and he exuded an air of increased confidence now that he had two pro fights under his belt. "I'm sure of a victory. If it goes six rounds, I'll beat him in six rounds and look good doing it. Whatever it takes is what I try to do. I'm sure the fans will enjoy the fight. I feel real good." One of the reporters cautioned Mike about what a tough guy his new opponent was. Mike just shrugged and in typical D'Amato style mumbled, "Yeah? I'm a tough fighter too. And I move my head and he doesn't." When Mike Tyson's quotes appeared in print, he often sounded like a braggart, but he wasn't. He was quiet and polite, but he was confident—very, very confident.[9]

Tyson arrived at the Convention Center on the night of the fight still unnoticed by the general public, but that comfortable situation was destined to change quickly. Within a few months his face would become familiar to most boxing fans thanks to a massive publicity campaign masterminded by his managers. But in May of 1985 he could still walk the streets without being recognized. He had increased the number of people in his unofficial retinue since his last visit to Albany however. Not only was he accompanied into the arena by his three trainers, but he was also followed in by two admiring blondes. After his usual warm-up period in the locker room, Mike headed to the ring decked out in white trunks and white shoes. Halpin was waiting for him, anxious to get it on. The Catskill teenager was also anxious, but he fought under more control in this fight than he did in the first two. He seemed to be maturing a little bit more with each passing month.

As round one got under way, it was apparent that Mike respected Halpin's ring expe-

Tyson knocked out Don Halpin at 1:04 of round 4 (courtesy Paul V. Post).

rience and his reputation as a scrapper. He didn't rush across the ring to meet his foe as he had in his previous two fights. This time he approached his man cautiously and tried to follow Cus's pre-fight plan. Cus wanted Mike to work his man inside with an intense body attack in order to open him up so he could get a clean shot at his chin. Mike followed Cus's instructions to the letter. In round two, he kept boring in, punishing Halpin to the body. In round three he suddenly switched his attack to the head and brought the crowd to its feet with a sharp left to the side of Halpin's face followed by a sizzling right to the cheekbone. These punches signaled the beginning of the end for the Massachusetts fighter. Although Halpin survived the round, the success that Mike had in getting through his guard only served to increase his confidence level. If there was one thing that Mike didn't need, it was more confidence. He rushed out of his corner in round four, looking for the knockout. A flurry of punches put Halpin in immediate trouble, and a dynamite left hand sent him to the canvas for an eight count. As soon as the referee waved the two fighters together, Tyson was back on the attack. In center ring, the Catskill Clubber caught his man with a right cross, staggering him. A left broke through Halpin's guard once again, and a follow-up left sent the Irishman reeling backward across the ring. Mike ran after his man and landed a paralyzing right uppercut that snapped Halpin's head back violently as he collapsed into the ropes. The Boston fighter bounced off the ropes, landing face-first on the floor, where he lay motionless for five minutes. The referee finished the count of ten at precisely 1:06, but he might just as well have counted to a thousand. Halpin didn't hear a thing.

Mike Tyson was an enigma in the violent world of boxing. He was one of the most vicious punchers in the ring, yet he also had a gentle side to his nature. After every knockout, he was more concerned with the welfare of his opponent than he was with the victory. Mike couldn't relax in his corner until he saw Halpin assisted to a stool that had been brought to center ring. Mike was at his side immediately, giving his opponent a loving hug and whispering words of consolation in his ear. It is doubtful that the bewildered Halpin heard Mike's words of sympathy. He was still dazed when his handlers led him back to the locker room and laid him on the examining table. The doctor immediately set about to restore his broken features, no mean feat when you realize it took 29 stitches to close the cuts on his face and a splint to straighten out his broken nose. Forty-five minutes after being knocked senseless, the battered Irishman dragged himself off the table, packed his bag, and went home. He would live to fight another day, but he chose not to. Don Halpin retired from the ring that very night.

It was too late for an 18-year-old to go out on the town to celebrate his victory, so Mike Tyson accompanied his trainers back to Catskill and enjoyed a quiet snack with Cus and Camille. The next night was different, however. Mike and his buddies peeled rubber up the New York Thruway to Crossgates Mall, a large, enclosed promenade five miles west of Albany. Over 150 concerns filled the two square mile complex, including a fine selection of clothing stores, jewelry stores, and restaurants (both quality and fast food), plus 12 movie theatres. The first stop of the night for the Tyson band was Ben & Jerry's, where the boys gorged themselves on homemade ice cream. After a boisterous 30 or 40 minutes reliving the glory of the night before and checking out all the girls in tight jeans, Mike and his crew jumped the escalator for the third floor where their favorite actor, Eddie Murphy, was cavorting across the screen in a wacky comedy, *Beverly Hills Cop*. By the time the movie ended, the gang was ready to eat again, so they fought their way down the "up" escalator to McDonald's on the floor below. Mike happily pigged out on Big Macs, fries, and Sprites. He was in heaven knowing that he could eat anything he wanted for two whole days, but he also realized that come Tuesday morning, he would pay dearly for it. Cus would make him toe the mark then, and would make him work twice as hard to take off the extra weight that resulted from his gluttony. But that was two days away. For now, it was just eat, drink, and be merry.[10]

Tom Sullivan was back in Catskill to work with Tyson once again. It was brutal work but the hours were good and the pay was excellent. The happy Hoosier had considerable experience sparring with Jerry Cooney and Carl Williams amongst others, but he had never been in the ring with anything like the kid from Catskill. "He's a much harder puncher than any of the other heavyweights. And he's relentless. There's no stopping him." After one of the sparring sessions, Mike took Sullivan back to Ewald House and introduced him to Camille. "I want you to meet my mother." Camille laughs at the memory. "I thought that kid's eyes would pop from his head when he saw my white skin."[11] From Mike's standpoint, it was just one more sign that he had finally settled into his new life and had accepted Cus and Camille as his family. Several weeks later, the former juvenile delinquent surprised his adopted mother with her first Mother's Day card. Mike wrote on it, "For someone I love, and wish you was my mother. Happy Mother's Day and I love you. By Michael, your black son." Not only was Mike becoming part of the family now, but he was also becoming financially independent, thanks to his earnings in the ring. After watching this situation develop for several months, Cus decided that Mike had earned the right to more individual freedom and responsibility.[12]

The Catskill teenager had wanted to build a pigeon coop in the front yard of the Ewald house for several years. Now, with Cus's blessing and Camille's permission, the youngster was given the go-ahead. He quickly recruited several of his buddies and, with their help and an ample supply of plywood and chicken wire, he constructed a small wooden structure along the banks of the Hudson. As soon as he had hammered in the final nail, the boyish Tyson set out to stock the coop with a large family of his cherished "street rats." It was a happy day for him when he placed the first pigeon in its new plywood home. At long last, he had everything he wanted. He was part of a loving family. He was being given the responsibility due an adult. And he had a new family of "babies" to take care of, his first flock in over five years. It was a great feeling just to be alive. The same week, the "new" Tyson stopped at Bob Meo's barber shop and had his hair redesigned. Mike always wore his hair close-cropped but, on this occasion, he took it one step further and shaved it clean all around about two inches above the ears, giving the impression that someone had covered his head with a soup bowl and then took a razor to it.

As the days passed, Mike was forced to step up his pace in the gym. With his next fight less than a month away, June 20 to be exact, he had to get in peak condition quickly and stay there. His new schedule consisted of a five-mile, early morning run, two hours of gym work, and four or five rounds of sparring. And it was relentless, every day, seven days a week. There was no relief in sight for a young man who was aiming for the stars. Cus, Jacobs, and Cayton met in New York City in late May and decided to make a change in promoters. Tri-State Promotions had been unable to provide the kind of publicity that Tyson's management committee felt was necessary in order to properly promote their "product." Therefore, Bob Arum, one of the top promoters in the country, was brought into the picture and took over the arrangements for Tyson's upcoming fight. He immediately scheduled it for the Resorts International Hotel in Atlantic City, on the undercard of the nationally televised Jesse Ferguson-Tony Anthony bout. It was even possible that Mike could get some television exposure if the main event ended in a quick KO. Some people in the Tyson camp were not too thrilled to learn that Bob Arum would be the promoter. His reputation was not exactly untarnished around the boxing world. Arum, a 52-year-old New Yorker, had been schooled as a lawyer at Harvard University, but a subsequent business project for the Internal Revenue Service soon convinced him that an enterprising young man could make big money promoting prize fights.

Bob Arum was a workaholic and for several years spent every waking hour negotiating with a multitude of managers and fighters to promote their bouts. His big break came in 1962 when he became acquainted with Muhammad Ali—then Cassius Clay—and started to promote Ali's fights. After Ali was stripped of his title for refusing to fight in Vietnam, Arum arranged a deal with the WBA and ABC-TV to promote an elimination series to find a worthy successor to Ali. Over the years Bob Arum's power has grown, but many people in boxing's inner circle have come to despise him. He has been labeled as a liar, a cheat, and a double-crosser, yet fight managers still deal with him. That's the way it is in boxing, even today. The man with the best deal gets the match. Period.

As the days wound down, concern grew in the Tyson camp over the condition of Mike's left hand, the same hand he injured in Finland. The hand throbbed constantly, and Cus was afraid that Mike had incurred more ligament damage. After a thorough medical examination, however, the considered opinion of the doctors was that nothing could be done to restore Tyson's hand to normal. They said it was one of the hazards of boxing, a condition that he would have to live with as long as he put on the gloves. Cus began covering the last two knuckles of Mike's hand with a sponge during the sparring sessions to protect it as best he could, but on fight night the sponge would come off and Tyson would have to endure the pain in silence. Sunday, June 16, was a special day in the life of Cus D'Amato. It was Father's Day and, on that day, Mike Tyson presented him with a Father's Day card, the first time that Mike had ever done that. Cus was truly touched, and it was something that he would always remember with misty eyes. Cus never married, but on this day he became a father.

Two days later, Kevin Rooney packed the station wagon with the necessary boxing gear, and the four-man crew set out for Atlantic City, a five-hour drive. They found things in turmoil when they arrived at the seaside resort. Mike's opponent had run out on the bout and with the fight less than 48 hours away, they needed an opponent quickly. The unlucky volunteer turned out to be Ricardo Spain, small for a heavyweight at 184 pounds, but aggressive and hungry, and better still—available. Cus was once again concerned about the small size of Mike's opponent, but Spain was very strong in the upper body. His thin legs accounted for most of the lack of weight, and Cus figured that Spain would come into the ring and run in order to survive a few rounds. How wrong he was.

The Tyson-Spain fight was the first bout on the card. Spain surprised everyone by coming right at Tyson, who met him in center ring. The tiny heavyweight threw the first punch, a left hook, but Tyson moved his head ever so slightly and slipped it easily. Then the Catskill Clubber began his own offensive. A thundering overhand right found its mark on the side of Spain's head, stunning the smaller fighter. He fell forward into Tyson, then collapsed backwards to the floor. Although dazed and hurt, the gutsy little fighter dragged himself to his feet, barely beating the ten count. Tyson was right back on the attack, backing his man into a corner where he unleashed a barrage of short, powerful, punches. The kid from Catskill threw a left, blocked a right, and then countered with a thundering right hand that snapped Spain's head back. A pawing left, another hard right, and still another right crashed against

Ricky Spain's face. The referee jumped in as Spain's knees sagged, and he caught the stricken fighter before he could fall. It was Mike's quickest knockout yet, with only 38 ticks off the clock.

The Tyson team was very upbeat after the fight, as you would expect. Cus D'Amato was beginning to beat the drum for his rapidly improving fighter. "He has great potential. Outside of Larry Holmes, the heavyweight contenders are a mediocre lot. Pinklon Thomas is probably the best of the lot, but the best fighters are the ones who are up and coming—Tyson, Henry Tillman, Tyrell Biggs." Rooney was so excited about the quickness of the knockout that he could hardly contain himself. "He's ready to step out. He's beginning to do things instinctively. We're going to fight again down here." When Tyson was asked how he liked fighting in Atlantic City, he just shrugged his shoulders. "No big deal. I feel more at home fightin' out of town. I fought all over the world in the amateurs. When I fought in Albany that was the first time I ever fought in my own area." Bob Arum crashed the scene and moved around the locker room yelling, "He looked awesome, awesome!" But it was left for former middleweight champion, Jake LaMotta, to get in the last word. When he encountered Cus D'Amato, the "Bronx Bull" congratulated him and said, "Cus, it looks like you have another world champion in that boy."[13]

Mike Tyson's Atlantic City debut was a smashing success. Even though the fight was not shown on television, the ESPN cable network was determined to televise Mike's next fight. The live crowd at Resorts International took the young slugger to their hearts immediately, and the hotel was anxious to get him back soon. Everybody associated with the fight card was talking about the unknown sensation from New York. Mike Tyson was a hit. Bob Arum, taking advantage of Tyson's sudden impact on the Atlantic City scene, scheduled another bout only three weeks later. This time his opponent was a tall, white boxer named John Alderson, and the bout was televised live by ESPN from the Trump Casino Hotel. This fight marked the actual beginning of "star buildup" for the Catskill phenomenon. Between Jim Jacobs, Bob Arum, and ESPN, they set out to make Mike's next fight an "event." The fight would also mark Mike Tyson's first experience at fending off media representatives while trying to concentrate on his opponent.

An ESPN film crew arrived in Catskill, New York, on July 2 to do a special on Mike and Cus D'Amato, a razzle-dazzle piece of film-making that would be shown on the cable station just prior to the Alderson bout. The commentators and camera crew spent the better part of the morning around the Ewald residence, then journeyed to Redman's Hall to catch Mike in the midst of his training routine. Somehow training went on in as normal a manner as the situation permitted. Cus tried to entice Tom Sullivan back to serve as Mike's sparring partner again, but he had a prior commitment. This left Tyson in a not-so-unusual predicament, stuck in the gym without a sparring partner. Mike made the best of it as usual and concentrated on the other aspects of his conditioning—the bag exercises, the calisthenics, and the road work.

The big sports news in Catskill over the weekend was tennis, not boxing. It was Wimbledon time again and merry old England was busy sipping tea and eating strawberries soaked with whipped cream. On the courts, Martina Navratilova and Chris Evert Lloyd battled for the women's championship for the fifth time, and for the fifth time Martina won. The scores were 4–6, 6–3, 6–2. On the men's side things were a little different. The top seeds, Ivan Lendl, John McEnroe, and Jimmy Connors, were all gone, and the final came down to a battle between eighth-seeded Kevin Curran and an unseeded 17-year-old West German player named Boris Becker. Becker, in all his youthful exuberance, was all over the court making acrobatic saves and subsequent winning volleys. When the smoke cleared, the young German had scaled the heights. He was the first unseeded player ever to win at Wimbledon. And he was the first German player ever to win there.

Mike Tyson wasn't a big tennis fan, but he could relate to Boris Becker's accomplishment. He himself was aiming to do a similar thing in the ring. After watching Becker's performance, he was more convinced than ever that he too could scale the heights. By fight night, Mike was beginning to feel the pressure. He was fighting on the undercard but he was, in reality, the main attraction. He was getting all the publicity and was being offered all the interviews. It was a lot for an 18-year-old kid to cope with, but he handled it with unusual maturity. John Alderson, all 6'5" of him, hailed from Cabin Creek, West Virginia, and he came into the fight with the same professional record as Mike Tyson, 4–0. Alderson had turned pro after compiling a tremendous 154–12 record in the amateurs, but as he entered the ring, he looked a little soft around the middle, a dangerous condition for a Tyson opponent to be in.

The fight got off the mark slowly. Alderson looked like a guy who just wanted to last six rounds, not win the fight, and he kept back-pedaling just out of Tyson's reach. Mike pursued him but refrained from throwing wild punches. He was intent on looking for a good opening. A Tyson jab bloodied Alderson's nose near the end of the round, and a left-right combination coming out of a clinch did more damage. In round two, the opening came. At the 1:42 mark, Tyson finally caught Alderson with a stinging left, opening a small cut over the West Virginian's eye. Another left dazed the big heavyweight, and a follow-up right hand dropped him for an eight count. Back on his feet again, he was fair game for the pride of Catskill, who moved in for the kill. A one-two, left-right combination did the damage. After absorbing the two vicious blows, Alderson pitched forward and Tyson obligingly stepped aside, allowing him to fall to the canvas. He rolled over into a sitting position and stayed there until the bell sounded, ending the round. Between rounds, referee Frank Cappuccino and the ring physician examined the battered fighter, and Cappuccino gave the young man some sage advice. "John, church is out. The fight is over. Come back and fight another day." Tyson's record now stood at 5–0 with five quick KO's. At the post-fight interview, Mike admitted that the pre-fight hype had bothered him slightly. "I felt a little funny because of the star buildup. It felt a little intimidating."[14]

The Tyson star was in its ascendency now, and the management team of Jacobs, et al, was determined to keep it there. Jacobs' crew of experts sat down to map out the publicity campaign that would make Mike Tyson's name a household word from coast to coast. Publicist Mike Cohen, a short, 30-year-old organization type with close-cropped black hair, mustache and beard, was assigned to keep Mike's name in all the major newspapers and on all the large television networks. To augment that plan, video cassettes containing the complete footage of all Mike's professional fights were mailed to every sportswriter and top TV personality in the country. Electrifying knockouts were viewed in hundreds of press rooms and TV stations from Bangor to Burbank. As Wallace Mathews of *Newsday* said, "It really brought Mike Tyson to the attention of a lot of people who hadn't seen him, myself included." Bill Cayton, the advertising genius of the group, with over 30 years experience in the field, knew how to sell a product. "It's said the press can either make you or break you, but if you're Mike Tyson, its value is priceless. The press' attention is really basic to the success of a fighter in terms of the money that fighter can make. The bigger the press, the more prominent the fighter becomes, the greater purses he commands, the more interest he generates."[15]

The following Saturday, July 19, Mike made his sixth pro appearance in the ring, this time in Poughkeepsie, New York. The program in the Mid-Hudson Civic Center featured the Catskill Clubber and Larry Sims, a chubby black boxer from Cleveland. Sims, a 30-year-old club fighter with a 10–10 record, approached Tyson very cautiously and stayed out of harm's way for the first two rounds. At the beginning of round three, Mike trapped his man in the corner and delivered a series of crushing body shots. As soon as Sims dropped his hands to protect his ribs, Tyson caught him with a clean right hook and put him in Never-Never-Land for a full ten minutes. Cus was duly impressed with Mike's quick ending. "A fighter, once he hurts his man, takes him apart. He opens up with everything. The ability to finish a man is what makes Mike Tyson exciting to the crowds. But he still needs more experience. He needs to go to the body more." Cus never let Tyson get complacent. He always found an area where Mike needed more work, and he always commented on it to let Mike know that he wasn't perfect, that he still had to work hard in order to improve his skills further. Cus always had complete faith in the ability of his protégé, and the Sims fight only served to reinforce that faith.

> I'm a sculptor. I can picture the ultimate fighter and I keep chipping away until I have created that fighter. I don't know how long it will take Mike Tyson to become the champion, but if he maintains his discipline and dedication, he can become champion before he's 22. Mike believes in himself so much, his actions in the ring become intuitive. And once they're intuitive, nobody can beat him. He can take anybody out. If he hits Holmes, then Holmes will go down too.[16]

Mike Tyson's bank account was beginning to grow substantially now, but he was very frugal with his money. He did afford himself one luxury, however. When he got back to Catskill, he rushed out and bought a used car, a snappy-looking Cadillac El Dorado, white with a blue top. At 18 years old, Mike was already a seasoned professional boxer, but as one of his boxing buddies at the gym recalled, his driving expertise did not match his ring prowess. When he first took the Caddy out for a road demo, the car salesman sat frozen in the front seat as Tyson bounced over the curbstone and careened down the highway, seemingly out of control. Mike thrilled to the ride, but the salesman was traumatized. After several minutes of sheer terror, he insisted on driving the car back to the lot himself. In spite of the man's lack of confidence in Mike's driving capabilities, the teenager was noticeably impressed with the performance of the vehicle and purchased it for his very own. It was his first sizable acquisition. The fancy car made a big hit with his buddies around Catskill, but it was obvious from the outset that Mike Tyson was not the world's greatest driver. In fact, his misadventures on the road scared the hell out of his manager, who was sure that Mike would kill himself someday. Not only that, but Mike himself didn't enjoy driving that much, so it was just a matter of time before the experiment died under its own weight. Mike had also accumulated four driving violations in a relatively short period of time and was grounded by the New York State Registry of Motor Vehicles. It was one of the happiest moments in Cus's life when Mike told him that he was selling the car. Cus slept easier after the car was gone.

Being a celebrity, even a small one, meant impositions on one's time by a variety of people out to sell a cause. One cause that Mike was happy to be associated with, however, was the athletic program at the Greene County Correctional Facility. Don Shanagher brought Kevin Rooney and Kevin Breen, the director of the facility, together one day and before long Rooney had organized an active boxing program at the prison. Whenever he could, he recruited Mike Tyson to accompany him inside the walls to talk to the inmates and demonstrate some of the finer points of the sport to them. Mike was delighted to go, and he was a good influence on the inmates, having been where they were, and having survived the incarceration to begin a new and productive life. When he spoke to them, it was the real thing. "I was a bum, too. I was an inmate. I spent my time in the joint, and look at me." Don Shanagher used Mike as an example, reminding the inmates, "Mike was destined to sit in an electric chair some place, but he got his breaks here."[17]

Two newsworthy events occurred in the baseball world in early August, both on the fourth of the month. Tom Seaver, one of baseball's finest pitchers, achieved his 300th victory in his 19th major league season, beating the New York Yankees, 4–1. To make the honor even sweeter, Seaver accomplished the feat in front of his favorite fans, the people of New York. On the same day, 3,000 miles away, another 19-year veteran of the Bigs smacked out his 3,000th major league hit. Rod Carew went one-for-five in the Angels' 6–5 win over the Minnesota Twins.

Seaver and Carew were relaxing in the soft glow of recognition that followed an illustrious career in sports. Mike Tyson's life, on the other hand, in the infancy of his professional career, was becoming a blur since the initiation of the new publicity campaign. His fights seemed to come one after another in rapid-fire succession. The days and weeks between the fights were filled with business obligations as well as his rigorous training responsibilities. Newspaper reporters by the dozen sought him out, and his manager, Jim Jacobs, was most obliging. Anybody who could get Mike's name in the newspapers was welcomed in Catskill with open arms.

But when all was said and done, the fight was the thing, and the fight must go on at all costs. After sparring with Carlos DeLeon in Catskill for a couple of days, Mike was matched against another old pro in the gym. James Broad, rated number four by the IBC, brought his 16–4 professional record to Redman's Hall. Broad, who had been in with the likes of "Terrible Tim" Witherspoon and Marvis Frazier, stopped over for seven days to stretch Tyson's skills a little further. After Broad departed, the Tyson group broke camp and made the long trek down to Atlantic City, this time to take on Lorenzo Canady at Resorts International. People questioned Canady's credentials as an opponent, but as Cus explained, "We don't ask about records anymore. We just thank God we have an opponent. I know the fans would like to see him fight top contenders, but that doesn't make any sense yet. We can't make any money doin' that. First Mike needs to establish a reputation and then we'll take on the top fighters, maybe in a year. In the meantime, we can get the experience fightin' them in the gym."

The Canady fight was short and merciful. Twenty seconds after the bell sounded, a Tyson left put the tall, lean Ohio fighter down on one knee in his corner, wondering how he had ever gotten into such a mess. Fifteen seconds later, the two adversaries met in center ring. They both missed haymaker rights simultaneously, but Tyson followed up with a left that found Canady's jaw, buckling his knees. The Detroit fighter seemed to hang motionless in space for an eternity and then slumped to his knees and fell over on his side for the full count. It was another electrifying knockout for Mike Tyson, the entire proceedings lasting only 58 seconds. In his first seven professional fights, the kid from Catskill had labored in the ring for only 25 minutes and 27 seconds, slightly more than one round per fight.

The truth was that Mike was getting more competition in the gym than in his official fights. In addition to Carlos DeLeon, James Broad, Tyrone Armstrong, and Tom Sullivan, Mike had traded blows with the likes of Carl "The Truth" Williams, Tyrell Biggs, Jimmy Young and Frank Bruno. Needless to say, it was a picnic when Mike stepped into the ring against his nondescript opponents, if and when he could even find a nondescript opponent. His next scheduled fight, on August 20, was cancelled when five possible candidates pulled out rather than step into the ring with the Catskill Cruncher. Finally, Michael "Jack" Johnson, a cruiserweight who had been inactive for over two years, volunteered to face the Catskill assassin. He should have stayed inactive. As WTEN CH-10 News in Albany reported, Tyson attacked the body immediately, and a left hook to the liver area put Johnson down for the first time. As soon as he arose, Tyson was after him. Rooney was yelling from the corner, "The 8–2, Michael, the 8–2." Tyson got the message. The 8–2 maneuver, a right hook to the rib cage followed immediately by a right uppercut to the jaw, was executed with pinpoint precision, and Jack Johnson was history, another victim of the New York "Hit Man." Total elapsed time, 39 seconds. And the loser was on his way to the hospital for observation.

On Friday, September 13, Cus D'Amato travelled to Albany, New York, to address a sales meeting at a local investment company. The subject of the talk was positive thinking, something that many people think was invented by Cus during his years in the Grammercy Gym. The talk eventually got around to his young ward, Mike Tyson, a subject that Cus loved to talk about.

> Now I have presently a young fighter, a fella by the name of Tyson. You must have heard of him already in this area. Tyson will be a champion of the world, and the only thing that will stop him is if he allows anything to interfere with his objective and dedication. Now what could interfere? Well, when boys are young and, at that age very healthy, his interest in girls may be so that it becomes a distraction. Now interest in girls is a healthy thing, it isn't a problem. But it can become a problem. When you're trying to achieve an objective everything can become a problem when the problem causes your objective to be secondary rather than primary. Everybody knows it, yet when we live it, we somehow don't observe it. Now what do I do? I put 'em on a track. And as he goes along on the track, he goes off. All I do is put him back on the track. Now I could do it in such a way where I can be right on him, and have my hands on his shoulders so to speak, with complete confidence, until he reaches his objective, but in the end he'll have confidence in me, not confidence in himself, because he can feel my hand on his shoulder. He's got to be able to do it himself. And I know how I do it at least. I start him on the track and when he goes off, I just put him back on the track. Let him continue. Follow behind him, but without touching him. Let him continue doing it until he reaches his objective. If a person believes he's gonna win, he will win. And he will generate the qualities necessary to win, the competitive spirit, the determination, the will to win, just like this young Tyson. He's beaten fellas that have four, five times, even ten times more experience than he has. He'll make mistakes a great deal more, but he'll overcome them because of this quality that he was able to generate. Mike Tyson has meant everything to me. If it weren't for him, I probably wouldn't be living today. He's got my adrenaline flowin' again.

Cus's voice was raspy during the talk, causing him to clear his throat frequently. It was the first symptom of the insidious illness that would take his life less than two months later. Cus's final battle with death was another vivid reminder that boxing was, after all, only a sport and not a microcosm of life. But Cus believed he had done his job well. He believed he had prepared Mike Tyson for every eventuality, including his impending death. Cus had put Mike Tyson on the track to the championship, and he believed that Mike had developed the necessary independence to continue on his own after his adopted father was gone.[18]

Real life, and its associated tragedies, were being painfully experienced on September 19 by countless thousands of people a continent away in Mexico City, where a devastating earthquake wreaked death and destruction over 20 percent of the mountain metropolis. Earth tremors measuring 7.8 on the Richter scale struck the Mexican capital early Thursday morning, flattening entire neighborhoods and destroying large sections of the business district. Fortunately the quake struck before the workday began, minimizing the number of casualties but, even so, estimates of the dead were put at a staggering 20,000!

Back in Catskill, New York, the Mexican tragedy was just an item in the newspaper, a catastrophe that seemed almost unreal, certainly incomprehensible to a young man whose whole life was concentrated in a 324-square-foot padded enclosure surrounded by ropes. As Tyson's regimen continued, the heavyweight championship was changing hands. On September 21, Michael Spinks, an inflated light heavyweight, took the title away from an over-the-hill Larry Holmes. It was a dull, 15-round affair. Spinks wouldn't fight, and Holmes was too tired to fight. When Mike saw the debacle, he told the *Daily Mail*, "I'll fight him right now. That fight disgraced the heavyweights. Spinks is only a light heavyweight. It's unbelievable. He should give me a title shot right now." Cus was a little more cautious. "Tyson has five more fights scheduled and then we'll see." With visions of heavyweight championship belts dancing in his head, Mike Tyson took a new oath of dedication to his profession. "I want respect. That's what it's all about, to get the respect of everybody. No more girls. No more night life. I'm gonna show everybody."

Once again, however, Tyson's career was slowed by a lack of qualified adversaries. A scheduled bout in the Felt Forum was called off when the opponent took a powder after concluding that the $700 payday wasn't worth the pain and suffering he would experience in the ring. Subsequently, Tyson's next fight was moved to Atlantic City where the larger $1,500 purse would entice more opponents out of the woodwork. After several frustrating weeks, an opponent and a date were finalized. Mike's adversary was to be Donnie Long, who had replaced Tony Anthony, who had replaced Dion Simpson. And the merry-go-round continued. It was impossible to tell Tyson's many prospective opponents without a scorecard. It was easy to keep track of his sparring partners. There were none. As a result, Tyson was forced to take out his frustrations in the ring by pounding away at Kevin Rooney's big catcher's mitts, and by working over his body bag. He also jogged his usual five miles a day. Even at this early stage in his career, Mike spent much of his free time promoting his home town, getting involved in various anti-drug campaigns, and generally trying to be a model citizen. He had already learned to handle the media politely, no matter how aggressive or insensitive they might be. "I can always afford to be a gentleman. I think everybody should. I'm a good guy basically. And I wanna help other kids go straight. Kids shouldn't be involved with drugs. They should be involved with academics, school, sports."

On October 9, Donnie Long brought a respectable 15–3 record and ten KO's into the ring at the Trump Hotel and Casino. Although both fighters tipped the scales at 215 pounds, Long's 6'2" height made him look bigger than his stockier foe. Tyson, attired in white shoes and trunks, had not yet assumed the intimidating all-black dress that would become his trademark as a top-rated contender, but his approach to the fight was just as black and just as simple—seek and destroy. The fight as usual was short-lived and took longer to write about than it did to experience. Tyson stalked his foe from the outset, and before a minute had passed he took command. As he maneuvered his man back toward the ropes, Mike faked a right hand, then leaped in with a thundering left hook to the jaw that bounced Long off the bottom strand of ropes and onto the seat of his pants. The courageous kid from Youngstown, Ohio, bounced up in a flash, but he was unable to stop the Tyson onslaught. The Catskill assassin came right at him as soon as referee Cappuccino satisfied himself that Long was able to continue. Tyson moved in quickly, his face a study in concentration. In center ring, he unleashed a right-left combo that put Long in full retreat. A roundhouse left staggered the taller fighter, and another bounced him off the ropes. Rights and lefts rained all over Long's head, two uppercuts snapped his head upright, and a crushing left hook put him down on one knee.

The battered Long still insisted on continuing. It was a bad decision. Tyson, beginning to show his youth and immaturity now, met Long in center ring and prepared for the final assault. The excited 19-year-old, trying unsuccessfully to control his emotions, threw a wild left hand that sailed two feet over Long's head. The two men wrestled momentarily, then a rapid-fire left-left combination by Tyson found Long's unprotected right cheekbone. The Ohio boxer wobbled for a split second, then his body went limp and he fell backwards to the canvas. Still determined, he tried to sit up, but his glassy-eyed stare was proof that he could no longer function, and he collapsed on his right side, a beaten fighter. The referee rushed over immediately, waved off a count, bent down and removed Long's mouth guard. Mike Tyson was still beaming at the post-fight press conference. "Everything was timed. I was very calm and relaxed. I put in so much trainin' and effort. As you can see, I'm a master at evadin' punches at me." Rooney was equally happy. "Michael passed his test with flyin' colors."[19]

The beginning of the end finally arrived for Mike Tyson's manager, trainer, adopted father, and confidante in early October. Cus D'Amato was admitted into Mt. Sinai Hospital suffering from a painful upper respiratory problem. He never left the hospital again as his condition gradually deteriorated, and his 77-year-old body was unable to fight off the ravages of the disease. Tyson spent as much time as possible at Cus's bedside while at the same time preparing for his next test, another Atlantic City bout, this one with Robert Colay. Like the nine men before him, Colay was greatly overmatched.

Tyson was adorned in blue as he entered the ring on the night of October 25. His adversary, a hometown kid who grew up within a stone's throw of the famous boardwalk, appeared nondescript in white shoes and blue and white trunks. When the fight started, the two combatants advanced to the center of the ring. Colay threw the first punch, a left hook that Tyson adroitly bobbed under. A Tyson return left grazed Colay's cheekbone. Tyson moved forward again, bobbing and weaving, working his way inside, while Colay tried to keep him at bay with a series of weak left jabs. Another harmless jab by Colay was countered by a stiff Tyson left. Suddenly the determined New Yorker unloaded his Sunday punch, an electrifying left hook thrown with perfect leverage and with all the animal ferocity that he could muster. It exploded against Colay's chin like a .357 Magnum, driving the New Jersey fighter backward to the canvas. The referee tolled the fatal ten count as the stunned Colay struggled vainly to regain his feet. It was a 37-second fight.

The Tyson express rolled on, without pause or reflection. Fight number 11 was confirmed for the Latham Coliseum for the night of November 1. The opponent was Sterling Benjamin, a chubby club fighter from Trinidad who had a misleading 11–4 win-loss record. Benjamin was chosen, as were all Tyson's opponents, because D'Amato and Jacobs felt that he could provide their protégé with a further learning experience, but had virtually no chance to win the fight. Sterling Benjamin's main claim to fame was that he had once gone the distance with the Olympic gold medal winner, Willie De Witt of Canada, and had survived into the seventh round with another gold medalist, Tyrell Biggs. Promoter Lorraine Miller of Tri-City Promotions lamented the lack of adequate facilities in the Albany area to showcase the increasingly popular local heavyweight. Mike Tyson was rapidly outgrowing the cramped upstate New York boxing arenas. The Latham Coliseum seated only 3,000 people, and it was sold out within days of the Benjamin fight announcement, even with ticket prices ranging up to $20 for a ringside view of the spectacle.

Lorraine Miller was looking ahead to future Tyson matches. Possible sites that might still be large enough to house the growing number of Tyson fans included the 8,000-seat Renssalaer Polytechnic Institute (RPI) Fieldhouse, the Glens Falls Civic Center, and the Syracuse Carrier Dome. Once Mike outgrew those sites, his fights would have to be moved to the "big time" locations like Madison Square Garden, Las Vegas, and Atlantic City. In addition to larger arenas, larger purses also became a reality for Mike Tyson fights. The asking price for Tyson opponents rose dramatically and now stood at $3,000 for an eight-round bout. The main event boys were asking $10,000 and up. It was strange to talk about eight- and ten-round fights when discussing the Catskill Clubber, however, since most of his fights were over before the first round was history.

The Benjamin match was no different. Tyson chased his man from the start. The Trinidad heavyweight tried to protect himself from Tyson's power by keeping his chin tucked tightly behind his gloves and holding his elbows close to the body. But it was to no avail. Two left jabs and a right to the head started Benjamin's downfall. A solid left hook toppled the big heavyweight at the 30-second mark. Benjamin managed to drag himself to his feet and immediately went into the famous Ali rope-a-dope in an effort to discourage his energetic assailant. But Tyson was unmoved. He continued to pummel his man with a torrent of body punches, leaving the battered Benjamin gasping for air. A crushing left to the liver, a similar right hand to the rib cage, then a crunching right uppercut, three lightning-fast rights in succession, and one last left hook that dug deep into the fat in Benjamin's side, and the chubby one collapsed to the canvas, a knockout victim at 54 seconds of round one.

The Latham Coliseum was in an uproar as 3,000 fans jumped to their feet whistling and screaming in celebration of another Tyson massacre. Cries of "We want Spinks, we want Spinks" reverberated through the tiny arena. A legend was being born. Sterling Benjamin shook his head in disbelief after his battle with the Catskill teenager. "Tyson hits like a sledgehammer, man. That's the hardest I've ever been hit."[20] Tyson and Rooney were both pleased with Mike's performance, particularly Rooney. "He's a corner man's dream. I don't have to do any work. The work is done in the dressing room. I think Mike is tryin' extra hard the last coupla fights in order to please Cus." The violent side of the sport was reflected in Tyson's final comments. "It was just a left hand to the right side of the body. I heard the crunching sound like click, click, click. I thought it was his ribs breakin'." The fight marked the beginning of Mike Tyson as a bona fide celebrity. Everyone in the sold-out arena was straining to pat him on the back, to wish him well with "way to go champ," and to get his autograph for posterity. A trailer belonging to a national television network was parked next to the Coliseum during the fight, and the TV crew recorded every second of the exciting event. After the final curtain, Mike was led outside the arena, still saturated with the sweat of his brief encounter. Inside the trailer he was brought to a small interview room where he patiently answered every question thrown at him by an inquisitive interviewer.[21]

In spite of his thrilling victory, Mike's first thoughts were of his mentor and friend, Cus D'Amato. Early the next morning, Mike traveled to Mt. Sinai Hospital in New York to update his teacher on his most recent fight. Cus was growing increasingly weak now, and it was becoming obvious that this might be the final round for the cagey old boxing manager. Cus, at 77, had many famous battles under his belt, including the one with the IBC, and he had always come out a winner. But now it looked like he might finally lose one. Mike tried

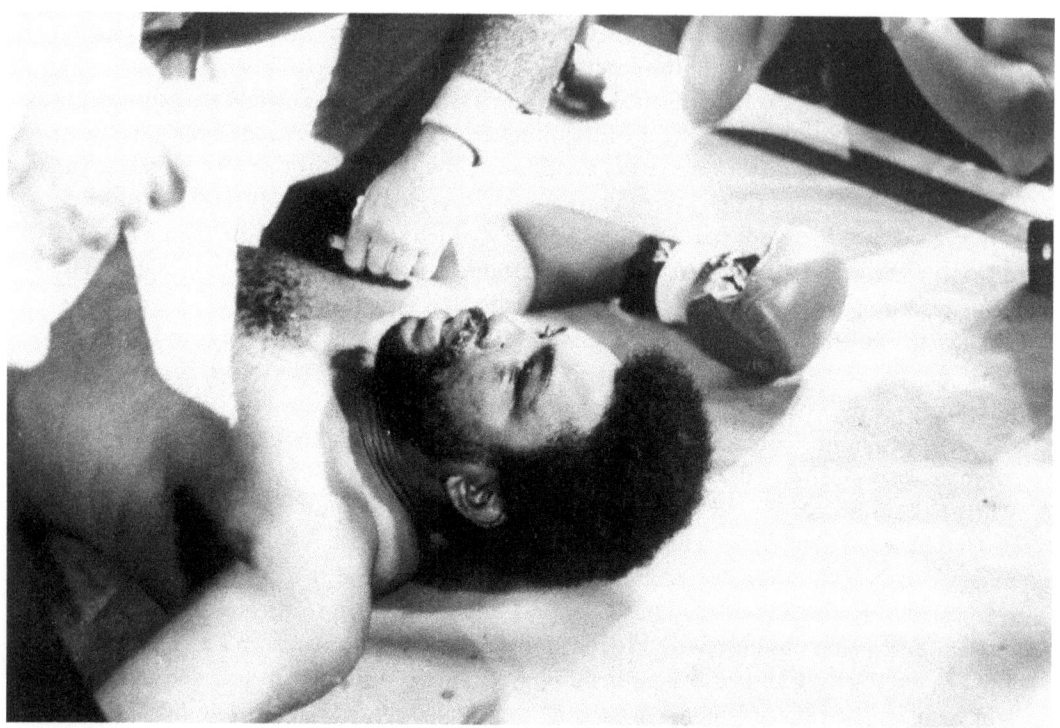

Sterling Benjamin was another first-round knockout victim (courtesy Paul V. Post).

to comfort his adopted father while Cus, on the other hand, constantly talked to his young protégé, to prepare him for the inevitable. Cus had brought Mike Tyson a long way along the road of life. He had taken a young hoodlum from Brooklyn and had transformed him into a model young man. Along the way he probably also created a heavyweight boxing champion but, strangely enough, that was less important to Cus than developing a good human being. "If somethin' should happen to me, Mike, if the time comes when I'm not here, you'll be all right. I've taught you to be independent, and now you're ready to be on your own. Just remember all the things we talked about and, someday, you'll be the heavyweight champion of the world. As long as you don't allow anything to distract you, you will be a success."

Cus's parting remarks to his young charge were wishful thinking on his part. It is possible that, at this juncture in his life, Mike Tyson was indeed working hard to be the model citizen that Cus wanted him to be, but the base on which his character was molded was like quicksand. His public comments before and after fights and during press conferences in 1985, his anti-drug efforts, and his public persona all depicted him as a polite young man and a good role model for the younger generation. If that were true, then it unfortunately all fell apart when he came under the influence of the slick con man, Don King, whose permissive attitude and lack of direction created the post-D'Amato Mike Tyson whose antics in and out of the ring demonized him and cost him his fortune and his reputation after a decade of hedonism and violence.

Mike usually left Cus's bedside in tears, trying to cope with the possibility that the old man would soon be gone. Kevin Rooney, another successful D'Amato project, was also trying to cope. "Michael and myself included are holding up well. There was one day I think it was botherin' him. Cus believed in mind over matter. I think he's been fightin' this for a long time. Now he's critical. It's a rare case of pneumonia affecting, not only his lungs, but the tubes leadin' to the lungs." As the days passed, Cus gradually slipped into a coma, leaving his fighter desolate and depressed. November 4, 1985, was the saddest day in the life of Mike Tyson. His "strong backbone," Cus D'Amato, passed away at precisely 4:30 p.m. from the ravaging effects of interstitial pulmonary fibrosis. Mike and Camille were alone in their grief, and they tried to find solace in each other's arms. The tears flowed uncontrollably in the Ewald house during the week-long vigil for the departed head of the family, but relief was a long time coming. The old woman and the young boxer particularly would feel the emptiness of the old Victorian mansion for many long months.[22]

Cus's family, friends, and associates, along with dozens of scruffy street kids, converged on Catskill, New York, to pay their last respects to the venerable trainer. Following a service of Christian burial at St. Patrick's Roman Catholic Church, Cus's remains were interred in St. Patrick's Cemetery, escorted to the graveside by eight somber bearers, including Tyson, Jay Bright, Floyd Patterson, Jose Torres, Jim Jacobs, Kevin Rooney, Tom Patti, and Cus's brother Jerry. Former light heavyweight champion Jose Torres gave the eulogy for his friend and mentor. "While some people were obsessed with money, power, or fame, Cus's obsessions were decency, integrity, and compassion. He treated his boxers like his own children, and I was one of them. Cus left us with a valuable legacy, not the obvious and superficial world championships, but rather he taught us to be better people. He taught us to become teachers. He was a fighter to the end, and he retired a champion."[23]

Once Cus was laid to rest, Tyson's quest for the championship resumed, just as the old man would have wished. A major challenge loomed immediately on the horizon. During the second week of November, the Tyson entourage traveled south to Houston, Texas, where his next stumbling block, Eddie Richardson, lay in wait like an old-time desperado. Richardson was attempting to re-establish his once promising career. He, like Tyson, had started out impressively in the pro ranks, winning his first 12 bouts, but in 1985 the bottom fell out. He suffered two consecutive defeats, including a nationally televised knockout at the hands of flashy newcomer Tyrell Biggs. Now it was the moment of truth for the 6'6" Texan. This fight would determine whether he could pull himself together and become a logical heavyweight contender again or would become just another "opponent" for young fighters on the way up. It was also a tough situation for the teenage Tyson to be thrown into. He was facing a determined opponent who was intent on regaining his lost promise, and he himself was in no condition emotionally to participate in an event of this magnitude, having buried his mentor and friend only six days previous.

Mike Tyson sat alone in his hotel room on the day of the fight. He had brought a photo of Cus to Houston with him, and he sat fondling it, tears running down his cheeks, as he tried to concentrate on the task at hand and to remember all the things that Cus had taught him, all the things he would have to do in order to win. He clutched the photo tightly, hoping it would somehow give him strength. When evening came, he carried Cus's picture to the dressing room with him, again looking for some magical transfer of power from Cus's image. He sat hunched over on the bench for what seemed an eternity, his head in his hands, and he squeezed the photo one last time as he contemplated the challenge ahead.

Whatever the reason, the long meditation seemed to work. Both fighters appeared nervous as they entered the ring, but Mike Tyson, with Cus behind him, was calm and determined by fight time. Kid Dynamite, as Cus had called him, wanted to win this fight for his mentor, and he was driven by an unstoppable force. Eddie Richardson never had a chance. He would have had to bring the Texas judges into the ring to hold Tyson while he hit him, in order to win the fight.

Wearing black trunks and shoes for the first time, perhaps in mourning for Cus, Mike Tyson looked like death and destruction as he stood in his corner waiting for the bell. The fierce look on his face, a look that would become a Tyson trademark, sent shivers up the backs of ringside patrons. Perhaps Richardson too was intimidated. In any event, only nine seconds into the fight, a Tyson right hand sent the tall Texan to the canvas. Tyson was bent on mayhem. He continued to stalk his man when the fight resumed, eventually backing the Texan into a corner. Tyson unleashed a right that grazed Richardson's temple. Then he went into a crouch and came right up with a torrid left hook that caught Richardson flush on the chin, felling him like a tree. John Tate never fell better. Referee Barry Yeats hovered over the prone Richardson and tolled the fatal count, "8–9–10." Mike Tyson rushed over to the fallen fighter as the count reached ten and helped his battered adversary to his feet. The timekeeper's clock read 1:17. It was a great win for the Catskill teenager, his first step on the road to independence and self-sufficiency. Cus D'Amato was gone but his legacy lived on. Eddie Richardson attested to the fact that Mike Tyson had lost none of his power during his long ordeal. When asked if he had ever been hit that hard before, Richardson replied, "Yeah. About a year ago, I was hit by a truck."[24]

Manager Jim Jacobs continued to be amazed by the prowess of his juvenile giant slayer. Dressed like a country gentleman in a tweed jacket and English cap, Jacobs confided to the press, "I've never been exposed to a fighter like Tyson in my life. He can beat seven of the top ten heavyweights right now." Mike Tyson felt satisfied with his performance, but he still felt alone in the world. Surrounded by dozens of well-wishers, the youngster from upstate New York yearned for a confidante, a father figure that he could cling to in time of need or success.

> People don't think I'm emotional because of the way I am in the ring, but I'm emotional when it comes to family. Now I'm alone. There's no Cus to tell me how I did. There's no mother to show my clippings to. No matter how I did, Cus would always find something wrong, something I needed to work on. He never let me get cocky. With Cus gone, I have to take my job more serious now out of respect for him. When I was 17 or 18 I was very cocky. I thought I was so good I didn't have to train, but Cus tried to keep me on track. I used to go into fights five or ten pounds overweight and still win. I had a bad attitude then, but Cus straightened me out. Now I have more discipline. I know that when two guys get into the ring together, anything can happen.[25]

Mike Tyson was beginning to grow up. He was maturing rapidly inside the ring and out. Soon he would be ready to tackle the rated fighters in the division. In just three months he would meet ESPN champion Jesse Ferguson. Then his star would soar heavenward in a hell-bent-for-election rush to glory. The Catskill man-child hardly had time to take a deep breath before his next fight was on him. Nine days after the Richardson bout, only 18 days after Cus's death, on November 22, Tyson climbed through the ropes at the Latham Coliseum to trade punches with a tall Jamaican fighter, Conroy Nelson, the number two Canadian heavyweight behind Willie DeWitt. Nelson expressed confidence that he could derail the Tyson express. "A shorter man always has a lot of problems getting in on a taller man. A tall man who can box and who can use his reach to good advantage will give the smaller man trouble." Tyson, as usual, sounded almost blasé about the upcoming battle. "I'm gonna go out there and put the pressure right on and see how he reacts from the first round on. If he's still around after four rounds, maybe we'll change our strategy, but probably not. Most likely, the pressure's gonna be on for the full eight rounds. I never anticipate a knockout. I always expect the fight to go the distance. Knockouts just seem to come."[26]

The tenor of the fight was established early in round one. Mike Tyson was on the attack, stalking his man from the outset. Conroy Nelson, on the other hand, wanted to feel Tyson out, to see how hard the youngster could punch. The big Jamaican didn't want to get involved in a slugging match early in the fight. He maintained good lateral movement throughout the round, staying just out of Tyson's reach. His hands were held high against his cheekbones and his elbows were tucked against his body, protecting his rib cage. He offered little in the way of an offense in round one, content to just get through the round. As round two began, Tyson was out of his corner like a big cat. He feinted with a left and then shot a straight right that broke through Nelson's guard, catching the taller man on the chin. Hurt now, Nelson forgot his fight plan and went on the offensive. He threw a left that missed its mark, and in the process he left himself wide open. Tyson immediately capitalized on the mistake, delivering the coup de grace, an explosive left hook to the point of the chin that sent Nelson sprawling backwards to the canvas for the full count. The fight had gone only 30 seconds into round two. This was Mike Tyson's first fight in the Albany area without Cus D'Amato, and he missed the old manager deeply, particularly at this time and in this town. After a quick shower, Mike left the Coliseum with some of his buddies and headed for the local pizza joint for some refreshment and relaxation. Mike stayed out on the town all night, making the rounds of his favorite Albany haunts, seemingly searching for something that wasn't there.

The youngster arrived back in Catskill as the sun was coming up, and he went directly to Camille's room for comfort. He sat on the edge of her bed and the tears were rolling down his face. "I did good in the fight, Camille, but I was lonely. Cus wasn't there. Everybody tells me I do good, but nobody tells me if I do bad. It wouldn't make any difference how good I did, Cus would always find somethin' I did wrong. I'm tryna get Cus's death outta my mind, but it's difficult. I used to talk to him before every fight. Now when I start to get nervous or scared, I have to deal with it myself."[27]

Mike returned to the gym two days after the Nelson fight to work on some of his weaknesses. He had only two weeks before he was scheduled to fight Sammy Scaff in New York's Felt Forum, so he was force-fed Kevin Rooney's condensed course in boxing strategy. To help Mike master his new lessons, another experienced heavyweight was brought to Catskill for five days of sparring. David "Big Foot" Johnson, out of Baltimore, had been in with some of the top names in the division—Witherspoon, Snipes, Tubbs, and Cooney. Mike and his team practically lived in the Catskill gym for one solid week, then packed their bags and set out for New York City to finish their training in Gleason's Gym, in the shadow of Madison Square Garden.

Located on a dirty, cluttered street just east of 30th Street and 8th Avenue, the two-story building sat unobtrusively next to a drab industrial structure. A plain white sign over the door beckoned to would-be boxing champions to come in and take the first step on their yellow brick road to fame and fortune. Gleason's was one of the few gyms left in New York, along with The Ringside and the Times Square Boxing Club, and for only $25 a month a guy could get a locker and use all the facilities. Gleason's was not one of those new, freshly painted gyms like Joe Frazier's in Philadelphia or the Boxing of the Americas Gym in Miami

Beach. Gleason's was a throwback to the old days when dingy, dimly lit athletic clubs were the focal points of urban America. It was a typical, smoke-filled school for pugs where the sweat and pungent odor of liniment permeated the atmosphere. Two rings dominated the room, and a quick look around at the 15 or so fighters who were busy working on their trade identified them as primarily Hispanics and African Americans, the usual street kids who were attempting to punch their way out of the big city ghetto. A wide assortment of punching bags occupied the perimeter of the room and, in the back, behind all the boxing paraphernalia, stood a lone shower, a hundred shabby lockers, and a single toilet stall.

The gym had a seedy, patriotic aura to it. Everything seemed to be painted or manufactured in red, white, or blue. The concrete floor, which had been given a glorious coat of red paint in the distant past, was now well worn by the shuffling and skipping feet of untold numbers of boxing hopefuls. The two 16-foot rings were gaily decorated with powder blue mats, surrounded by ropes of red, white, and blue. We've all seen Gleason's Gym, or others just like it, in dozens of Hollywood movies, from *The Champion* to *Rocky*. It has atmosphere. It also has slum kids looking for a way out, punch-drunk pugs mopping the floors and emptying the spit buckets, and the ever-present mobsters smoking cheap cigars and looking for talented but ignorant fighters to exploit. Ira Becker, the owner of Gleason's, ran a clean operation, but boxing is boxing, and the wolves are always on the prowl. Becker had even provided Gleason's with a status symbol. There was a balcony level overlooking the gym that served as a private dressing area for VIPs of the boxing world. It wasn't fancy by Gloria Vanderbilt standards, but it was a place to which all the apprentices aspired. It contained a maze of thin metal lockers, a shower stall, and a toilet. The shower, like the rest of the gym, was showing signs of age. The ceiling was falling down, the white tile walls were chipped and broken, and the sheet metal floor was coming up around the edges. It wasn't much to look at, but every kid in the joint would have given his eye teeth to be able to dress there.

Mike Tyson prepared for his match with Sammy Scaff under the dim fluorescent lights of Gleason's. James Broad was there to make sure that Mike stuck to his guns and concentrated on the basics. Kevin Rooney was draped over the top strand of ropes à la Cus D'Amato, yelling instructions to his fighter. "Work on the jab. Cover up. Protect yourself. Faster. Use combinations. Don't throw just one punch at a time. That's good. Keep punchin', Now practice the jab, straight and sharp." The sweat poured off Tyson's body like a September downpour, but his breathing was imperceptible, a sure sign that Mike was in tip-top shape. After completing five fast rounds of sparring, Tyson moved on to the heavy bag to improve his stamina and his punching leverage. Mike worked hard to control the big bag, much like he would work to control an opponent in the ring. He punched. He punched hard and often, circling, bobbing and weaving, using his weight and his balance to maneuver the bag into an advantageous position, then feinting and lashing out with a barrage of hard combinations to exact the maximum punishment from a foe. Mike Tyson was in good form, and he pursued his trade with enthusiasm. Come Friday night, December 6, 1985, he would be ready for war, and Sammy Scaff had better be at his rough, tough best. For the Tyson camp, Scaff was just one more stepping stone to boxing immortality.

The scene of the fight was the Felt Forum, the smaller sister arena to Madison Square Garden, located in the heart of metropolitan New York. Prestigious galas were staged in the Garden, while the Forum was used for the run-of-the-mill boxing cards. The Forum, seating 4,500 people, was the site of most New York City bouts now, primarily the popular but poorly attended club fights. The Garden had fallen into disfavor with the boxing entrepreneurs who usually opted for Las Vegas to stage the championship bouts. Over the last ten years, Vegas and Atlantic City had replaced New York as America's boxing mecca. But on this night, the Felt Forum was Mike Tyson's stage, and his already burgeoning reputation filled the arena to capacity. Sammy Scaff was the first one in the ring. Dressed in black trunks and blue shoes, the balding, 6'4", 250-pound Kentuckian looked old, fat, and out of shape. His hairy body, blubbery build, and mustache gave him the appearance of a lethargic walrus. When Tyson entered the ring, he was all business as usual, and the embodiment of a lean, well-muscled, and well-conditioned gladiator. He eyed his large, fleshy opponent with a look of disdain.

Scaff, just coming off a brutal beating at the hands of Tim Witherspoon on national television, looked awkward and inept as he tried to keep the determined Tyson at bay. Tyson advanced on the brawny Kentuckian quickly, driving him into a corner. A straight right hand smashed against Scaff's nose, spewing blood over his milky-white body. Fighting for survival now, the chubby heavyweight threw a wild left in Tyson's direction. The kid from Catskill weaved effortlessly to the left and the punch passed harmlessly over his shoulder. A return right by Tyson caught the top of Scaff's head, and a follow-up left uppercut snapped the big man's head back. Scaff backed off and threw out a stiff left that missed the mark. Tyson missed a left. Both fighters missed with uppercuts. Scaff missed yet another left hook. Tyson ducked under it and came back with two left hooks of his own that landed with full force against Scaff's jaw. Scaff's arms immediately dropped to his sides, his head slumped down on his chest, and he pitched forward on his face in a neutral corner. Doggedly, he pulled himself upright at the count of nine, but the vacant look in his eyes told everyone that the match was over. The referee wrapped his arms around the beaten fighter and called a halt at 1:19 of the first round. A concerned Mike Tyson rushed to Scaff's side to thank him for a valiant effort. As Sammy Scaff recovered on the table in the dressing room, he told the press, "I've gone four rounds with Tim Witherspoon and I've been in the ring with Greg Page, but I've never been hit that hard in my life."[28] Tyson, for his part, was matter-of-fact about it. "I was tryna connect with a good shot to the body, but he was a bit awkward, and after I hit him in the nose, he was wary of my punchin' power. It was difficult to get to him because of his height." When asked what he liked most in life, Tyson replied truthfully, "Bein' alone." Being alone was something that Mike Tyson would find harder and harder to do as his celebrity increased. He was quickly changing from a private person to a public figure, a personality whose life would never again be his own.

Within a period of one week in December, Mike Tyson was featured in several articles in such acclaimed journals as *Ring Magazine* and the *New York Times*. His boyish face adorned the cover of the prestigious *Sports Illustrated*, and even the popular television show, *Today*, escorted the young fighter to their studios where he was interviewed by Bryant Gumbel.

> He's a 19-year-old heavyweight who's had 14 fights, won all 14 of them by knockout, ten of those in the first round. In a world of hard punchers. Tyson's punch is devastating. It's been likened to a blackjack and a sledgehammer by opponents who have found it impossible either to avoid or withstand. Though he has been a pro fighter for less than a year, he has the experts raving, comparing him to all-time greats and saying he'd knock out men with bigger reputations but smaller hearts, like Gerry Cooney, in just one round.

The interview centered around Mike Tyson's drive for the heavyweight championship of the world and his life without his mentor and confidant, Cus D'Amato. The American public was exposed to Tyson, the person, for the first time. He came across on television as a typical 19-year-old kid, shy and unassuming. Life was beginning to move at a dizzying pace for the teenage slugger from upstate New York. His schedule was completely filled every day. If he wasn't fighting or training, he was suffering through interviews or photo sessions, or appearing on local or network TV shows.[29]

On December 27, Mike Tyson climbed through the ropes in the Latham Coliseum to take on foe number 15, Mark Young, from Charlotte, North Carolina. Young, unlike Scaff, was a competent young boxer in tip-top physical condition, a fighter capable of giving Tyson a run for his money. But as usual, the Catskill Clubber was ready. What was expected to be a long, tough fight turned out to be a short sojourn in the ring. Tyson came out of his corner with a look of intensity in his eyes. The two fighters exchanged punches in the center of the ring until a Tyson right cross jarred the Carolina fighter and sent him flying backwards across the ring. He bounced off the ropes onto his face like a rag doll and lay motionless for several minutes. The fight had lasted exactly 50 seconds. The look of intensity was still on Mike Tyson's face as his gloves were removed and the gauze was cut away from his hands. According to Tyson, the fight had no special meaning. "Boxin' is just a business to me. It's a job. I don't enjoy it. It's just a job." If it was just a job, it was a helluva job, and Mike Tyson was doing one helluva job at it. His record showed a total of 15 fights in 1985, 15 victories, all KO's, 11 in the first round. In his 15 pro fights, Mike had labored in the ring for a total of only 37 minutes and 21 seconds, an average of 2:29, or less than one round, per fight.

Anyway you look at it, 1985 was a resounding success for Mike Tyson. His professional debut was electrifying, and his relentless advance up through the professional ranks was unmatched in boxing history. The promoting of Mike Tyson was also unparalleled in the annals of the sport. Maneuvered adroitly by his co-managers and marketing geniuses Cus D'Amato, Jim Jacobs, and Bill Cayton, Mike Tyson's boyish face appeared to be everywhere. *CBS Evening News* did a feature on him. So did *NBC Nightly News*. And *Good Morning America* sent a limousine to Catskill at dawn one day to escort the young slugger back to Manhattan for a 7:30 interview with host David Hartman. Mike obliged everyone, but he was already beginning to yearn for his rapidly disappearing privacy. "I don't like the intrusion. I like bein' alone. Talking to the press is not important to me at all. I'm still 19. I'd like to hang out with my friends and have a kid's life, be a little wild now and then. I can't even talk to a girl without everyone knowin'."[30]

Mike was beginning to pay the price for fame. But if he thought 1985 was hectic, he would have been amazed and perhaps terrified at what lay in store for him in 1986. His career would continue at breakneck speed onward and upward toward the summit. The year 1986 was destined to be "The Year of the Kid."

8

The Road to the Championship—1986

The year 1986 was to be Mike Tyson's road to the title, the year when he would challenge the top pretenders to the throne and dismantle them, one by one. That was the plan. But before Mike would be turned loose on the top-ranked fighters, his managers had one other goal for him to reach first: Rocky Marciano's knockout record. Marciano had KO'd his first 16 opponents in the professional ranks, and Tyson's record now stood at 15. Jim Jacobs wanted to break that record before turning Mike loose to make a run for the gold. Opponent number 16, the man who would allow Mike Tyson to tie Marciano's record, was Dave Jaco, a tall, frail-looking white boxer fighting out of Bay City, Michigan. Jaco, at 6'5" tall, carried a deceptive 215 pounds on his lanky frame. Although he brought a respectable 19–5 record into the fight, the Michigan fighter was considered no more than another stepping stone for the new heavyweight sensation. The Empire State Plaza in Albany, New York, was jammed to the rafters on the night of January 11. A standing room only crowd of 3,000 screaming Tyson fans were on hand to witness his attempt at the KO record. Ticket prices were scaled from $15 for general admission to $40 for ringside, an unheard-of price for a relatively obscure boxing card, but the Tyson mystique in upstate New York gave the match an almost championship atmosphere.

Mike entered the arena carrying his usual small canvas gym bag long before the crowd arrived, and was followed to the dressing room by three pigtailed blonde admirers. Dave Jaco, another of Tyson's journeymen opponents, was not concentrating on a victory on this night. His objective was only to go the route with the new heavyweight sensation. Even that would be difficult according to Jaco: "It will take sheer will to keep me up for ten rounds." The main event was 45 minutes late starting, and the impatient crowd began their usual rhythmic hand clapping and foot stomping. They were understandably anxious to see the dynamic heavyweight in action and to participate in a small segment of ring history. When Jaco finally made an appearance and headed down the aisle to the ring, he was greeted with a generous round of applause from the congregation. Moments later, however, the building shook with tumultuous cheering as the crowd caught sight of the burly Tyson leaving the dressing room. The kid from Catskill forced his way down the crowded steps accompanied only by his trainer, Kevin Rooney, and his cut man, Matt Baranski. Every person in the arena was on his feet, screaming and whistling, some standing on their chairs to get a better view. The noise was deafening. As Tyson climbed through the ropes, his face was solemn. His eyes were fixed in a dark stare as he prepared himself for his next hurdle. He was unclothed as usual, save for his white boxing shoes and white trunks. He wore no socks. He wore no robe. He was once again the gladiator entering the arena to do battle to the death.

Tyson knocked down Dave Jaco three times in round 1 for a TKO win at 2:16 (courtesy Paul V. Post).

Jaco was visibly agitated at the sight of his muscular adversary. He tried to keep Tyson at a distance once the fight started, but he was not strong enough to prevent the aggressive 19-year-old from bulling his way inside. Jaco appeared to be wary of his notorious opponent, and he punched ineffectively off his rear foot while backpedaling away from the advancing Tyson. Jaco stuck a jab in the kid's face to keep him at bay, but Tyson walked right through it. Jaco missed with a right. Tyson had him in a corner now and dropped the outgunned Michigan heavyweight to his hands and knees with a stinging left hook. As soon as Jaco regained his feet, Tyson backed him into another corner, and another left hook buckled his legs. He crumpled to the canvas in a heap as Tyson watched and waited. Although Jaco's talent was non-existent compared with Tyson's, his heart was big, and he once again struggled to his feet. The game Midwesterner tried to stay out of harm's way but that was impossible. He managed to avoid one Tyson left, but a follow-up clubbing right hand to the top of his head sent him sprawling again, face-first to the canvas. The referee jumped in and stopped the fight immediately, invoking the mandatory three knockdown rule. It was over, mercifully in the first round, and Mike Tyson had equaled the record of the legendary Rocky Marciano by KO'ing his 16th straight opponent. Tyson was low-keyed and all business at the post-fight interview. "It's just a business. Jaco is a professional. He lost because of the three knockdown rule, but if there was no rule and I didn't catch him right, he would have kept gettin' up and I would have had to knock him down 10 or 15 more times."[1]

In January 1986, Tyson's celebrity grew significantly larger. After tying Marciano's knockout record, he began attracting the media like honey attracts bees. The January issue of *Sports Illustrated* carried a cover photo of Mike with the caption, "Kid Dynamite." The accompanying article called him the next great heavyweight. That was just the beginning of the hype. It would grow to unbelievable proportions by year end. The final test of Mike Tyson would not be how great a fighter he was, but how well Cus D'Amato had prepared him for the pressures and the demands of stardom. The major concern of Tyson's managers was not whether the young slugger could reach the top, but rather how he handled it once he got there. The major TV networks were beating a steady track to the Manhattan offices of Big Fights, Inc. to talk to Bill Cayton and Jim Jacobs about their fighter. Everyone wanted a piece of him. ABC-TV was the first network to cough up the big bucks, putting the teenager under contract for four exclusive fights in 1986 at a cost of $850,000. Mike Tyson was well on his way to making his first million.

Late in the month, a national tragedy took the nation's focus off the sports pages. On January 28, the space shuttle *Challenger*, the 25th flight in a frenzied NASA program designed to establish a permanent space station high above Earth, had lifted off from Launch Pad 39-B at precisely 11:38 a.m. with a seven-person crew including a New Hampshire school teacher. Seventy-two seconds into the flight, the *Challenger* exploded, sending the cabin section plummeting into the Atlantic Ocean, shattering on impact and killing all seven occupants.

January also saw the changing of the guard in one of the heavyweight groups, although the result was tainted and unpalatable. "Terrible Tim" Witherspoon decisioned WBA champion Tony Tubbs in a drab title fight but, more importantly, traces of marijuana were found in Witherspoon's urine during a post-fight examination. After a hasty meeting of WBA officials, it was decided that Witherspoon would be allowed to retain the title, but he would also have to give Tubbs a rematch within six months. He was also fined $25,000. The incident was just another example of the sorry state of affairs the heavyweight division was in. The heavyweights needed a champion who could set a good example for the youth of the country and serve as a positive role model for the inner city blacks. Mike Tyson was making his move and was as concerned about his image as he was about winning the title, telling Roy S. Johnson of *Penthouse*, "I want to work on being a good person. Some athletes have trouble when they retire because after awhile they start to believe what people think they are, and forget who they really are."[2]

Less than two weeks after the Jaco fight, "Kid Dynamite" was back in the ring, this time in Atlantic City. Mike's opponent was Irish Mike Jameson, a 31-year-old pro from Cupertino, California. Tyson's manager, Jim Jacobs, was not happy when he learned that Jameson was substituting for Phil Brown, who had to withdraw with an injury. Brown was a superbly muscled fighter, but one well suited to Tyson's brawling style. Jameson, on the other hand, was known as a survivor, a tough Irish kid who had carried several rated fighters into the later rounds. The statistics on the two fighters gave Tyson a decided advantage. The kid from Catskill was younger, stronger, and faster than his more experienced adversary. Physically he was as solid as a rock, built like a finely chiseled Greek statue. Jameson, carrying 236 pounds on his 6'4' frame, had a height, weight, and reach advantage, but the California heavyweight was soft around the middle and had little foot speed, two attributes made to order for a young bull like Tyson.

On fight night, the Trump Hotel and Casino, one of the many high-rise hotels that decorated the Atlantic City Boardwalk, was crowded with boxing buffs anxious to get their first look at the new heavyweight sensation. The match, promoted by the Houston Boxing

Association, was scheduled for eight rounds and was televised live by ESPN. Irish Mike Jameson, true to his heritage, entered the ring decked out in kelly green trunks with a white shamrock. Tyson made his appearance dressed in black once again. That color would be his trademark from now on. Tyson's managers thought black was an intimidating color, and along with Mike's menacing sneer, the image that he presented would strike fear into the hearts of many opponents. Jacobs and Tyson were convinced that the dark visage of the heavyweight executioner would win many fights before the first bell had rung. And they were right. Jameson paced nervously around the 20-foot ring as he awaited the pre-fight festivities. Tyson was more composed, standing quietly in his corner receiving last-minute instructions from Rooney. Referee Joe Cortez waved the two fighters to center ring to get their final instructions. A mustachioed Mike Jameson brought his 17–9 record with eight KO's with him. He was soon joined by the man the media was now calling "Iron Mike," perfect at 16–0. Tyson's face was expressionless as he listened to Cortez, like a man deep in concentration. He didn't even acknowledge the cheers of the crowd. He was mentally preparing himself for the task at hand, that of destroying Mike Jameson.

After the ritualistic handshake, the two antagonists returned to their respective corners to await the bell. Ringside commentators Ken Wilson and Murray Sutherland were previewing the fight, particularly as it reflected on the overall future of the heavyweight division. Sutherland added to the Tyson mystique with his glowing commentary. "Mike is a ray of sunshine coming to the heavyweight division—a division sadly lacking exciting opponents. There is a need for someone with Mike's explosive power to bring back the days of George Foreman, Joe Frazier, and Sonny Liston." Time would tell if Mike was the man.

The bell sounded and the Catskill strongboy advanced to the center of the ring to meet the journeyman from sunny California. An early right by Jameson caught Tyson on the side of the head, but the youngster responded with a sharp right uppercut of his own. Tyson stalked his man like a sleek jungle cat, weaving and bobbing, moving forward, always forward. Mike unleashed a short flurry on the ropes but Jameson escaped serious difficulty. The constant diet of body punches was already bringing the big guy's hands down. Tyson scored with a good uppercut and ended the round with a furious two-pronged attack to the head and body. Two hard rights to the head, one on top of the head that brought a grimace to his face, hurt Jameson, and he later said, "It felt like my neck went down to my belly button."

In round two, Jameson, the 1972 California Golden Gloves champion, landed a solid right to the side of Tyson's head, but it didn't seem to bother Mike at all. The Catskill Clubber came back with a fierce body attack, always moving forward. He didn't take a backward step the entire fight. A sharp uppercut opened a deep gash over Jameson's left eye, causing blood to flow freely down the side of his face. Jameson's lumbering style made him a sitting duck for the swift Tyson. He was unable to escape from Mike's withering attack, and he was frequently trapped on the ropes where the young New Yorker could bang away at will before Jameson could tie him up.

The scenario remained unchanged in round three. Tyson backed Jameson to the ropes at every opportunity and worked his body with dozens of rights and lefts, all of them thrown with bad intentions, a Tyson trademark. The big heavyweight from Cupertino began to hold more often now as he realized his chances of survival were becoming slimmer with each Tyson attack. Mysteriously, the bell sounded to end the round at the 2:01 mark—a two-minute round. Mike Jameson probably appreciated the thoughtfulness of the timekeeper.

In round four, Mike Tyson continued to follow his fight plan. Jameson was warned for

Mike Jameson was the first opponent to last more than four rounds with Tyson (photograph by the

butting a couple of times early in the round, but that didn't slow Tyson down either. The pride of Catskill quickly pinned the Irishman on the ropes, as had been his practice throughout the fight. A crushing left hook followed by two lightning left uppercuts dropped the Californian to the canvas in his own corner at 1:08. The speed with which Mike put together three-, four-, and five-punch combinations was unheard-of in the heavyweight division. He had the speed of a lightweight combined with the power of a heavyweight, a frightening combination for an opponent to ponder. Floyd Patterson had been credited with having the fastest hands in heavyweight history, but Mike Tyson was faster, according to the man who should know, Cus D'Amato. Jameson was on his feet quickly, shaking his head to clear the cobwebs, but Tyson gave him no relief. As soon as the referee waved the two fighters together, the determined Tyson rushed in for the kill. Jameson tried to tie up the rambunctious New Yorker with but moderate success. The Cupertino heavyweight proved his toughness in this round by surviving an all-out onslaught by the frenzied teenager.

Tyson was out quickly in round five and immediately maneuvered his man into a neutral corner. A hard combination followed by an overhand right put Jameson down on one knee. Referee Joe Cortez asked Jameson if he wanted to continue as he wiped off the big guy's gloves. Receiving no positive response after his third query, he stopped the fight. Mike Tyson was declared the winner on a TKO at 46 seconds of round five, his 17th successive knockout. Jameson appeared to be frantic and distraught when Cortez called it off, but boxing insiders claimed that Jameson's tantrum was all a charade. According to those in the know, Cortez put the question to Jameson three times. "Are you all right? Do you want to continue?" Having received no answer from Jameson, the referee had no choice but to stop the fight, at which point Jameson finally responded, "I'm all right. I'm all right." As all boxers know, the referee can't think for them. It is the boxer's responsibility to let the referee know if he wants to continue or not. Jameson obviously did not want to take any more punishment from "Kid Dynamite."[3]

With Rocky Marciano's knockout record tucked safely in his back pocket, Mike Tyson could now begin to move up in class. From now on, his managers would schedule world class boxers. The final phase of his long, arduous, and frenetic campaign toward the heavyweight championship was about to begin. From that day long ago, in September of 1980, when a scared 14-year-old street kid from Brownsville arrived at the Ewald house on the banks of the Hudson, the major effort of Cus D'Amato, Jim Jacobs, and Bill Cayton was directed toward placing the young boy on the heavyweight throne sometime before March of 1988, a timetable that would make him the youngest heavyweight champion in history. D'Amato's boxing expertise, Jacobs' management skills, and Cayton's promotional talents were carefully orchestrated to produce the best world class fighter in the world, a fighter who was known around the globe, and a fighter whose image could demand multi-million dollar purses whenever he fought.

The countdown had begun, and Jesse "Thunder" Ferguson was first on the list. Ferguson was the ESPN champion. Rated number 16 in the world, he carried a record of 16–1 with 10 KO's into the ring. His only loss was a tenth-round knockout at the hands of Carl "The Truth" Williams, and he had Williams on the canvas twice before his luck ran out. The fight would be a major hurdle for the youthful Tyson and would determine if he was ready to handle the top contenders.

Outside the ring, Mike Tyson was getting a taste of what it was like to be a celebrity. He completed his first television commercial in January, a 30-second slot for an Albany, New York, electronics store. Tyson was shown throwing punches at the air while an unseen voice said, "Heavyweight Mike Tyson is tough on the competition." At the end of the pitch from the electronics firm, Tyson pointed to the camera and said, "We knock out competition." At least it was a start. Also outside the ring, the boxing community was formulating

8. The Road to the Championship—1986

a plan to unify the heavyweight title for the first time in more than six years. Early in 1986 there were three men who all claimed to be the true champion. First there was Michael Spinks, probably the closest thing to a true champions there was. Spinks was recognized as the title holder by the International Boxing Federation. Then there was Pinklon Thomas, the WBC champion, and Tim Witherspoon, the WBA king, in truth nothing more than pretenders to the throne.

Boxing promoters Don King and Butch Lewis, under an umbrella called the "Dynamic Duo," after months of difficult negotiations with Home Box Office (HBO) cable TV, announced the details of an elimination tournament to crown a unified champion. The scenario had Witherspoon fighting Englishman Frank Bruno in March, Michael Spinks defending his newly won IBF crown against former titleholder Larry Holmes, and Pinklon Thomas putting his WBA belt on the line against Trevor Berbick. The WBA and WBC winners would then unify two-thirds of the title with a box-off in November, while the IBF champ defended his title against the European champion, Steffen Tangstad, on the same card. Finally, early in 1987, the two champions would meet in the final unification bout to crown the one true heavyweight champion.

Many talented heavyweights were excluded from the tournament, including Gerry Cooney, Carl Williams, and Mike Weaver, and their managers were screaming "foul" and talking about collusion and "deals" in all the national "rags." Mike Tyson was also ignored when the tournament was engineered, but that was as it should have been. Mike was coming on strong, but he still did not have the credentials to qualify as a serious contender. He was close, however, as witnessed by the fact that the HBO Vice President for Sports, Ross Greenberg, made the trip from Manhattan to Troy to study the new heavyweight sensation firsthand. Although Mike's mentor, Cus D'Amato, was no longer around to choreograph his career, his co-managers, Jim Jacobs and Bill Cayton, were still grooming him very carefully. His opponents were still hand-picked, and his rate of progress was monitored meticulously. His schedule would not be accelerated just to satisfy the whims of the Don Kings and HBO. When his time came, Mike Tyson would be ready. As Jacobs told HBO, "Our chief responsibility over the past year has been to select the right opponents for Mike Tyson. Nothing else has been more important. When people watch Mike Tyson fight, we want them to leave the arena saying, 'When can we see him again?' And that's where Bill and I are scrupulously careful in determining who he fights and the style of the fighter."

February 16 arrived, surprisingly sunny and pleasant for a winter day in upstate New York, and the city of Troy was buzzing with excitement. The author was on site to record all the sights and sounds of the big day as well as to report on the fight itself. The RPI Field House stood silent and peaceful as dawn broke over the blue collar community, and the people began to prepare themselves for another typical Sunday respite—church services, the Sunday newspaper, and pro basketball on TV. Those sports fans who were lucky enough to get tickets to the fight would head for the Field House about noontime, but the rest of the locals would have to be satisfied with the basketball game since the fight was blacked out for a 50-mile radius around Troy. As midday approached, the quiet serenity of the neighborhood was transformed into a three-ring circus as almost 8,000 rabid Tyson fans descended on the tiny area, media people by the dozens jockeyed for position in and around the Field House, and blue-uniformed lawmen struggled to maintain peace and order in the environs.

The crowd started to trickle into the arena as soon as the doors were opened at 1:00 p.m. one hour before the first fight would start and two-and-a-half hours before the hometown hero would enter the ring. A lonely 16-foot, eight-inch ring stood in the center of the gymnasium floor, visited periodically by various handlers from both the Tyson and Ferguson camps who were methodically checking the structure for defects. They tested the tightness of the ropes, the consistency of the canvas, and even the location of the television platforms to make sure that the scaffolds would not be a serious distraction to their fighter. ABC Sports was on hand to televise the fight, the first in their million dollar package with the Tyson group. The scaffolding had been erected in several locations around the ring to support the permanent TV camera installations that would provide a variety of camera angles of the event. In addition to the fixed units, a number of portable cameras would be present at ringside to portray the action "up close and personal." Sportscasters Jim Lampley and Alex Wallau were early arrivals to the arena to survey their territory, to assess the strengths and weaknesses of the Field House itself, to confirm the strategic positions of the permanent cameras, and to run through their pre-fight comments and analysis.

The $20 grandstand seats filled rapidly once the doors were opened as local boxing fanatics filtered into the arena jabbering and gesticulating, anxious to see everything that was being offered. They generally armed themselves with hot dogs and cold beer, then settled comfortably into their seats to witness the entire card, from the first four-round prelim to the final match of the day sometime around six o'clock. Beer and "dogs" were consumed voraciously in these seats. The $50 ringside seats filled less rapidly, some of them remaining empty until just before the 3:30 scheduled time for the Tyson-Ferguson main event. Many ringsiders were celebrity attendees, less interested in the bouts themselves than in being seen at a television event. Others were there on business—members of the New York Boxing Commission, promoters, managers, employees of HBO, and local and state politicians. They too were less enthusiastic than the grandstanders.

Mike Tyson, adorned in his favorite leather jacket and carrying a small gym bag, slipped into the arena unnoticed at about 2:30 and made his way to the dressing room. His usual entourage of three pigtailed blondes trailed obediently behind like puppy dogs. As one preliminary fight after another went the distance, the crowd became larger and more raucous. When the hands of the clock passed the 3:30 mark, the anxious crowd began to hoot and clap their hands. Within minutes, Jesse "Thunder" Ferguson finally came into view and was welcomed into the ring with but a smattering of applause from the pro–Tyson crowd. Ferguson climbed through the ropes with a confident smile on his face. He looked well warmed up and ready to go, and his pre-fight comments to ABC were brought to mind once again. "I think I can beat Mike Tyson. I'm gonna stand there and fight him. I won't run. I think my experience and my punching power will win the fight for me." Perhaps he was right, but there were 7,600 people in attendance who were of the opinion that, if Ferguson stood toe to toe with the Catskill assassin, he would leave the ring on his shield.

The buzzing that filled the arena during the minutes immediately preceding the fight suddenly erupted into a deafening roar as the pride of New York emerged from the dressing room. He was not yet in full sight of the crowd but already the rafters reverberated with thunder as 7,600 frenzied fans screamed, whistled, stamped their feet, and began the rhythmic chant, "Ty-son, Ty-son, Ty-son." If the roof had separated from the building as a result of the tumultuous welcome for their hometown hero, not one person in the building would have been surprised. Ross Greenberg, Vice President of Sports for HBO, at ringside, looked around incredulously at the wild scene. He said he had never in his life witnessed such an enthusiastic welcome for an athlete. Although the noise continued unabated for a full three

8. The Road to the Championship—1986

minutes, Mike Tyson was oblivious to it. He was stone-faced and impassive as he strolled down the aisle to the ring, the omnipresent black shoes and black trunks his only attire, his moist bronze body glistening threateningly in the glare of the Field House lights. Once inside the ring, Mike stood quietly in his corner while his trainer laced on the eight-ounce thumbless gloves that are mandatory in the state of New York. Rooney then spread liberal amounts of Vaseline around his fighter's eyebrows and cheekbones, as a normal precaution against cuts. The lubricant reduces the friction on a fighter's face, allowing an opponent's glove to slide off his face harmlessly instead of grabbing the skin and opening a nasty wound in the process. It doesn't prevent all cuts, but it does minimize those caused by friction.

When Tyson was formally introduced to the crowd, another wild demonstration was ignited. A group of enthusiastic Tyson fans at ringside stood and waved placards to the crowd glorifying their hero's professional achievements. One man held a card aloft reading "Fight 1–KO," another "Fight 2–KO," another "Fight 3–KO," and so on all the way up to Fight 17. The group vigorously urged Mike to continue the string and make Ferguson knockout victim number 18. Mike did not acknowledge the roar of the crowd, although later he remarked, "It was great, but I like to hear my name announced, you know."[4] As referee Luis Rivera gave the fighters their final instructions, Alex Wallau at ringside summarized the importance of the fight for television viewers. "Tyson is stepping up from fighting journeymen fighters to fighting a quality opponent. The heavyweight division right now is in chaos with three champions. If Mike Tyson is for real, he could be the star that this division and this sport need very badly."

Tyson's emotions appeared to be under control as fight time approached. He calmly bounced up and down in his corner, pounding his gloves together in anticipation. At the bell, his placid countenance suddenly changed. A cloud came over his face and his expression turned dark and sinister. He was once again the gladiator, and it was killed or be killed in the arena, with no quarter asked or given. Tyson was a man on a mission, and his mission on this day was to club Jesse Ferguson into submission as quickly as possible. Tyson met the ESPN champion in center ring and immediately maneuvered him into a neutral corner where he exploded six vicious body punches to the ribs and liver area. Five more body shots were delivered with bad intentions. Ferguson tried to fight back but his single punch was drowned out by a Tyson avalanche. Two thundering rights dug deep into Ferguson's side. The round was only a minute old and already Ferguson had taken enough body shots to last an entire fight. Two dynamite left uppercuts straightened the lanky Ferguson up and forced him to respond with four or five punches of his own in sheer desperation. Tyson brought three more crushing lefts up from the floor to crash against Jesse's liver area. Whomp! Whomp! Whomp! Lesser opponents would already have called it a night against Tyson's onslaught, but Jesse Ferguson was no average fighter. He was a cut above Tyson's previous opponents. Tyson's attack became more varied now, as he shifted from body punches to occasional lefts and rights to the head that stunned Ferguson. The round was less than half over when two tremendous left hooks found the side of Ferguson's face. Tyson had already thrown 40 or 50 punches in this fight, and every one of them was designed to maim or kill. Ferguson landed his first good punch of the fight, a short right uppercut that snapped Tyson's head back. The action continued at a rapid-fire rate for the rest of the round with Ferguson fighting back but Tyson still landing the more telling blows.

Rounds two and three were fought on the ropes with Tyson maneuvering for position and Ferguson trying to keep the Catskill strongboy at bay. A crushing right uppercut thrown

Jesse Ferguson lost to Tyson by disqualification in round 6 when he refused to break from a clinch when ordered by the referee (courtesy Paul V. Post).

by Ferguson found Tyson's chin, but Mike's only response was a counterattack of his own. In round four, Ferguson was able to keep Tyson at arm's length. As a result, most of the action took place in the center of the ring. Tyson became more tentative in this round, perhaps beginning to pace himself for a possible ten-round match, perhaps just looking for the one big opening. There was a minor fracas at the end of the round when Tyson landed a hard right hand to Ferguson's body after the bell. The infraction inflamed Jesse and caused his handlers to leap into the ring, but order was quickly restored before things got out of hand.

As round five started, Ferguson came out boxing and jabbing more than at any time in the fight. Tyson didn't throw a punch for almost a minute, choosing instead to stalk his man, biding his time and waiting for a clean shot. Several times Tyson had the ESPN champion backed into a neutral corner without throwing a punch. Once again, he pushed Ferguson's body against the ropes. This time a flurry of body punches brought Ferguson's guard down, which is exactly what the kid from Catskill was looking for. A Tyson left uppercut connected, but with not much on it. That was followed by a hard right to the rib cage, then a lightning right uppercut that broke Ferguson's nose, snapping his head back and driving him back against the ropes. The big man's knees buckled, his body crumpled, and he pitched forward to the canvas. He rolled over on his back and lay motionless, his hands held high as if shielding his eyes from the lights. His smashed nose spurted blood. Tyson was an eerie sight as he turned away from his fallen foe and walked slowly to a neutral corner. His hands were straight down by his sides, and a strange, almost evil leer covered his face. Mike explained the reason for his reaction to Paul Post of the *Daily Mail* after the fight. "I was laughing because when you know somethin's gonna happen, it's amusing."

Jesse Ferguson survived that punch and escaped another 30-second pummeling by Mike Tyson to end the round. But the former Marine from Harrisburg, Pennsylvania, was still not fully recovered when round six started. He tried to give himself time to clear the cobwebs by holding whenever Tyson moved in close, a tactic that brought several warnings from the referee. Rivera had difficulty separating the two fighters on several occasions, and when Ferguson continued to grab and hold in defiance of his directives, Rivera had no choice but to stop the fight, disqualifying Ferguson and awarding Tyson a technical knockout at 1:19 of the round.[5]

In interviews after the fight, Tyson insisted that Ferguson's tactics did not discourage him. "They can't beat me by hittin' and holdin'," he said. "It's a ten round fight and sooner or later I'm gonna get him." Asked why he changed his tactics after the first three rounds, Tyson volunteered, "In the fourth round I was watchin' his shoulders and watchin' the punches he was throwin' so I could counter them. At the end of the fourth round, I saw an opening and I knew I was gonna hit him with an uppercut and finish him." Alex Wallau noted that Tyson didn't appear to be winded at all after his six-round battle, and he also noted that Mike had taken some good shots from Ferguson without any noticeable ill effects, two areas that the critics were leery about. Tyson just shrugged off their doubts. "I can't change any opinions. Perhaps some people still have doubts about me, but as I continue to win and to meet all the contenders in the near future, then I will quiet all doubts." Trainer Kevin Rooney rated Mike's performance a "B." "He'll never get an A+, but I expect to give him a lot of straight A's. We mark on perfection."[6] All in all, it was a stunning start to Mike Tyson's charge to the top of the heavyweight ranks. One national boxing magazine called it "electrifying." And electrifying it was. His performance was dominating, his demeanor terrifying. Perhaps it was time for Rocky Balboa and Apollo Creed to step aside. The real "Master of Disaster" had arrived on the scene. And his name was Mike Tyson.

Ross Greenberg was another who considered Tyson's achievement to be monumental. He hurried back to his HBO offices greatly impressed with the new heavyweight challenger. He immediately informed his staff that it was almost certain that Mike Tyson would have to be included in the heavyweight unification tournament before it reached its final resolution. Negotiations were ordered to begin at once with Big Fights, Inc. After weeks of discussions between the two parties, Jim Jacobs made the momentous announcement. Big Fights, Inc. had just concluded a package deal with HBO that would put one million dollars in Mike Tyson's pockets for appearing exclusively on HBO in four fights during the upcoming year. Coupled with the ABC offer, Mike was assured of earning almost two million dollars for eight matches in 1986. The date was March 19. The Tyson camp still had not committed their valuable property to the heavyweight elimination tournament, but they had made assurances to the HBO-Don King group that they would continue to negotiate through the summer and would make a final decision by Labor Day.

During this period, Mike began driving automobiles again, his license having been returned by the Registry of Motor Vehicles. Mike had spent the previous year being escorted around in a bright new chauffeured limousine, placed at his disposal by his manager, Jim Jacobs. Now he could chauffeur himself around again. He didn't rush out and buy a new car this time, however. Remembering his previous experience, he was more cautious the second time around. One of the Catskill city administrators owned a yellow Cadillac convertible, and he put the car at Mike's disposal from time to time. Mike got a lot of use out of that yellow Caddy during the summer of 1986. He was spotted driving all over the north country, from Albany, New York, to Pittsfield, Massachusetts. Many days he drove the Caddy up to Catskill High School to visit Mr. Stickles, Mr. Turek, and some of his favorite teachers. Occasionally he took a bunch of the high school kids out for a joy ride. Mike was a hero to most of the teenagers in Catskill, and he delighted in the adulation and the responsibility. He was still a big kid himself, and he loved to impress the youngsters. It was hard to believe, but he was only a year or two older than some of them.[7]

Being a celebrity was not all fun and games for the teenage idol, however. There were always people searching for the dark side of a public figure's life. An article in the *Boston Globe* accused Mike of using lewd and obscene language to female patrons in an Albany department store. A security guard at the mall also stated that Mike and several of his friends were asked to leave the local cinema for cursing at customers. True or not, it created reams of adverse publicity in the sports pages of the nation's newspapers. Articles like this one made Mike painfully aware of the tremendous impact his actions could have on his life. He was no longer just a private citizen. He was now a public figure, and as such would spend the rest of his life in the journalistic fishbowl. The eye of every reporter and the ear of every freelance journalist would be on him continually from now on. His smallest transgression would be noticed, and it would be magnified and twisted beyond recognition by the purveyors of sensationalism, and elaborately displayed to the world on the cover of one of the weekly scandal sheets.

Mike had only three weeks to prepare for his next opponent, journeyman Steve Zouski, a scheduled "breather" strategically slotted between two name opponents, Ferguson and James "Quick" Tillis. But Mike Tyson was still experiencing growing pains at this time, still maturing emotionally. His mind continued to play games with him, telling him that he could

Tyson thought he looked like a tank in this photograph (courtesy Paul V. Post).

coast through certain matches without giving a full effort and without preparing for the fight properly. Such was the case with the Zouski match. Mike did not train with his usual zest, occasionally skipping a day completely and, on other days, engaging in half-hearted sparring sessions with Charles "Tombstone" Smith. In Mike's juvenile mind, Zouski was a stiff who didn't have to be taken seriously. He confided to a friend, "He's nothin'. I can beat him easily." As a result of his confused thinking, fight day found Mike Tyson mentally unprepared for battle. To make matters worse, he fell off his pigeon coop in the morning, damaging the cartilage in his ear and laying the foundation for a full-scale infection. To Mike's dismay, the Zouski bout was a lackluster affair from start to finish. Mike exhibited few of the skills that had vaulted him into the top ten in the WBC's latest ratings. He seemed to be fighting in a daze, throwing far too few punches and getting hit too often in return.

The 6,000 Tyson fans that crowded into Long Island's Nassau Coliseum began to wonder what was wrong with the Catskill assassin. True, Steve Zouski had gone ten rounds with current IBF cruiserweight champ Lee Roy Murphy, and his 25–10 record included 14 knockouts, but the Brockton, Massachusetts, native was not around to see the sixth round against either Marvis Frazier or Tony Tubbs. His fleshy midsection was ample proof that his conditioning program left something to be desired. Tyson contented himself with working Zouski's soft middle during round one, leaving a series of bright pink welts wherever his thumbless gloves made contact. Mike landed several telling uppercuts in round two but took a number of hard shots in return, uncharacteristic of a mentally prepared Tyson. As round three got underway, Kevin Rooney grew impatient with his charge, at one point yelling, "If you don't start punchin', this bum will go ten rounds with you." Perhaps Tyson heard his trainer's admonition, perhaps not. In any case, he suddenly unloaded the big artillery. A left hand followed by two whistling rights staggered his courageous foe. Another right hurt Zouski, and one final powerful left hook that smashed against the right side of Zouski's head sent the challenger to the canvas face-first for the full count. Referee Arthur Mercante counted the dazed Zouski out at precisely 2:49.

According to Rooney, Tyson rated a C+ for his effort, but based on the questions and answers at the post-fight press conference, most journalists, and even Tyson himself, gave the Catskill boxer a much lower score. Mike admitted that it was his worst performance ever, saying that he was suffering from a cold and that he had "a lot of personal problems." Within three days of the Zouski fight, Mike Tyson was back in the gym sparring with Marc Machain and "Tombstone" Smith, readying himself for the Tillis fight, only 16 days hence. Mike was forced to don the unaccustomed headgear in order to protect his injured ear, which was becoming more irritated with each passing day.[8]

The following week, Mike was the recipient of a prestigious honor, official recognition by the New York State Legislature. Mike and his trainer, Kevin Rooney, traveled to the state capital at Albany on Tuesday, March 19, to receive the honor. Assemblyman C. D. "Larry" Lane introduced Tyson to the legislature, and Assembly Speaker Stanley Fink presented the young boxer with the framed resolution. It read, in part, "It is the sense of this legislative body to publicly recognize and commend ... [Mike Tyson] ... an individual of singular and

Tyson took out Steve Zouski in round 3 (courtesy Paul V. Post).

Tyson was honored by the New York State Assembly March 19, 1986, with a framed resolution commending his "singular and truly compelling distinction" (courtesy Paul V. Post).

truly compelling distinction ... for his outstanding professional career." With all the adverse publicity that Mike Tyson had received in recent weeks, it was questionable whether or not he could live up to the accolades he had just received. But fate entered the picture at this point and gave the New York teenager a much-needed break in his grueling schedule. The ear infection that had been developing since the Zouski fight suddenly hit Mike with full force, sending him reeling to the hospital for ten days of rest and treatment. It forced a postponement of the Tillis fight until May 3, and gave the beleaguered 19-year-old time to reexamine his recent escapades and get his head back together. He thoughtfully reviewed his behavior and his attitude over the past few months, his recent frivolous nighttime activities with people who were supposed to be his friends, but who in fact turned him away from his objective and caused considerable consternation in the Ewald household and in the offices of Big Fights, Inc. Headlines in the nation's sports pages referred to "nights away from home," "a girl a night," and "lewd behavior in public places."

As Mike rested in his hospital bed, he utilized his convalescence to full advantage. He rededicated himself to the goal that he and Cus had first set back in 1980, to win the heavyweight championship of the world. He would not be distracted by girls or by the exciting city nightlife. And he would choose his friends more carefully in the future. Former stablemate John Chetti was confident that Mike would regain his common sense and renew his dedication to the task ahead. "Now that he's famous, everyone wants to be his friend. But Mike's smart. He knows who his friends are." While Mike Tyson recuperated, a British citizen was creating something of a furor in far-off London Town. Heavyweight challenger Frank

Bruno destroyed former champion Gerrie Coetzee at 1:50 of round one to guarantee himself a title fight with the new WBA king, Tim Witherspoon, during the summer, as part of the HBO box-off. The hard-punching Bruno improved his record to an impressive 28–1 with 27 knockouts, his only loss being a tenth-round KO at the hands of the unpredictable James "Bonecrusher" Smith.

When Mike Tyson took leave of Mt. Sinai Hospital and returned to Catskill, New York, to resume his training program for the Tillis fight, he was a new man. He had matured considerably in the ten days spent in isolation, making full use of his time away from home to reflect on his short but hectic career as a sports celebrity, and on the distractions that had caused him to ignore his trade and to betray his promise to his deceased manager. Cus D'Amato had warned him about the dangers he would have to face when he became a celebrity. They discussed these very possibilities many times over the years as the former Brooklyn street urchin was growing and developing, both physically and emotionally. Cus told Mike that the hardest thing he would have to face was how to handle himself once he became a celebrity. "It is difficult getting to the top," Cus had said, "but it is more difficult handling the success once you have achieved your goal." Now Mike understood what the venerable old trainer was trying to tell him. Now he was back on track, and he promised not to make the same mistake twice.

He returned to the gym on April 7 to begin his training program for the "Quick" Tillis fight, and he was all business. He knew he had only four weeks to get ready for the toughest fight of his career, and he didn't want to waste a minute of it. Mike Tyson attacked his training program and his sparring partners with a vengeance. The kid from Catskill knocked out the lower front teeth of one sparring partner, Charlie "Tombstone" Smith. And he punished former world class heavyweight Jimmy Young, dropping him with a vicious left hook. Young, who had driven George Foreman into retirement and who had lost a controversial 15-round title fight to Muhammad Ali, was impressed with the youngster's talent. "You're not allowed to bat your eye. He knocked me down the first day and the second day, and I don't get knocked down in the gym."[9] In the opposition camp, "Quick" Tillis was also busy mastering the fundamentals. The 28-year-old "fighting cowboy" from Tulsa, Oklahoma, was on a four-fight losing streak, including decision losses to Gerrie Coetzee and Tyrell Biggs, but those bouts were now ancient history. Admittedly, Tillis was out of condition for those fights, but against Tyson he had something to prove. He had the best reason of all to get in top condition, incentive. Mike Tyson was the hottest piece of boxing property to come along since Jack Dempsey, and Mr. Tillis wanted to show the world that he was the better man. Come May 3, Mike Tyson had better be in the best shape of his short career because James "Quick" Tillis was coming to the fight loaded for bear.

In spite of his recent setbacks, Tillis still had an impressive set of credentials. His overall record showed 31 victories against only eight losses, and 24 of his opponents were put to sleep before the final bell sounded. Tillis arrived in Glens Falls, New York, brimming with confidence for his big match, and he was sure he knew how to beat Tyson. "You gotta keep movin' against Tyson. You gotta go side to side and in and out, keep movin' so he can't catch you. Hold him, rope him, all that stuff. My great grandfather was a cowboy, so it's in my blood. From the root to the fruit, I'm in this game to make big money. I wouldn't want to work hard and train hard just to be a punchin' bag for somebody. I want to get back on top—in the limelight."[10]

More than 7,500 screaming fans were on hand to welcome "Kid Dynamite" to the Glens

Falls Civic Center. He was glad to be back after a seven-week layoff caused by the ear infection that pushed the Tillis fight back from its original March 29 date. "(The hospital) was the best thing that ever happened to me. It was like a vacation. Not being in the gym took off a lot of pressure and gave me time to think and relax. I thought about what I wanted to do; did I want to be a playboy and hang out or fight. I found out I wanted to fight." The parade to the ring encompassed the usual Tyson entourage—local security people, followed by Rooney, Tyson, assistant manager Steve Lott, and cut man Matt Baranski. Needless to say, pandemonium reigned while the somber Tyson pushed his way through the crush of people. A hint of a smile crossed his face as he slipped between the ring ropes. There was a joke around town about the new Mike Tyson doll. You just wind it up and it comes out punching. Sure enough, when the bell sounded, the Tyson "doll" came out swinging. Mike was his usual aggressive self, bobbing and weaving, moving forward, mixing hard rights and lefts to the body with an occasional shot to the head. It was obvious that he intended to try and take Tillis out early. But "Quick" Tillis came prepared. He was in great physical condition, and he was ready for Tyson's tactics. He slipped most of Mike's rushes rather easily, although he did take a few hard shots in the process. Mostly he kept the young brawler at bay, pushing him away when he got close and landing several good counterpunches of his own in the process. One uppercut in particular caught Tyson clean but left no ill effects on the youngster's sturdy chin. Tyson landed a solid right to the head early in round two, but Tillis grabbed and clinched immediately. Tyson continued to pursue his man throughout the round but couldn't catch the dancing cowboy.

The Catskill teenager shifted tactics in the next round, becoming more of a boxer and less of a brawler. The early part of the round was dominated by frequent clinches as the man from Tulsa wouldn't let the young slugger cut loose on him. But that scenario finally ended when Mike trapped his man on the ropes and unloaded. A hard right to the body was followed by a left hook to the head. Now the punches came fast and furious as Tyson unleashed a vicious attack to press his advantage. Left-right-left. A hard right to the side of the head knocked Tillis sideways along the ropes. Half a dozen more punches found their mark before Tillis could tie up his energetic adversary. In spite of all Mike's punishment, the "fighting cowboy" was back on the balls of his feet, dancing away from danger and bringing feelings of doubt to the young boxer. Tillis caught Tyson with several good left hooks in round four, but Tyson walked right through them like nothing had happened. That was a plus for Tyson because Tillis was a known hard puncher. He had Marvis Frazier on the canvas, he had Greg Page down, and he dropped Carl Williams twice. But the tough New Yorker didn't even acknowledge that he had been hit. At one point in the round, Tyson went into a low crouch that left the top of his head even with Tillis' knee. After a subsequent clinch, the Oklahoma cowboy lunged at his man with a hard left to the head that missed. Tyson slipped the punch as Tillis went by, spun around and caught the off-balance fighter with a left hook, dropping him to the canvas, more surprised than hurt.

As the middle of the fight approached, Mike Tyson became very tentative. He wasn't his usual busy self in the clinches, he put together no rapid-fire combinations, and he seemed to have lost some of his drive. The crowd became curious. Was it out of respect for Tillis? Was he now in awe of his crafty opponent? Was he tired? Was he pacing himself? What was his problem? On one scorecard, Tyson had won rounds 2, 3, 4, and 6, with rounds 1 and 5 being scored even. Tillis had not won a single round at that point, but suddenly he began to come on, and Mike Tyson began to fade. Tyson managed to come out on top in a sluggish round 7, but rounds 8 and 9 were dominated by the Oklahoma cowboy, although they were so dull that Kevin Rooney implored his young charge to "keep punchin'. Don't stop in the clinches." The final round was no different. Mike Tyson kept the lid on until the final 30 seconds, when he opened up and finished with a flurry. Tyson eked out a close decision by a 6–4, 6–4, 8–2 count, but he left many questions unanswered in the process. He certainly did not impress anyone with his lackadaisical performance in this fight.

The days following the Tillis fight were times of soul-searching for the Tyson camp. The fight itself had been less than an artistic success, and unkind guttural murmurings could already be heard throughout the boxing world. First of all, the fans were unhappy. Tyson followers across the country had expected Mike to claim his 20th consecutive victim via the knockout route, and his inability to do so left them disgruntled and angry. Boxing fans, in general, are a bloodthirsty lot, and Tyson fans in particular crave their share of the sticky red stuff. Nothing less than witnessing an opponent being bludgeoned into unconsciousness will satisfy the appetite for gore and mayhem. Boxing experts around the nation were also dissatisfied with Tyson's lethargic performance, and they continued to question his determination and his stamina over the ten-round distance. Certainly his inactivity over the last four rounds of the fight fanned the flames of that still raging controversy. Mike had been content just to lay on his opponent and rest whenever Tillis tied him up in rounds seven through ten, his dynamite right hand hanging useless at his side. At a time when he should have been taking Tillis apart piece by piece with devastating body shots, Tyson did nothing. Stamina. Did he have enough stamina to compete in the heavyweight ranks over a grueling ten- to 15-round route, or was he strictly a six-round fighter? The jury was still out on that question, according to sportswriters.

The brain trust of the Tyson group set about to answer that question to their own satisfaction. One thing that all members of the Tyson camp agreed upon was that a fighter's first ten-round bout is more than a punishing physical effort. It is a frightening excursion into the unknown. It is a mind-boggling psychological obstacle that must be overcome, a mysterious, tenuous wall that has to be breached before a boxer can pass from the club fighter stage into the arena of the professional pugilist. Self-doubts play on one's mind, making the task at hand larger than life-size, until it appears to be an insurmountable barrier of mammoth proportions. A boxer's character is tested at times like these. He needs to keep his goal in the proper perspective and proceed toward it one step at a time. He must challenge the training regimen day by day, always keeping sight of his objective and determining what will be required of him in order to achieve it. And on fight night, the same procedure must be followed. The fighter must maintain absolute concentration, focus all his energies on the fight one round at a time, and not let the big picture overwhelm him. If he does this, and if his conditioning has been satisfactory, he will succeed and the ten-round demon will be crushed forever.

Tyson had breached the wall, although in retrospect it seemed at times as if he had tiptoed over it. Still, the ten-round hurdle was a thing of the past, and a sigh of relief could be heard emanating from the secluded confines of Catskill, New York. Jim Jacobs, for one, was more than satisfied with Mike's performance. He passed the test and, in the process, he had laid a good beating on Tillis for the first six rounds. Had he not gone into a shell over the last four rounds in order to conserve his energy, it is very likely that he would have made Tillis knockout victim number 20. Kevin Rooney had rated Mike's achievement a C+ in his school of hard knocks. The young trainer grades his students just like a college professor,

8. The Road to the Championship—1986

marking their level of skill and execution in such areas as defense, aggressiveness, ringmanship, effort, and consistency. According to Rooney, none of his students will ever achieve a perfect mark of A+ on their report card, as noted previously. Tyson's C+ was considered satisfactory for this stage of his development, although it was far from outstanding.

Rooney predicted, however, that Mike would be advancing to the B level in his upcoming fights, and should be producing straight A's consistently by the end of the year—just in time to challenge for the title. Certainly Rooney could breathe a little easier after the Tillis fight. He had done his job and he had done it well. Tyson was in superb physical condition and was able to compete at a high level of consistency over the ten-round distance. From the looks of it, he could have extended his effort to 12 or 15 rounds without a problem. Mike finished the fight with a lot of gas left in his tank, and the fact that he became ultra-conservative as the fight progressed was not Rooney's fault. The mind plays strange tricks on a person. Mike Tyson had struggled with the mind game for weeks prior to the Tillis fight. He was troubled and tormented by the demons of self-doubt, but in the end he emerged victorious. From now on, the ten-round bugaboo would be a piece of cake. With that hurdle behind him, it was time for Mike to look ahead to his next hurdle, another ten-round test against the WBC's seventh-rated contender, the Bronx bad boy, Mitch "Blood" Green. Mike had only 17 days to prepare for the fight, which would be held in the high temple of boxing, New York's Madison Square Garden. This fight would be not only a boxing match, it would be an "event." Jim Jacobs, Bill Cayton, and HBO would see to that. This was Mike's first fight for HBO under his million dollar contract, and both his managers and the people at HBO wanted to make the most of it.

The fight was being promoted by HBO in conjunction with Don King Productions. Don King, the flamboyant one, was a typical American success story. Born in Cleveland in 1933, King, his sister and four brothers were raised by their mother after their father was killed in an industrial accident. As a teenager, King operated on the fringes of the criminal element in town, eventually working his way into the position of the "Numbers Czar." King's world came crashing down around his ears, however, one night in 1965, when he accidentally killed a man during an argument. His conviction on a manslaughter charge resulted in a four-year stint in the Marion Correctional Institution. Once released, King decided that he could make as much money legally as he could running numbers, and with none of the risks. In a short time, he became a boxing manager, his first notable fighter being "The Acorn," Muhammad Ali's favorite name for the tough, hard-hitting, and bald Ernie Shavers, whose contract Don King purchased from former major league pitcher Dean Chance for $8,000. Two years later, King branched out into promoting fights, eventually snatching the brass ring with the Foreman-Ali match in Zaire on October 30, 1974. In addition to his multi-faceted business acumen, Don King is also a showman of the first magnitude. He wears his hair in a long, wild, Afro style, looking like a man with his finger in a light socket. The gaudy, diamond-studded rings that dominate his hands complement his sequined tuxedos, frilled shirts, and gold necklaces. One national magazine probably came closest to characterizing Don King when it referred to him as "Flamboyant, ostentatious, cunning, ruthless, part businessman, part con-man, part riverboat gambler, part revivalist preacher. And brilliant." And the man knows how to make money, too.

This group—Jacobs-Cayton, HBO, and Don King—were embarking on the final phase of the campaign to sell Mike Tyson. The Green fight would mark the beginning of the gigantic promotion that was designed to culminate in a Tyson title fight on HBO late in the year.

The first step in the plan was to move Mike Tyson's training camp to New York City, where a major media blitz could be initiated. During the second week of May, the Tyson camp was uprooted and moved from the back woods of Catskill to the Grammercy Gym in Manhattan. Rooney insisted on Grammercy this time because, as he told Bob Smith at the *Daily Mail*, "everybody goes to Gleason's, but I would always train in the Grammercy Gym because it was Cus's gym. It's cleaner and bigger than most of the other gyms in the area." In the boxing world, the Grammercy Gym was known as "the gym that Cus built." Mike Tyson's first task in the big city was not sparring. It was not running. And it was not doing calisthenics. It was playing another game of "meet the press," a chore that Tyson always despised. He got tired of answering the same old questions over and over. "I'm looking forward to fighting in Madison Square Garden. All the great fights in history have been fought in the Garden. It's a great opportunity. I love what I do. I'd fight three times a week if I could." And on. And on. And on.

There was a slight possibility that the fight would not even be held in Madison Square Garden, but would be pre-empted by a professional hockey game. The New York Rangers were playing in the Stanley Cup Playoffs and, should they make it to the finals, the sixth game would be played on May 20 in the Garden. If this remote possibility came to pass, the fight would be moved next door to the Felt Forum, the smaller, 4,000-seat arena in the Garden complex. Shortly after Tyson arrived in New York, Don King scheduled a press conference in the Waldorf Astoria to introduce both fighters to the press and, hopefully, lay the groundwork for a crowd-appealing and money-making hate-hate relationship between the two fighters. Mitch "Blood" Green did his part to bring about that hate-hate relationship. Mitchell Green was a native of the Harlem section of the Bronx, a tough street kid who had to fight for survival from the time he was old enough to walk. When he was still a youngster, his fights often ended with the other guy cut and bleeding, causing one of his buddies to remark, "They oughta call you Blood." And so Blood it was. Mitchell Green had earned a nickname. But that was all Mitchell Green had. That and his life in the streets. He became the leader of one of the local street gangs, The Warriors, and his life became one constant conflict with the dedicated minions of the law. During his teenage years, Mitchell "Blood" Green spent a great deal of time in and out of courtrooms and jails, much to the dismay of his poor mother. Charlene cried herself to sleep many nights, worrying about her son. She was afraid to answer the phone at night for fear it would be someone telling her that Mitchell had been killed. According to Charlene, boxing proved to be a salvation for her son. He could fight legally, and he could vent his anger and his frustrations on his opponents in the ring instead of in the streets.

And Mitchell Green made good copy. He certainly perked up the press conference for the Tyson fight. As he paraded back and forth around the head table, decked out in an outlandish outfit complete with a long gold earring and a Panama hat, Blood Green boasted about how he would destroy the Tyson legend. "I'm not no bum! Tyson, as for you, I'm gonna break your neck. You can't whup me. Look at me good like I tole you before. This is 'Blood' Mitchell Green. I'm not one of those duffle bags who lay on the ropes. If you show up at Madison Square Garden, you're gone." Poor Green should have listened to those young kids on the streets of the Bronx who warned him, "I don't think you can mess with Tyson, buddy." Mike Tyson is a quiet man. He doesn't say much, and he doesn't make disparaging remarks about his opponents. He also doesn't like people to make disparaging remarks about him. As he eyed Green's histrionics, his expression remained placid, but his steely eyes were already planning revenge. Mike's revenge always took place in the ring. His only public remarks were, "If he makes a mistake, he's gonna find out for the first time how it feels to get knocked out. You can do a lot of things to Mike Tyson, but intimidating him is a different matter."[11]

The week proceeded quietly in training camp, with Mike doing his road work in Central Park and his ring work at Grammercy's. He got in a lot of sparring with heavyweights Wes Smith and Melvin Epps under the watchful eye of trainer Kevin Rooney. Rooney also worked Mike hard on the bags, the jump rope, and the exercise equipment. Still the media blitz continued unabated, making it difficult for Tyson and Rooney to concentrate on the task at hand. One day Mike appeared with Bill Mazer on *Sports Extra*, Channel 5, New York. During the interview, Mike emphasized the fact that he was going to be champion of the world someday, and he impressed his host with his knowledge of boxing trivia, although he was openly flustered at being asked to parade his wisdom before the American public. When Mazer asked Tyson who Mickey Walker was, Mike replied, "Oh God. Don't do that to me. You embarrass me." He also exhibited the humorous side of Mike Tyson to the TV audience.

Mitchell "Blood" Green went the distance with Tyson on May 20, 1986, losing by unanimous decision after ten rounds. Green also fared poorly in a highly publicized street fight with Tyson two years later (courtesy Paul Antonelli).

Mazer: You're so young. Don't you worry about burnout?

Tyson: No. The old fighters fought hundreds of fights. One guy had three fights in one day. If you like what you're doin', you can do it frequently. You guys come to work every day and you like your job.

Mazer: Yeah, but nobody's hitting me.

Tyson: Nobody's hitting me either.

The next night, on the *David Letterman Show*, Mike commented on the sacrifices that a boxer has to make in order to be successful.

Q: It must be tough for a fighter to have girlfriends with all the training that's required. Do you have any?

A: I don't have a girlfriend. I'd like to but I'm a fighter and I have to train all the time.

The Friday weigh-in was a noisy affair with Green storming around bare-chested, complaining about his share of the purse, and threatening to pull out of the match. Green was guaranteed $30,000 for the fight, while Tyson was being paid a cool $200,000. While Green strutted his stuff and boasted about his Adonis-like physique, Tyson just shrugged and noted, "If a body was the only factor, then Arnold Schwarzenegger would be world champion." At another press conference following the weigh-in, Tyson let the public in on the other side of a celebrity's life.

> People wouldn't want to be in my shoes. They think so because they say, "Wow! I can get money. I can be rich." But if they had to go through some of the things I have to go through, they would cry. Sometimes it's so depressing. Everybody always wants something. They want to find some way to get your money. It's always people. Just as hard as you work, people are working as hard to separate you from your money.[12]

Fight night. The Garden was theirs, and 6,529 boxing fans pushed their way through the turnstiles to witness another Tyson demolition derby. Don King and HBO billed the fight as an interborough war with Mitchell "Blood" Green representing the Bronx and Mike Tyson upholding the honor of Brooklyn. Most of the crowd was hoping to see Mike Tyson score a quick and awesome knockout, but Mike himself had other plans. Mike Tyson was angered over Green's insulting remarks during the week preceding the fight and was determined to make Green pay for his braggadocio. His plan was to punish Green for the full ten rounds, giving him a sound beating, but never taking advantage of an opportunity to knock him out. Mike wanted to make Green quit if he could.

Larry Merchant was at ringside extolling the virtues of Mike Tyson as Mitchell "Blood" Green came jogging down the aisle decked out in a flowing white robe with white fringe on the shoulders and arms. He was loud and noisy and he flicked jabs at the air. The voice of Merchant could be heard in the background. "He's a spirited, tough kid in the ring, not a classic style but he'll fight you. He wants to get in there and go dukes with Mike Tyson. The question is can he do it?" The answer wouldn't be long in coming. Mike Tyson paced his dressing room like a caged tiger thirsting for blood, Mitch Green's blood. He had listened quietly to Green's tirades all week, but now the moment of truth had arrived. It was time to put up or shut up. As he left his dressing room, it was a different Mike Tyson that made his way down the aisle. Gone was the look of nonchalance and relaxed gracefulness that had defined the Tyson countenance in previous fights. Now he was all business, dressed in black and unrobed as usual, his face twisted into a grotesque sneer that could only mean trouble for Mitch Green. On this night, Mike Tyson hated the Harlem tough guy with a passion that could not be extinguished. Tonight Mike Tyson would make Mr. Green pay for all those disparaging remarks of the previous week. He vowed to punish Mitch Green for ten long rounds. He would beat him thoroughly and painfully to show Green who was the tougher of the two. And if Green wanted to end the fight prematurely, he would have to quit.

The ringside commentator's voice was drowned out by the roar of the crowd as the future champion came into view.

> Mike Tyson is an awesome prospect, in the process of becoming a fighter, a challenger, a champion. It does seem already, prematurely, he's being treated like some sort of human trash compacter, expected to just go out there and grind everyone into powder, and if he does anything less, it's failure. So let's just remember that even the greatest fighters left some opponents standing and the critics clucking—that he is just 19—and that he's been a professional for only 14 months.

Announcer Charlie Hull introduced Mitch Green to the crowd amidst polite applause. The 6'5", 225-pound Bronx bomber looked in tip-top condition, his shoulder-length black hair hanging in tiny ringlets, his mustache and goatee neatly trimmed, and his statuesque body glistening in the glare of the ring lights. His ring record was almost as impressive as Tyson's. Winner of 16 fights with one draw, Green had lost only once, on a close decision to WBC champion Trevor Berbick. This fight was to be his stepping stone to a rematch with Berbick for the title. Tyson glared at his man threateningly during the briefing by referee Luis Rivera and then returned to his corner to receive last-minute instructions and a kiss on the lips from his trainer.

Mitch Green's dream of glory lasted less than 30 seconds in actual combat. Mike Tyson came out fast and he came out swinging. After the first 20 or 30 Tyson hooks, a look of doubt came over Green's face. Tyson was a man on a mission, and Green was the target. The big man's eyes showed concern almost from the start, and he was forced to backpedal and fight a defensive fight before the onslaught of the teenage tiger. To his credit, he fought back when cornered, and he caught his assailant with some telling punches. Still, Tyson took the shots without notice and moved inexorably forward. In round two, the stone-faced Tyson hit Green with a straight jab that sent his mouthpiece flying into the crowd. Green responded by holding Tyson behind the head with his left hand and banging four solid shots to Mike's head with his right. There were some good exchanges in the early going with both fighters winging and landing some good punches. In round three, a Tyson hook knocked Green's mouthpiece out again, this time with a bridge and two teeth in it. By now, Mitchell "Blood" Green was becoming very discouraged. The red stuff that covered his trunks was coming from his own mouth instead of his opponent's. In between rounds, he sat dejectedly on his stool and shook his head in disbelief. Mike Tyson was too much for him. In the other corner, Mike Tyson was enjoying himself. He had the fight well in hand, and he was executing his moves with complete confidence. He continued mixing his punches well, throwing a stiff jab, followed by vicious hooks to the body and a variety of punishing uppercuts and head shots. And every punch was thrown with bad intentions.

In round five, Tyson taunted Green for a minute or so. After talking to his opponent, Tyson laughed at Green and dared the big man to hit him. Mike moved forward, bobbing and weaving, not throwing any punches, slipping every punch that Green threw at him, thoroughly enjoying his defensive abilities. Between rounds eight and nine, Tyson's exuberance surfaced once again. In the middle of a Rooney lecture, Mike glanced up at his intense trainer, smiled, then kissed him on the cheek. All was well in the Tyson camp. In the end, it was a Tyson runaway. He won the fight handily with Green winning one round at most. Mike was still not winded after 30 minutes of constant activity where he threw almost 500 punches.

At the post-fight interview, Mike confirmed his fight plan. "I don't want to sound brutish or anything. I didn't want to knock him out. I wanted to put a lot of pressure on him and make him decide himself whether to give up or not. I hit him with some rugged punches but not devastating punches. I knew he was a professional and if he went down from those punches, he would have given up. And I must take my hat off to him. He's a very tough individual." Mike summed up the fight best a little later when he said, "I'm just a 19-year-old kid havin' a lot of fun."[13]

With the Green fight history, the selling of Mike Tyson took off in high gear. Bill Cayton's strategy for the rest of the year was to keep Mike close to New York City, the media capital of the world, with an occasional side trip to her west coast counterpart, Los Angeles. Mike was scheduled to fight in the New York City area another eight to ten times before challenging for the title in November or December. In between fights, Cayton and Jacobs would see to it that Mike attended as many noteworthy events as possible, making sure to be photographed with famous people in the process. He would also be seen in the company of the world's most beautiful models and starlets. The New York newspapers were soon full of Mike Tyson photos. His gold, gap-toothed grin was everywhere. One day he was at Gracie Mansion trading jokes with Mayor Edward Koch, and the next day he was at Yankee Stadium autographing a baseball for superstar Dave Winfield. He even found time to make the newsprint in the clutches of Penthouse Pet Cody Carmack. No wonder he was smiling.

Kevin Rooney and Jim Jacobs had to be very careful they did not overdo the promo bit to the exclusion of Mike's conditioning program. After all, Mike was first and foremost a boxer who was still in pursuit of the title. Getting him in condition for his next fight, only 24 days away, was paramount. His opponent, Reggie Gross, was already in training, and he was intent on derailing the Catskill Express. Gross, out of Baltimore, Maryland, was no pushover. His record showed 18 wins and four losses against some stiff competition, mostly in the cruiserweight division. In his two most recent fights, Gross had scored an impressive eighth-round knockout over highly rated Bert Cooper, then lost a tough ten-round decision to Mike's old nemesis, Henry Tillman. Come June 13 in Madison Square Garden, Reggie Gross would be standing in front of Mr. Tyson, determined to make him his 19th victim. The sparring sessions in the Cus D'Amato gym were fast and furious during the early part of June as Mike Tyson tangled with some tough competition. In addition to his regular sparring partner, Dion Burgess, Mike was forced to contend with tough Anthony Davis. As everyone knew, Tyson's sparing sessions were no different from regular bouts. They were wars, with no quarter asked or given. And Mike Tyson fought them without the protective headgear, which he was not allowed to wear unless there was a medical problem that necessitated their use. "We want guys who aren't afraid to throw bombs," said Rooney. Anthony Davis was like that, and Rooney appreciated it. But Anthony Davis was no match for a fired-up Mike Tyson, and he had to call a halt to one sparring session after Mike had bloodied his nose. "Whoa. He's like a rock. I got to stop."[14]

Sharing the spotlight with Mike Tyson in Catskill was Edwin "Chapo" Rosario, who was headlining the June 13 Garden card in a WBC title fight against champion Hector "Macho" Camacho. Tyson usually worked out in the gym from 12:30 p.m. until 2:30 p.m. followed by Rosario from three to five. Chapo, at 16–1 with 16 KO's, was extremely confident of taking the title away from the Macho man, whose record stood at 29–0 with 16 KO's. While Tyson was focusing his energies on Reggie Gross, his manager, Bill Cayton, was busy announcing his next three fights. On June 28, according to Cayton, Mike was scheduled to meet William Hosea in the RPI Field House in Troy, New York. Less than two weeks later, he would step into the ring at the Stevensville Country Club in the Catskill Mountains to take on Lorenzo Boyd, and on July 26, Mike would be paired with Marvis Frazier in the Glens Falls Civic Center.

When fight night arrived, 10,000 fans filed into Madison Square Garden on what was billed as "Resurrection Night" by the metropolitan media, who were intent on rebuilding the Garden's reputation as a major boxing arena. The Tyson fight, in fact, was only a secondary fight that evening, yielding the limelight to the WBC lightweight title fight between Camacho and Rosario. When Reggie Gross stepped into the ring, it looked like it would be a long night for the kid from Catskill. Gross, who stood six feet tall, had filled out as a heavyweight and carried 218 pounds on his sturdy frame, one pound more than Tyson. Mentally, Gross was ready for the challenge. He was determined to carry the fight to the youngster. And he was confident that he would destroy the Tyson myth during the course of the evening. The fight turned out to be short and sweet, at least as far as Mike Tyson was concerned. Mike came out quickly as usual, determined to take Gross out in the first round. Gross was just as determined to stand his ground and mix with the young New Yorker. Midway through the round, Gross went on the offensive, throwing a flurry of punches at the teenage sensation. Tyson ducked under a hard right thrown by the determined Gross and took a short left uppercut that caught him flush on the chin. Another short left missed its mark, and a hard right failed to connect as Tyson calmly moved out of harm's way. Still another right and left found nothing but air as the elusive Tyson bobbed and weaved like a magician. A solid right uppercut finally found its mark and stood Tyson straight up, but the New Yorker's bull-like neck absorbed most of the force of the devastating blow, leaving Mike alert and ready to counterattack, which he did. After another Gross right sailed over his head, Tyson leaped out of his crouch with a roundhouse left that found Gross' right cheekbone, dumping the Baltimore fighter on his back. Gross crawled to the ropes on his hands and knees, and pulled himself upright at the count of seven, but his glassy-eyed stare was evidence that the fight was almost over. Tyson followed up his advantage with determination, and two more left hooks put his courageous opponent down again. Gross was beaten but his heart wouldn't admit it, and once again he pulled his battered body upright. Referee Johnny LoBianco grabbed the wobbly fighter and waived an end to the fight at 2:36 of round one. The fight had been short but not easy.

After the fight, Tyson was ecstatic over his quick victory. "I was lookin' forward to fightin' Gross because of his good performances against Cooper and Tillman. I wanted to prove somethin' tonight. I was determined to knock him out in the first round."[15] When his manager, Jim Jacobs arrived, Tyson was all smiles. "I can't believe how I avoided all those punches he was throwin'. It was weird." Jacobs smiled. "That's because you're elusive, Mike. You're very elusive." One of the reporters questioned Mike about the right uppercut that Gross laid on him. "I saw the punch comin' and I braced myself for it. It looked devastatin' but it wasn't. I wanted him to stand there and trade punches."[16]

Tyson's stablemate, Edwin Rosario, was not as fortunate as Mike, losing an unpopular 12-round decision to Hector Camacho. Twice the rugged Rosario had Camacho on the verge of a knockout but couldn't finish the job. As soon as Camacho regained his senses, he got on his bicycle and ran away from his tormentor for the rest of the fight, salvaging his title only through the good graces of the judges, not through any effort of his own.

Mike Tyson had only 15 days to bask in the glory of his most recent victory. On June 28, he entered the RPI Field House to trade punches with yet another graduate of the cruiserweight division, William Hosea from Peoria, Illinois. Hosea carried an impressive 17–4 record with 15 knockouts into the ring with him. During his career, Hosea had beaten Mitch Green, KO'd former heavyweight contender Renaldo Snipes, and had the highly touted Greg Page on the canvas before losing a ten-round decision. One of his claims to fame was the fact that he had never been knocked down in 21 professional fights. Mike Tyson intended to change that statistic. As usual, the kid from Catskill was the aggressor from the opening bell, keeping the pressure on his 29-year-old opponent. As the two fighters exchanged punches in center ring, Hosea suddenly got in a thunderous left hook that caught Tyson right between the eyes. The teenager's head snapped back on impact, but he shook off the blow with no apparent damage. Seconds later, Tyson was on the attack, pounding Hosea with both hands. A jolting right uppercut buckled Hosea's knees and spelled the beginning of the end for the Illinois heavyweight. The punches came in flurries now, mostly heavy, sickening shots to the body. The barrage continued for about 15 seconds, then one-two-three hooks found the side of Hosea's head, dropping the 205-pounder on his face. Hosea quickly got up on his haunches, then made it to one knee, but remained fixed there as the fatal count reached ten.[17]

The knockout, coming at 2:03 of round one, culminated a 57-punch demolition, and improved Tyson's record to a perfect 23–0 with 21 knockouts, including 14 first-round knockouts. "I hit him with two good body punches and I felt his strength disintegrating and leaving his body," Tyson said. "He took a better punch to the head than to the body." "Mike's got a pretty potent punch," Hosea noted. "I'm sorry the people didn't get their money's worth." Tyson's trainer, Kevin Rooney, added, "He took some shots and could have continued. But the count got to 6,7, and 8, and he said, 'What the hell.' He knew he couldn't beat him."[18]

The Tyson express was back on track and headed for "Titleville." Mike was already ranked number two by the World Boxing Council, and he was in a position to demand a title shot any time he chose. His managers chose instead to schedule another four to six fights before sending their teenage gladiator into the ring against the champ. There was no urgency to challenge for the title. The end of the year would be soon enough. Two days after the Hosea fight, Mike Tyson quietly celebrated his 20th birthday and then slipped away to one of the Catskill resorts near Swan Lake to rest and promote his upcoming fight against Lorenzo Boyd.

The metropolitan New York area was celebrating a birthday during the week also, but not Mike Tyson's birthday. The Statue of Liberty, the graceful lady who stood peacefully in New York harbor welcoming visitors to our shores, was turning 100 years old on July 4, and all America was gathering to wish her well. Miss Liberty's beauty had been restored to its former brilliance during the past year thanks to a $66 million face-lift paid for by public donations. As the big day dawned, ten million people crowded into lower Manhattan to witness the spectacle. President Reagan was on hand to press the button that sent a laser beam darting across New York harbor to illuminate the statue and begin the festivities. Thousands of boats in the harbor sounded their fog horns and sent streams of water skyward in celebration. Pope John Paul II sent a "God bless America" message to the people of the United States by videotape. Tourists consumed three million hot dogs and seven million cans of soda. Twenty tons of explosives were used in the fireworks displays. A good time was had by all and, when the weekend was over, Miss Liberty settled back to welcome immigrants to the "Land of the Free" for another hundred years.

Mike Tyson returned home to Catskill after the holidays to prepare for the Boyd fight. The serenity around the Ewald house was comforting to a young man who had risen to celebrity status almost overnight. As he told the *Daily Mail,* "I like the peace and quiet of the country. And I like animals. I still have my pigeons. And I just bought a Shar-Pei. I've always wanted to get a Shar-Pei." The Shar-Pei breed was developed in ancient China to hunt wild boar. It's a mass of wrinkles to look at, a homely little dog, but warm and loving.

Mike Tyson was anything but warm and loving to his sparring partners in the gym on Monday morning. Dion Burgess and Anthony Davis brought out the best in Tyson and, as a result, they took a fearful beating. Davis, in particular, gave Mike a torrid workout, with some vicious in-close exchanges. There was good reason for Davis' courage during these sessions. Every vital area of his body was covered by some type of protective equipment. The most recent addition was a full face mask, which he donned to prevent further damage to his broken nose. As a result, Davis had little fear of being hurt by Mike Tyson when he traded punches with the pride of Catskill. It made for an interesting week, and it gave Tyson a solid foundation for his impending battle with Lorenzo Boyd. The Tyson entourage made the 100-mile trek up to Swan Lake the night before the fight. Fight day dawned hot and humid, with the temperature creeping up into the '90s, but it was still more comfortable than it would have been had the fight been held in New York City or Albany.

Mike spent a relaxing Friday in the cool environs of the country, communing with nature, enjoying the animals, and getting himself mentally prepared for his 24th search-and-destroy mission. The New York fighter was gunning for another quick knockout against Boyd in order to propel himself into the upper echelon of the heavyweight division. From here on, he would fight only contenders as he scrambled toward the top of the heap. Lorenzo Boyd, another Oklahoma cowboy from the same stable as "Quick" Tillis, sported a solid 17–5 record as a professional, but he was still considered to be just a journeyman fighter by most boxing experts. Boyd sounded confident in his pre-fight comments, but the words had a hollow ring to them.

When the match got under way, Mike Tyson immediately assumed the role of the pursuer and Lorenzo Boyd became the pursued. Boyd fought like a man trying to survive, not like a man who had come to town to defrock a myth. He stood cemented in the center of the ring, hands held high to protect his face, and elbows in close to the body, as he waited for Mike Tyson to start beating on him. Tyson didn't disappoint. His first punch of the fight, an awesome right hand to the rib cage, forced all the air out of Boyd's lungs, accompanied by an eerie hissing sound. Boyd recoiled from the blow, grimacing in pain, but before he could recover, an even more damaging punch smashed against his nose, shattering it and sending a shower of blood cascading over both contestants. Tyson worked Boyd's body unmercifully during the remainder of the round, maintaining an almost non-stop offensive. At one point, Mike narrowly missed scoring with a sizzling uppercut that might well have ended the fight then and there, but it was only a temporary reprieve as far as Lorenzo Boyd was concerned.

Round two was more of the same. Body punch after body punch found its mark as the relentless and ruthless Tyson kept on top of his outgunned foe. He was poetry in motion now, a pugilistic virtuoso who was performing to perfection as 2,300 excited patrons cheered him on. Tyson moved in on his man once more, unleashing a lightning left-left combination to the body and head that spun Boyd around. The predator was in full pursuit now, and he closed in for the kill. Another rapid-fire left-left sequence finished the job, with the final uppercut lifting the man from Cushing completely off his feet and depositing him on his back, out cold. Only one minute and 33 seconds had elapsed. Lorenzo Boyd never moved as the referee hovered over him and showed him his fingers, from one to ten. Boyd lay unconscious for a full five minutes, his head resting comfortably on the bottom strand of rope. When he was finally revived, he was propped up on his stool in center ring, where the doctor worked over him for another five minutes. Boyd looked like a man who had just been run over by a truck.

Mike Tyson was ready for the big time, and the big time was only 15 days away. On July

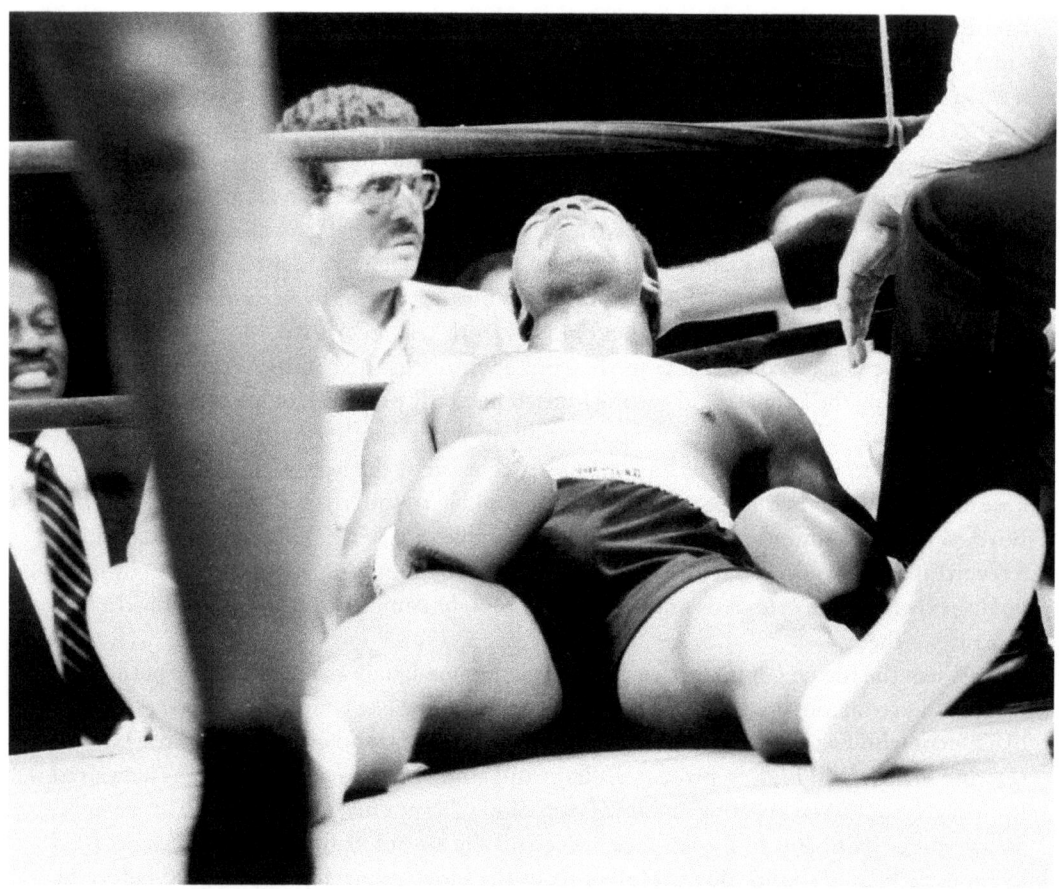

Lorenzo Boyd went to sleep in round 2 (courtesy the *Times Herald-Record* [Middletown, N.Y.]).

26, Tyson, now ranked eighth by the WBC, would climb through the ropes at the Glens Falls Civic Center to "go dukes" with the number 11 heavyweight, Marvis Frazier, before a live audience of 8,000 wild boxing fans, plus thousands more who would be watching the action on ABC's *Wide World of Sports*.

9

Everest Conquered—
November 22, 1986

Mike Tyson was entering the final phase of his long climb to the top of the boxing world. The Marvis Frazier fight was intended to be the event that would catapult him into international prominence. No longer would he be a sports figure, known only to those who followed the sweet science of pugilism. Henceforth, if all went as planned, he would be a citizen of the world, known to all and admired by most. It was only fitting that this fight should evolve into a contest of minds rather than a war of clenched fists. "Smokin' Joe" Frazier, Marvis' famous father, initiated the mind game and, when the final hand had been played, he regretted having done so.

Joe Frazier always looked for the edge in a boxing match. In this contest, Joe felt that he could destroy Mike Tyson's nerves by constantly belittling his talents and achievements. He insulted and embarrassed the Catskill youngster at every opportunity. At press conferences, during TV interviews, even in everyday conversation, "Smokin' Joe" preyed on Mike Tyson's inner character. During the four weeks preceding the big encounter, Joe Frazier played the matador to Mike Tyson's bull. The boxing world waited to see if the matador could humble his courageous foe, or if the bull would turn on his tormentor and disembowel him.

Eleven days before the fight, baseball unwrapped its annual showcase of stars, the All-Star Game. The 1986 extravaganza, held in the Houston Astrodome, was unique in many ways. To begin with, the American League All-Stars eked out a 3–2 victory, only their fourth win in 29 games dating back to 1960, and their first win in a National League park since 1962. The winning margin in the game came on a two-run homer by Detroit's Lou Whitaker off Dwight Gooden, early in the game. Fernando Valenzuela, Mexico's gift to the Los Angeles Dodgers, equaled the feat of another great screwball pitcher, Carl Hubbell, when he fanned five consecutive batters.

Four days after the American League's victory, boxing came center stage once more, this time in Wembley Stadium, London, England. The pride of Great Britain, Frank Bruno, challenged "Terrible Tim" Witherspoon for the WBA Heavyweight Championship. Bruno entered the contest with perhaps the most imposing statistics in the heavyweight division. The former European Champion had won his first 21 fights by knockout, surpassing Mike Tyson's total of 19. The lone blemish on an otherwise magnificent career came on a tenth-round KO at the hands of James "Bonecrusher" Smith in this same stadium on May 13, 1984. Since that setback, Bruno had gotten back on the winning track, disposing of another seven challengers, six by KO, giving him 27 knockouts en route to a 28–1 record. The WBA champ,

Tim Witherspoon, appeared fat and flabby at fight time, carrying 235 pounds on his 6'3' frame. Bruno, on the other hand, was in top physical condition, his superb physique displaying 227 pounds of solid muscle. Sadly, with all the hype, and with 43,000 screaming fans in Wembley Stadium, the bout was a dull affair, and the hero of Great Britain proved to be no match for the chubby one. A flurry of punches by the champion ended Bruno's dream of glory in the 11th round, leaving the overrated challenger slumped in a neutral corner bloody and battered. Bruno was suddenly exposed as another hyped-up heavyweight who carries dynamite in either hand but who is hampered by a crockery chin.

Back in the States, the HBO Unification Series was heating up. IBF Champ Michael Spinks, having defeated the aging Larry Holmes twice, was set to defend his title against European Champion Steffen Tangstad in September. Two months later, WBC king Trevor Berbick would put his title on the line against an, as yet, unnamed opponent. Then, in December, Tim Witherspoon was scheduled for a rematch against former WBA champ Tony Tubbs. A February box-off would unify the WBA-WBC crowns, with the winner taking on the IBF champ in the Unification finale in late spring. The Tyson-Frazier hookup might well determine Berbick's next opponent. Other possible new entrants in the series included Gerry Cooney, he of the devastating punch but questionable heart, and gold medal winner Tyrell Biggs.

As a recent celebrity, Tyson's every move was now being scrutinized by the men of the press, in hopes that a sensational story might surface to tarnish his reputation. Every slight transgression was faithfully blown out of proportion by the vultures of the news beat and colorfully reported to an equally cynical public thirsting for scandal. A visit to a Latham pizza joint with a group of friends that became somewhat boisterous, as teenage gatherings are wont to be, became a "disturbance" according to the local scandal sheets. A day away from the gym was reported as a major training and attitude problem if you listened to the "impartial" sports writers. The rumor mill buzzed with the latest Mike Tyson tidbits. Mike had an apartment in Albany. Mike was a regular participant in the Central Avenue swinging singles scene. Mike was looking for a house in Loudonville. Mike had a new girlfriend every week, his latest amour being Cody Carmack. Mike was frequently AWOL from training camp, much to the chagrin of trainer Kevin Rooney. The truth is that Mike Tyson was neither saint nor sinner. He was not perfect. Yet neither was he a teenage degenerate as some of the "yellow journalists" would have the public believe. He was still just an adolescent, one year out of high school. He did miss an occasional day in the gym in order to hang out with his buddies at Crossgates Mall. He did have a lot of girlfriends. And he did have an apartment in Albany, close to his favorite hangout, Septembers. But he also kept his nose to the grindstone more than most fighters do, sparring up to 200 times a year. Mike Tyson was a professional boxer, and he was dedicated to his profession. Taken in context, Mike Tyson was as normal as his friends, and more disciplined than most.

At this time, in July 1986, Tyson and his trainers were working hard, preparing for the Frazier fight. The newspaper comments by Joe Frazier drove them to work even harder. "Mike Tyson is no heavyweight. He's just an overblown middleweight." "Mike Tyson hasn't fought anybody, just a bunch of bums." "He's got no punch." "He's never been in the ring with anyone like Marvis." Mike Tyson read the reports, and he seethed at Frazier's audacity. Outwardly he remained calm and cool, but inside he was an inferno ready to explode. He vowed he would get even with the Frazier family—on fight night. Tyson sparred with increased intensity. Joe Frazier spurted venom. "Mike Tyson's a baby. He talks like a girl."

Tyson read and listened. He took out his anger on the body bag and the speed bag. He made his sparring partners pay for Joe Frazier's big mouth. Kevin Rooney observed the mental jousting between the two camps and smiled with satisfaction. He confided to the *Daily Mail*, "Mike Tyson's not a boxer. When the bell rings for round one, Mike is released." The boxing sessions with Dion Burgess and Anthony Davis were violent and exciting, bringing a round of applause from the local fans who crowded into the Spartan gym to view the future champ. Rooney was impressed with his fighter's progress. "I've sparred him a lot. I know he's in shape. He doesn't have time to get out of shape. And he doesn't have any bad habits. He doesn't drink or do drugs. Plus his fights are scheduled one on top of the other. That's the way it should be."[1]

The press conference held in Glens Falls on July 25 was typical of the pre-fight buildup. Joe Frazier did most of the talking. "Marvis will slug it out with him, and will beat him. It's gonna be a rumble. Marvis is a truck. Tyson is only a wheelbarrow, a wheelbarrow that's gonna get run over." Tyson listened intently, but when his turn to talk came, he was much more subdued than "Smokin' Joe," although quietly confident. "I know what Marvis Frazier has got. I'm sure he's seen what I got. I'm ready to fight."[2]

Other reports emanating from the Glens Falls area all predicted a Tyson's victory. Former opponents of the two fighters didn't give Frazier much of a chance to topple the kid from Catskill. James "Quick" Tillis, commenting on Joe Frazier's statement that there would be a rumble, said, "That's Tyson's fight. He does that, Tyson's going to beat that little *bleeper* to death." Journeyman Steve Zouski had no doubts about the outcome. "I give Frazier three or four rounds and he'll be sitting outside the ring. Frazier takes a pretty good punch and he's busy. But there's nothing behind his punch to worry Tyson."[3]

Cus's old friend, hypnotist Dr. John Halpin, drove up from Manhattan to spend a few minutes with Mike on the day of the fight. Together they talked about Cus's philosophies of positive thinking and mind over matter. It didn't take Dr. Halpin long to realize that Mike needed no special pep talk for this fight. He was well prepared, mentally and physically. Joe Frazier had given the young warrior all the incentive he needed to win this fight, and his approach was positive and aggressive. Across town, in another hotel, the Fraziers spent the pre-fight hours discussing their fight plan. The preparations for this fight contained more than the average amount of psychological jousting with "Papa" Joe Frazier trying to destroy Mike Tyson's confidence. Frazier had ranted and raved for weeks leading up to this big event, denouncing the 20-year-old fighter's manhood as well as his boxing ability. He attempted to work Mike into such a frenzy by fight time that the Catskill youngster would forget his fight plan and throw caution to the winds, allowing Marvis to take advantage of his carelessness and control the fight, possibly winning by a knockout. Joe Frazier didn't know it at the time, but his strategy had backfired as no other strategy had ever backfired in the history of professional boxing. He had created, in Tyson, a monster of immense proportions, a monster seething with pent-up fury and hostility, a monster seeking revenge, but a monster who would be fighting intelligently and under control. Joe Frazier had gotten Mike Tyson worked up all right, but Tyson didn't let it destroy either his fight plan or his concentration. Instead he channeled his anger into an increased determination and aggressiveness.

Saturday, July 26, turned out to be an oppressive summer day in upstate New York, hot and humid, with the mercury approaching the 90-degree mark. The entire country, in fact, was locked in the throes of a punishing heat wave. In the southern states, a drought had parched the earth and destroyed the crops. Chickens and cattle lay starving by the thousands.

Farmers as far west as Illinois and Indiana pitched in to assist their brethren south of the Mason-Dixon line. They sent train loads of hay to the stricken area to help fight the crisis, but it was more of a goodwill gesture than a cure. Only a change in the weather could end the suffering.

The atmospheric conditions in Glens Falls were still more comfortable than the conditions inside the Civic Center, where the air conditioning units were never activated and the only relief from the stifling humidity came from circulating fans that moved the hot-sticky air round and round in never-ending currents. The Civic Center felt more like a Turkish Bath than a sports arena, and boxer and spectator alike, including this author who was in Glens Falls to report on the action in the ring, perspired freely. Spectators began filing into the arena shortly after noontime although the Tyson-Frazier fight was not scheduled to start until approximately 4:30 p.m. Only 5,102 spectators were willing to travel to Glens Falls and fork out from $30 to $75 to witness the event, leaving over 2,000 empty seats in the Civic Center at fight time. Most boxing enthusiasts in the area had already seen Mike Tyson fight on numerous occasions, and for a lot less money than $75. The inability to sell out the auditorium spelled doom for Glens Falls as a site of big-money boxing matches. Hereafter it would be considered only for the less popular fight cards, the $12 ringside cards. World class matches would be held in New York, Atlantic City, and Las Vegas.

Marvis Frazier entered the ring first, as was customary for Tyson's opponents. He looked

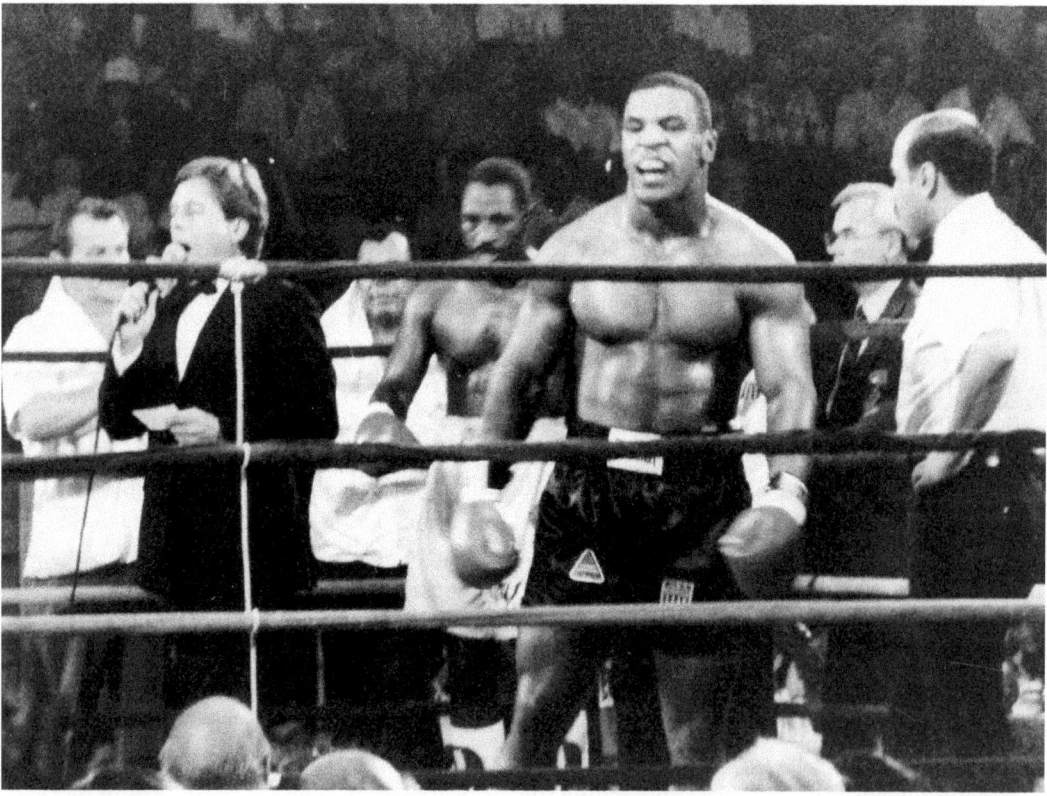

Tyson and Frazier met in the ring July 26, 1986, for a scheduled 10-round fight (photograph by the author).

calm and confident as he went through a preliminary warm-up routine. Minutes later, Mike Tyson made his entrance into the auditorium, and the hushed silence in the great building suddenly exploded in a cacophony of noise. The 5,102 fans stood and applauded, screamed, whistled, and stamped their feet, to welcome their favorite gladiator into the arena. "Ty-son, Ty-son, Ty-son." Mike Tyson was oblivious to the reception. Gone was the casual, unexpressive look that usually covered his face. In its place was an unsettling sneer, a look that bordered on total hatred. Not only was Tyson angry at the Fraziers, father and son, but he was also upset at many so-called friends in the Albany area who had predicted a Frazier victory. Mike was determined to prove them wrong. Today the world would know how good Mike Tyson really was. Tyson stalked around the ring scowling, anxious to get the proceedings under way. As he stood in his corner staring at Joe Frazier, the kid from Catskill mentally vowed to dismember the younger member of the Frazier clan quickly and decisively in round one. He was determined not to let Smokin' Joe's son hear the bell for round two.

The referee, Joe Cortez, kept the fighters separated for almost a minute before round one, waiting for a cue from the television crew. When at last the fight began, Tyson lurched into the center of the ring like a man chasing a streetcar. Frazier pawed at his attacker with a looping left, but Tyson slipped it easily. Tyson countered with a hard right that only caught Frazier on the arms but still drove the Philadelphia fighter back several feet. The young New Yorker missed two wild punches but, in the process, backed Frazier into a neutral corner. Four jabs from the intense Tyson brought no retaliation as Marvis slid along the ropes to a point midway across the ring. A right cross to the side of the head rocked Frazier, and a

Tyson beat Frazier by TKO at 0:30 of round 1—the fastest knockout of his professional career (photograph by the author).

follow-up right to the rib cage sent him reeling backward. Marvis seemed to be intimidated by Tyson's awesome power at this point, and he withdrew into a defensive shell. This was exactly what Tyson wanted. Without any offensive weapons, Marvis Frazier was a sitting duck.

The Master of Disaster bobbed and weaved while flicking out light jabs, trying to maneuver his man into a vulnerable position. Then Marvis made the fatal mistake. He slipped away from Tyson and moved back along the ropes, into the neutral corner again. Tyson stalked his man like a predatory jungle cat. Three more Tyson jabs backed Frazier deeper into the corner so his back was now touching the padded ring post. The cat had played with the mouse long enough. He was ready for the kill. One more left jab occupied Frazier's attention, then a quick right uppercut buckled his knees. As he straightened up, another uppercut crashed against his unprotected chin, almost decapitating him. With the second devastating punch, the muscle tone completely disappeared from Frazier's neck. His head, now without any muscles to support it, lurched upwards and backwards grotesquely. His vacant eyes stared out into nothingness. As he bounced off the ropes and pitched forward, his head hung helplessly in front of his limp body, beckoning to Tyson like a seductive speed bag. The Catskill assassin responded with two more crushing punches, a right cross and a left hook, that had Frazier's head bouncing back and forth like a yo-yo. He collapsed sideways into the ropes and slid helplessly into a sitting position against the ring post. Referee Joe Cortez stepped in immediately and waved Tyson to a neutral corner. He got down on one knee next to the fallen Frazier and picked up the count, but at five, seeing no response from Marvis and fearing for his safety, he waved the fight over. Then, with fatherly affection, Cortez reached under Frazier's right arm to support him and gently removed his mouthpiece. The carnage had lasted only 30 seconds.

Mike Tyson was in the forefront of those who rushed to the side of the stricken fighter, but Matt Baranski and Kevin Rooney pulled their charge back across the ring. As he was being led away, a worried Mike Tyson looked back over his shoulder and pleaded with Marvis' father, "Please go check on him. I'm sorry it happened like this."[4] Once back in his corner, Tyson, still concerned for the well-being of his opponent, ran to the ropes and yelled down to one of the attending physicians, "Get in here quick." But Dr. Jock Ford, another physician, was already leaping through the ropes yelling, "Don't move him. His neck may be broken." Ford, who had witnessed the savage attack close-up, feared that Frazier might have suffered serious neck damage from the ferocity of Tyson's blows. Later Tyson would remark, "I didn't want to hurt him, because I wouldn't want to get hurt myself." As Tyson's thoughts drifted from Frazier's condition to the fight itself, he remembered once again Joe Frazier's vitriolic comments and the predictions of his Albany detractors. His face darkened, and the look of anger and hatred returned. The arena was sheer bedlam now, brought on by the terrifying destruction of the world's 11th-best heavyweight boxer, and the young D'Amato protégé got caught up in the electricity of the moment. Sneering with disdain, he stared out at the cheering throng and almost spit the words at them. "I'm from Catskill, New York, and I'm the best fighter in the world."

The scene was reminiscent of a scene 26 years earlier when young Floyd Patterson, another D'Amato protégé, leaned against the top strand of ropes and yelled down into the press row, deriding the reporters who had been denouncing his boxing ability for 12 long months. In 1959, Patterson had been dethroned as heavyweight king during a seven-knockdown humiliation at the hands of Ingemar Johansson. The press, almost to a man, ridiculed Patterson in print, calling him a poor imitation of a fighter and a man who was totally unequipped to compete in the ring. Patterson read the stories and absorbed the hurt deep in his psyche. The anger grew little by little for a year until, by fight time, he was thirsting for Johansson's blood. He dominated the fight from start to finish, finally KO'ing the battered Swede with a thunderous left hook in the fifth round. The picture of the unconscious Johansson lying on the canvas, his eyes open and his feet twitching grotesquely as if with brain damage, remains indelibly imprinted on the minds of boxing fans everywhere. It was a frightening moment. Patterson said later, "I never want to go into a fight that mad again. It was not a good feeling."

Back in Glens Falls, Joe Frazier's strategy lay in a bloody heap in a neutral corner. This fight was a warning to all future Tyson opponents: do not get Tyson angry. It turns him into a wild animal. As he himself had said only weeks before, "There are a lot of things you can do to Mike Tyson, but you can't intimidate him." Sweating profusely at the post-fight interview, the youngster from Catskill, New York, was pleased and excited with his performance.

> I was calm. I was relaxed. I knew deep inside that I was gonna catch him early in the fight because of that little mistake he makes. When he first comes out, he comes straight down. He doesn't bend his knees.[5] As soon as he went against the ropes, I knew the fight was over. I saw his head comin' down and I said, "This is a perfect time to throw the uppercut." The left jab and him bendin' down set up the uppercut. It was such a precise punch I don't even know how hard it was. I didn't even feel the punch, it was so precise. I just said, "Boom" and that's all she wrote.

Marvis Frazier was still trying to clear the cobwebs from his head an hour after he was counted out. The last thing he remembered was backing into a neutral corner. "I wanted to see what Mike had. I guess I found out too late." When asked what he would do differently next time, Frazier sagely remarked, "I wouldn't get hit with that uppercut."[6] Mike Tyson's first test as a contender was an unqualified success. As Cus D'Amato once remarked, "When he hits them, they go down." Trainer Kevin Rooney updated D'Amato's comments by adding, "He's ready to fight anybody in the world."

The seamy side of boxing reared its ugly head outside the Civic Center late in the afternoon. A young Albany middleweight named Stephen Frost was seated on a bench outside the arena in obvious distress after having won his eight-round match earlier in the day. Frost had traveled to Glens Falls by himself and was left to fend for himself once the match ended. A spectator, noticing the troubled boy, sat down to offer assistance. Frost pulled away and stumbled to his feet. "Don't talk man, OK? Just be quiet for a minute." With that, he walked away, apparently nauseous. Approaching the side of the building, the young boy bent over and vomited. With each passing minute, Frost's condition deteriorated. He returned to the bench and lay down, sick and incoherent. Eventually the medical staff from the Civic Center was alerted to the situation, and they assisted Frost back to the First Aid room for an examination and treatment.

A brutal beating in the ring. The vanquished man slumped in a corner with a possible broken neck.

A victorious fighter wandering aimlessly outside the arena, ill, incoherent, and alone. This was the downside of boxing.

The upside of boxing could be seen in the Tyson camp. The Catskill phenom was now a premier drawing card in the division, in fact, in the entire sport of boxing. Offers poured in to Big Fights, Inc. from all sectors of the boxing world, and were carefully scrutinized by messieurs Cayton and Jacobs. Bob Arum wanted to arrange a match between Mike Tyson and Gerry Cooney, which he referred to as the "Fight of the Century," a $50 million extravaganza. The Larry Holmes camp expressed an interest in a contest between their man and Tyson that would determine "the real heavyweight champion of the world." Bob Gutkowski, President of Madison Square Garden Boxing, proposed the closed circuit event and offered Tyson $500,000 to meet the former titleholder. HBO Sports and Dynamic Duo Productions wooed the Tyson group to join the HBO Unification Series by challenging Trevor Berbick for the WBC heavyweight title in October. Cayton and Jacobs promised a decision by the end of August, following a scheduled match with Jose Ribalta in Atlantic City on August 17.

Mike Tyson took a brief holiday following the Frazier fight, but it was a working vacation. He spent a week away from the gym, but he did make a series of personal appearances in New York City before beginning his training. One morning, Mike did an anti-drug television commercial for the FBI. In the afternoon, he visited Shea Stadium for a publicity session with several members of the New York Mets. The photographer captured several light moments of Tyson clowning with Dwight Gooden and Darryl Strawberry. Tyson autographed several sets of boxing gloves during his visit, including one pair for third baseman Ray Knight, "From one slugger to another." Later in the week, Mike occupied a front row seat at Yankee Stadium, where he chatted with Dave Winfield and Rickey Henderson. His Yankees buddies presented him with six autographed bats for his trophy room.

The closer Mike Tyson got to the heavyweight championship, the more intense the pressure became, and the more demands were made on his time. His life was no longer just training and fighting. As his celebrity grew, more of his time had to be allocated to promotions, TV commercials, public appearances, and community relations. These commitments came at the expense of his training time. Solitude would be hard to come by for Mike Tyson for many months. Fortunately for the young boxer, Cus D'Amato had anticipated this eventuality several years before and had worked hard to prepare his young charge for this day. Mike recalled his friend and adopted father fondly.

> Cus and I, it was a very close and intense relationship. We always talked about bein' successful. Because he always knew I would get there. He would say, "There's always people telling you if you work hard, stay on a straight line, you'll be very successful. But there's never anyone tellin' you how to handle it. A lot of people tell you how to be a success, but after you get there, that's the hardest part." Sometimes when I used to get an attitude, he used to say, "So whatta ya gonna do when you become a big-time fighter, a champion, whatta ya gonna do, say the hell with me now." See, I learn these things now because a lotta things I didn't wanna listen to.

Mike Tyson was trying to prepare himself for stardom.

While Tyson's people weighed all the offers and pondered the various alternatives, trying to predict which strategy would have the best long-term financial benefits for their fighter, another young boxer was attempting to thrust himself back into the title chase. Tyrell Biggs' career had more ups and downs that the proverbial roller coaster, as he traveled the treacherous road from amateur sensation to professional contender. Along the way, the former Olympic gold medal winner achieved numerous victories, with almost as many of them occurring outside the ring as inside. As Biggs' amateur reputation grew, he gradually fell in with a bad crowd. Wild parties, fast girls, booze and drugs quickly followed, and before long Tyrell Biggs was hooked on cocaine. By the time he defeated Italian super heavyweight champion Francesco Damiani in the Olympic finals in Los Angeles, the Philadelphia boxer was free-basing the deadly white powder. His pro career ended suddenly after only one fight. Following his six-round victory over club fighter Mike Evans, Biggs wisely checked himself into the Care Unit Hospital in Orange, California, in an attempt to kick his chemical dependency habit, a decision that kept him inactive for four months. Once he returned to the ring, Biggs ran off a string of eight straight wins, but in the last one, a ten-round decision over Jeff Sims, he broke his collarbone in round two and, although he courageously hung on to corral a unanimous decision, the injury put him back on the shelf for another five months. In the fall of 1986, the big heavyweight made yet another comeback, his second in only two years of professional boxing. Tyrell was clean and healthy, and his sights were set on a title match before the end of 1987. His first step along the path to a championship ended impressively on August 14 as he knocked out Rod Smith in round six of a scheduled ten-rounder. The Tyson camp was talking about possible fights against Holmes, Spinks, Berbick, and Gerry Cooney, but they also kept a wary eye on the big man from the City of Brotherly Love. Tyrell Biggs was immensely talented and clever. And now he was also hungry.

After a week and a half of light duty, Mike Tyson was sent back to the musty old gymnasium on Main Street to sharpen his skills for the next challenge. Dion Burgess was on hand to hone Mike's ring reflexes, and this time he was joined by former Tyson opponent Irish Mike Jameson and a Hawaiian heavyweight named Enok. Mike Tyson's heart wasn't in training for the Ribalta fight, however. He was still decompressing from the spectacular win over the Frazier boys, Marvis and Joe. That was unfortunate, because 1500 miles away in Miami Beach, a sinewy 6'5", Cuban heavyweight named Jose Ribalta was working out feverishly in preparation for his big opportunity. The rangy Ribalta jogged five miles a day in the sands of sunny Florida, beginning his run in the early morning darkness, and finishing it as the sun was just breaking through the shimmering blue waters of the Atlantic Ocean. Midday found the dedicated boxer at the gaily decorated Boxing of the Americas Gym, where manager Lou de Cubas drove him unmercifully through his conditioning program. Both men were determined that "Nino" would be in the best condition of his life for this fight. If Ribalta lost to Tyson, it would not be for lack of training. It would be because Tyson was the better fighter.

As the final countdown to fight day began, Kevin Rooney was on the verge of a nervous breakdown. He couldn't seem to establish a regular training routine for his fighter. On Tuesday, August 12, a small group of locals positioned themselves on and around the small stage in the Cus D'Amato Gym to view Tyson's 12:30 sparring session. Jameson and Enok were well warmed up as they shadow boxed in the ring, awaiting the arrival of Tyson. As the minutes ticked off the clock, Lori Hoey, manager of Peloke's Motel, home base for Tyson's sparring partners, whispered to the author, "Sometimes he doesn't show up." Another spectator came to Tyson's defense. "He's a good kid." Finally, at 1:10 p.m. the telephone rang and Rooney grabbed the receiver like an expectant father. Within seconds, the trainer returned, and announced disgustedly to the audience, "Mike isn't gonna spar today. He's under the weather." Lori Hoey just smiled. "He has his moods. He never smiles in the gym unless someone does something stupid."

Mike Tyson was handling his meteoric rise to the top of the boxing world as well as could be expected. But he was, after all, only 20 years old and still a kid. Occasionally the constant pressure and demands on his time, 12 hours a day, seven days a week, got to him and he rebelled. But the rebellions were fleeting, and they had little effect on the performance of the boy who ate, slept, and breathed boxing 12 months a year. When he failed to spar again on Wednesday, Kevin Rooney was outwardly distressed. "The fight may be called off. Mike has an intestinal infection and he may not be better till Monday. We still have to go to Atlantic City and have Mike checked by the doctors. They might give him a medical discharge." On Friday, two days before the fight, Rooney, Tyson, and the corner men made the 200-mile trek to Atlantic City in their new customized van. Mike Tyson was still not fully recovered from the flu, but he passed the physical and the fight went on as scheduled. Jose Ribalta completed his training sessions on Friday and was pronounced ready to go. Ribalta, ranked number eight by the WBA, had been in with some of the top talent in the division. In spite of two tough losses in 1986, ten-round split decisions to both Bonecrusher Smith and Marvis Frazier, his record still stood at a strong 20–3–1. Although Mike Tyson's training schedule was severely limited, trainer Kevin Rooney was confident about the outcome of the battle. "Ribalta is an awkward fighter, but I don't think he'll last long against Mike. Michael will work his body until he sees an opening, then he'll knock Ribalta out."[7]

Sunday night, a capacity crowd filled the Trump Plaza Hotel and Casino to see if the New York youngster could add the clever Ribalta to his growing list of knockout victims. Most people were hoping for another Tyson massacre. At ringside, the HBO broadcasting team of Barry Tompkins, Larry Merchant, and "Sugar Ray" Leonard, decked out in formal black tuxedos, were busy preparing themselves for the main event. Outside the arena, a stiff breeze, coming in off the Atlantic Ocean, was an ominous harbinger of things to come. Hurricane Charlie was rushing violently up the North Carolina coast, leaving death and destruction in its wake. By morning, the storm would strike Atlantic City with all its fury, destroying property and threatening lives. The business community had been working hard all day to protect itself from the ravages of the deluge. Storefronts were boarded up and dykes were built around vulnerable areas to keep the water out.

Mike Tyson's appearance in the ring supported the contention that he had been ill during the preceding week. He came in at only 213½ pounds, four pounds below his normal fighting weight and his lightest weight as a professional. His features were gaunt and drawn. Still, he managed to get in a good warm-up session in the dressing room, as attested to by the heavy blanket of perspiration that covered his body. He entered the ring with his usual menacing sneer. Referee Rudy Battle, one of the few black referees in the sport, beckoned the fighters to center ring. During the introductions, the 6'6" Ribalta towered over the stocky Tyson, causing one wag to compare them to the comic strip characters, Mutt & Jeff. Another spectator marveled over the big height and reach advantage enjoyed by the Cuban heavyweight, whereby an annoyed Tyson backer retorted, "Don't give me height and reach. Give me a guy that can fight."

When the bell rang, Mike Tyson was prepared to show everyone that he could fight. He was in center ring in a flash, raining rights and lefts on his surprised opponent. Before the end of the round, a Tyson uppercut straightened Ribalta up like a tree. Still, Rooney was not happy with his charge's performance. Between rounds, he instructed the Catskill youngster, "Looks like you're a little lazy. Turn the intensity up, you unnerstan?" Tyson understood, coming out in round two still the aggressor. Both fighters threw punches with bad intentions. Ribalta's stiff left jabs annoyed the pressing Tyson who, nonetheless, forced his way to the inside to work the body. Midway through the round, Mike executed a perfect 8-2, a sharp right hook to the rib cage followed by a rapid-fire right uppercut that knocked Ribalta on the seat of his pants. Although the punch was devastating, Ribalta's expression was one of shock rather than one of pain. He had never before witnessed such hand speed from a heavyweight. He became more respectful of Tyson's power after the knockdown. There were still 55 seconds left in round two, but Jose Ribalta was still fresh and not ready to be taken. A heated exchange ensued as both fighters unloaded their Sunday punches. Tyson landed a hard left to the chin at the bell.

As the fight progressed, the lanky Cuban used a stiff jab to keep Tyson at arm's length, occasionally stopping to bang with the young New Yorker in short but torrid flurries. Whenever Tyson was able to work his way inside, Ribalta tied him up. The Catskill fighter appeared to get frustrated by these maneuvers and began head-hunting. He did fight with extreme intensity during the first three rounds, however, repeatedly scoring with tremendous body shots. The pace slowed noticeably during the middle rounds, causing an annoyed Rooney to chastise his fighter. "Michael, you're stinkin' up the joint. You're not throwin' combinations. You're only throwin' one punch at a time, and you're not throwin' them with bad intentions." Mike Tyson was obviously not fully recovered from his intestinal infection. His mind was willing, but his flesh was too weak to give an all-out effort for a full three minutes each round. In spite of the heated activity of the first five rounds, Tyson's body was barely wet, indicating that the young fighter had been dehydrated by his illness. In round six, a Ribalta jab bloodied Tyson's nose, the first time in his career that Mike had bled. In the seventh round, Tyson unloaded a big right hand to Ribalta's cheekbone with 33 seconds left, snapping the big guy's head back and spewing perspiration all over the front row spectators.

The crowd showed its appreciation for Ribalta's courageous effort by chanting, "Jose! Jose! Jose!" as round eight began. Mike Tyson was not impressed, and he answered the crowd's chants with a flurry of punches to Ribalta's body. A hard right hook found the Cuban's head with one minute gone, sending his mouthpiece out of the ring. Another right hook knocked a bridge out of Ribalta's mouth. The Catskill Assassin, sensing an opportunity to end the fight, calmly stalked his man. Another stiff right sent the big Cuban careening off the ropes. Again Tyson was on top of him, and again he hurt the Miami fighter, this time with a crunching right uppercut that turned Ribalta's legs to jelly. The big heavyweight was taking a lot of punishment now, and his only defense was to try to tie Tyson up whenever the New Yorker got within arm's reach, but that didn't happen nearly often enough. A long left hand crashed into Ribalta's head with 30 seconds left in the round, dropping him onto the lower strand of ropes in a neutral corner. Referee Rudy Battle gave the beleaguered Cuban a much-needed standing eight count.

Mike Tyson was back. He had overcome his earlier fatigue, and the adrenaline was flowing again. Unfortunately, his physical condition wouldn't allow the number two contender to sustain the pace indefinitely, and round nine was a lethargic affair. Tyson waited for his man in the middle of the ring as the round started. A big, looping left hand staggered Ribalta, who leaned against his adversary. Tyson had an opportunity to put his man away now, but he got overanxious and let the Cuban off the hook. In round ten, both fighters came out determined to destroy their opponent. They stood toe to toe in the center of the ring for several seconds, flailing away with both hands in a lively exchange. Tyson came back with a right from left field that caught Ribalta on the nose, dropping him on his back. The gallant Cuban, hurt but still defiant, struggled to his feet at the count of three and waited as Rudy Battle tolled the mandatory eight count. The referee stared at Ribalta's glassy eyes. "How ya doin'? Wanna continue?" "Yeh. Hell, yeh."

As soon as Battle bade the fight continue, the pride of Catskill pushed his big adversary to the ropes and unleashed five solid shots to the head. That was all Battle needed. He quickly stepped between the two fighters and ended the punishment at 1:34 of round ten. Tyson by a TKO. As Tyson paced back and forth in his corner trying to relax, he caught sight of Jim Jacobs and rolled his eyes in a sign of relief, whispering an almost inaudible "Whew" at the same time. It was not one of Tyson's greatest fights but, under the circumstances, with the debilitating effects of his illness and the resultant sparse training he had endured in preparation for the event, it was certainly an acceptable performance. At best, Ribalta won one round. As Tyson noted, "He was discouraged and he was desperate. He was scared. Every time he threw punches, his head stayed in the middle, and I wanted to take it off. But he took them, and he brought the best out of me."[8]

Mike Tyson's strategy committee was not long in announcing the Master of Disaster's plans. On Thursday, August 21, Big Fights, Inc., Dynamic Duo Productions, and HBO Sports called a press conference to make the long-awaited announcement. Mike Tyson would enter the HBO Unification Series immediately and would challenge Trevor Berbick for the WBC title in November. First, however, the Catskill boxer would honor his commitment to fight Alfonso Ratliff in Las Vegas on September 6, on the undercard of the Michael Spinks-Steffen Tangstad IBF championship match. At a glance, Alfonso Ratliff did not appear to belong in the same ring with Mike Tyson. Ratliff, the former WBC cruiserweight champion, was a talented boxer in his weight class, but the Catskill sensation was a talented fighter in the heavyweight division and outweighed the challenger by 20 pounds. Tyson's opponents usually attempted to bolster their own confidence by downplaying Mike Tyson's previous adversaries and, in some cases, his skills in the ring. Alfonso Ratliff of Chicago was no exception. At an early press conference, Ratliff, gaily bedecked in a dark suit with a pink open-necked sports shirt, remarked, "His opponents have all been fat little Pillsbury Doughboys, fat and flabby around the middle. Most of them looked like they would fall over without ever taking a punch."[9] Mike Tyson listened with amused interest as the native of the Windy City produced his own irritating breeze. Ratliff's tirades didn't impress the Las Vegas oddsmakers, however. Mike Tyson was installed as an overwhelming 28–1 favorite to win the fight. As a matter of fact, It was impossible to place a bet on the winner of the fight. The only bets that were being accepted were on whether or not Ratliff would last longer than five rounds.

On Thursday, September 4, another press conference was held, this one in the press room of the Hilton Hotel in Las Vegas, the site of the fight. Although the Tyson-Ratliff match was on the undercard of the Spinks-Tangstad fight, it was being treated by the media as the main event. Mike Tyson, the man who had brought excitement back to the heavyweight ranks, was the focus of attention around town. The conference room was jammed with newspaper and television reporters as "Iron Mike," his new media sobriquet, and "Windy City Al" faced off verbally for the last time. Ratliff, cool in a baseball cap, was still trying to talk himself into the match. "Tyson says he'll take me out in five. Well, I'll take him out in six. If he beats me, I'll quit boxin'. I'm not gonna stand toe-to-toe with him. When he's throwin' those wild punches, I'll be stickin' and movin'." Mike Tyson, the master of understatements, had only one comment to make. "If there's any knockdowns, I'll be the one makin' them." Michael Spinks, the IBF king, was well aware of Tyson's capabilities, and he was kinder to the kid from New York than Ratliff was. "He's dangerous, big, rugged, and awesome. He's another guy for me to be afraid of, to worry about." Michael Spinks knew that, somewhere down the road, he and Michael Tyson would square off in the ring, and he was not looking forward to it.[10]

Except for the boxing excitement in Las Vegas, Thursday, September 4, was a sad day for the sports world, a day when it mourned the passing of one of its most admired participants, baseball's Hank Greenberg. Greenberg, a star slugger for Detroit Tigers during the 1930s and 1940s, lost a courageous battle with cancer at the age of 75. As a player, "Hammerin' Hank" was one of the most feared batsmen of his time, along with Ruth, Gehrig, and Jimmie Foxx. His lifetime statistics included 331 home runs and a batting average of .313. The high point of his career occurred in 1938 when he made a run at Babe Ruth's single season home run mark of 60. Greenberg deposited 58 balls into the distant reaches of American League parks in the first 148 games, but failed to connect over the last seven games of the season. Still, Greenberg's record stood proudly as the fourth-highest total ever hit in one year, trailing only Roger Maris (61) and Babe Ruth (60 and 59), until the steroid era made a mockery of the feat.

Tyson's 20-pound weight advantage held up at the weigh-in as he tipped the scales at 221½ pounds to 201 pounds for the 30-year-old cruiserweight. Even though Ratliff had a record of 21–3 with 16 KO's, most of his victories were against cruiserweights. His occasional forays into the heavier weight class had ended in disaster, knockouts at the hands of Tim Witherspoon (seven rounds) and Pinklon Thomas (ten rounds). Mike Tyson hoped to improve on those performances, hence the five-round betting limitations. Saturday found young Tyson ready and waiting. Alfonso Ratliff, however, seemed to leave his bravado in the dressing room. Like so many of Tyson's opponents, Ratliff talked a good game but, when the chips were down, he wilted under the Tyson mystique. He was intimidated by Iron Mike's awesome record of mayhem and mutilation in the ring, and his pre-fight courage was replaced by fear as he slipped through the ring ropes to face his destiny.

Both fighters came out on the balls of their feet, dancing like ebony clones of Mikhail Baryshnikov. Tyson was the aggressor, as everyone expected him to be, and Alfonso Ratliff was the runner, constantly backing away and circling the ring to keep the young slugger at long range. Tyson advanced on his man, gloves held high against his cheekbones in the time-honored peek-a-boo style developed by Cus D'Amato, and used to maximum advantage by Floyd Patterson and Jose Torres. Tyson stalked his man but was unable to work his way inside or trap him on the ropes. At the 1:11 mark, Ratliff changed direction from counterclockwise to clockwise and was met immediately with a stinging right hand to the chin. The kid from Catskill tried to follow up his advantage, but the tall, lanky Ratliff tied him up. Two Tyson jabs held Ratliff immobilized on the ropes, and a left-right combination dropped the overmatched Chicago fighter to one knee. Referee Davey Pearl inexplicably called it a slip. Ratliff scrambled to his feet and got back on his bicycle, content just to survive the round. Announcer Barry Tompkins referred to Ratliff's behavior as resembling that of a startled fawn. The round ended without further action and Tyson returned to his corner in obvious disgust at his opponent's antics. If Mike had his choice, the two fighters would stand toe-to-toe in the center of the ring, banging away at each other until one of them dropped. Trainer Kevin Rooney implored his fighter to go back to the basics. "Work the body and cut the ring down, you unnerstan?' You got him scared. Now don't let him get brave. Punch in combinations and then cut it down. Cut it down the right way. Cut the angles down quick." Ratliff's corner was pleased with their fighter's imitation of Fred Astaire. "That's it. You're doin' good. Now, combinations and don't stay still. Move around and punch in combinations this time."

Ratliff disregarded his corner's instructions and moved in closer at the start of round two, intending to trade punches with Tyson more often. It was a big mistake. After about three seconds, Mike set his man up with a flicking left jab, then bobbed and weaved under a Ratliff right and countered with a short, chopping left to the side of Ratliff's head that sent the former cruiserweight champ sprawling over the bottom strand of ropes. Tyson watched in disbelief as Ratliff dragged himself to his feet at the count of nine, intent on continuing the battle. The kid from Catskill was on his injured prey like a buzzsaw, unleashing a fusillade of punches to Ratliff's body and head. The Chicago fighter was wobbly, but finally managed to tie his man up. As soon as the referee separated the two fighters, Tyson maneuvered his outgunned opponent back to the ropes again. A devastating right hook turned Ratliff's legs rubbery, and he sagged against the ropes. Another flurry of punches ended with a jolting left to the side of the head that dropped Ratliff to his hands and knees. The fight ended without a count as Davey Pearl waved an end to the slaughter at 1:41 of round two. A concerned Mike Tyson was one of the first people to approach his vanquished foe, putting both hands behind Ratliff's neck and whispering some words of consolation into his ear. The sneer disappeared from Tyson's face as soon as the fight ended, and the boy was a boy again, loose and jovial as Kevin Rooney cut the tape from his hands.

It was a good fight for Tyson, another valuable lesson in ring generalship. The young contender fought a tall, rangy boxer who tried to run, and he cornered the man and destroyed him. Before his career was over, a lot of fighters would try to run and hide on Mike Tyson, and it was imperative that he become proficient at cutting the ring down and trapping his man on the ropes. The Ratliff fight provided another learning experience for Tyson, and he showed continued progress in his trade. Watching the 20-year-old kid solve the Ratliff puzzle brought to mind, once again, the words of the immortal Joe Louis: "He can run but he can't hide." The kid from Catskill added a few words of his own. "Runnin' doesn't work at all, because they can't win the fight by runnin'. I keep the pressure on them, and the more they run, the more I throw punches, so I'm ahead either way."[11] Tyson donned earphones and joined "Sugar Ray" Leonard and Barry Tompkins at ringside before the Spinks fight. The Catskill sensation was very relaxed and at ease. The maturing process appeared to have reached completion as Mike learned how to handle his new-found celebrity with grace and patience.

The victory against Ratliff moved Mike Tyson into a title match with WBC champion Trevor Berbick. The fight, already booked, was scheduled for the Las Vegas Hilton on November 22. Michael Spinks was still alive and well in the HBO Unification Series thanks to a fourth-round knockout of the mechanically equipped Steffen Tangstad. Spinks had little trouble with the Norwegian heavyweight, picking his spots carefully and sending the European champion to the deck three times. After the last knockdown, Tangstad politely informed referee Richard Steele that he no longer wished to continue. Tangstad just wanted to take his money and go home. By virtue of his victory, Spinks received a bye until the final Unification fight tentatively scheduled for spring. Before the fight could become a reality, the winner of the Berbick-Tyson match would have to meet the Tubbs-Witherspoon WBA survivor to unify the WBC-WBA shares of the title.

At a Las Vegas press conference to present the upcoming Berbick-Tyson confrontation, champion Trevor Berbick was already having reservations about tangling with the young Adonis, and the fight was still 11 weeks away. "This guy is like a tank. This guy's a young, strong monster. I don't know if I want to be in the ring with him longer than 12 rounds."[12] Mike Tyson wasn't around to hear the tribute paid to him by the champ. The number one challenger had already departed Las Vegas for a well-earned three-week vacation. On October 1, Mike would resume training for the big fight. Until then, he would just relax, enjoy life, and do a little promotional work for Big Fights, Inc.

As Trevor Berbick vacillated and Mike Tyson relaxed, controversy raised its ugly head in the heavyweight Unification Series. The dispute was triggered by none other than Bob Arum, the controversial promoter who was left out in the cold in this series. Desperately trying to get a piece of the lucrative heavyweight action, Arum declared that Trevor Berbick was not committed to putting his WBC title on the line against Mike Tyson. According to the crafty Arum, Berbick's contract with Don King and HBO was a promotional contract only, and did not require a defense of his title against the Catskill strongboy. The wily one courted the Canadian titleholder for weeks, promising him $3 million to meet Gerry Cooney for the WBC crown in December. Berbick, obviously confused and flattered by all the attention, declared his November contract with Don King to be invalid and said he would sign to fight Cooney for Top Rank, Inc., Bob Arum's production company. It didn't take the HBO group long to respond to the attempted coup by Arum. Don King, Carl King, Butch Lewis, and the Hilton Hotel officials all attacked Arum publicly, insisting that Trevor Berbick was committed to defending his crown against Mike Tyson in November and would honor his contract.

Don King and the Hilton people vowed to take Berbick and Arum to court if necessary. The Hilton chain had reportedly spent over $10 million on the four-bout HBO Series and was ready to do battle to protect its interests. Don King was quoted as saying, "A rival promoter has stooped to an all-time low. Berbick has a contract and it is registered with the WBC and its president, Jose Sulaiman. Trevor has been given a $125,000 check expressly for Mike Tyson." Once the King boys, father and son, got to Berbick, he wilted under the combined pressure and agreed to honor his contract. A press conference, announcing the date, was quickly scheduled for the following day, September 9. Trevor Berbick capitulated publicly, to the relief of all parties associated with the tournament. After being threatened by Jose Sulaiman with having his title taken away, the Jamaican-born heavyweight returned to the fold, hat in hand. Don King helped to make Berbick's decision easier by sweetening the pot for the title fight, upping Berbick's end of the take from $1.6 million to $2.1 million.[13]

At the splashy New York City press conference, Don King, the John Barrymore of the squared ring, proudly pronounced "Judgement Day" to John Q. Public. And the hype was on. Nattily attired in a black tuxedo, hair in a straight-up electrified style that was his image, the effervescent promoter titillated the crowd of media people jammed into the ballroom of the Waldorf Astoria with the prediction that the Berbick-Tyson fight would be the fight of the decade. "Mike Tyson is the hottest thing in boxing in a long time," said Berbick's manager, Carl King. "He is knocking guys out left and right, and that's what the people want to see." Berbick, always one to verbalize a victory for himself, downplayed Tyson's talents. "I'm the best fighter in the world today. Tyson is a good fighter, but he's going to get a boxing lesson. Not only am I going to knock him out, but I'm going to give him a good whooping. If he comes at me like he's been going after all those other guys, it will end early. This is going to be a tuneup fight and nothing more." The soft-spoken Tyson was more modest. "This is the biggest opportunity of my life. I've been trainin' for eight years with this fight in mind. My managers feel I belong here. I feel I belong here."[14]

Once the hoopla had died down, Mike Tyson and Kevin Rooney could concentrate on the real business at hand, to get Iron Mike in the best condition of his short career, both physically and mentally. Mike Tyson had had 44 amateur fights and 27 professional fights. Now his life-long quest was down to a single fight, a battle for the championship of the world and an opportunity to make a prophet out of his late manager, Cus D'Amato. A victory over Berbick would fulfill D'Amato's prediction that Mike Tyson would become the youngest heavyweight champion in history. The Catskill youngster was determined not to let the opportunity slip away. He would dedicate this fight to his beloved mentor.

Out in Las Vegas, the Hilton people were hard at work preparing the physical facilities for the final three bouts in the Unification Series. The Berbick-Tyson fight would necessarily have to be fought indoors in the Hilton Pavilion, with its seating capacity increased to 9,000. By the time the WBC-WBA title fight was held, however, a new outdoor arena would be in general operation. The arena, being constructed in the parking lot of the hotel, would seat more than 15,000 spectators.

Tyson's preparations began with one thought in mind, winning the championship of the world. Becoming a world champion is like breaking the four-minute mile, achieving a perfect score of ten in Olympic gymnastics competition, or breaking Babe Ruth's single season home run record. On the surface, it appears to be impossible, but it isn't impossible. Athletes with adequate skill and superior dedication appear on the sports scene from time to time and achieve the impossible. They succeed where others fail because they believe in themselves and they believe in the quest. Tyson believed he would be the heavyweight champion of the world someday. He believed it with all his heart, and he was willing to work hard in order to prove it. He dedicated himself to one objective, to be the best. Cus D'Amato had instilled many valuable qualities in his young protégé. One of the most important was a positive attitude. Mike Tyson never thought in terms of losing. He firmly believed he could never lose. One day, a reporter asked him, "What if you lose?" Mike looked at the man incredulously and replied, "I can't relate to that. I never think in terms of losing. Besides, that's a negative question and I'm not a negative person. I don't see me losing."[15]

Outside the ring, Mike Tyson's life was good. He had money, friends, girlfriends, and a host of admirers. Although Mike still maintained his primary residence at Ewald House, he began to gravitate more and more toward Albany, where he had a host of buddies and where the after-dark activities were exciting. One of the first things Mike Tyson did after the Ratliff fight was to get an apartment on Clifton Avenue in Albany, near his friends and close to the action along Central Avenue. Mike was a local celebrity, and hangouts like Septembers, one of the city's more popular dating bars, attracted him like a moth to the flame. According to his Albany roommate and close friend, Rory Holloway, Tyson was also on the market to purchase a house in Loudonville, a suburb of the state capital. Mike enjoyed the night scene. He related well to the people and loved spending time with people his own age, people that he could swap stories with and exchange jokes with, people on the same emotional and chronological plane. Mike also loved the dancing opportunities and the camaraderie that pervaded the late-evening atmosphere along Central Avenue.

Saturday afternoon often found the Catskill sensation at the Crossgates Mall with his hometown cronies, hanging out and watching the girls. It was just like the old days. Hardly anything had changed outwardly in the last two years. Except for the heavy gold chains and diamond-studded gold bracelets, Mike Tyson was still the enthusiastic high school kid. As usual, the gang cruised the town in the early evening hours, visiting some of their old haunts at the Latham Circle Mall as well as at Crossgates. The routine might include a pizza at Papa

Gino's before catching a flick at Cinema 7. Then it was on to Septembers and an evening of light-hearted conversation and dancing.

As Tyson frolicked, the HBO Unification Series was heating up yet again. Word out of Philadelphia was that Butch Lewis was going to pull his man out of the series. Ostensibly, Lewis wanted to match Michael Spinks against Gerry Cooney in a super-spectacular that would generate more income than would a title match against a WBA-WBC champion. The rumor mill, however, indicated that the real reason Spinks was pulling out of the tournament was much more basic. Spinks wanted no part of Mike Tyson, and he was worried about being seriously hurt if a match with the Catskill man-child ever became a reality. Don King was livid at Lewis' remarks. HBO, having invested $20 million to televise the series, was upset, and the Las Vegas Hilton, contributor of $10 million to the kitty to host the four fights, threatened legal action. Just to confuse the issue even more, Bob Lee, the president of the International Boxing Federation, warned Spinks that if he didn't defend his title against the number one contender by January 15, the title would be declared vacant.

Amid all the heavyweight furor, life went on as usual in the rest of the boxing world. Tyson's stablemate, Edwin Rosario, challenged Livingstone Bramble, destroyer of "Boom Boom" Mancini in two epic lightweight encounters, to a title match in Miami Beach on the evening of Friday, September 20. Bramble, thought to be invincible in most quarters, was installed as a heavy 4–1 favorite in pre-fight betting. Apparently Rosario paid no attention to the odds. He carried the fight to the champion from the outset, winning the first round easily. As round two started, Rosario drove Bramble into the ropes with a hard right hand and buckled the champ's knees with a torrid left hook. Bramble, bleeding profusely from a cut over the right eye, tried to backpedal out of danger, but Rosario could smell the title and wasn't about to let his man escape. A final right hand dropped the champ to his knees. As the referee tolled the ten count, Bramble tried unsuccessfully to regain his feet. Edwin Rosario, a 4–1 underdog, was suddenly the new WBA lightweight champion, improving his record to 24–2 with his 20th knockout. The Jacobs-Cayton stable finally had its first titleholder since Wilfred Benitez and, hopefully, another would follow in less than two months.

As the first of October rolled around, it was goodbye to the Central Avenue strip and hello to the gym for Mike Tyson. The young challenger had eight weeks to work off the excesses of a three-week journey into dissipation and prepare himself to meet the champ, but at 20 years old, that wasn't a difficult task. Conditioning is relatively easy at that age. It is the 30-year-old boxers that have a problem working themselves into shape after an extended layoff. Trainer Kevin Rooney welcomed his fighter back to the training camp with open arms, telling the *Albany Times-Union,* "I'm not gonna ask him what he did on his time off. He needed a break from everybody. The three weeks off rejuvenated him. All I know is, he's alive and back in trainin'." The Cus D'Amato Gym was bustling with activity for the first time in three months as the Tyson quest resumed. The first week was restricted to light workouts of about an hour duration, to get Mike loosened up. As week two began, the training schedule became more rigorous, with a full slate of sparring sessions in addition to the usual gymnasium regimen. Mike's ring opponents, those men designated to get him in top condition to battle Trevor Berbick, were big Mike Jameson and Walter Santemore. Rooney was happy with the selection. "Jameson has been here before and he's a tough guy. We saw Santemore out in Vegas and he wants to work with us. He's been with Cooney and Holmes. From now on, we'll go from Monday to Saturday, and give him Sundays off. We're just tryin' to get him back in shape." Rooney might also have noted that Santemore, although his professional record was only a so-so 22–15, had been in the ring with some of the biggest names in the division, men like John Tate, Mitch Green, James Broad, James Tillis, Ernie Shavers, Frank Bruno, Tony Tucker, and Trevor Berbick, almost a who's-who of the top 20. Mike Tyson, with the glitter of Las Vegas and the constant media harassment waiting to transform him into a screaming schizophrenic as soon as he set foot on Nevada soil, tried to maintain his equilibrium. "I feel all right. I don't get too excited. It will hit me when I get out to Las Vegas. I'm not gonna let myself get bothered with all the hype. I'm just gonna concentrate on my home life and my trainin'."[16]

Controversy, confusion, and confrontation continued to be the order of the day for the Unification Series even as Mike Tyson squared off against Mike Jameson in the ring on the third floor of the Village Building in the tiny hamlet of Catskill in upstate New York. Butch Lewis continued his threats to pull Michael Spinks out of the HBO Series. Lewis, who was promoting the Series with Don King under the banner of Dynamic Duo Productions, called on the WBA to sever its ties with South Africa and to publicly denounce its policy of apartheid. "If the WBA doesn't respond, Spinks will not fight in the Series. I refuse to sell my soul for a dollar," screamed the histrionic Lewis, knowing full well that the WBA would not yield to his threats.[17]

After two weeks of training in Catskill, it became obvious to Kevin Rooney that a change of scenery was in order. Originally the Tyson group was scheduled to move its base of operations out to Las Vegas on October 28, but Rooney moved it up to the 19th in order to escape the hometown distractions. The crowd of locals that crammed into the tiny gym to watch their hero in action impeded Mike Tyson's progress and prevented Mike from achieving complete concentration, something that was critical to his success. In addition, the magnetism of the Albany scene and the attraction of one particular female friend resulted in several episodes where Mike was AWOL from camp completely. As a matter of fact, during the second week of October, Mike was away from the gym for six straight days. Rooney tried to gloss it over. "He looked so good workin' in the gym that I gave him a few days off. Then he got tied up in New York with business deals with the managers. They're workin' on a million dollar promotional deal with several large companies." That excuse didn't wash, however, and Mike Tyson packed his bags and headed west. According to the trainer, "We're ready. We're leavin' early to set up camp and get situated. We want to get out there and get used to the climate, plus get away from any distractions. We'll have five weeks to get ready and get him in shape." As Mike Tyson departed Catskill, he made the first prediction of his life. "I'm fightin' for the title. This is it. I'm ready. [He'll go] in the sixth." Kevin Rooney was even more confident. "We're goin' for an early knockout, maybe even the first round." Apparently the Las Vegas bookmakers agreed with Mike's and Kevin's assessments, installing the challenger as an early 4–1 favorite to dethrone the Canadian champion.[18]

Mike was lodged in a private residence a couple of miles outside of town to give him the maximum amount of privacy. The house, owned by Dr. Bruce Handelman, a friend of Jim Jacobs, was put at his disposal for as long as he remained in the area. Training camp was set up at Johnny Tocco's Gym, about a mile from the house, and the doors were barred to keep the public out. Even the press was excluded from witnessing the workouts. Tyson and Berbick both trained at Johnny Tocco's, with Mike using the gym at 12:30 p.m. daily and Berbick's entourage arriving at 4:30. Both camps insisted on the utmost secrecy, so all the windows were covered and iron bars secured the doors. Two new sparring partners were added to the Tyson training camp in Las Vegas, Mike's old friend and top ten contender,

James Broad, and young, up-and-coming heavyweight sensation Mike Williams. There were even rumors that the hard-punching Williams had put Mike Tyson on the seat of his pants during one workout, but trainer Kevin Rooney discounted that story as being a figment of someone's imagination.

Although the Tyson camp maintained a Spartan atmosphere in Las Vegas, Mike's newfound celebrity status still required his meeting certain commitments to enhance his public image and promote the fight. In early November, for instance, Mike appeared on the *Joan Rivers Show* in L.A. for a few minutes of verbal jousting with the syndicated talk show hostess. Strangely enough, Mike got no worse than a draw with the sharp-witted Rivers. During one exchange, the blonde comedienne asked Mike why he wore so much gold jewelry. Without blinking an eye, the young fighter, who was weighted down with a heavy gold necklace and an enormous gold and diamond-studded bracelet, deftly replied, "I'm a Catholic." Later, in answer to a question about his out-of-the-ring hobbies, Mike gave them as "ice cream and women in that order."[19]

While in L.A., Mike also attended a press conference at the Beverly Hilton Hotel to promote the upcoming fight. A 5–1 favorite, the challenger exuded confidence when he stated, "I'm a man and I'm ready to fight for the man's crown." Trevor Berbick, the 32-year-old champion from Jamaica, had his own ideas about the outcome of the fight. "No question it's going to be a knockout, and I'll be standing at the end." Poor Berbick was rapidly getting himself into a macho state of mind, a condition that would prove his undoing on "Judgement Day." The proud champion was talking tough in order to psyche out his young opponent, but the more he talked, the more he believed his own rhetoric. As the days passed, Berbick became determined to prove his manhood in the ring by standing toe-to-toe with the 20-year-old slugger and exchanging full firepower with him. Trevor Berbick intended to show the world that he could take anything that Mike Tyson could throw, and then go on the offensive himself and bring the kid from Catskill to his knees. That was Berbick's plan. It was a bad plan.

As soon as the Los Angeles schedule was complete, Mike and Kevin Rooney flew back to Las Vegas to resume workouts. Mike rose bright and early his first day back in the desert and stepped out into the Vegas darkness for his usual five-mile run through the outskirts of town. It was 5 a.m. and Mike had the streets to himself. After a leisurely morning agenda and a light lunch, Tyson and Rooney drove to Johnny Tocco's Gym for the day's training session. The focal points of the workouts were the ring wars, two rounds each with Jameson, Santemore, Broad, and Williams. As Rooney reminded everyone, Mike Tyson's sparring sessions were not run-of-the-mill workouts. They were real matches with no holds barred. "I always make it a point to say [to the sparring partners], 'I want you to go out there and do the best you can. I don't want you to go out there and hold back. My man is here to fight. My man is gonna go hard.'" Tyson nodded in agreement. "I train like a fight. If someone comes to spar with me and they're not serious, I think they're makin' a very foolish mistake. I think the best profit from it is when you have a sparrin' partner in there that's not intimidated, that's throwin' punches and tryin' his best to get the edge and win, like in a fight, tryin' to knock you out."[20]

Most of Mike Tyson's sparring partners didn't fare too well in their wars with the young gladiator. A point of proof was the fact that Mike had gone through 24 spar mates in the past 17 months. Rooney smiled when reminded of that statistic. "I've had guys walk right out. They say 'This isn't for me,' and they go, or they don't come back, ya know. They say they'll call, but they never do. Bein' a sparrin' partner for Mike Tyson is not an easy job. The punishment is brutal, but it does have some benefits. The hours are good. You get to travel and see new places. And the pay is good, $600 a week." While Mike Tyson concentrated on the task at hand in Las Vegas, back home in Catskill, New York, new billboards were being proposed for the tiny hamlet. The billboards, to be strategically located on all major highways leading toward town, would advertise the region's latest product, Mike Tyson. The preliminary artwork showed the good-looking boxer in a contemplative mood, accompanied by the enticing statement, "Welcome to Catskill, home of Mike Tyson, WBC champion." The Catskill Village Board of Trustees enthusiastically approved the construction of the billboards in hopes of promoting tourism in the area.[21]

As the days passed, the verbal quotes from the two camps predicted dire consequences for the other guy. Berbick, sporting an impressive 31–4–1 record with 23 knockouts, continued to feed his ego with boasts about his future accomplishment. "I love breaking those bubbles that have never been busted. I'm going to give him a good whipping, then knock him out. I'm going to take him to school. All these years I've been chasing guys around the ring; Greg Page, Pinklon Thomas. Now here's a guy who comes at me, and I love it. He hits just hard enough to make me mad." Mike Tyson listened to Berbick's comments and he smiled with approval. "He's a very tough, determined fighter, but he's not gonna take my punches for twelve rounds. He says he'll be right there, and that's fine with me. He won't be there for long, though."[22] Most of the hype for the fight centered around Mike Tyson's attempt to become the youngest heavyweight boxing champion in history. Floyd Patterson was the current record holder, having defeated Archie Moore for the title when he was exactly 21 years and 300 days old. If Mike Tyson were to unseat the WBC champion, he would only be 20 years and 145 days old, and would surpass Patterson's record by more than 17 months, or 520 days.

As training wound down, the atmosphere around the Tyson camp seemed much more relaxed than usual. For most fights during his professional career, Mike's training regimen lasted approximately three weeks, the average time between matches, and it was an intense three-week preparation for his next opponent. Now there was an 11-week hiatus between the Ratliff fight and the title encounter with Trevor Berbick. As a result of this extended interlude, the preparation could be developed more slowly and more systematically over a longer period of time, without the frenetic, helter-skelter activity that surrounded his previous non-stop schedule. Even so, everyone in camp knew that the pressure would begin to mount about 30 days prior to the fight, and by fight time it would be suffocating.

On Friday, November 21, the day before "Judgement Day," both Tyson and Berbick made their way to the Las Vegas Hilton around midday for the ritualistic 1 p.m. weigh-in and final press conference. The weigh-in was held in one of the hotel meeting rooms, complete with stage. The official scale, the fighters, their assistants, the promoters, and state and local boxing officials assembled on the stage, with several hundred media representatives vying for the choice positions near the front of the stage. A huge Lite Beer sign provided a somewhat incongruous backdrop to the proceedings. Mike Tyson, as challenger, was first to step on the scales. Clad only in blue briefs, the confident New Yorker weighed in at 221¼ pounds, the heaviest of his career. Trevor Berbick was next, and the WBC heavyweight king stood proudly before the press gathering and held the championship belt over his head for all to see and admire. Dozens of cameras flashed as the photographic contingent scurried for pictures for the evening editions of the nation's newspapers. The champion tipped the scales at a svelte 218 pounds. There was no doubt that Trevor Berbick was taking the challenger seriously. This would be Berbick's third title fight and his first defense of the crown. On April 11, 1982, Berbick became the first fighter to take Larry Holmes 15 rounds, although he lost the decision. Then, on March 22, 1986, the 6–1 underdog won the WBC title by taking a unanimous 12-round decision from Pinklon Thomas. This time, Trevor Berbick would enter the ring as the champion, but would still be a heavy underdog.

Over the years, Trevor Berbick had become an enigma in the boxing world. A member of the 1976 Jamaican Olympic boxing team, Berbick lost in the second round to Romanian Mercea Simon. After turning pro and moving his residence to Canada, the big heavyweight battled his way into the top ten rankings with impressive victories over such renowned boxers as Greg Page, Muhammad Ali (finally forcing the Great One into retirement), John Tate, and Thomas. He also carried the aforementioned title fight to Larry Holmes for 15 rounds. Yet, along the way, he suffered mysterious losses to the likes of Bernardo Mercado, Renaldo Snipes, and cruiserweight S. T. Gordon. Characteristically, Berbick was always ready to explain away his losses with such diverse excuses as managerial problems, illness, and having been drugged before the fight. Excuses would do Trevor Berbick no good this time. In one more day, he and Mike Tyson would go to war to determine who was king of the hill. One of them would remain standing at the end. The other would be counted out. As the weigh-in broke up, a reporter noted that Mike Tyson didn't appear to be in the least bit nervous. Mike shrugged and remarked, "I always have butterflies. But as far as being intimidated, no one intimidates me." Another reporter yelled out to the young challenger, "Mike, anything to say?" This brought a thumbs-down gesture from the Catskill kid and the prediction, "Knockout."

After lunch, the final press conference got underway with the same cast of media characters on hand to record the historic event. Champion Trevor Berbick arrived, nattily attired in white from head to foot—shirt, tie, suit and shoes—projected the good guy image top to bottom. It was reminiscent of another champion who, 71 years earlier, appeared at a prefight press conference decked out all in white. On that occasion, Jack Johnson went on to lose his title to the "Potawatomie Giant," Jess Willard, in a 26-round KO under a brutal Havana sun. Mike Tyson showed up for the press conference much more casual, dressed in a white warm-up suit trimmed in black and red. The 6'2" Berbick left no doubts as to his intentions during the fight. "I'm going to knock him out in the seventh round, but first I'm gonna put a whippin' on him." The challenger was more succinct, but just as determined. "This is the third press conference we've had. I can't answer any more questions. The time for talkin' is over. Now it's time to fight." Before the press conference ended, Berbick played one more mind game on the Catskill neophyte in an attempt to rattle the youngster and throw him off his fight plan. As the champion, Berbick had the first choice of colors for his boxing trunks. Knowing that Tyson always wore black trunks and shoes in his fights, the wily titleholder surprised the audience when he announced, "I'm the judge. It's Judgement Day and I'm the judge. My robe is black, my trunks are black. I'm the judge." "It doesn't matter. We're not changing. We'll wear black too," Rooney stated, ignoring the automatic $5,000 fine for wearing the same colors. After all, a $5,000 fine was pin money for a guy who stood to reap a $2.1 million reward from the big event.[23]

Tick. Tock. Tick. Tock. The hands of the clock moved inexorably ahead. Then—it was Judgement Day, November 22, 1986. The hype was over, the verbalizing had ceased. The training camps stood dark and silent. All the remained now was the main event. Mike Tyson slept late. The sun filtering through the shaded window finally rousted him out of bed on this fateful day. He dawdled over a light breakfast, read a couple of boxing magazines, watched TV, and generally wasted away the morning in indolence. It would be a long day for champion and challenger alike. Tyson was visited by a constant stream of well-wishers during the day, including former D'Amato world champions Floyd Patterson and Jose Torres. Patterson predicted that Mike Tyson would break his record and become the youngest heavyweight champion in history. "That's what Cus wanted," said Patterson. "I hope for Cus's sake that Mike wins." Apparently Mike Tyson was ready. As he told Patterson, "I have been preparing for this day since I was 12 years old. I always wanted to be a world champion. This is a man's crown, and I'm gonna wear it."

Tick. Tock. Tick. Tock. The hands of the clock inched closer to showdown time. As evening approached, the impatient challenger ate a hearty dinner, a high-protein meal designed to give him the strength and stamina to go 12 tough rounds if necessary. About 7 p.m. Tyson, Rooney, cut man Matt Baranski, and assistant manager Steve Lott set out for the "Strip," that neon glitter dome that was Las Vegas, for the Hilton and for destiny. Fight time was scheduled for approximately 10:30 p.m. Eastern Standard Time. HBO would begin its television coverage at precisely 10 o'clock with personal profiles of both fighters, then a preview of the match. Tyson's dressing room for the big event was a portable trailer that had been set up in the Hilton parking lot next to the Convention Center. The evening was cool, the sky starry. The atmosphere was charged with electricity. A sellout crowd of 8,500 excited fans packed the Hilton Center to view history in the making. It was a strange scene, this title fight, almost eerie in some respects. Trevor Berbick was the champion, but it was Mike Tyson whose name was on everybody's lips. The fight was "The Mike Tyson fight." It was Mike Tyson this, Mike Tyson that. The kid from Brownsville was already considered to be the new savior of boxing.

The heavyweight division at the time was in chaos, with three relatively uninspiring fighters reigning as the IBF, WBA, and WBC champions. Suddenly, a young, refreshing teenager appeared on the scene, a man-boy who carried dynamite in either hand. As he stepped over one victim after another, en route to a string of 19 consecutive and sometimes electrifying knockouts, he brought excitement back to the heavyweight division. Here was someone who could unify the title. Here was a fighter cut from the same mold as Jack Dempsey and Rocky Marciano. Here was a destroyer of men, a true champion who would dominate the world of boxing for a decade or more. The air tingled with expectation. As one wag announced, "This is more than a title fight. This is a coronation."

As fight time drew near, Mike began his usual warm-up routine in the trailer, shadow boxing to the strains of Sam Cooke coming from his tape system. Flailing away at an unseen opponent, the kid from Catskill bobbed and weaved, jabbed and flurried, until the perspiration ran down his sleek brown body in steady rivulets. The stillness of the night was broken by a knock on the door. A voice yelled through the steel wall, "OK, this is it. You're on." Suddenly the trailer exploded in a cacophony of noise as half a dozen managers, trainers, and handlers all began speaking at once. Someone noted that the desert air was cool at this time of day in Las Vegas, and that Mike might get chilled if crossed the parking lot to the Hilton Center uncovered. Mike was well loosened up by now, and the last thing he wanted was for his muscles to tighten up on the way to the ring. Fortunately a quick solution was found. One of the trainers grabbed a large white towel from the bathroom and cut a circular hole in the center of it, just big enough for Mike's head to fit through. Wearing his homemade poncho, the young challenger prepared to meet his destiny. As he stepped from the trailer, a reporter asked, "When do you put on your game face?" Mike almost spat out the reply. A sneer crossed his face as he said, "This is no game." Mike was already preparing himself mentally for the task ahead. From now until the end of the fight, Mike's mind would be on only one thing, defeating Trevor Berbick and capturing the WBC title. And that was serious business.

The walk to the hotel was short and silent. Then they were inside. The Hilton Center burst into thunderous applause as the ecstatic crowd caught sight of the young 20-year-old sensation. Kevin Rooney led the entourage down the aisle, followed by Tyson, Matt Baranski, and Steve Lott. Except for the bath towel that covered his shoulders, Mike presented a threatening image, black trunks and high black shoes covering his dark, menacing body, the whole set off by a sinister sneer that prophesied doom. It was a visage that had sent chills up the spines of numerous opponents over the previous 20 months, a visage that won a dozen or more fights for the Catskill assassin before the first bell had rung. It was now 76 days since Mike Tyson's last fight, and he was anxious to get back into action again. Mike slipped calmly through the ropes and surveyed the crowd, the sneer becoming even meaner and more ominous than before. Trainer Kevin Rooney, on the other hand, looked like the cat that ate the canary. A smile played around the corners of his mouth. He looked like a man who knew something that no one else knew.

HBO was on the air, profiling the powerfully destructive challenger. Its cameras scanned the audience to locate and identify the many celebrities in attendance. It was a gala evening in Las Vegas, an "event," and as such it was attended by dozens of famous people, most of them lavishly dressed in fancy tuxedos and extravagant evening gowns. The boxing world was well represented by WBC lightweight champion Hector "Macho" Camacho, IBF heavyweight king Michael Spinks, and former champions Larry Holmes, Muhammad Ali, Thomas Hearns, and the old "Mongoose" himself, the legendary Archie Moore. Also in attendance were celebrities from the arts, the sciences, and the business world. Even the silver screen lent many of its superstars to the gala event, mammoth talents like Kirk Douglas, Sylvester Stallone, and Jack Nicholson. All were here for one primary reason, to see the next legend of sport win his first title.

The hands of the clock approached the witching hour. The crowd waited expectantly. The challenger paced the ring nervously. It was time for the main event. The heavyweight boxing champion of the world entered the arena looking very much like the executioner on Judgement Day. He was clothed entirely in black from head to foot. He wore black shoes, black socks, and a black silk robe. His face was hidden from view behind a large black hood. The only hint of opulence in the otherwise somber scene was the jewel-studded WBC championship belt that circled the champion's waist. His procession to the ring was much more subdued than that of the charismatic challenger. The 8,500 people in attendance greeted him with polite applause. Trevor Berbick was a pleasant champion of average talent. He was neither liked nor disliked by the boxing world. In general, the average fan was apathetic toward the gentle giant. As the champion approached the ring, he caught sight of his adversary walking back and forth around the ring like a caged animal, his face a study of impending doom. The bravado that the champion had slowly built up in the weeks preceding the fight began to ooze from his body almost as soon as he caught sight of the menacing challenger. He suddenly became apprehensive about the outcome of the match, but he was still determined to take the fight to the man-child. It had become a macho cause for the Canadian champion, and he had to prove his manhood in mortal combat.

Tyson continued to pace nervously during the introductions, but as referee Mills Lane brought the two men together for their final instructions, the nervousness was gradually replaced by quiet resolve. The voice of his mentor played on his mind. "If you do what I tell you, you can be the champion of the world." Tonight Cus would be in his corner once again. Tonight they would be together one last time, the old man and the boy. This was the culmination of their quest, the top of Everest. One final time the venerable trainer would counsel his charge between rounds, assessing the fight, setting the strategy. He would instruct, and the young challenger would listen. He would direct, and the young fighter would carry out his orders. Together they would scale the mountain. Together they would claim the coveted championship belt.

The bell sounded for round one and the fight was on. Tyson came out winging, meeting the champion in the center of the ring with a flurry of lefts and rights. Berbick stood toe-to-toe with the challenger, attempting to overpower the younger fighter. That strategy turned out to be the mistake of the fight. One minute into the round, Berbick responded to a Tyson barrage with a flurry of his own, landing a solid right hook to the side of Tyson's head in the process. The kid from Catskill walked right through it as if it had never happened. Mike Tyson was like a man on a mission, always moving forward, his face frozen in that frightful sneer, his eyes riveted on the center of Berbick's chest, looking for the slightest sign of an opening. The New Yorker used his stiff left jab to great advantage, keeping Berbick at arm's length, then connecting with a right and left to Berbick's face. A hard right hurt the champion at the 1:15 mark, but the big Jamaican kept boring in. There was very seldom more than a foot or two separating the fighters during the round. Often they battled head to head. Tyson connected with two more shots and Berbick beckoned him to keep coming, a show of bravado as if to say "you didn't hurt me." A left hook, then another right and left found their targets on unprotected areas of Berbick's body. After about 20 seconds of close in-fighting, the referee separated the two men. The determined challenger came back quickly with two rights that hurt the champion. A following left hook sent the big man reeling backwards into a corner. Tyson was on top of him with 18 seconds left in the round and dazed him with a right uppercut and still another left cross. A right cross found its mark before the beleaguered titleholder could tie his man up.

The crowd was on its feet screaming at the bell. Berbick tried to stick his tongue out at his adolescent antagonist as he wobbled back to his corner, but he couldn't get it past his mouthpiece. The futility of the attempt mirrored the futility of Berbick's strategy in round one. Angelo Dundee was frantic in the champion's corner. He was distraught over Berbick's performance, and he let his man know it in no uncertain terms, screaming into his ear, "You're fighting like a damn dummy." Across the ring, Kevin Rooney offered encouragement to his fighter. "You're doin' great. Stay calm."[24]

The challenger came out fast in round two, hands held high against his cheekbones in Cus D'Amato's famous "peek-a-boo" style. A wide, looping right hand to the head stunned the confused champion. The challenger quickly followed up with two big left hooks followed by a hard right that lifted Berbick off his feet and dropped him on his back. Eight thousand, five hundred shocked fans leaped from their seats, anticipating the end. The arena was complete bedlam now, but the 32-year-old champion was not yet ready to throw in the towel. He was up immediately, hurt but also embarrassed by his inability to slow down the Catskill brawler. Trevor Berbick was breathing heavily, obviously agitated by the humiliating turn of events. He could see his title slipping away, slowly but surely, and he didn't know how to prevent it. Tyson continued the assault, pummeling Berbick in center ring. The fight became all Tyson now. Berbick retreated, trying only to survive the round, to give himself time to regroup. His macho plan of overpowering the youngster from upstate New York had long since disappeared in a fusillade of punches from the 20-year-old challenger. It appeared to be only a matter of time now before Tyson would lift the crown from the head of the battered champion.

Only one minute had expired in round two and, as far as Trevor Berbick was concerned, a lifetime remained before he could retreat to the safety of his corner stool. The challenger relentlessly pursued his man for the next minute, punching selectively as openings occurred. Berbick backpedaled and spent most of his time covering up. There was no offense now in the champ's repertoire, only self-preservation. At the 2:13 mark, Mike Tyson landed a savage right to the kidney and barely missed with a following uppercut. He backed away momentarily, then stepped up and caught Berbick with a short left hook to the temple. The punch traveled less than 12 inches but it completely incapacitated the valiant champion. Berbick hung motionless for a split-second, then slumped backwards to the canvas. Courageously he tried to right himself. He struggled to all fours but, as he attempted to stand, his legs refused to support his huge torso and he toppled sideways into the bottom strand of ropes. Still, his champion's heart pushed him onward, and once again he fought to pull himself upright. Again his limbs failed to respond, and he stumbled completely across the ring, finally collapsing in the corner. It was an eerie and terrifying sight. He thrashed about on the floor like a fish out of water, his equilibrium completely destroyed. Already there was concern at ringside that Trevor Berbick might be seriously injured. Finally achieving a vertical position on the third attempt, the game Canadian turned to face his tormentor, but it was obvious that he was in no condition to continue the fight. Mills Lane stepped in and wrapped his arms around the champion just as he was about to collapse again.

Mike Tyson had done it. He had taken the WBC title in a most convincing manner, thereby becoming the youngest man ever to wear the crown. At 20 years, four months, and 22 days, he had eclipsed the old record of Floyd Patterson by more than a year and a half. Tyson's first thoughts, naturally, were of Trevor Berbick. He pushed his way across the ring to put his arm around his vanquished foe, to ascertain his physical condition, and to console him in defeat. The ring was pandemonium. The defeated champion sat stunned in his corner, still unable to comprehend what had happened. Jim Jacobs jumped into the ring and was met with a kiss on the lips from the jubilant new titleholder. Kevin Rooney was ecstatic.

The post-fight interview with Larry Merchant revealed the immense confidence the young challenger had in his abilities.

Q. How does it feel to be wearing this belt?

A. It's a moment I've waited for all my life. Berbick was strong, very strong. But I was calm. I was timing my punches, and I threw every punch with bad intentions in a vital area.

Q. How were you prepared for this fight?

A. I anticipated a knockout because I had so much confidence, so much belief in myself. My trainer, Kevin Rooney, and I sacrificed so much, we couldn't fail. My plan was to stick my jab in his face, and every punch I threw with bad intentions. Now I'm the youngest champion in the history of the sport. My record will never be broken.

Q. Did he hit you with anything?

A. He hit me with a few glancing punches, but even if he connected, I refused to get knocked down.

I refused to lose. There was no way I was gonna go outta this ring walkin'. I woulda hadda been carried out. There was no way I was gonna leave this ring alive.

Q. He looked like he was just trying to survive as early as the second round.

A. I don't know about that. If that was so, that was his problem. I come to destroy and win the heavyweight championship of the world, which I done. I want to dedicate my fight to my great guardian, Cus D'Amato. I'm sure he's up there, and he's lookin', and he's talkin' to all the great fighters, and sayin' his boy did it. Now I want to unify the title.

Q. When Cus first saw you at 13 years old, he said, "Stay with me and you can be the heavyweight champion of the world." And you said, "How do you know that?"

A. That's not what I said. I said, "He's a crazy, ole white dude. But he was a genius. Everything he said, happened. Isn't that true? Everything he said, happened."

Mike closed the interview by vowing to be a fighting champion. "I want to fight the Witherspoon-Tubbs winner. I'll fight any man alive. I can beat any man in the world. And I'll take on all comers."

Trevor Berbick, still unsure of himself, graciously consented to give his thoughts on the fight. "I still can't believe I got caught and fought the wrong fight. I was trying to prove to myself that I could take his best shot, and I got caught. I still can't believe it. He hits hard. I don't know if I saw the knockdown punch or not. His punches came from all directions." And so it was. Tyson's punches came from all directions, and they brought him the championship of the world. As the arena emptied and the silence returned once again to the Hilton Center, the new champion's words still echoed softly through the immense nothingness. "I come to destroy and win the heavyweight championship of the world. Now I'll take on all comers. I can lick any man in the world."[25]

10

The Unification and Beyond—1987

Early Sunday morning, before the sun came up, Mike Tyson awoke as usual. But this time he didn't have to force himself out of bed to jog five miles through the Las Vegas darkness. This morning was different. As he lay there, slowly stretching his muscles, the events of the previous night flashed through his mind like a kaleidoscopic fairy tale. He suddenly realized he was not just Mike Tyson anymore. Now he was the heavyweight champion of the world, the larger-than-life hero he always dreamed about being. It was an exhilarating feeling, a feeling to be inhaled and enjoyed. Little did Mike know that there was more to being a champion than just the money and the glory. There was celebrity to contend with, and there were the myriad of professional responsibilities that go hand in hand with the championship.

Mike Tyson had been trained for stardom since he was 13 years old by his astute mentor, Cus D'Amato. But no one can be completely prepared for the sudden and suffocating avalanche of personal commitments, business proposals, and other intrusions on one's time that accompanies fame. The young New Yorker's private life was over, and in its place was a tight schedule of interviews, photo sessions, promotions, and civic responsibilities orchestrated by the duo of Jacobs and Cayton. The champ was, at first, amused by all the attention, but soon became annoyed when he realized he couldn't even walk down the sidewalk in a major city without being accosted by crowds of hero worshippers, well wishers and autograph seekers. Over the next year, the hectic pace and associated mental stress in Mike Tyson's life would, at times, reach unbearable proportions, particularly in the weeks leading up to a title fight. So much so, in fact, that the strain on his nervous system would cause a small patch of hair to fall out near the front of his scalp. The bald spot would become most prominent on fight night and would fill in somewhat between fights, but it would be a full year before Mike Tyson would feel comfortable enough in his new position to relax and accept his celebrity status.

The new heavyweight king spent the better part of Sunday morning walking around the Las Vegas Hilton with his WBC championship belt strapped around his midsection, accepting congratulations from many of the hotel's 4,000 guests. Back home in Catskill, his fellow "townies" were still reliving his stunning victory over Trevor Berbick. There was even talk of a big parade down Main Street the day after Thanksgiving. But Mike Tyson was too emotionally and physically drained to be guest of honor in a parade, and his managers begged off. In fact, they cancelled all his personal appearances for two weeks to give the new champ time to rejuvenate himself. Tyson was off first thing Monday morning, jetting to the coast for two glorious weeks of fun and sun, alone and away from the drudgery of training camp. He partied and cavorted with a gallery of Hollywood luminaries including beautiful Lisa Bonet, one of the stars of the Bill Cosby television show.

Still, the young champ could not escape from his responsibilities, even for two weeks. In rapid succession, he appeared on the *David Letterman Late Night* television show and the *Joan Rivers Show*. To Letterman, he confessed the sacrifices that a professional boxer has to make in order to be champion. "I would like to date women, but I can't give them the attention they deserve. Except Lisa Bonet. I'd make time to give her attention." He parried successfully with the irreverent Joan Rivers, queen of night-time comedy. When she reminded the boyish Tyson that kids looked up to the heavyweight champion, Mike replied in his soft, high-pitched voice, "I love kids. That's the best part, having kids around. That makes everything worthwhile." And to her statement that, as a kid, he was a delinquent, Mike just smiled, "But I was a sweet delinquent." As a celebrity, Mike Tyson's comments now carried considerable weight. Children listened to what the heavyweight champion of the world had to say, and they followed his example. Even adults paid more attention to his advice now that he was famous. Tyson expounded further on his responsibilities to the youth of the nation during an HBO interview. "When you're the champion, you can't use foul language. You can't drink in public. Can't smoke. Can't do any of those things around kids. It shouldn't be tolerated."

As the WBC champion drifted through December in unsupervised indolence, basking in the Southern California sun, his next opponent was being selected in far-away New York City. Originally, the WBA had scheduled a title fight between the champion, Tim Witherspoon, and the former champion, Tony Tubbs, for December 12, 1986, in Madison Square Garden. Four days before the big event was to take place, however, Tony Tubbs withdrew with an apparent injury. Fortunately, the dangerous James "Bonecrusher" Smith was in training for an upcoming fight against Mitch Green, and he gladly seized the opportunity to replace Tubbs and challenge for the title. It was the chance of a lifetime for the number eight contender. On December 12, "Bonecrusher" stepped into the ring to meet the man who had dealt him a brutal beating only ten months before. Determined to do the first damage this time, Smith attacked the champion from the outset. Stunningly, he dropped the lethargic Witherspoon three times in the first round, taking the title and winning the dubious distinction of squaring off against Mike Tyson in a WBA-WBC unification match in early 1987.

The politics of boxing once again raised its ugly head immediately after the Smith-Witherspoon fight and, for a brief time, threatened to destroy the WBA-WBC unification fight between Smith and Tyson. WBA chairman Alberto Aleman insisted that Smith defend his title against the WBA's number one contender, Tyrell Biggs, rather than Mike Tyson. When Biggs management declined the offer, Aleman opted for the next highest contender. The WBA chairman did approach the unification series in a positive manner, however and, after the WBC and the promoters agreed to follow all WBA rules including the 15-round championship distance, he agreed to Tyson as an opponent. The date and site were quickly agreed upon. The big event would take place at the Las Vegas Hilton on March 7, 1987, in a newly constructed outdoor arena located in the Hilton parking lot. The final unification battle against the IBF champion, hopefully Michael Spinks, would also be in the Hilton outdoor arena in May or June. After that gala attraction, the site for future heavyweight title fights would be up for grabs. Among the leading contenders for staging future fights were Alan Fields of Madison Square Garden and Donald Trump of Trump Plaza in Atlantic City.

James "Bonecrusher" Smith was boxing's newest Cinderella story. The WBA king was the heavyweight division's first college graduate, having earned a Bachelor of Science degree in Business Administration from Shaw University in Raleigh, North Carolina. Bonecrusher was a late-comer to the boxing ranks, having first taken up the sport in the United States Army in 1978 when he was 24 years old. Now, at the age of 33, the former prison guard stood on the threshold of immortality. If he could get past the immovable object, Mike Tyson, he would probably be favored to unify the title against the IBF champion in late spring. If he could get past Mike Tyson....

The present WBA champion was a complete surprise, but at least the WBA had a champion. The IBF titleholder was fading out of the picture completely, a situation that would leave the title vacant. Late in the month, HBO obtained an injunction against Michael Spinks, prohibiting him from fighting Gerry Cooney until after he had fulfilled his obligations to the Heavyweight Unification Series. As events unfolded, however, it was obvious that the injunction was without substance. As long ago as October 2, Butch Lewis stated his intention of entering into a big money fight against Gerry Cooney outside the Heavyweight Unification Series. As a pretext for taking the fight, Lewis said that Spinks would no longer compete in the series unless the WBA severed its ties with South Africa. Lewis was quoted as saying, "I will no longer associate myself with any activities with which the World Boxing Association is involved." Future events would show that Butch Lewis' statement was the epitome of hypocrisy. Butch Lewis apparently wasn't interested in apartheid at all. Butch Lewis was only interested in money—and how much of it he could make. His actions typified the sleazy side of the boxing world.

As the new year got under way, it was business as usual for the WBC king. He spent several days in New York making a series of public service television commercials. He spent one full day filming an anti-drug commercial for the FBI, and another day on a film clip for the State of New York. The 15-second promo showed the champ punching the speed bag in the gym, then turning to face the camera with the advice, "Say no to crack—and live." Mike's primary thrust in civic projects was aimed at educating the youth of the country to the dangers of drugs. He spent considerable time with the kids of New York City, speaking out loudly against the perils of drugs and alcohol. Later in the month, he shared the stage with New York Yankees left fielder Dave Winfield at one of the inner city junior high schools to promote Drug Awareness Day. Mike, casually dressed in a white silk shirt and gray slacks, entered the auditorium with his green and gold WBC championship belt encircling his waist. He spoke to the student body like a big brother, in terms they could understand. "I'm only four years older than the oldest person in here. I love the championship. I love bein' rich. I love havin' beautiful girl friends. But I'd give it all away before I'd belittle myself by putting a joint to my mouth or putting some white poison in my nose. I love myself too much."[1]

Honors began to pour in to the Tyson household early in the year as he was voted "Fighter of the Year" by the Boxing Writers of America, an award he shared with undefeated featherweight champion Julio Cesar Chavez, winner of 54 straight fights, 44 of them by knockout. Tyson was also named "Fighter of the Year" by *Ring Magazine*. In this same issue, *Ring Magazine* previewed a possible future Tyson opponent when it named Texas heavyweight Mike Williams boxing prospect of the year. The muscular Williams, a former Tyson sparring partner, sported a 9–0 professional record with six KO's. His most recent outing was a knockout win over "Quick" Tillis.

Mike's dizzying business schedule and his frequent coast to coast commuting came to the attention of the *Catskill Daily Mail* Sports Editor, Bill White. "How do you keep your life balanced? You spend so much time in New York and L.A. with celebrities and then you come back to Catskill." "I don't want to forget my roots. Catskill is home. That's where my family and my real friends are. I'm always aware of the bloodsuckers that try to latch on to celebrities. I keep my distance from them."

Tyson also kept his life in perspective by socializing with his buddies in Albany and Catskill and avoiding the celebrity scene. He would rather hang out at his favorite joint, Septembers, or take in an Albany Patroons basketball game in the Washington Avenue Armory than rub elbows with the likes of Jack Nicholson at an L.A. Lakers game. The Patroons were only a high minor league club, a member of the Continental Basketball Association, but they were exciting to watch, and Tyson loved to visit the old castle-like structure with his buddy Rory Holloway to root for his team against teams like the Mississippi Jets.

Be that as it may, the champ's life took on a surrealistic quality. His social and business activities were all-consuming, and his boxing career was relegated to a minor hobby. His management team of Jacobs and Cayton were busy laying the groundwork for Mike Tyson's financial future at the expense of his preparation for the upcoming WBC-WBA unification fight with "Bonecrusher" Smith. They engaged Ohlmeyer Communications Co. to market Tyson to the public. Ohlmeyer's responsibilities included locating marketing and licensing opportunities related to book publishing, television, toys, games, and advertisements, evaluating the various projects, and making recommendations to Jacobs and Cayton, who retained the final decision making themselves. Jacobs, Cayton, and the Ohlmeyer people were also negotiating with three major studios for a two-hour television film of Tyson's life. To oversee this new venture, the managers formed a new company, Reel Sports, Inc., which had a personal services contract with the heavyweight champion. Media exposure continued unabated in January, much to the chagrin of trainer Kevin Rooney, whose sole responsibility was to have his charge in top physical and mental condition by fight time. It was an impossible task under the prevailing conditions. Photograph sessions with people like the model, Iman, took precedence over sparring. Interviews with *Life* magazine correspondent Joyce Carol Oates took precious time away from Mike's gym work. Over 300 requests for interviews and photos sessions were received in the offices of Big Fights, Inc., and were meticulously evaluated for media value and for economic considerations.

Finally, on January 14, Mike Tyson attempted to go back into serious training in the gym in Catskill, but the attempt had a circus atmosphere associated with it. As champion, Tyson attracted visitors to the Cus D'Amato Gym in droves. Friends dropped by to congratulate the champ and to wish him well. Boxing fans crowded the little training camp to catch a glimpse of the king in action. And media representatives scrambled for position on a day-in, day-out basis, always pushing for one more interview, one last photo. *Time* magazine did a photo spread on the new champ, the session taking up most of the day. The usual assortment of directors moved into the D'Amato Boxing Club late in the morning and immediately took over the facility. Moving about with all the paraphernalia common to a magazine camera crew, e.g. tripods, cameras, and lights, the *Time* group completely upset Kevin Rooney's schedule, leaving the trainer annoyed and frustrated. By the end of the day they had accumulated numerous photos of Tyson clad in a woolen warm-up suit, working out on the heavy bag and doing floor exercises. Right on the heels of the *Time* crew came a Japanese film crew. They were doing a TV spread on the new champion, Japan's newest hero, and they wanted to record his workouts in Cus's old gym. Considering his growing popularity in Japan, there was a definite possibility that he might fight there in the fall, possibly against Gerry Cooney. According to inside sources, a major Japanese corporation and a large bank were willing to bankroll such a venture—and money was no object.

Rooney was rapidly becoming disgusted with the situation in Catskill. He could not concentrate on the task at hand, that is getting the champ ready for a title fight in six weeks. Mike needed a lot of work. After his six-week sojourn in Hollywood, the WBC champion came into the gym a chubby 230 pounds, 11 pounds overweight. The sharply delineated stomach muscles that usually marked his magnificent physique were missing on January 14. Instead of muscle, a noticeable layer of fat covered his midsection. It was obvious that the good life had gotten to Mike Tyson and had made him a poor imitation of the 20-year-old "Iron Mike." Rooney immediately put Tyson under a strict training regimen, working him mercilessly until the pounds of ugly fat began to melt off the champ's body. In a week, the conscientious trainer had his fighter down to a more manageable 225 pounds, and had sparred him for 20 rounds over a three-day period. Still the distractions persisted. Rooney took steps to rectify the situation before it was too late. He made all training sessions closed-door affairs. That only partially solved the problem, however. It corrected the situation in the gym, but the atmosphere outside the gym continued, and Rooney was helpless to stop that. Mike was constantly pressured for interviews, autographs, personal appearances, and just plain handshakes. A few sparring sessions were held with regulars Mike Jameson, Dion Burgess, and Anthony Davis, but it was like shoveling against the tide. Rooney was convinced that it would no longer be possible to conduct a meaningful training program in Catskill.

On January 27, Tyson had to appear in Los Angeles for a press conference heralding the upcoming fight, labeled "Superfight" by promoter Don King. As soon as the press conference ended, the champ was whisked off to New York City, where he was honored at a luncheon by the World Boxing Council and received another "Fighter of the Year" award. His managers, Jim Jacobs and Bill Cayton, were also honored, being recipients of the "Manager of the Year" award. As the days turned into weeks and Tyson's business commitments continued to keep him away from the gym, Kevin Rooney brought the situation to a head. He telephoned Jim Jacobs and notified the manager that he and Mike were going out to Las Vegas two weeks early to get acclimated to the desert environment and to escape the circus atmosphere in Catskill. Jacobs agreed.

Following Rooney's decision, the congenial heavyweight king made the rounds of Catskill to visit all his friends one last time. He started the day by visiting Werner and Elfie Murkowski, owners of Bell's Coffee Shop, where he gulped down a double order of toast and two glasses of orange juice. Within an hour, the affable giant was at Burger King finishing off a fish fillet, salad, and a vanilla shake. Along the way, he took time to walk up and down Main Street visiting friends and greeting his neighbors in Catskill. Eventually the champ made his way over to Catskill High School to visit principal Dick Stickles, assistant principal John Turek, and gym teacher Jim Franco, and to mingle with the kids themselves. Mike even shot a few baskets in the gym before tearing himself away to return to the Cus D'Amato Gym for yet another interview. Before facing the bright lights and exposing himself to the battery of questions that constituted the media zoo, Mike confided to a friend, "I'm in a bad mood today." Still, he was patient and polite to the reporters. After several minutes, he excused himself and went to the locker room to dress for the day's workout. The omnipresent eyes of the cameras followed his every move as he worked out on the bags or moved around the ring during his sparring session. Another interview followed the workout, but the sweaty, tired heavyweight champion graciously answered all questions. There were very few original questions, and the youngster answered many of them automatically.[2]

His trainer, obviously happy to be leaving for Nevada, sounded very positive about the upcoming bout. "We're ready to go. He's in good shape. We'll take a few days off when we get out there, and then get back to work. We'll have five weeks to get ready. Right now, we're right on schedule." When asked to comment about Tyson's apparent weight problem, Rooney shrugged it off. "He hasn't been able to run because it's been too cold." It's always cold in the Catskills region of upstate New York in late January, but this year the weather turned frigid, with sub-zero temperatures, howling winds, and blowing snow, preventing the young boxer from taking his early morning jaunts. "When we get out there, we'll do plenty of runnin'. The weight doesn't matter. He's a little heavy, but he's still all muscle. He'll come in around 218, 219. It doesn't matter."[3]

The Tyson entourage, consisting of Mike, Kevin, Matt Baranski, Mike Jameson, Oscar Holman, and Tyrone Armstrong, left Albany airport at 1:17 p.m. on Tuesday, February 3, aboard an American Airlines 757 bound for the City of Lights, Las Vegas, Nevada. Once in the desert country, Rooney breathed a little easier. Safely ensconced in a comfortable condominium outside town, the training crew could relax in privacy except for the two hours spent in Johnny Tocco's Gym. Even that was conducted under tight security. Team Tyson was now completely isolated from the outside world, a situation that aided them in preparing for the upcoming fight. From here on, any press conferences or interviews would be tightly controlled and scheduled well in advance so as not to upset the training regimen. It was now time to focus on only one thing, the fight. Meanwhile, the promoters had to increase their propaganda campaign if they wanted to prevent a disaster. Only five weeks remained before the big event. Ticket sales were sluggish and time was getting short. The apparent lack of interest in the fight was due to the fact that boxing fans were reluctant to fork out from $75 to $750 to see a match that was expected to end in an early Tyson knockout.

The key was to stimulate interest in the big fight, and that could only be realized if the fans envisioned "Bonecrusher" Smith to be a viable challenger. The marketing of "Bonecrusher" got under way with a flourish. He was immediately given a substantial dose of media visibility, including guest appearances on various radio and television talk shows as well as national sports programs. On one such show, "Sports Look," he told host Roy Firestone, "I believe I'm the most devastating puncher in the world today. Mike Tyson has never faced anyone who could put him out with one punch. If I hit Mike Tyson with my best punch, he will go out. There's no doubt about it." Tyson quietly rebutted that statement to Bill White, the sports editor of the *Catskill Daily Mail*, "I'm nervous. No, not nervous, I'm excited. I'm ready and I'm confident I'll be successful. I'll take out anyone they put me in against. No man is my equal."

Kevin Rooney was now in his element. He had full control of Mike Tyson's everyday activities. With help from assistant manager Steve Lott and Matt Baranski, he kept a tight rein on the champ, a situation that frustrated Tyson at times. "I can't do anything. They watch my every move." After the daily workouts, Baranski would escort the sparring partners back to the Hilton, while Tyson, Rooney, and Lott would head for the condo and an evening of rented videos. As the trio left the gym, Rooney assured the *Daily Mail*, "We haven't changed our game plan. We'll take no prisoners." Now the regimen got down to the boring, repetitive drills that Mike Tyson disliked so much, but the drills that would make him rock solid, both mentally and physically, when he stepped into the ring to face a man named Smith.

At 4 a.m. Monday morning, Mike Tyson climbed out of bed, donned a gray warm-up suit and stocking cap, and stepped out into the cool Nevada darkness to loosen up his body with a leisurely five-mile jog through the strangely deserted side streets of the now quiet gambling mecca. After breakfast, the young New Yorker watched a cartoon show on video cassette and chatted with cut man Matt Baranski, who stopped by for an early morning visit. Baranski, an almost unknown member of the Tyson party, was one of its most valuable contributors. A lifetime boxer and trainer, Baranski was an expert at controlling cuts and reducing swelling. A cut man was something Tyson had not yet needed in his amateur or professional career, a total of 72 matches. But someday, the unexpected could happen. Mike Tyson could have his eye sliced open by a sharp punch or by a head butt. If that should happen, Matt Baranski's sweet science could mean the difference between winning or losing a title. The cut man is a key part of every fighter's team. If the fighter has confidence in his cut man, he will perform at a higher level in times of severe difficulty, knowing that his condition is being treated by the best man possible. Matt Baranski was the best man possible. At noon, Tyson, Rooney, and Lott climbed into the back seat of their chauffeur-driven limousine and made the two-mile trek to Johnny Tocco's Gym in downtown Vegas. Once inside the barricaded building, Tyson quickly changed into his boxing gear and, after several minutes of floor exercises, he readied himself for his daily wars—his sparring sessions against Jameson, Holman, Ferguson, Burgess, Davis, and Broad.

Tyson's sparring partners were always ready to go. As Davis noted, "It's like a fight. You get yourself geared up to face this guy every day. You try to hurt him because he's trying to hurt you." Dion Burgess nodded in agreement. "You must do nothin' but concentrate on Mike Tyson for three minutes. And before you get in the ring, you have to prime yourself up for that. If you don't, then that could create problems for you." Still, in spite of the punishment they absorbed daily from the heavyweight champ, the sparring partners seemed to enjoy their work. As Burgess once put it, "Believe it or not, as ludicrous as it sounds, I might have done it for nothin'." Davis was not quite that blasé about it. He did, however, put the job in its proper perspective. "Top pay, travel, you get to see the country, and you get treated well. There's a lot of advantages here."[4] Besides, the sparring partners were protected against injury with a maximum of body gear. They wore padded head gear that covered their entire head except the front and top. Their critical body areas, including the kidneys and liver, were covered with a protective jacket, up to and including a flak jacket. A groin protector completed the safety equipment, making Tyson's opponents almost impervious to pain. For his part, the champion wore minimal protection, again harking back to the philosophy of Cus D'Amato, who claimed protective equipment made a fighter careless. One change was made to Tyson's equipment now that he was champion, however. Specially designed headgear was now worn during all sparring sessions. As champion, Mike Tyson was now a valuable property and had to be protected from an accidental training camp injury that could delay or postpone a multi-million dollar fight, resulting in substantial losses to the promoters. The headgear was much smaller than that worn by the sparring partners. It protected his ears but did not protect his jaw or forehead.

The Tyson camp seemed to run like a well-oiled machine, quietly and efficiently. There were numerous jobs to be done in the course of a day's routine, but each man knew his responsibilities and handled them flawlessly. Matt Baranski, for instance, was not merely Tyson's cut man. He had many other responsibilities as well. One of his most important responsibilities was riding herd on Tyson's sparring partners during their stay in Las Vegas. While Tyson, Rooney, and Lott stayed in the condo outside of town, Baranski and the rest of the entourage were housed in town at the Hilton. Baranski's first job of the day was to drag Holman, Jameson, and the rest of the crew out of bed at 5:45 for a three-mile jog through town. He also had to make sure they arrived at Johnny Tocco's on time and were loosened up and ready to fight by the time Tyson got to the ring. Many of the sparring partners had the talent to become world class boxers, but they lacked the self-discipline needed to realize their potential. While they trained with Mike Tyson, Matt Baranski became their "self discipline."

Tyson's weight gradually dropped from 227 to the 220 range. He appeared as strong and as fast as ever, causing Jesse Ferguson to remark, "He's in a class by himself as a fighter. He comes right at you with only one thing on his mind, to take you out of there. He's out to win." As the days passed, Tyson's training activities became more and more mechanical, an early morning run of three to five miles, an early afternoon two-hour gym session, and an evening on the exercycle at the local nautilus club. In between the training programs, the time dragged by painfully slowly. In fact, the only reason Mike started going to the nautilus club was to relieve the boredom back at the condo. Except for small talk with his trainers, Tyson's time in the condo was spent just lying around relaxing, reading, or watching videos. After five weeks, Mike had seen almost every video in Las Vegas. The idle time affected everyone, even Matt Baranski. "We have a lot of time on our hands. I lay in the sun. I only eat twice a day. I'd shoot craps sometimes. Used to shoot a lot." Then he thought about the big fish that were biting on Lake Mead nearby. "I love to fish. I've got my pole with me this time. The fight is four weeks from Saturday. I'm counting the days. After a month, I'm not the only one who's ready to leave. So are Kevin and Mike. We leave the next day [after the fight] and very happy to go."[5]

On February 26, the International Boxing Federation made an announcement that stunned the entire boxing world. Michael Spinks had been dethroned for not signing to fight the top contender, Tony Tucker. Instead, Tucker and James "Buster" Douglas would square off in May to crown a new champion, the man who would meet the Tyson-Smith winner in the finale of the HBO Unification Series. The announcement was a big disappointment for all those associated with the tournament—HBO, Jacobs and Cayton, and Don King. Michael Spinks was a bona fide champion, and his presence lent credibility to the box-off. With him gone, the tournament lost some of its luster. A Tyson-Tucker fight or a Tyson-Douglas fight was nowhere near as big a fight as a Tyson-Spinks fight would have been. Don King, as co-promoter of the tournament with Butch Lewis under the forum of "The Dynamic Duo," said, "It's Dynamic Uno now. What Butch Lewis has done to the reputation of Michael Spinks is a tragedy."

The name of Mike Tyson still made the boxing headlines around the country during February, but an old, familiar name suddenly appeared on the sports pages. Former heavyweight champion George Foreman began a comeback ten years after retiring from the ring. The 39-year-old Foreman, in his prime, was one of the most destructive punchers in boxing history. Holding the record for the highest knockout percentage in the heavyweight division with 43 KO's in a 48-fight career, the big Texan stepped into the ring in Sacramento, California, against journeyman Steve Zouski to resume his career and, hopefully, earn another title shot. The man who destroyed Joe Frazier in less than two rounds, and who left Ken Norton a battered hulk, drew only 5,307 fans to Arco Arena to witness his second debut. Foreman had whittled his weight down from 320 pounds to 267 for the fight, but he was still a long way from his prime fighting weight of 227. Even so, the blubbery ex-champ was too much for Zouski, who was rescued by the referee in round four. In a post-fight interview, Foreman, a preacher since his boxing days, stated that his primary purpose in returning to the ring was to raise funds for his favorite charity, "The George Foreman Youth and Recreation Center" in Houston, Texas.

Another announcement that disturbed the HBO tournament officials was the news that Michael Spinks and Gerry Cooney had signed contracts for a big money, closed circuit fight to be held in Atlantic City, New Jersey. The bout, sanctioned for 15 rounds by the New Jersey Athletic Commission, was being promoted as the "People's Championship" by the garrulous Butch Lewis and his co-promoter, millionaire business tycoon and owner of the Trump Hotel and Casino in Atlantic City, Donald Trump, who was bankrolling the affair. With Spinks out of the picture, managers Jacobs and Cayton had to evaluate alternate competitors to match their young champion with throughout the remainder of 1987. With Tyson fighting every two-and-a-half to three months, the Jacobs-Cayton duo always tried to keep three bouts ahead. The planning strategy now called for Tyson to defend his title against Tyrell Biggs in May, meet the Tucker-Douglas winner in August to unify the title, then possibly fight in Japan against an unknown opponent late in the year. Jim Jacobs had, in fact, been working with Biggs' manager, Shelly Finkel, to provide Biggs with credible but beatable opponents for two or three fights prior to the proposed May meeting. Jacobs had succeeded in convincing Renaldo Snipes and James "Quick" Tillis to meet Biggs late in 1986, and Biggs responded with convincing victories. The March 7 Tyson-Smith title fight would also showcase the flashy 1984 Olympic superheavyweight champion against rough, tough David Bey. Biggs remembered sparring with the then 18-year-old Mike Tyson during the Olympic Trials. "He was trying to knock me down," he said almost incredulously. "There's no doubt about that. That's the way he always fights. He tries to nail you. I've always thought that, with his style of fighting, he'd be a much better pro than he was an amateur." Tyrell Biggs considered himself to be the ultimate fighting machine, a dazzling boxing master, who was a thinking man in the ring and who had knockout power. In his mind, Mike Tyson was nothing more than a street fighter, a ruffian. He dreamed about the day he would dance circles around the kid from Catskill and take his title away in the process.

Two days before the "Superfight," a final press conference was held in the Hilton Showroom. James "Bonecrusher" Smith appeared on the scene, properly programmed by Don King. "I don't like being considered a contender going into this fight. I'm the WBA Champion. Mike is going to bite the dust. He is fighting the hardest punching heavyweight in the world. 'Iron Mike'—that's a lot of bull. I want to see if he's made of iron, or if he reacts to pain. Everybody I've hit has shown a reaction." Tyson listened to the harangue nonplussed as usual. His only comment in rebuttal was "I'll do whatever it takes to win." As Tuesday dawned, Tyson's training program began to wind down. He finished his sparring agenda with six rounds against Broad, Ferguson, and Jameson. The next day, a three-mile run through town and four rounds on the heavy bag completed Rooney's preparations, and the young trainer appeared satisfied with his fighter's condition. "We're ready. Trainin' is over and we'll just keep him loose until fight time." Mike Jameson felt the sparring partners had done their job creditably when he commented, "He's solid. He's in great shape. He won't have any problems." Many outside observers felt otherwise. They thought Mike Tyson might be overtrained this time out. There was a feeling in the Tyson camp that Mike peaked a week and a half before the fight, a sentiment voiced by Rooney himself. "We wanted to fight last week. Now we'll just wait it out. He'll just run now. If he gets bored, he'll probably go to the health club and ride the bike. Otherwise, he'll just lay around the house."[6]

Tyson was up Thursday morning at precisely 4:30, ran the required three miles, then slipped back into bed until nine. Breakfast consisted entirely of a fruit diet, but Mike more than made up for it at lunch, devouring a two-pound steak washed down with eight glasses of water. At 9:30 p.m. it was bedtime. The same routine was followed both Friday and Saturday with two exceptions. Mike didn't run on Saturday, but he did make one trip into town for the official weigh-in at 11:00. The WBC Champion scaled a tight 219 pounds while the big man from Magnolia, North Carolina, tipped the scales at a trim 233. The next nine hours were a time of waiting for both Tyson and Smith. Time weighs heavy on the mind and the nervous system in the hours before a heavyweight championship fight. The tension builds, the fighters pace their respective hotel rooms nervously, and the hands of the clock move ahead at an agonizingly slow pace. Mike Tyson was new to the celebrity game, having been the WBC Heavyweight Champion for a little over three months, and the circus atmosphere in Las Vegas, combined with all the pre-fight hype, had taken its toll on the young fighter, both emotionally and physically.

His frayed nerves became visible by fight time as he made his way down the center aisle of the Hilton outdoor arena and climbed the steps to the ring. A bald spot had appeared on the front of his scalp, caused by a nervous disorder according to the doctor. The same ailment caused his neck and jaw to twist grotesquely to the left at sporadic intervals. Tyson's physical and emotional problems, combined with "Bonecrusher" Smith's sudden timidity in the presence of the WBC king, resulted in one of the dullest heavyweight title fights in recent years. "Bonecrusher" did not come out and attack the kid from Catskill as he had promised. Instead, he kept away from Tyson's potent left jabs and right uppercuts, using a pawing left jab to maintain a reasonable distance between himself and his adversary. When the WBC champ did venture inside, Smith wrapped his huge arms around the youngster, tying him up until the referee was forced to step in and separate the two.

For his part, the 20-year-old slugger fell right in with Smith's tactics, showing none of the typical Tyson aggressiveness during the fight. He continually walked through Smith's ineffectual parries, but once tied up he made no effort to free himself, being content to just lay on Smith and wait for the referee's intercedence. When he did mount an offensive, he threw only one punch at a time. Gone were the patented lightning-fast Tyson combinations. Gone were the punches thrown with bad intentions. In their place were lackadaisical, mechanical punches executed by a man completely devoid of emotion and incentive. "Bonecrusher" Smith was severely criticized for his performance in the fight, but it takes two to tango, and Mike Tyson was an equal, albeit unintentional, collaborator to the fiasco. Iron Mike did unify the WBC-WBA titles handily, winning all 12 rounds, but his image was severely tarnished in the process. The contributing factors for Tyson's poor showing were many. There were the early indications that he was overtrained. As Rooney had said, Mike was ready to go two weeks before the fight, and just marked time during the final two weeks. Tyson certainly fought like a man whose reflexes and incentives had long since passed their peak. There were also the newly experienced pressures associated with being the heavyweight champion of the world, with all the invasions of privacy and intrusions on one's time that accompany it.

The final stressful incident that befell the troubled boxer occurred during the fight. An unidentified person telephoned the Hilton Hotel, threatening to kill the WBC champion. As soon as the fight ended, Hilton security personnel surrounded the fearful boxer and escorted him from the ring with the admonition "Stay low." The ensuing post-fight press conference was chaotic as Tyson tried to be as inconspicuous as possible. When asked to pose for photographers with his new WBA belt, Mike declined, saying, "Someone threatened to kill me." Again, when a photographer asked Mike to stand up for a picture, the champion replied, "And get shot? I stand up and 'boom.'"[7]

Before the press conference ended, Jim Jacobs informed the mass of reporters that the new WBC-WBA champ would fight again on HBO on May 30 against an unnamed opponent. Jacobs had hoped to announce that Tyson would meet the highly publicized Tyrell Biggs on May 30, but Biggs' performance on the undercard of the Tyson-Smith bout erased that possibility. Tyrell Biggs fought a tough journeyman fighter named David Bey in a match that was supposed to give Biggs increased credibility and induce the public to clamor for a Tyson-Biggs confrontation. It failed in all respects. In fact, the Biggs-Bey fight was a near disaster. The former Olympic king inexplicably decided to stand and slug it out with the brawler from Philadelphia instead of dancing and boxing as he was trained to do. He played right into Bey's hands and, in the fourth round, he took a sharp right hook to the head that opened a gaping hole over his left eye. To Biggs' credit, he was able to regroup and launch a two-fisted offensive that dropped the tubby challenger to the canvas in the sixth round. Although Bey regained his feet, referee Richard Steele stopped the onslaught seconds later, awarding Biggs a TKO victory. Thirty-two stitches were required to close the ugly wound over Biggs' eye, causing any possible title fight to be postponed for at least six to eight months. Mike Tyson's next logical opponent for the May 30 date appeared to be Pinklon Thomas, the former WBA champion, who had KO'd Danny Sutton on the same card.

Tyrell Biggs was a semi-tragic figure in the world of professional boxing. A fighter endowed with unlimited natural ability, a perfect physique for a heavyweight boxer, and the necessary courage to fight back in the face of adversity as he did against David Bey, he was a fighter who could be categorized as a "loser." Tyrell Biggs lacked two of the essential ingredients necessary to become a world champion. First, he lacked the discipline to establish a fight plan and then stick to it in the ring. Invariably, the Philadelphian got drawn into a slugging match with his opponent when he should have been exercising the boxing skills that made him an amateur champion. Biggs had exceptional speed, both of hand and of foot. He was an outstanding boxer with a good jab and superior ring generalship. But in a macho mix-up of elementary thinking, he felt he must be a knockout artist in order to be a respected heavyweight champion. As a result, at some point in almost every fight, Biggs threw his fight plan to the winds and slugged it out with his opponent. The most critical flaw in Tyrell Biggs' makeup however, was his lack of confidence. The young boxer sounded confident in pre-fight conversation, but it was all a charade. Biggs had a deep-rooted feeling of inferiority that obscured his artistic strengths. He would never be a professional heavyweight champion because of the demons that plagued his soul, the demons that told him he was not good enough.

Don King, the flamboyant one, threw his usual post-fight celebrity bash in the Hilton Skyroom, but Tyson and Rooney made only token appearances. Mike Tyson is not a partygoer. "He likes to have fun on his own," Rooney said. "He doesn't drink or smoke." Mike Tyson shuns the spotlight whenever possible and, on this night, with a death threat hanging over his head, he was less inclined than usual to expose himself in a wide-open ballroom. After greeting the host and making small talk with some of the guests, Tyson and Rooney excused themselves and headed back to the safety of their rooms. As the nervous duo sneaked down the corridor, their apprehension was evident. "When we were walkin', I kept looking for someone to come out of the blue," stated Rooney. "I kept my eye out."[8]

The Tyson entourage left Vegas in force the next morning, Tyson and Rooney off for several weeks of well-earned vacation, and Jacobs back to New York to review and evaluate potential new contenders for the champ's crown. Pinklon Thomas loomed on the horizon, as did former champion Tony Tubbs, British heavyweight Frank Bruno, Italian boxer Francesco Damiani, and former Olympic boxers Tyrell Biggs, Henry Tillman, and Evander Holyfield. Of the group, Tyson wanted desperately to meet Tillman and Biggs. He had to stand in their shadows during his amateur days, and he thirsted for revenge. He resented Biggs intensely because Tyrell was the fair-haired boy of the U.S. Olympic Committee and was always treated in a royal manner. The Philadelphia fighter was a tall, handsome man, with the face of a movie star and the physique of a Greek God. He was a fast, clever boxer who was made to order for the rules of amateur competition. He was given maximum media exposure in international competition in order to groom him carefully to represent the United States in the 1984 Olympic Games. Mike Tyson, on the other hand, was looked upon as a street fighter by the pretentious Olympic officials. Henry Tillman was the man who defeated the inexperienced Tyson in the Olympic Trials elimination matches in 1984, preventing the Catskill teenager from realizing one of his childhood dreams. Tyson never forgot that humiliation.

Tyson was destined to meet Tyrell Biggs in the near future, but the chances of a return match with Henry Tillman were exceedingly remote. Tillman was a cruiserweight and not a world class cruiserweight at that. He did get off to a fast start in the professional ranks, winning the NABF Cruiserweight Title in less than 18 months by knocking out Bashiru Ali in the first round in Las Vegas on April 22, 1986. He subsequently lost the title to "Smokin'" Bert Cooper in his first title defense the following June. After racking up four more victories, the California fighter tried to recapture his past glory by winning the WBA cruiserweight belt from his old friend, Evander Holyfield, in a February bout in Reno, Nevada. It was no contest from the start. The talented Holyfield made Tillman his 14th consecutive victim, and tenth knockout victim, in a convincing manner. The classy champion staggered his Olympic buddy in every round, flooring him in the second. Tillman demonstrated great courage, but the rapidly improving Holyfield had the heavier artillery. In the seventh round, Carlos Padilla stopped the carnage after Holyfield dropped Tillman to the canvas for the third time. Tillman would probably never fight Mike Tyson, but the impressive Holyfield loomed as a definite threat to the heavyweight champion, perhaps in 1988 or 1989.

Mike Tyson and Kevin Rooney spent several weeks basking in the sun and unwinding from the pressure cooker of a Las Vegas championship fight. They would have to return to the ring wars soon enough to get ready for the next title defense, against the dangerous Thomas. But for 14 glorious days, Kevin Rooney and his family lounged around the snow-white sands of the Bahamas, while Tyson alternated his time between New York and Los Angeles. As a guest on the *Today* show, Mike told an amused Bryant Gumbel, "I'm still a kid and I don't know what I want to do with the rest of my life when I grow up." While

Tyson and Rooney were taking it easy, it was business as usual in the offices of Big Fights, Inc. Jacobs and Cayton were trying to lure former champ Larry Holmes out of retirement à la Joe Louis and Muhammad Ali. Negotiations continued unabated for three days, but ended in failure when Holmes' demands became unreasonable. The Easton entrepreneur demanded half a million up front, another $3.5 million after the fight, plus a percentage of the gate. Cayton wanted to get Holmes in the ring to add luster to Tyson's record. "Larry Holmes is a highly skilled fighter. He would make the fight very competitive." But $4 million plus was too much to pay for luster.

Mike Tyson rolled into Catskill one weekend just long enough to indulge himself in two new automobiles—a chauffeur-driven 1987 Rolls Royce and a sleek 1987 Jaguar. Then he was off again, back to Hollywood to hang out with his entertainment buddies. It was there that the young champion's life made a sudden and irreversible change. During dinner with friends one evening, the Catskill boxer was captivated by a young, female patron nearby, an ivory-skinned beauty named Robin Givens. Mike imposed on comedian John Horne to introduce him to Robin, and from the first moment he met her, the champion was lost, bitten by the love bug—and it was a fatal bite. The sophisticated Givens, one of the stars of the television show *Head of the Class*, quickly replaced Lisa Bonet in Mike Tyson's heart. On their first date, the young couple dined at Le Dome Restaurant in Hollywood, accompanied by Robin's mother, Ruth Roper, and her sister, Stephanie.

Before Tyson could begin a courtship, however, he had to return to New York for a business obligation, followed by a visit to England to attend the heavyweight fight between the pride of Clapham, Frank Bruno, and the ever-present James "Quick" Tillis. At La Guardia Airport, the American press were still pressing the champion to explain the bald spot and the neck twitch that were evident during the Smith fight. Jim Jacobs' explanation, obviously the party line, was that the bald spot was the result of a mistake by a Las Vegas barber, and the neck twitch was just Mike's way of loosening up. Funny, Mike never loosened up that way before. The explanations were weak. The cause was obvious (nerves), and the prognosis was good (the nervous disorder would disappear by the end of the year as Mike Tyson became more comfortable in his new celebrity). When asked about a prediction for the Bruno fight, Tyson declined to comment, but Kevin Rooney volunteered his opinion. "I hope Bruno wins. He's a big, strong guy. He'd be a good opponent for Mike." Remembering the time in 1983, when the 16-year-old Junior Olympic Champion stepped into the ring to spar with the British professional at Grossinger's Resort in upstate New York, Rooney said, "They boxed five or six times. Mike held his own then. Now he has more experience so he should do better."[9]

Across the big pond, the Tyson group was surrounded by British newsmen as soon as they deplaned at Heathrow Airport. The world champion politely posed for photos, decked out in a new British "bowler," with his WBC and WBA belts slung over his shoulder. After a day of rest, Tyson and his managers sat down with representatives of Frank Bruno to discuss a possible future championship match. Initial talks revolved around money, location, and date. British promoter Mike Barrett pushed for a late-summer date in Wembley Stadium, a time frame and location that was amenable to Jacobs and Cayton. As Cayton stated, "We want Mike to do what Muhammad Ali did, fight all over the world." The final arrangements, of course, would depend on Bruno's performance against Tillis, as well as Tyson's schedule in the Unification Series.

On Wednesday, March 24, with Mike Tyson at ringside, 3,000 spectators filed into the vast soccer stadium to witness the British Commonwealth Champion in action. The powerful Brit didn't disappoint. He scored an impressive fifth-round KO over the Oklahoma cowboy, racking up his 29th knockout in his 29th victory. His only two losses were also via knockout, to former WBA champions Tim Witherspoon and "Bonecrusher" Smith. Mike Tyson was impressed with Bruno's performance. "Bruno did a tremendous job and I'm looking forward to meeting him in the ring." Manager Bill Cayton was equally impressed with the British heavyweight. "I have never seen anyone destroy Tillis like this. Bruno was brilliant, and remember, Tillis gave Mike his hardest fight."

While Tyson was out of the country, the Nevada State Supreme Court lifted its injunction against Michael Spinks. Now that Spinks had been stripped of his IBF title, he was automatically eliminated from the HBO Unification Series and was free to fight whomever he pleased. Butch Lewis immediately announced that the "People's Championship" between his fighter and Gerry Cooney would be viewed on closed circuit television from the Atlantic City Convention Center. The arrangements called for Spinks to receive a guaranteed $7 million, while his opponent was assured of $5 million against a percentage of the gate.

Back in the States again, the love-sick Tyson headed straight for the west coast, determined to woo and win the ravishing Givens. The 22-year-old beauty was, like Tyson, a New Yorker. Born on Seymour Avenue in the Bronx, she managed to escape the inner city syndrome thanks to the efforts of her strong-willed mother. Ruth Roper scrimped and saved so she could send her daughter to private schools, determined to see to it that Robin would marry rich. After attending the exclusive Sarah Lawrence College in Bronxville, the statuesque Givens applied to Harvard University for entrance into its pre-medical program but, on the advice of actor Bill Cosby, changed her plans in mid-stream and entered the acting profession instead. The Givens-Tyson relationship got off to a stormy beginning, mutual attraction being interspersed with frequent heated arguments. Mike Tyson had been a conqueror of women throughout his early life, and he was used to pursuing a woman until she succumbed to his charm and his advances. Then, having won the prize, he would discard her and move on in search of another challenge.

In Robin Givens, Mike Tyson more than met his match. Givens was not a starry-eyed teeny bopper in pursuit of local athletic heroes. She was a strong-willed, well-educated, confident individual whose goal in life was to be famous and wealthy. She had associated with celebrities for years and had dated such well-known personalities as comedian Eddie Murphy and basketball superstar Michael Jordan. She was not overly impressed with the heavyweight boxing champion of the world. She enjoyed being in Tyson's company, but she was not a hero worshipper and did not fawn over the champ like his usual female companions did. Many times, when the refined Givens resisted his will, Tyson would go into a tirade, often resulting in a physical punching match between the two. At one point in their relationship, the champ presented Robin with a four carat diamond, which he coyly referred to as a "friendship" ring. Within weeks, Robin returned the ring following another of their domestic wars. The Tyson-Givens duo was the entertainment world's new "odd couple." Tyson, the tattooed Brooklyn street thug, and Givens, the refined beauty from Scarsdale, were 180 degrees out of phase with each other culturally. Yet, strangely enough, they also seemed to complement each other. They had many common interests—a sense of humor, the love of music, the need for close family ties, and the value of a career. In their differences, they tried to teach each other love and respect. The street kid imparted his wisdom on positive thinking, a strong work ethic, and love of children. For her part, Robin instructed Mike in culture, financial management, and the value of publicity to one's career.

It was a strange, stormy relationship that should have ended as soon as it began. Unfortunately, the two protagonists yielded to lust and would be married on February 7, 1988. The marriage would end one year later on Valentine's Day, after 12 months of what Robin told Barbara Walters during a televised interview was "pure hell." It was pure hell on both their parts. But the beginning of the marriage seemed to be idyllic. Robin and Mike spent the Easter weekend in Catskill, quietly enjoying the upstate New York scenery and solitude. Mike taught Robin how to shoot pool in the upstairs bedroom. He introduced his new girl to his "family" of pigeons in the front yard, even letting her hold them and pet them. And he displayed his beautiful girlfriend to all his friends in town. Robin took time to get to know Camille over the weekend, impressing the older woman with her manners and her charm.

Tyson's life became a whirlwind of activity following his demolition of the WBA king "Bonecrusher" Smith. The demands on his personal time became much greater, with hundreds of offers pouring in to the headquarters of Big Fights, Inc. Even so, the new heavyweight king had more time for himself as champion. In the old days of Cus D'Amato and the Catskill Boxing Club, Mike Tyson trained seven days a week in preparation for his bi-weekly bouts. As champion, he was limited to four or five title defenses a year, requiring a maximum total training time of 30 weeks. The remaining 22 to 28 weeks were divided between business commitments and vacation time. Mike Tyson, the heavyweight champion of the world, had an excess of free time to enjoy himself and an unlimited amount of money to indulge his every whim. But once he had become infatuated with the bewitching young actress, much of Mike's free time was spent in the air between New York and California.

Early one spring day, the champ received a phone call from Jim Bouton, a former major league pitcher with the New York Yankees and author of the controversial baseball expose, *Ball Four*. Bouton was now a member of the board of directors of the Young Adult Institute (YAI), an agency that served mentally retarded and developmentally disabled young adults in New York City. He was looking for a celebrity who would devote not only his name but also his time to the forgotten individuals of YAI. He found the perfect person in Mike Tyson. The former Brooklyn street urchin knew what it was like to be underprivileged and emotionally handicapped, and he approached the project as he would a fight. He waded in with both fists flying, determined to help the kids singlehanded. These young adults wanted to make a useful life for themselves, but they needed help, the kind of help that a Mike Tyson could give. YAI members were handicapped, but not to the point of having to be institutionalized. They could support themselves if given the opportunity. Jim Bouton and the other YAI volunteers were trying to purchase private brownstone homes in the city to house the young adults in a supervised, dormitory style environment, giving these people a chance to experience a normal, dignified life.

YAI also created a workforce that contracted jobs from private industry, small packing-type operations, or other types of manual functions that could be carried out under close supervision. But the institute suffered, as do most organizations of its type, from a lack of funds necessary to purchase and staff a private home for young adults. There were still 1,400 New Yorkers waiting to get into a home, the average wait being an agonizing ten years. Mike Tyson, for one, was appalled by that statistic. He did contribute his name to help the Institute raise funds to support their programs, but he did much more. He also contributed his time, spending several days with Jim Bouton in New York, visiting one of the brownstones, working with the young adults, and playing games with them. His visits were dutifully recorded by several news organizations including ABC, HBO, and Don King and Mike Tyson Productions. The residents of YAI were thrilled to be in the presence of the heavyweight champion. One bashful young lady, wearing a Pepsi Cola baseball cap, expressed the feelings of all the young adults when she said, almost unbelievingly, "It's a great big thrill. Michael Tyson is here." She timidly approached Mike in the playground to shake his hand and, after the champ gave her his hand, he patted her on the shoulder, a simple gesture that overwhelmed the girl. "Oh my God. He touched my shoulder." Later in the day, Tyson worked with the young adults in their basement workshop, helping pack plastic utensils and sugar into wax paper bags, one of the menial tasks performed by them to earn money. At one point, Mike Tyson leaned over and gave his working companion an affectionate kiss on the cheek. The young girl blushed and shyly bowed her head, embarrassed. "I do love you, Mike," she giggled. To a visitor, she exclaimed, "I love this guy a lot."

That was the effect Mike Tyson had on all the members of the YAI. He could relate to them on their own level. He played basketball with them, worked alongside them in the basement, listened to music and danced with them, exchanged stories with them, hugged them and gave them love. He even boxed with a few of the young men in the gym and took a knockout punch from one excited opponent who nipped him on the chin. The champ toppled backward to the floor and lay motionless on the mat while another boxing enthusiast tolled the fatal ten count. As most people discover when they work to help others, they receive much more than they give. Mike Tyson was no different. "I hurt when I see these people. They are sentenced and they never did a crime." Arnold Schwarzenegger, who watched Mike work with the challenged athletes at the Special Olympics, said, "You can see the love he has in him. He wants to share." Tyson confirmed that statement. "I never realized, but I'm the kind of person that gets the biggest satisfaction from giving more than receiving."

The heavyweight champion sought to help the less fortunate wherever he was, visiting handicapped children in Atlantic City, feeding homeless people in Cleveland, handing out truckloads of turkeys to poor people on Thanksgiving in Cleveland, and marching in parades and soliciting financial support for charitable causes in New York.

The idyllic nights of March soon gave way to the rainy spring days of April, and soon it was time to go back into the gym and prepare for another title defense. Mike's extended social life had taken a bigger toll on his body this time than before the Smith fight. He reported to Rooney weighing a blubbery 237 pounds, 21 pounds over his best fighting weight. The layer of fat that covered his midsection when he began training in January had turned into a noticeable paunch this time, and hung grotesquely over the top of his trunks. A friend described him as looking like a fat, little old man. As before, the atmosphere in Catskill was not conducive to getting the fighter in top condition. The champ played hooky the second day of camp, opting to wheel his 12-cylinder Jag to Albany to visit friends instead of enduring the painful grind of the gymnasium routine. Mike's life in the fishbowl made it difficult for him to concentrate on his work. He went into training for Pinklon Thomas on Thursday, April 16, with some light gym work. The following Tuesday, the Cus D'Amato Gym was ablaze with floodlights as Mike Tyson worked on one of his many television commercials, this one a 30-second shot for Kodak. The actual shooting took seven and a half hours to complete, as the champ was photographed going through his normal paces such as shadow boxing and jumping rope. The training session was cancelled again on Wednesday to allow Mike to travel to New York City to attend a press conference for the upcoming fight. And on Thursday, a Japanese film crew moved back into the dingy gym to film a television special on the young heavyweight sensation. Life in the fishbowl was hectic, and occasionally nerve-wracking.

Even Robin came east for a visit. Mike sent a stretch limo to New York to meet her at the airport and escort her back to Ewald House. She spent the following day at the gym watching the champ in action. Relaxation for the pair consisted of shooting pool, playing ping pong, "sloppin'" the pigeons, and taking long hand-held strolls along the banks of the Hudson. Mike Tyson was in the process of becoming domesticated, but he didn't know it at the time.

Life continued hectic in the tiny New York hamlet. Training camp was only a minor diversion instead of the all-consuming crusade it must be for a heavyweight champion. Outside the gym, Mike was involved in numerous civic functions. One night, he threw out the first ball at the season opener for the Class AA Albany-Colonie Yankees. Another night, he made a guest appearance at the Empire State Convention Center boxing matches featuring the number one WBC featherweight contender, Buddy McGirt.

On Wednesday, April 29, Mike Tyson and Kevin Rooney traveled to New York for another press conference at the Waldorf Astoria. Pinklon Thomas, like most of his predecessors, arrived with his courage on his sleeve, deriding and denigrating the champion. "Hey, little man with the squeaky voice," pointing to Tyson, "Is your name Michael Jackson or Mike Tyson?" Tyson eyed the challenger disgustedly. "Show a little respect in front of your lady." Thomas continued to rant and rave during the proceedings, predicting dire consequences for the kid from Catskill. "I'm not gonna tell you how, but I'm gonna whup him. He doesn't belong in the same ring with me." Tyson told reporters that he expected a short fight. When pressed as to when the fight might end, Tyson said, "As soon as he gets hit."[10]

The following week, 2,000 miles west of Catskill, the eyes of the boxing world were focused on Las Vegas, Nevada, for what would turn out to be the boxing event of 1987. It was the highly publicized match between the undisputed middleweight champion, Marvelous Marvin Hagler, and the charismatic challenger, "Sugar Ray" Leonard. This was the richest fight of all time, as thousands of boxing fans crammed into theatres and arenas all over the country, paying an estimated $60 million to watch the Sugar Man, with a record of 34–1 with 22 knockouts, attempt to wrest the middleweight crown from the head of the awesome champion, whose record was an imposing 62–3–2 with 52 KO's. Hagler was a heavy favorite. Not only was Leonard moving up in weight class, but he had been relatively inactive in recent years, having fought only once since retiring in 1982 with a detached retina. His last fight, against Kevin Howard on May 11, 1984, was unsatisfying to him, and he went back into retirement. But a match with Hagler gave him the incentive he needed, and he returned to the ring wars one more time, determined to carve out a niche in boxing history. The fans who crowded the closed circuit TV outlets, and the 15,336 fans who paid to witness the event live in the parking lot outside Caesars Palace, were not disappointed. It was a great strategic battle, particularly on Leonard's part. Leonard fought the perfect fight, maintaining a safe distance between himself and the aggressive Hagler most of the time, his circling and jabbing tactics frustrating the Brockton brawler, who wanted to stand toe-to-toe and mix it up. Leonard occasionally did stop and slug it out with the Marvelous One, but only for brief intervals. Leonard danced on the balls of his feet like a Broadway ballet star for three rounds, but the long layoff took its toll. His motion slowed noticeably from the fourth round on, and by the ninth round his tank was empty. Only his champion's heart spurred him on and allowed him to trade punches with the middleweight king. Leonard actually won two of the last three rounds on guts alone. His late-fight heroics clinched a split decision.

Another important fight, at least from Tyson's point of view, took place several weeks later. Former Olympic teammate Evander Holyfield took on Rickey Parkey for the IBF cruiserweight title. Holyfield, the WBA Junior Heavyweight Champion, at 15–0 with 11 KO's, had ambitions of moving up to the heavyweight division in 1988 and eventually challenging Tyson for the big crown. His performance against Parkey only added to his reputation as a possible future heavyweight contender. The action was head-to-head for two rounds but, in round three, the powerful Holyfield dropped the tough Parkey twice to end the fight and annex the IBF crown.

Next it was Tyson's turn. May 30 arrived almost without notice. The day before the fight, the champion was surrounded by a crowd of yelling, screaming fans as he pushed his way into the Hilton for the official weigh-in ceremony. It was a new experience for the 20-year-old hero. He was mobbed by fans wherever he went—New York, Los Angeles, Brooklyn, even Catskill. But he was learning to deal with it and to accept it as the price for fame. "I prefer to be alone, but it's no problem. They don't mean any harm. It's not like they're tryin' to assassinate me. I'd probably do the same thing if I saw Mickey Mantle on the street." The champion, seeking his 30th victory, watched the balance beam stop at 218¾ pounds as dozens of flashbulbs popped, recording the event for posterity. The challenger came in a pound lighter. Angelo Dundee, Thomas' trainer, tried to unsettle the New York youngster by announcing he had a hidden camera in Johnny Tocco's Gym and had recorded Tyson's training sessions. "Tyson is vulnerable. He was off balance. Pinklon can and will beat him." Kevin Rooney, openly amused by Dundee's statements, retorted, "If they had a hidden camera watching Mike Tyson sparrin', then Thomas wouldn't show up for the fight." Tyson was equally unimpressed. "I don't recall Angelo ever scoring a knockout." The heavyweight king was looking forward to this match with great anticipation. After his lackluster performance against "Bonecrusher" Smith, Tyson was determined to make amends against Thomas. "He's a very worthy opponent. I was lookin' forward to this fight even before I was champion. This is the fight in which I'm gonna prove I'm the best fighter in the world."[11]

The 6'3" Thomas, out of Pontiac, Michigan, was considered by many experts to be the cream of the crop, the best heavyweight in the world, outside of Tyson. He boasted a 29–1–1 professional record and had scored 24 knockouts over a ten-year career. The big heavyweight was, at one time, the WBC Champion, having taken the title from Tim Witherspoon on a 12-round decision. He subsequently defended his crown with an impressive eighth-round KO of hard-punching Mike Weaver, but relinquished the crown to the smiling Jamaican, Trevor Berbick, on a 12-round decision on March 22, 1986. Now it was revenge time for Pinklon Thomas, time to reclaim the crown. But first he had to destroy the man who stood between him and his objective, "Iron Mike" Tyson, or the "Baddest Man on the Planet," as Tyson likes to call himself. Thomas promised he would challenge Tyson on a man-to-man basis. "I'll be there. He won't have to look for me. And I'll throw the first punch." Manager Jim Jacobs was under the weather physically, complaining of back problems, but he made the effort to attend the festivities in the desert. His partner, Bill Cayton, was not so fortunate. Laid up in the hospital with a heart ailment, Cayton would have to view the fight on HBO.

Saturday, May 30. Fight night. Another sellout crowd of 12,000 people surrounded the ring in the parking lot of the Las Vegas Hilton. The desert air was stifling, with the temperature approaching the 90-degree mark by the time Tyson and Thomas entered the ring at approximately 10:45 p.m. Eastern Daylight Time. Thomas desperately wanted his title back. Mike Tyson wanted to obliterate the memory of the "Bonecrusher" affair. Tyson had the greater incentive. The champion from upstate New York attacked the taller fighter ferociously in round one, intent on ending the brawl quickly and decisively. He stunned the challenger with a two-fisted attack early in the round. A left hook to the head hurt the Michigan fighter, and Tyson quickly followed with two more damaging hooks. It was a blazing start for the newly crowned champion, and he continued his non-stop rampage into the second minute of the fight. It was obvious that Mike Tyson was bent on the complete destruction of his more experienced foe. Pinklon Thomas tried to fight back in center ring, but his feeble jabs and hooks were ineffective against the Tyson onslaught. Mike literally overpowered him. As the round drew to a close, a big left hook by Tyson, thrown out of a crouch, staggered the confused ex-champion, and a following right drove him into the ropes. In the final 30 seconds, a 15- to 20-punch barrage by the 20-year-old Catskill native had Thomas on the brink, but failed to put the rugged heavyweight away. Although it was a big round for the champion, it was to Thomas' credit that he survived the frantic three-minute attack. Pinklon Thomas was a tough, experienced heavyweight who had never been knocked off his feet as a professional. He had a granite chin, a chin that had absorbed some mighty blows from the best of the heavyweights during his ten years in the ring, and he showed that side of his character to young Mike Tyson in round one.

As round two progressed, the fight slowed noticeably. Tyson, realizing that his opponent was not going to cave in at the first opportunity, and mindful of the oppressive desert heat that beat down incessantly on the exposed ring, decided to conserve his energy and wait for an opening. Thomas, after seeing Tyson's aggressive tactics in round one, also changed his fight plan. He chose to keep away from Tyson's heavy artillery, tying his man up whenever the two came to close quarters. As the rounds ticked away, the tempo of the fight seemed to swing slowly toward the challenger, Pinklon Thomas. But that was only so much smoke. Actually Tyson could feel his adversary tiring, and he was determined to press the advantage in round six. Kevin Rooney implored his young charge to return to the basics. "Go to the body hard." But the kid from Brownsville could smell the end coming. "Give me one more round." The patient champion stalked his man for the first minute of the round. Then, as the two fighters lay on each other's shoulders, the final act began to unfold. Tyson initiated the old 8–2 as laid out by Cus D'Amato. A right hook sank deep into the challenger's rib cage. At the same instant, the champ took one step back and to the side, and unleashed a lightning-like right uppercut that drove Thomas' head skyward. Seconds later, a sizzling left hook found Thomas' unprotected chin, knocking him back on his heels. A follow-up right put the Michigan heavyweight on Queer Street. Now it was just a matter of time. A vicious 15-punch assault, led by left hooks and right uppercuts, ensued. Thomas stumbled backward, eyes glazed, hands hanging helplessly at his side. A final left hook crashed into his jaw, putting the courageous challenger on his back for the ten count. It was an impressive performance by the young king of the heavyweights, more so against a man who had fought the biggest bombers in the division and had never been off his feet. After the fight, an excited Tyson said, "I knew from watching his previous fights that he tended to get tired around the seventh round. I had seen him gasping for air."[12]

In the other bout of the evening, Tony "TNT" Tucker became the new IBF heavyweight champion by knocking out James "Buster" Douglas in the tenth round of a scheduled 15-rounder. Tucker, fighting out of Houston, Texas, ran his undefeated skein to 34 straight with his 30th knockout, as he disposed of Douglas, 23–3–1, a 4–1 underdog, with a furious flurry that left the Ohio heavyweight defenseless on the ropes. The final fight of the HBO Unification Series was now a reality. WBA-WBC king Mike Tyson and IBF Champion Tony Tucker would square off in the ring at the Las Vegas Hilton on the evening of August 1 for 15 rounds of boxing—or less. The winner would be the proud owner, and the sole owner, of all three belts, and would be the undisputed heavyweight champion of the world. Mike Tyson was sure to be an overwhelming favorite to own those three belts when the sun rose on August 2. Time would tell if that scenario would become a reality.

There were many interested observers at the fight, but none more personally involved than Gerry Cooney and Michael Spinks. Cooney's manager, Dennis Rappaport, watched the proceedings with dollar signs reflecting off his eyeballs, anticipating a possible Tyson-Cooney matchup. "If Tyson keeps knocking out his opponents, and when Gerry knocks out Spinks, the two will lock horns in what will be the biggest heavyweight championship fight in boxing history." Butch Lewis and Michael Spinks were beating their own drum at the same time. Spinks, who referred to himself as the "People's Champion," scoffed at Tyson's titles. "Tyson won a couple of meaningless belts, but the people know who the real champion is." Tyson, annoyed at the constant badgering from the Spinks camp, retaliated, "Anyone who thinks Spinks is the heavyweight champion, you have to question their mentality."[13]

Now that the Tyson-Thomas match was history, "The War at the Shore" between Michael Spinks and Gerry Cooney hit the front pages of the sports papers. It was being advertised as the "People's Championship." It was hardly that, but it would produce a bona fide challenger for Tyson's crown, someone who could attract a generous gate. The great hype for "The War at the Shore," unfortunately, fell far short of its objective. The event turned out to be a financial disaster. The live gate at the Convention Center was a sellout, but the closed circuit outlets across the country experienced a lack of fan interest, many of them cancelling the telecast due to slow ticket sales. One Philadelphia promoter's show was typical of the situation across the country. "I sold 80 to 85 percent of all available seats for Hagler-Leonard. If I do 20 percent for this fight, I'll be lucky." Still, all the principals in the boxing business made sure they were in Atlantic City to witness the battle and to wheel and deal for future attractions. Mike was there, accompanied by his lady.

As the two combatants made their way to the ring, Cooney was a slight favorite. The big Irishman, all 6'7" of him, looked to be in excellent condition at a solid 238 pounds. Spinks, at 208¾, was still looked upon as a light heavyweight in most quarters. The feeling was that his 30–0 record with 20 knockouts wouldn't hold up against the big New Yorker. "Gentleman Gerry," 28–1 with 24 KO's, was expected to chop the smaller man down within five rounds. As 15,732 fans looked on with curiosity and some amusement, the little man showed no respect for his bigger foe in the opening round. Spinks boxed beautifully, dancing around the slow-footed Cooney, keeping him at bay with solid, well-timed jabs. Occasionally, the former IBF champ even stepped in and mixed it up with the Long Island slugger. It was obvious that Cooney was confused. He didn't know how to combat Spinks' strategy. Spinks was in and out, jabbing and dancing, then moving in quickly with a flurry of solid shots to the big man's head. "Gentleman Gerry" could see openings, but he was too slow to react to them. By the time he set up to punch, the will-o'-the-wisp Spinks was gone.

Rounds one and two went to Spinks easily, as the plodding Cooney followed his man around the ring helplessly. A clash of heads opened a gash over Spinks' right eye in round three. Even though the corner controlled the cut effectively, Spinks fought from a defensive posture in round four, losing the round on all cards. By round five, the former IBF champion had regrouped mentally and came out firing at the start of the round. He attacked the big heavyweight with abandon, raining more than 50 telling punches on Cooney's body. A right hook dropped Cooney in a neutral corner for a five count. Spinks was on his man again, bombarding the disillusioned Irishman with numerous punches to the head. Again Cooney slumped to the canvas under the accumulation of blows, only to arise to absorb more punishment. Referee Frank Cappuccino was finally forced to step in and halt the action as Spinks unleashed a constant barrage of unanswered punches on his timid opponent.

In less than 15 minutes of boxing, Michael Spinks' image changed drastically. No more was he considered to be an inflated light heavyweight. His total destruction of Gerry Cooney vaulted the Philadelphia fighter into the forefront of the heavyweights, a logical challenger for Mike Tyson's crown. Michael Spinks may have been the smartest fighter in the ring at that time. His philosophy, "I know I'm going to win. I just don't know how," had served him in good stead through ten years of professional challenges. Spinks liked to get in the ring and see what his opponent had. Then he did what he had to do to win. Whether that strategy would suffice against the pressing, hard-punching champion remained to be seen. Manager Butch Lewis orchestrated Spinks' escape from the HBO tournament in order to reap monetary rewards from a Cooney fight, although most boxing experts felt he had committed a monumental blunder. The victory vindicated Lewis and cast him as a promotional genius.[14]

Down the street at the Sands Hotel/Casino, another fistic challenge was in progress as "Smokin' Joe" Frazier tangled with Larry Holmes in a clash of former champions. This time, however, the field of battle was a stage instead of a ring, and the weapons were microphones and electronic amplifiers instead of boxing gloves. The two heavyweights exchanged musical jabs and uppercuts for 90 minutes, backed up by their respective groups, the Knockouts and the Marmalades. Though serious musical talent was lacking on both sides, Frazier's greater experience and stage generalship gave him the victory by a wide margin. The winner happily danced offstage to the mournful cries of "I'm still Smokin'."

Another potential challenger for Tyson's crown took his second step forward on the comeback trail. Big George Foreman, still a flabby 249 pounds, disposed of club fighter Charlie Hostetter at 2:01 of round three. Foreman looked better than he had in his previous fight. He was 18 pounds lighter and showed a stiff left jab, but it was a crushing right uppercut that put Hostetter's lights out. It was doubtful that Foreman could ever come back far enough to seriously challenge Mike Tyson, but the Cruiserweight Champ, Evander Holyfield, was still making noises in that direction. After disposing of Oscar Ocasio to up his record to 16–0, the Alabama youngster announced his plans to move up in weight class. He added a physical fitness expert to his staff to design a program to make him a full-fledged heavyweight à la Michael Spinks. Carrying 186 pounds on his 6'1" frame, Holyfield anticipated adding 30 pounds to bring him up to a solid 215 pounds before he challenged Tyson. He launched his first challenge at the heavyweight king. "I hope nobody busts Mike's bubble before I get a chance."

Back in Catskill, Mike Tyson had to listen to more criticism of his boxing ability. In spite of his sixth-round knockout of Thomas, his performance was still panned by boxing writers in some quarters. "He doesn't punch out in clinches." "He doesn't work the body

Rooney taping Tyson's hands in the gym (courtesy Paul Antonelli).

enough." "He head hunts." "He doesn't use the jab enough." "He's a slugger, not a boxer." His defensive skills were still going unnoticed, largely because all attention was focused on his electrifying offensive skills. But Mike Tyson was a superb defensive fighter. After 43 amateur fights and 31 professional fights, his face was unmarked. As Jim Jacobs was fond of stating, "If you met Mike immediately after a fight, you wouldn't know what his profession was. He carries no scars of battle."

Six weeks till Unification time. Rooney and Tyson set up camp on Main Street to begin the champ's conditioning program. According to the recently vanquished Pinklon Thomas, Mr. "TNT" Tucker was going to have his hands full on August 1. "It was the first time I was down. Mike is going to be one tough cookie to crack."[15] The final weekend of June, the championship team of Tyson, Rooney, Lott, and Baranski boarded a 3 p.m. flight at La Guardia and headed west—to Las Vegas—to the Hilton Hotel—and to glory. Along the way, the heavyweight champion continued to learn the steep price he would be forced to pay for fame. Each day, in some way or other, he discovered that his private life was a thing of the past. Every action and comment was put under a microscope and meticulously dissected by the men and women of the press. More often than not, these so-called journalists searched in hope of uncovering some sensational tidbit of information that could be made into an "expose." Violence and sex were preferred.

Before starting his final training program in Vegas, the kid from Catskill paid one last visit to his girlfriend in Hollywood. He and Robin attended a rock concert at the Greek Theatre, where they were entertained by Run-DMC and the Beastie Boys. After the show, an incident in the VIP parking lot brought the champ more unwelcome headlines. Allegedly, the energetic Tyson grabbed a female parking lot attendant, Tabita Gonzalez, and tried to kiss her. Supervisor Jonathan Casares heard her screams and raced to her rescue on an electric golf cart, only to be faced with the menacing visage of the heavyweight champion of the world. According to Casares, as he attempted to free the girl, Tyson grabbed him and struck him in the face with the heel of his hand, bloodying his lip and nose. Casares and Gonzalez filed a complaint with the City Attorney's Office, and Tyson was subsequently charged with two counts of assault and battery with a dangerous weapon—a professional boxer's hands. A hearing was scheduled for August 26. In the meantime, the champ was released in his own recognizance. If found guilty, Mike Tyson faced up to 18 months in jail plus a fine of $12,000.[16]

As the newspapers were having a field day with the 21-year-old king of the ring, manager Bill Cayton raced to his defense. "Things are blown all out of proportion if there's a way to make a gain."[17] Mike Tyson himself professed his innocence. "Anyone can think and say what they want. But those who know me know what happened. That's all I have to worry about. Those who I love and who love me." The young boxer was glad to get back to Las Vegas. He was well protected in the training camp, and Kevin Rooney made sure that Mike had an escort wherever he went. Still, the tight security did not guarantee peace and quiet. There were rumors of a rift between the fighter and his trainer, a charge that Rooney strongly denied. "All that talk is bull. It's like a joke to me. It doesn't affect me or Mike. We're stickin' to our plan and not lettin' all the distractions bother us."[18]

On July 24, Mike Tyson mysteriously disappeared from camp, once again giving the boys in the tabloids new fodder to digest. "Tyson deserts training camp." "Tyson and Rooney feud in Vegas." "Tyson becoming basket case now that he's champ." The men of the press did not know where Mike Tyson was, nor did they know why he left camp. But they talked like they did. They pieced together fragments of stories from several different sources. They deduced the events of the day based on previous rumors. Or they just concocted the stories out of their vivid imaginations. In any case, the stories would titillate their readers. Their stories, as usual, were wrong. Mike Tyson's adopted mother, Camille Ewald, was sick, bedded down in Catskill with the flu. Mike was worried about her health and eventually had to tear himself away from camp and go back to Catskill to visit her. Mike's friends knew where he was at all times. In fact, the champ made a surprise guest appearance in the paper hat parade at the Old Catskill Days street festival on July 26. In spite of all the outside legal problems, the rumors of a rift between Tyson and Rooney, and the AWOL incident, business went on as usual in the Tyson compound. Mike Tyson diligently pursued his quest to unify the heavyweight title.

The Catskill youngster no longer measured himself against his contemporaries, but against the legends of the ring. His goal was to be recognized as the greatest fighter of all time. That goal was within his grasp. He would not let it slip away. Assistant manager Steve Lott praised Mike's work ethic. "He's in terrific shape. We're boxing 6 to 8 rounds now, but it's still early. We'll get up to 10 and 12 rounds, and one day 15."[19] The Tyson camp had a tremendous advantage over their opponents when it came to attracting sparring partners. In the Tyson camp, money was no object. They paid top wages and they got the best opponents. As Kevin Rooney said, "We used to have problems sparrin' with Mike. But now we pay them so well, they can't turn the money down." The workouts were intense, and the sparring sessions, with such willing opponents as James Broad, Oscar Holman, and Anthony Witherspoon, were shockingly violent, as attested to by the ugly red welts that decorated the bodies of the champ's adversaries. "You get in there and it's war—war at the gym," said Holman, a journeyman heavyweight with a 13–7–1 record. "It ain't no boxing. It's fighting. It's different fighting this guy. He's just too full of energy and too strong. Believe me, the money has to be good or I wouldn't be doing this. I'd get an eight hour a day job rather than take this punishment." James Broad echoed the feelings of all the fighters. "Every time I throw a punch, I try to knock him out."[20]

Johnny Tocco's Gym was sweltering. The perspiration ran off the fighters' bodies like running water. The outside temperature was 106 degrees, and the temperature inside was about the same. Mike Tyson wanted to work in the heat so he'd get used to it. He was anticipating the stifling desert air in the Hilton parking lot on fight night, and he wanted to be ready to go a hard 12 rounds, heat or no heat. Anthony Witherspoon was sent to the hospital one day with bruised ribs. Witherspoon, the brother of "Terrible Tim," marveled at the power of "Iron Mike." "It makes you freeze, getting hit so hard like that. I've never been hit so hard by anyone." When he returned to the ring wars, young Witherspoon was decked out in a full flak jacket to protect his tender body. At a different time of day, in the same city, in the same gym, IBF Champion Tony Tucker was busy preparing himself for the trial to come. The 6'5", 221-pound Tucker was a determined fighter. Sporting an undefeated 35–0 record embellished with 30 knockouts, he was not to be taken lightly. He was strong, mobile, and confident, three traits that spell winner. And he was a champion.

As the days wound down, the rumor mill quieted and the interest centered around the fight itself. Tyson's manager reiterated the champ's strategy for the fight, saying that it's the same as it's always been. "Attack at the sound of the bell." The rhetoric emanating from Tucker's camp prior to the fight was low-key compared to previous Tyson opponents. Tony Tucker himself expressed quiet confidence that, when the smoke cleared, he would be crowned champion. "Here I am, a man who don't know nothin' about losin', and I'm a 12–1 underdog. I get motivated when I hear these odds. I don't get mad about it. I've got somethin' to prove. Somebody's gonna get rich bettin' on me." Kevin Rooney was another one who respected Tucker's talents. "Deep down, I feel that Tucker will come out to fight. He has a snappy right hand, and it could go longer than most people think, but I will say that it will be an excitin' fight."[21]

As the sun set beyond the stark Nevada desert on the evening of August 1, referee Mills Lane brought the two champions together in the center of the ring at the Hilton Center before a near-capacity throng of 8,000. The IBF King and the WBA-WBC Champion eyed each other warily as they listened to their final instructions prior to the long-awaited Unification shootout. The HBO Series had begun over one year ago with three separate titleholders and a dozen or more claimants to the throne. Now the field had dwindled down to only two, the IBF Champion, Tony Tucker, and the WBA-WBC King, Mike Tyson. The time had come to pit champion against champion in the final gladiatorial encounter. Two gladiators would enter the arena, clad only in sandals and loincloths, unarmed except for their fists. One of them would emerge as the undisputed king of the heavyweights.

The fight itself was an exciting one. Tony "TNT" Tucker did, in fact, come to fight, and he gave a good account of himself. His best moment came only one minute into the fight, when he caught a pressing Tyson flush on the chin with a sizzling left uppercut. The force of the blow lifted the smaller man completely off his feet and drove him back on his heels. A lesser man might have hit the canvas immediately and called it a night. To his credit, the kid from Catskill absorbed the blow with his mighty neck and came right back on the attack as if nothing had happened. As Mike admitted later, "I kind of took him for granted, and that was a big mistake." Tucker's strategy was well thought out and proved effective against the WBA-WBC Champ in hand-to-hand combat, flurrying for a few seconds, then dancing out of harm's way one more time. On those occasions when Tyson successfully worked his way inside, the Texas heavyweight tied him up to prevent the patented Tyson body attack from materializing. For his part, Mike Tyson maintained the pressure constantly, following his man, working his way inside, and unleashing punches with bad intentions whenever the opportunity presented itself. There were no knockdowns in the fast-paced affair, although Tyson landed numerous hard left hooks and jarring rights to Tucker's head. For the most part, they were one-shot forays as Tucker's clinching tactics stalled the New Yorker's attempts to initiate multiple combinations. Tucker's strategy made the fight interesting but Tyson was still winning most of the rounds. His punches were the most effective and, little by little, they wore down the IBF Champion. Tyson noticed a change in the big slugger as the fight progressed. "But after six or seven rounds, he stopped fighting and started running. He knew he couldn't win, so he was just running to go the distance. He was looking for miracles. There are no miracles here."[22]

When the final decision was announced, it was no surprise. Mike Tyson was declared an easy winner, yielding only two rounds to the former IBF Champion. The kid from Catskill now stood alone at the top of the heavyweight division, holding all three crowns, the WBC, WBA, and IBF. August 1, 1987, was a day to be remembered in boxing history. It was the beginning of the Tyson era. As soon as all the ringside formalities were completed, Don King staged a garish coronation ceremony in the hotel ballroom. The champion good-naturedly attended the festivities and permitted himself to be escorted to the stage via a long, red carpet. He was seated on his royal throne wearing the purple robe trimmed with ermine, the royal scepter in his hand. He graciously allowed Don King to place the ermine crown upon his head, a crown described by the flamboyant promoter as studded with "baubles, rubies, and fabulous do-dads." According to King, "England never had a coronation like this." Mike's only comment was an embarrassed, "I feel like a freak."[23] And he should have felt like a freak, because on this night he was.

Cus D'Amato must have turned over in his grave at such a disgraceful exhibition.

Michael Spinks and his mentor, Butch Lewis, watched the Tyson-Tucker fight from the cheap seats. Lewis got on his soapbox at every opportunity, trying to sell the public on the ultimate fight—the WBA-WBC-IBF Champion against the real champion, the "People's Champion," his man, Michael Spinks. "This is the ultimate fight. It's unpredictable. No one knows how it will turn out." Jim Jacobs for one was annoyed at the constant bantering from the Spinks-Lewis duo.

> They had their chance to fight Mike Tyson, but they chose to break their contract with HBO. They withdrew from the tournament to fight Gerry Cooney. We keep our commitments. We are fighting Tyrell Biggs in October. We have another match scheduled for January, and we will fight in Tokyo in March. Michael Spinks is not on our agenda. We have no plans to fight Michael Spinks, and you can write that with an exclamation point.[24]

For the first time since he fought for the championship, Mike Tyson would not be fighting in Las Vegas. The Tyrell Biggs fight would be held on October 16 in the Trump Plaza in Atlantic City, New Jersey, the first title fight under business magnate Donald Trump. On Tuesday, August 25, a press conference was held at the Grand Hyatt Hotel in New York City to announce the fight formally, to present the new boxing entrepreneur Donald Trump, and to introduce the combatants in what Don King called "The Clash for The Crown." Six days later, the sports world was saddened by the death of one of its legendary sports columnists, Dick Young of the *New York Daily News* and *New York Post*. Young, who spent 50 years behind a typewriter, had covered such magical names as DiMaggio, Louis, Williams, Marciano, and Man O War. The king is dead. Long live the king.

A major concern permeated the offices of Big Fights, Inc. during the early days of autumn: how badly Mike Tyson's image was damaged by the Greek Theatre incident in June. The whole ugly episode was dragged through the papers again on September 29 when Los Angeles judge Maral Kirakosian dismissed the charges after Tabita Gonzalez and Jonathan Casares, the alleged victims, said Tyson had paid them damages. It was reported that the champ had paid the two in excess of $60,000 not to pursue the criminal charges. One source close to the Tyson camp said, "Forget the cover of the Wheaties box now. This will cost him millions." Not so, said Wheaties spokesman Bill Schaeffer, who was quoted as saying that the Wheaties policy did not infringe on athlete's private lives, but on the individual athlete's outstanding sports accomplishments. "It's how a champion handles adversity in their sport, not in their private lives," insisted Schaeffer. "No question, he's a champion athlete. Tyson could very well be the winner of the Wheaties award some day."[25]

Meanwhile, back on the fight scene, things were heating up at the Trump Plaza press conference in Atlantic City as Jim Jacobs and Lou Duva went head to head. Don King couldn't have written a better script. "These two teams don't like each other," he said as Jim Jacobs and Lou Duva traded barbs. Duva jumped to the front as he predicted victory for his fighter. "Biggs would have beaten you if you two had met in the amateurs and now he will beat you and beat you good in the professionals." Jacobs countered Duva's attack on his fighter, revealing that members of the Biggs camp called their number one contender a "mental case." Biggs added, "I'm already an admitted drug addict if that makes me a mental case," but he promised, "We're going to see a whole different Mike Tyson when he feels my punches. He hasn't really fought the caliber of fighters that I have. Mike could barely knock out guys who could barely stand up in the beginning. All the pre-fight hype, I've had it. I'm ready to fight." Tyson's response was short and sweet. "I don't think there's a human being on this planet that can kick my butt." As usual, Kevin Rooney had the last word. "Talk is cheap. I hope and pray Tyrell Biggs comes to fight and we'll find out just what he's made of."[26]

As Mike Tyson's training camp got under way in Atlantic City, it focused attention on the struggle between the two great gambling meccas, Atlantic City and Las Vegas, for control of the major championship boxing extravaganzas. For ten years, Las Vegas had controlled the big fight purses. Now it was a toss-up, with a slight edge going to the east coast. The sudden shift in location came about with the arrival of millionaire business magnate Donald Trump on the scene. Trump, a self-made tycoon from New York City, purchased land adjacent to the 20,000-seat Atlantic City Convention Center in 1986. There he constructed the magnificent 39-story Trump Hotel and Casino. And there he threw his hat in the ring to attract major boxing events to the city, because boxing fans are reputed to be notorious gamblers and, more important, gamblers that lose big! Boxing and gambling have always gone hand In hand. Trump's first big coup was staging the Spinks-Cooney match, the much publicized "War at the Shore." Although the fight was a major disaster for the closed circuit TV business, it was a financial success for Donald Trump and Atlantic City. The Convention Center was a complete sellout, and the boxing crowd dropped millions at the tables. Now Trump had cornered the popular Tyson-Biggs confrontation, and he was determined to use this match as a launching pad from which to attract more such events in the future.

Trump and the Jacobs/Cayton duo got along well together. They trusted each other and enjoyed their business relationship. Donald Trump hoped that such a feeling of mutual respect would allow him to stage many more Tyson fights in the years to come. In addition to Trump, Atlantic City had many other advantages to offer Mike Tyson and boxing fans. It was close to Tyson's home town of Catskill, New York, making it easy for him to commute back and forth if he so desired. It was also in the middle of the country's major metropolitan area and was easily accessible from New York or Philadelphia. Once settled in Atlantic City, Mike Tyson quickly became involved with one of his pet projects. He visited the local Hospital for Disabled Children, to be with the kids, to give them hope, and to bring smiles to their faces. "When I see them, I feel so bad for them, and I realize that I really shouldn't complain about things like I do, or take things for granted. And I say, damn, I don't have any problems like them. No one has problems like they do." The nurses smiled as they watched the heavyweight champion of the world, dressed in a gray warm-up suit, sitting on the hospital floor playing with the kids, holding them and hugging them. It was incongruous, this picture of "The Baddest Man on the Planet," the heavyweight assassin, gently distributing love and affection to those less fortunate than he. Mike Tyson, the fighter, stepped into the ring with only one thought in mind, to physically destroy his opponent, to hurt him and make him quit. But Mike Tyson, the man, was concerned about the underprivileged and disabled people in the world, particularly the children. He committed his private life to helping those children whenever and however he could.[27]

The "Tyson Team" this time around included several new sparring partners: Glenn McCrory, Melvin Epps, "Quick" Tillis, and young Oliver McCall. McCall was a strapping 6'2", 227-pound heavyweight whose 11–1 professional record and outspoken personality had intrigued Tyson and Jacobs. The two had seen McCall when they attended the Edwin "Chapo" Rosario match. McCall KO'd Richard Scott on the undercard that night and, following his knockout, he raced over to the side of the ring where Tyson was sitting and yelled at him, "I'll whip you too. You're next." Three weeks later, Jacobs invited McCall to Atlantic City. McCall, in fact, caused some consternation in the Tyson camp. The 22-year-old Chicago boxer, known as the "Atomic Bull," sparred 22 rounds with the champ, landing some good punches along the way. One week before the fight, he caught the champ flush on the nose with a right hook, splattering blood all over the ring and turning Tyson's gray warm-up a bright crimson. The cocky McCall immediately corralled the reporters, being his own best PR man. "I'm gonna get Mike Tyson. I can beat both Tyson and Spinks in the same month."

Tillis, Epps, McCrory, and McCall prepared the champ well for the Biggs fight, showing him good hand speed and excellent lateral movement. Rooney was impressed with Tyson's conditioning, as evidenced by the muscle tone in the champ's stomach. He appeared to be in better shape for this fight than for any of his previous title matches. Pointing to the six protruding stomach muscles that Robin Givens fondly called "his washboard," Rooney noted, "It's about there. You can see 'em." The intensity in the champ's training camp continued right up to the last day. The makeshift gym in the theatre section on the fourth floor of the Trump Hotel bustled with activity as a half-dozen fighters went through their training regimen. The rat-a-tat-tat of the speed bag was constant as it was attacked by one fighter after another. In the ring, Tyson faced two, three, and four opponents a day, all bent on bringing him to his knees. "Quick" Tillis, dressed in enough armor to mount a S.W.A.T attack, blasted away at the champ for four rounds. The head gear, groin protector, and flak jacket provided the challenger with an excess of courage. Mike Tyson, whose only protection was the specially designed mini-headgear, had to be a defensive specialist in order to keep his sparring partners from putting serious hurt on him. Melvin Epps danced and survived two rounds. Glenn McCrory moved in and out, harassing the champ and trying to avoid his heavy artillery. Inside the dressing room, Steve Lott flipped on the TV and grabbed a Perrier. The weary Tyson slumped in a chair and gulped water from an ice bucket. "Steve, turn it to MTV." After three songs, the champ pulled himself up, showered, and dressed. It was a good day. The workout had been brisk and challenging. Lott, Baranski, and Rooney were all satisfied with their boxer's progress. The champ was ready.

All was well with "Team Tyson" except for the venomous sounds emanating from the Biggs camp. Headlines abounded nationwide as the bad blood between the camps simmered and boiled. Don King and co-promoter Donald Trump drooled at the verbal conflict between Jacobs and Duva. Publicity of a hostile nature could only ensure a blockbuster gate on fight night. Poor Lou Duva should have followed Mike Tyson's career more closely, as any good manager would. If he had, he would have known that whenever Tyson was verbally assaulted and insulted prior to a match, he entered the ring in a fit of rage and proceeded to dismember the opponent as the mood suited him. In Marvis Frazier's case, he destroyed the challenger in just 30 seconds flat. When Mitch Green derided the Catskill boxer, however, Tyson punished the Bronx bully for ten full rounds, choosing to administer a severe beating to him rather than knock him out. It was certain that Duva's remarks and insults would bode ill for his fighter. Based on past performances, the only question was whether Mike Tyson would choose to take his revenge quickly or would ration it out painfully over a number of rounds before applying the coup de grace.

After the press conference, Tyson was whisked away to a local studio to film a promo for the upcoming fight, all part of the Don King razzle dazzle for the "Clash for the Crown." Shown in a gymnasium setting, a confident Mike Tyson faced the camera. "Hi. I'm Mike Tyson. One day I'd like to be associated with boxing greats like John L. Sullivan, Rocky Marciano, and Joe Louis. Names like Tyrell Biggs, I have no use for. So on Friday October 16, I'm going to the Trump Plaza with bad intentions to put Tyrell Biggs in his proper place in boxing history—great amateur career—Olympic Gold Medalist—got creamed by Mike Tyson."[28]

Mike spent the last two days lounging around the boardwalk and the hotel. He strolled through the casino amidst a sea of well-wishers. "Good luck, son," said one old gentleman. "Would you sign this please?" asked another. The young champion approached his public with the aplomb of a veteran. Twelve months in the spotlight had taught Mike Tyson how to relax amid all the fanfare, how to mingle with his fans on a one-on-one basis, and how to deal with the constant media attention that dogged his footsteps. He was now a major celebrity, and his time was in constant demand. But he was in control. He could deal with the pressures and the public attention like a true champion. As Rudyard Kipling wrote in his famous poem "If," "If you can talk with crowds and keep your virtue—or walk with kings, nor lose the common touch—yours is the earth and everything that's in it and—which is more, you'll be a man, my son." Mike Tyson was a man.

The men of the press cornered Kevin Rooney in the lobby to get his assessment of the fight. "My guy is goin' after him. We're ready to roll. We'll find out if Biggs has a mature heart or if he has some dog in him." Tyson, still fuming at Duva's remarks, muttered to Baranski, "If I don't kill him it doesn't count."[29] The two fighters found it difficult to keep their minds on their training regimen with all the distractions around them, the interviews, the publicity photos, and the press conferences. It was to the credit of both Tyson and Biggs that they arrived at the Convention Center on fight night in tip-top physical condition. As fight time approached, the champ was a study in relaxation. Sitting casually on the rubbing table in his makeshift dressing room, the Brooklyn-born boxer, attired in a hooded gray warm-up suit, quietly listened to the music of Sam Cooke. He nonchalantly kicked his legs back and forth to the strains of "You Send Me."

At precisely 10:20, the door opened and a visitor peered in. "Mike, you're on." The champ smiled, gave him a thumbs-up sign and a wink, and slipped off the table. "Let's go." Matt Baranski grabbed his bag and quickly checked it to be sure he had everything he would need in case Mike got hurt. Fresh adrenaline ... coagulants ... Thrombin and Avitene ... an ice bag ... surgical scissors ... gauze pads ... Q-tips ... and a pressure plate to help reduce swelling or to move blood away from a critical area, such as a swollen eye. As the champ moved toward the door, his expression suddenly changed from one of contentment to one of hate. It was as if a dark cloud had passed across his face. His thoughts became instantaneously focused on only one thing, destroying his opponent as quickly as possible.

Tyrell Biggs slipped from his dressing room almost apprehensively and descended the stairs to the Convention Center surrounded by a large entourage of handlers and security people. He was decked out in a white satin Nehru shirt, with his name and the logo "realize your potential" emblazoned across the back in bright red letters. Outwardly, the Philadelphia fighter looked fit and ready, but as the great Roman orator, Marcus Tullius Cicero, once noted, "the eyes are the windows of the soul." And Tyrell Biggs' eyes gave him away. They revealed to the world what was lurking in the deep recesses of the challenger's soul as he climbed into the ring to do battle with the heavyweight champion. The emotion that Biggs felt was fear. "Iron Mike" almost ran to the ring, so anxious was he to get his hands on his amateur nemesis. Tyson's somber appearance, in his black sockless and robeless dress, stood out in dark contrast to the challenger's flashy attire. It was only in their eyes where the champion had the advantage, the eyes and the head.

As round one got underway, the challenger showed excellent lateral movement and a stinging jab, two weapons that could give Tyson trouble over the distance if they could be maintained. Tyson was out fast, as usual, applying immediate pressure on the challenger. A hard right to the ribcage drove Biggs across the ring at the start of the round. Biggs was on the balls of his feet, backpedaling away from the champion's advances, trying to throw him off balance with constant movement. Tyson patiently stalked his man, bobbing and weaving from a low crouch, trying to work his way inside the tall Philadelphian's defenses. It became obvious early that Biggs had one serious weakness that could be exploited by the Catskill assassin and result in the challenger's early exit from the fight. Biggs carried his left hand very low, down by his waist, offering an inviting target for a Tyson right hook. Biggs kept his man at bay successfully throughout the early part of the round with his side-to-side maneuvers and his ability to stay at long range and not allow Tyson to trap him on the ropes. Tyson maintained his low peek-a-boo crouch like a well-disciplined student. A stinging right cross brought blood from Biggs' mouth as the round neared an end. Biggs had already slowed noticeably under the Tyson attack and, inexplicably, stopped dancing after the first two minutes. In a pre-fight press conference, the Olympic champion told reporters he had a plan to defeat the champion, whereby Tyson remarked, "They all have a plan until they get hit the first time."

Apparently, that's what happened to Biggs in round one. As soon as he took one good shot from the champion, he forgot his fight plan and fought just to survive. At a post-fight interview, Biggs stated that he lost his confidence in round one. The truth is that he never had any confidence. It was the one chink in his athletic armor, a weakness that haunted him throughout his career. The big man had plenty of heart and an abundance of talent, but he lacked the confidence necessary to become a champion. Heart allows a person to absorb tremendous punishment, to survive. But confidence is that special trait that makes a person a winner. When you know you are going to win, you will do whatever it takes to win. Tyrell Biggs was a courageous fighter, a survivor. But Mike Tyson was a winner. The Philadelphia fighter began to unravel in round two, pushing his jab instead of throwing it, and forgetting all about alternating his line of retreat. The outcome of the fight soon became a foregone conclusion. Tyrell Biggs was emotionally overwhelmed by the determined champion. His effort lacked enthusiasm, and he seemed bent on surviving rather than on winning. If Tyrell Biggs could regroup and begin moving and jabbing, he could still win the fight. But as a stationary target, he couldn't hope to survive 15 rounds. It was only a matter of time before Mike Tyson recorded his 28th knockout.

The kid from Catskill took the challenger apart methodically round after round, thrashing him with crushing body shots, then shifting to the head with stunning left hooks to Biggs' unprotected chin. Blood had flowed from Biggs' mouth after Tyson split his lip in the first round, and a nasty gash was opened over his left eye in round three. It was the same eye David Bey had slashed open on March 7. The wound would require more than 20 stitches to close. Biggs' chest and trunks were covered with his own blood as he came out to face the onslaught in round four. He desperately grabbed the champion around the ears with both gloves in an effort to stop the punishment. But Kid Dynamite continued to dish out a systematic beating. Between rounds four and five, trainer Kevin Rooney admonished the champion. "You're layin' back. Takin' it easy. You can't take it easy with this guy. You gotta keep the pressure on. You gotta move your hands. You gotta throw the combinations. You gotta put 2,3,4, punches together. Do you unnerstan' what I'm sayin?'" Across the ring, Lou Duva tried to encourage the embattled challenger. "One more round, he won't be there baby." Both fighter and trainer knew the emptiness of that statement.

Tyson started the fifth round by walking straight across the ring and unloading a thunderous right to the side of Biggs' head, buckling the big man's knees. Duva was still inside the ring when the punch landed. The pummeling continued throughout the round as the stronger Tyson overpowered the game but outgunned Olympic champ. Biggs tried to fight back, but his punches fell like harmless drops on the body of the former Brownsville street kid. A solid Tyson right hand found its target at the 1:30 mark, and a short, chopping right to the ribs caused the Philadelphia fighter to wince in obvious discomfort. Biggs' face looked like something that had gone through a meat grinder. In addition to the bloody mass above his left eye, an ugly swelling appeared underneath his right eye, and a constant trickle of blood oozed from the corner of his mouth. Biggs corner worked frantically to inspire their charge between rounds, but it was all in vain. Duva pleaded with his fighter, "Now look, don't give in to this kid. Keep your hands up when you jive. Don't trust the guy."

Round six began like every other round, Tyson walking through Biggs' defense to score with combinations to the head and body. The champ's punches were landing with increasing ferocity and accuracy as he stalked his man like a jungle predator. A sizzling right cross to the temple was followed by a similar punch from the left side. Tyson advanced on his man with 37 seconds left in the round and unloaded a flurry of punches to the head and body, each punch thrown with bad intentions. Biggs had a look of panic on his face as the round came to an end. Rooney implored his man to step up the attack. "More 7's. 6–5–1, 6–5–2–1. Get to the side. Play with this guy now. You unnerstan?' This guys got nothin'. Give him a fake. Step to the side." In the Biggs corner, the attempt to rebuild the challenger's destroyed confidence continued. "You've taken the best he's got, so what the hell's wrong with you? C'mon, this guy's gone. C'mon, you're a better fighter than him. If you got no legs, fight him inside."

As the two fighters clinched at the beginning of round seven, Tyson came up with a forearm that knocked Biggs' mouthpiece into the second row of spectators. Biggs' legs appeared to be gone, and Tyson pummeled the stationary target around the ring with an avalanche of blows. The champ moved in low, bobbing and weaving to avoid the challenger's jabs. The pain of the fight was evident in Biggs' actions, as he frequently covered up in anticipation of a Tyson barrage, even when one was not forthcoming. This action was the ultimate admission of intimidation on Biggs' part. The challenger tried to get inside Tyson's hooks, hoping to land a lucky punch, but he was no match for the energetic New Yorker. With 32 seconds left in the round, Tyson caught Biggs with a glancing left hook to the temple, similar to the punch that destroyed Berbick. The big heavyweight toppled backwards through the ropes, onto the apron of the ring, with Tyson falling against the upper strands, straddling the fallen fighter. Biggs' face was a study in pain and disbelief. His body and trunks were drenched in his own blood as it gushed from the jagged wound above his left eye. He valiantly volunteered to continue the battle, but it was a foolhardy gesture. Six seconds later, a thundering roundhouse right put Biggs on Queer Street, and a follow-up left hook to the point of the chin found its mark. The challenger stumbled back several feet before collapsing in a neutral corner, his head resting comfortably on the bottom strand of ropes. Referee Tony Orlando immediately stopped the fight without a count, fearing for the safety of the Philadelphia fighter.

At the post-fight interview with HBO analyst Larry Merchant, the champion brimmed with confidence. "I was havin' a great time out there. I felt good. I was in the best condition of my life, and I did what I was supposed to do. I hurt him with body punches. Actually he was cryin' in there, makin' woman gestures like 'oo—oo.' I knew he was breakin' down—perhaps from the fourth round on."[30] It was obvious that Mike Tyson was maturing as a boxer with each fight. In this match, he exhibited a good left hook, better use of his jab, and more body punches than in recent outings.

He had just won his fifth championship fight in a little less than 11 months, and he deserved a long rest. But there was no rest for the champ yet. He had promised his fans he would be a fighting champion, and he was already scheduled to meet four new opponents in the next year. Mike Tyson, the youngest champion in heavyweight history, had set his sights on a new goal. He wanted to be recognized as the greatest heavyweight champion of all time.

11

The People's Champion—June 27, 1988

The headline on October 17 trumpeted the news: "Tyson Carves Up Biggs to Win in 7th." The defeated manager, Lou Duva, solemnly read the eulogy. "[Tyrell Biggs] lost confidence in the second or third round. He didn't quit in his heart. He quit in his head." On the sidelines, several interested spectators sought out the media. Larry Holmes, anticipating a title fight in the near future, spoke of dirty tactics on the champ's part and threatened retaliation if the champ attempted to use those tactics on him. "Tyson was dirtier than I've ever seen him. Whatever he does to me, I'll do back. He's going to think it's Hulk Hogan vs the Junkyard Dog."[1]

The Spinks-Lewis duo were visible and vocal as usual, trying to force the Tyson camp into a match. Jim Jacobs reemphasized the champion's agenda. "Michael Spinks is certainly in our future, but not our immediate future." He did propose a winner-take-all match between his fighter and Spinks, with the loser taking home $1 million and the winner getting the bulk of the purse, as much as $20 million. Michael Spinks quickly shrugged off that suggestion. "What if I lose? I got to go home sad and poor too."[2]

As the renowned boxing historian Jim Jacobs saw it, Mike Tyson had to meet these two adversaries in the ring before he could take his rightful place alongside boxing's legends. First, he had to defend his crown successfully against the "old guard," Larry Holmes. Then he had to defeat Michael Spinks, the so-called "People's Champion," and *Ring Magazine*'s heavyweight titleholder. Jacobs, a stickler for the line of succession, admitted that Spinks won the true championship when he beat Larry Holmes for the IBF crown, since Holmes' lineage could be traced all the way back to John L. Sullivan. In the manager's eyes, a champion can only lose his title in the ring, not have it stripped away by some petulant boxing authority. Therefore, Mike Tyson had to take the "real" title from Michael Spinks in the ring before he could follow in the footsteps of the great John L.

Even though Larry Holmes appeared to be the next man who would climb into the ring with the heavyweight champion, the countdown had already begun on an eventual Tyson-Spinks confrontation. The media propaganda increased daily as the big city publications heralded the credentials of the two men, the champion Mike Tyson standing astride the boxing world with a record of 32–0, and the challenger, the undefeated former light heavyweight and IBF heavyweight champion of the world, Michael Spinks, sporting an equally impressive 31–0 mark. The tall, lanky Spinks was certainly a deserving challenger, equally effective attacking or counterpunching. His awkward style confused his opponents and created openings for his two-handed combinations. *Ring Magazine* championed boxing tradition by recognizing Michael Spinks as the true heavyweight champion by reason of the revered "line of succession" from John L. Sullivan to Larry Holmes. Assuming that the Tyson camp kept its pledge to fight in Japan in March, it would be possible for a Tyson-Spinks match to take place later in 1988, possibly as early as June.

But first things first. Before the heavyweight king could even begin to think about tangling with Michael Spinks, he first had to get by Larry Holmes and then possibly Tony "TNT" Tubbs in Tokyo. The Holmes fight was scheduled for the Atlantic City Convention Center on January 22, only three months after the Biggs demolition. Before returning to his training regimen, however, Mike Tyson had a personal commitment to keep, helping his old friend, Father George Clements of Holy Angels Church in Chicago. Father Clements, a maverick inner city priest, had for years kept the Catholic Church's Chicago diocese in an uproar with his unorthodox behavior. The good Father worked with the poor and neglected people of the Windy City, helping them become useful citizens. Although some of Father Clements methods were unconventional—he strove to educate the citizens in their voter registration rights, for instance—they were results oriented. Over the years, the black priest became such a champion of people's rights that a TV movie, starring Lou Gossett, Jr., was made about him.

Father Clements had the painful experience of watching his beloved church burn to the ground on June 9, 1986. Shortly thereafter, friends of the good Father began a drive to raise the necessary funds to rebuild the structure. As part of that drive, a professional boxing program was held at De Paul University's Alumni Hall on the evening of November 13, 1987. Heading the impressive card was a seven-round heavyweight exhibition match between champion Mike Tyson and his old adversary, James "Quick" Tillis. By all accounts, the match was a competitive one. Even though the champ wore headgear for this one, the encounter was described as a typical Tyson war. There were no official scorecards kept, but Tillis gave a good account of himself, even carrying the fight to the champion in the final two rounds. Thanks to the efforts of people like Tyson and Tillis, the event drew 5,000 fans to Alumni Hall and added over $50,000 to the church fund.[3]

Two weeks later, the promotion for the Tyson-Holmes match began in earnest. A press conference was held in the ballroom of the Grand Hyatt Hotel in New York City to kick off the event, labeled "Heavyweight History" by the pugilistic huckster, Don King. Mike Tyson was first on the scene and politely posed for photographs with Meghan Coutineri, the March of Dimes Poster Child. Meghan's mother said later that "Mike came right over and hugged her. She told me afterwards that she liked him." Mike Tyson liked Meghan also—but he didn't like Larry Holmes. He thought Holmes had a bad attitude and was rude and petty. Holmes' behavior on this day only served to reinforce that opinion. The "Easton Assassin" kept everyone waiting for over an hour. When he finally did enter the ballroom, an angry Mike Tyson refused to shake his hand. Once at the podium, Tyson was asked why he hadn't welcomed Holmes to the affair. His reply was curt and to the point. "Because I didn't want to. I don't like Larry Holmes." That was all Don King and the media representatives needed. The reports of bad blood between the two combatants were like music to the ears of the promoter and the men of the press. Stories of the hate war were fed to the fans on a daily basis. For eight weeks, the press corps kept up the barrage, reporting on the hostility that existed between the two boxers and their camps.[4]

In mid–December, the Tyson team moved its base of operations from Catskill to Atlantic City and set up operations in the Beach Club condominium on the Boardwalk.

Tyson brought about a dozen old photographs of former boxing greats with him, and he spent the better part of the first afternoon taping them to the walls of the apartment. The action photos of great fighters like Jack Johnson, Henry Armstrong, and Battling Nelson would constantly remind the young champ of the dedication and discipline required to be the best. They would be his motivation, his driving force, for the next six weeks. Once the young slugger geared himself to the training regimen, he blocked out all outside distractions, maintaining perfect tunnel vision on the job at hand. "New Year's Eve is on Thursday night," Rooney explained. "We have a workday on Friday with sparring. It'll be a quiet New Year's Eve this time. We'll do our celebrating after the fight."[5] Rooney added, "We're gonna have Mike sparrin' as much as we can. Cus always said that the best way to prepare for a fight is to spar as much as possible. We teach our fighters to avoid punches. As long as our fighters don't get hit, sparrin' can only help. Plus Mike loves to fight. Some of these guys enter the ring only once a year. There's no way you can reach your peak doin' that." Including sparring sessions, Mike Tyson entered the ring more than 150 times a year.[6]

Training camp life can be dreadfully tedious, particularly in a Spartan atmosphere like Tyson had. Mike's day began at 4 a.m. long before the sun made its appearance over the Atlantic horizon. Within 20 minutes, the kid from Catskill was doing his three-mile run along the boardwalk and white sandy beach of the seaside resort. Some days he relaxed briefly by feeding the seagulls, from two loaves of bread he brought with him. After a light breakfast, the champ and his roommates, Rooney and Lott, killed the morning flipping through newspapers and magazines. At noon, the three men motored to the Pleasantville Recreation Cen-

(Left to right) Donald Trump, Don King, Bill Cayton and Tyson at the Tyson-Holmes press conference (courtesy Paul Antonelli).

ter for the daily two-hour workout. They were joined there by Matt Baranski and sparring partners "Quick" Tills, Oliver McCall, and James Broad. By mid-afternoon, the 21-year-old was back in his condo, pacing the floor like a prison inmate. Even the meals were eaten in, to protect the heavyweight king from his adoring but disruptive fans. In the evening, the group either rented videos or analyzed video tapes of the day's training camp activities. "Early to bed, early to rise, makes a man, healthy, wealthy, and wise," goes the old saying. For Mike Tyson that meant hitting the sheets no later than 9 o'clock. Soon it would be 4 a.m. and the cycle would begin all over again.[7]

As the days wound down, the champion's mental and physical condition was honed to a fine edge by Rooney. Tyson, particularly, was happy to see fight day approach.

> 80 percent of the trainin' is all emotional. I try not to think about the fight ... but when I'm trainin', I would think about the fight, and I always dream that I lose, and it's very scary. I'd say "Oh, my god, what am I gonna do now?" It's funny when you dream you lose. You wake up and you wake up thinkin' that you lost. It's scary. The most difficult part of fightin' is the trainin'. Believe it or not, the easy part of fightin' is the fightin'.[8]

On fight night, both boxers were in a determined mood and ready to mix it up. The 21-year-old champ tipped the scales at a svelte 215¾ pounds, his lowest weight in many months. The aging former heavyweight king, now 38 years old, was also well prepared, carrying a tight 225¾ pounds on his 6'3" frame. The big question in the Holmes camp was how many rounds his old legs would carry him. At his age, it would be a question of stamina. Unfortunately for the Easton Assassin, he made a strategic blunder just before the match. Like Joe Frazier and Lou Duva before him, Larry Holmes decided to play a mind game with Mike Tyson. As it always had in the past, it backfired. The former champ refused to make his entrance into the cavernous arena at the specified time, choosing to keep the champion waiting an extra 15 minutes. That final rudeness on Holmes' part threw the champion into a rage. An angry Tyson threw a savage left hook at the locker room wall, as reported by most news outlets. The flimsy wallboard shattered before his explosive fist, sending plaster dust in all directions. A gaping hole suddenly appeared through the haze, exposing the outside world. As the team of Rooney, Lott, and Baranski stood in shocked silence, cars and pedestrians could be seen through the hole, moving briskly along Pacific Avenue. A stunned Tyson just hung his head in embarrassment, while a handler whispered, "My God, he broke the wall."

Holmes parade to the ring was quiet but nostalgic as the PA system blared his familiar pre-fight tune, "Ain't No Stoppin' Us Now." As soon as Holmes stepped through the ropes, the Tyson team entered the great hall, anxious to get on with the match. The stare-down during the referee's instructions was a draw as both Holmes and Tyson wore their meanest faces. Tyson was an angry young man. He disliked Holmes as a person and he resented being kept waiting in his dressing room. Now he would get even. He would make Holmes pay for his behavior.

The kid from Catskill was out fast at the bell and pinned the 38-year-old Holmes on the ropes, unleashing a flurry of punches. The cagey old pro tied up the young champion before any damage could be done. Holmes' strategy quickly became evident. He intended to keep the shorter man at a distance by utilizing his reach advantage, constantly keeping his left in Tyson's face. Most of the time, he simply used a straight arm to fend off the champion rather than employ his famous snapping jab. Holmes kept out of harm's way by circling

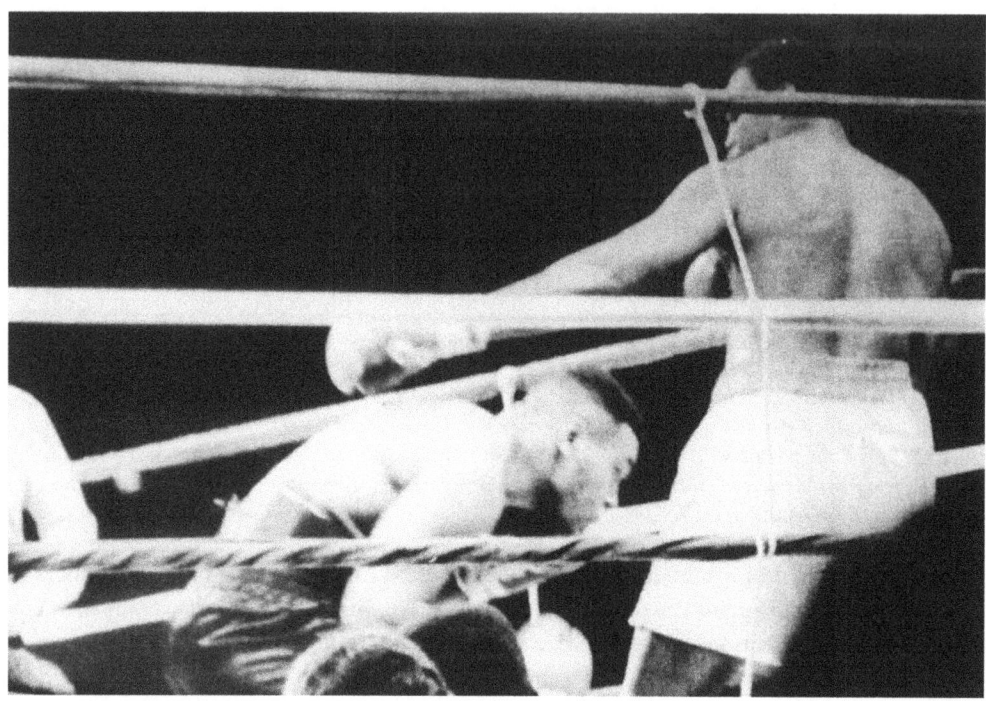

Tyson stalking Holmes, the former champion (courtesy Paul Antonelli).

to the right. This maneuver prevented Tyson from throwing a right hand over the Holmes left which he always carried waist-high, and which left him vulnerable to a right hand lead. That flaw in Holmes' style resulted in three knockdowns during his reign, by such sluggers as Renaldo Snipes and Ernie Shavers.

The champion ran across the ring and started dancing as he pursued the former champ in round two. Holmes was still not ready to mix it up with the young New Yorker, choosing instead to conserve his energy. His only sign of aggression was trying to nail Tyson with a right hand when the champ moved in, a strategy that had been attempted by other Tyson opponents. Thomas, Tucker, and Biggs had all tried to time their right hands against a charging Tyson. All failed to land a solid punch against the bobbing and weaving champion. As usual, Tyson proved to be elusive, constantly slipping Holmes' jabs. He picked up the pace in round two, scoring with several punishing left hooks to the head as well as some crunching body shots. Holmes' infrequent attempts at retaliation were ineffective as the champ deftly avoided the blows. Round three was another slow round, with Tyson chasing his man and Holmes circling and keeping a stiff left jab in the champ's face. Tyson caught the Easton Assassin with a big right hand at the bell and followed up with a left hook before referee Cortez could jump in and separate the fighters. Between rounds, Larry Holmes realized he didn't have the stamina to maintain good lateral movement for a full 12 rounds. His legs were already giving out on him. The moment of truth had arrived for the cagey veteran, and he decided to make his stand now. Round four would be the last round, one way or the other.

To everyone's surprise, Holmes came out on his toes at the bell and danced like a 20-year-old kid. The crowd screamed in anticipation. The old Holmes jab was evident once more, snapping Tyson's head back when the champ tried to move inside. This looked like the Larry Holmes who ruled the heavyweight division for seven years, the man who destroyed all challengers to his title, including Ali himself. Holmes was determined to carry the fight to the young champion in this round. His strength was gradually slipping away and it was obvious to him that he could not last much longer. If he were to win, it would have to be by an early KO. At the one-minute mark, the kid from Catskill caught Holmes standing straight up, resting against the ropes, his left hand low. The alert champ immediately sent the big man reeling backward with a solid left hook. Seconds later, Tyson parried with a soft left, then came across with a lightning-like right hook that broke through Holmes' guard and smashed against his left temple, just above and behind the eye. Holmes wobbled momentarily and then toppled backward like a giant redwood, his equilibrium gone. It was reminiscent of the blow that spelled lights out for Trevor Berbick. The gallant challenger rose quickly, but it was obvious he was in serious trouble. He stood in the corner, shaking his head to clear the cobwebs, as Cortez tolled the mandatory eight count. Holmes would note later that the punch destroyed his balance, and he was never able to recover fully.

With his legs gone, the former champion could not avoid the determined young slugger. His only hope was to stand still and try to tie his man up. But Tyson would not be denied. He was in quickly, throwing punches in bunches. Even though none of them landed cleanly, a glancing right to Holmes' head sent the unsteady challenger to the canvas a second time. As he tried to rise on shaky pins, he fell backward into the ropes. A concerned Cortez wiped off the old champion's gloves and took a good look at his eyes. He bade the fight go on, allowing an embattled Holmes to leave the ring on his shield. There was still one minute to go in the round, and the fired-up champion pursued his man around the ring. For 35 precious seconds, the proud Holmes absorbed a fusillade of punches, but he would not quit. Just when it seemed he might survive the onslaught, Tyson backed him against the ropes and stunned him with a paralyzing right to the side of the head. Holmes' instincts told him to cover up, but he was no match for the strong, young champion. Tyson smashed a left hook to Holmes' unprotected jaw, then dug a hard right to the challenger's rib cage. The champion immediately stepped to the side as he had done a thousand times in the gym under the watchful eye of Cus D'Amato. He unleashed a powerful right hook, thrown with all the bad intentions he could generate. The punch barely grazed the side of Holmes' head, but a swift follow-up right hand caught the old pro on the point of the chin, snapping his head violently to the right and dropping him straight down as if his legs had been cut out from under him. There was no count. Referee Joe Cortez, realizing that the former champion was unconscious, signaled an end to the carnage.

It was a good outing for Mike Tyson. He overcame frustration, learned patience, and followed his trainer's between-rounds instructions. He had fought a wily old ex-champion who knew all the tricks. He learned from the older man, he benefitted from the lesson, and he came away victorious. At the post-fight press conference, the undefeated champion was matter-of-fact about the significance of the fight. "I made it clear to Larry Holmes that his career is unquestionably over. Larry was a great champion during his time, but this isn't his time anymore. He had his reign, and his reign is over. This is my era now."[9]

While Cayton and Jacobs struggled to put together a Tyson-Spinks match for early summer, a warm-up fight was scheduled for Tokyo, Japan, on the evening of March 21. The fight was part of a week-long celebration to dedicate the capital city's new domed arena. Korakuen Stadium, labeled "The Big Egg" by the natives because of its enormous white oval roof, could accommodate 65,000 spectators. The Japanese promoter, Akihiko Honda, specifically chose Tony Tubbs to be Mike Tyson's next opponent because of his durability as well as his ring prowess. He had never been knocked out in eight years as a pro and had compiled a solid 24–1 record along the way. The former WBA champion had fought ten rounds or more on seven different occasions, his only loss coming on a close 15-round decision to "Terrible Tim" Witherspoon. Honda, ever mindful of the 1973 title fight between George Foreman and Jose "King" Roman, an embarrassing two-minute fiasco, and realizing Mike Tyson's proclivity toward early knockouts, wanted to assure himself of the longest and most competitive fight possible; hence Tony "TNT" Tubbs.

Jim Jacobs and Bill Cayton started negotiations with Butch Lewis for a Tyson-Spinks matchup while Iron Mike was preparing for his January title defense against Holmes. The big stumbling block in the deal was money, as usual. On Saturday, January 23, Team Tyson offered Lewis $10.8 million compared with $16.2 million for Tyson. Lewis threw his nose up at that offer, blatantly holding out for $15 million. Cayton was livid. "You mean if you don't get $15 million, there's no fight?" he screamed. "That's it," said Lewis as he headed for the door. Cayton's eyes followed him closely. "If you walk out, don't come back." Butch Lewis slammed the door in his face. Getting the two premier heavyweights together in the same ring appeared to be about as easy as getting President Reagan and the Ayatollah Khomeini to dine together in Jerusalem. The personalities of the principals, particularly Jacobs and Lewis, were incompatible, and their participation in the negotiations exacerbated an already delicate situation. Enter one Shelley Finkel. The smooth-working promoter was rushed into the negotiations by Bill Cayton to formulate a package acceptable to both parties. Working like a fine diamond cutter, Finkel did just that. Stroking everyone's ego, the erudite businessman actually had Lewis and Jacobs smiling and shaking hands in a matter of days. The finished arrangement had Tyson guaranteed a minimum of $17 million and Spinks $13.5 million. Both fighters could add to their take depending on the closed circuit television revenues.[10]

Donald Trump, with some fancy footwork of his own, obtained the rights to the fight without having to engage in a bidding war with Las Vegas. Trump had been massaging the Tyson group for many months, going all the way back to the Ribalta fight in September 1986. The New York millionaire paid an exorbitant price to snare the Ribalta match, but he established a good rapport with Jacobs and Cayton along the way. The two groups worked well together and, most importantly, they trusted each other. When Trump purchased the rights to the Holmes fight, he also received the right of first refusal to any future Michael Spinks match. Don King subsequently offered the Spinks fight to Donald Trump for the astronomical price tag of $11 million. If Trump refused the offer, King could peddle it on the open market for the same amount. Trump quickly accepted the deal. The long awaited heavyweight battle would take place in the Atlantic City Convention Center adjacent to the Trump Hotel and Casino on June 27.

A vacationing Mike Tyson wasn't interested in the business aspects of the fight. He just wanted to get Michael Spinks in the ring. The histrionics of Lewis and Spinks disgusted the young champion to the point where he once remarked, "Sometimes I just wanna take him [Spinks] and slap him alongside the head." Another time, he suggested, "We'll both go down into a cellar, and the one that comes out is the champion." Naturally Spinks declined the offer. Before the final chapter of the Tyson-Spinks saga could unfold, however, the champion first had to fulfill the commitment with Tony Tubbs in Tokyo, a bout that was considered to be nothing more than a showcase event, to present Tyson to his millions of admiring fans in the "Land of the Rising Sun."

11. The People's Champion—June 27, 1988

One week before Tyson's scheduled departure for Japan, however, the young champion's world was turned upside down, and things would never again be the same. On Sunday morning, February 7, Tyson and girlfriend Robin Givens planed to Chicago to attend the annual NBA All-Star Game. They watched in admiration as the top players in the game put on an incredible ball handling and scoring exhibition, led by Givens' old boyfriend, Michael Jordan. "'Air' Jordan, as he was reverently referred to by the fans, waltzed off with the Most Valuable Player award after netting a game-high 40 points. Still, the prolific East All-Stars hung on to win the game by a 138–133 margin. As the crowd filed out of the huge arena, Mike Tyson suddenly grabbed Givens by the arm and started dragging her toward the exit. "Let's get married," he whispered nervously. Caught up in the excitement of the moment, Givens nodded assent, and the two youngsters raced for a cab. They sought out Mike's old friend, Father George Clements, who agreed to marry them in the chapel of the Holy Angels rectory. Before half a dozen witnesses, gathered together hurriedly, the 21-year-old Tyson and the strikingly beautiful 23-year-old Givens were united in holy matrimony.

Immediately after the final blessing, the newlyweds sped to O'Hare Airport to catch the return flight to the Big Apple. On the way, Mike made a hurried telephone call to Camille with the good news, and she, in turn, informed his manager. Jim Jacobs was caught completely off guard. "Bill and I are surprised by the move. It's sort of a shock." As an afterthought, Jacobs confirmed Mike's schedule for the Tubbs fight. "Mike's training will go on schedule. He will leave the U.S. on February 16. I'm not sure if Robin is going, but if she does, it won't be a problem."[11] The Tysons were married a second time in New York, two days later, this time in a civil ceremony performed by Judge Charles E. Ramos in the City Clerk's office. In spite of the recent change in the champ's marital status, the Tyson entourage departed Kennedy Airport as planned and began their grand adventure to the Far East. After 14 hours in the air, a weary and disheveled Tyson, wearing a fleece-lined brown leather flight jacket, walked through the gates of Tokyo's Narita Airport, to be greeted by a sight as incredible as man's first moon walk. Hundreds of reporters and photographers had spent the night in the terminal awaiting their hero's arrival. Now they swarmed all over him, bombarding him with questions in a mish-mash of Japanese and pigeon–English. Flashbulbs popped continuously as the Tyson-hungry media representatives frantically struggled to satisfy the demands of their editors. At the ensuing press conference, reporters continued to deluge the young American with dozens of questions, all of them in

Tyson and Robin Givens (courtesy Paul Antonelli).

Tyson and Rooney at the Tyson-Tubbs press conference in Tokyo March 1988 (courtesy Paul Antonelli).

Japanese. A quizzical smile played on Tyson's face as he whispered to his trainer, Kevin Rooney, "No one here speaks English."

The circus atmosphere at Narita Airport carried over into Tyson's everyday activities. The adulation bestowed upon the world's heavyweight boxing champion by the Japanese people continued unabated right up to fight time. Wherever the young American went, he was surrounded by hundreds of adoring fans, both young and old, male and female. The men admired his strength. The women thought he was sexy. Even his 4 a.m. runs through darkened Tokyo streets brought out droves of photographers, who either ran with him or followed on bicycles or in autos. The city kid from Brownsville was bewildered. "It's scary. It's frightening to me because I never wanted to be a superstar. I just wanted to be champion of the world. I feel like I left earth and went to another planet. I never experienced anything like that before in my life."[12]

In spite of the many distractions, Kevin Rooney made sure his intense training program was followed to the letter. There was no letup in the gymnasium workouts or in the sparring sessions. When the bell rang for round one on the evening of March 21, Mike Tyson would be ready. Even so, the training camp was not as Spartan as in previous Tyson camps. This time, the kid from Catskill found time to tour Tokyo with his new bride—and five security guards, all karate experts. They visited the Ueno Zoo several times, strolled through many of the colorful gardens that decorate the capital city, and paid homage to the famous old Tokyo boxing arena, Korakuen Hall. Along the way, the Tysons visited the children's hospital and made an appearance at the sumo wrestlers gym, where photographers had a field day snapping pictures of the heavyweight champion facing off in the ring against the 400-pound Hawaiian sumo wrestler, Sally Konishiki. Bill Cayton arrived in Tokyo just eight days before the fight, but he came alone. His partner, Jim Jacobs, for the first time in his life, was unable to attend one of Mike's professional fights. Jim remained in New York, reportedly recovering from a minor illness. Korakuen Stadium was buzzing with anticipation as fight time neared. The champion appeared ready to go, weighing in at a trim 216 pounds. The challenger, for all his good intentions, came in carrying a blubbery 238 pounds on his 6'3" frame. Although Tubbs, a former WBA champion, had impressive ring credentials, his poor physical condition prevented this fight from being a major pugilistic event.

A great, noisy welcome ushered the kid from Brownsville into the huge arena. Clad in his usual somber black attire, the champion looked calm and peaceful as he walked down the aisle but, by the time he reached the ring, his expression had darkened and he was once again a man whose mission was to search and destroy. The bald spot that had once decorated the front of Tyson's scalp was no longer visible. Now he knew who he was. He was the champion, and he was comfortable in his new position. The nervous tension that accompanied Tyson's rapid rise to the top of the professional ranks and had caused the temporary baldness was a thing of the past. It had been replaced by confidence and self-assurance.

The first 30 seconds of round one was a feeling-out process, with each fighter sizing up the other. Tubbs, showing a stiff left jab and good lateral movement, had come to fight, not to run. It was obvious that Tubbs was not intimidated by the champion's press clippings. He treated Tyson just like any other opponent. Both fighters landed some good exchanges as the action was brisk in an even round. Midway through round two, the "Baddest Man on the Planet" caught Tubbs with the old 8–2, the uppercut jolting the challenger, who fought back with a stiff uppercut of his own. The two fighters mauled each other at close quarters. Then Tyson unloaded a short left hook to the side of the head that rocked Tubbs. He immediately drove the Ohio fighter to the ropes and worked the body with a series of left-right combinations. A hard left to the top of Tubbs' head stunned the big man. In center ring once more, Tubbs fired a three-punch combination, but failed to slow down the champ. Once again Tyson scored with a vicious 8–2 combination, causing Tubbs to hold on. As soon as the action resumed, Tyson exploded a short, chopping left hook to the temple. Tubbs' hands went up to his head immediately and he turned his back on his tormentor, blood gushing from a nasty cut over his right eye. He stumbled toward a neutral corner on wobbly legs and, with Tyson in hot pursuit, made a grab for the ring rope, missed, and collapsed in a heap on his back. Trainer Odell Hadley was in the ring in a flash, stopping the contest without a count at the 2:54 mark.

Tony Tubbs was no match for Iron Mike (courtesy Paul Antonelli).

Commentator Jim Lampley informed the television audience

that "the fight ended with stunning swiftness." Mike Tyson had successfully defended his title for the sixth time, ending it with another paralyzing punch to the temple, much like the blows that destroyed the equilibrium of both Trevor Berbick and Larry Holmes. The champion himself was surprised at the way the fight ended. "He's very crafty. When I hit him, I thought he was like one of those cute guys who appear shaken, but don't fall." He also took time out to make a promise to the "People's Champion," Michael Spinks. "Michael Spinks knows what he's got comin'. I'm comin' after him."[13]

Two days after the Tubbs fight, tragedy struck the Tyson household. Manager Jim Jacobs succumbed to pneumonia in New York's Mt. Sinai Hospital at the age of 57. Jacobs had been suffering from chronic lymphocytic leukemia for nine years, a fact known only to his wife Lorraine, his partner Bill Cayton, Camille Ewald, and Kevin Rooney. The ugly truth had been kept from Mike Tyson in order to let him concentrate on his career without the traumatic distractions of the impending death of a loved one. The bereaved champion went into seclusion for several days, trying to deal with and accept the loss of his closest friend and advisor. Cayton was the spokesman. "He's not up to making any statements. He's totally distraught." Assistant manager Steve Lott eulogized his employer as an honest and decent human being. "After Cus died, the only person with Cus's information was Jim. But what Cus had was character, and Jimmy had that same unwavering character. Whatever was proper, no matter what other people thought about it, was the right thing to do. And he would never veer from that."[14]

With the death of Jim Jacobs, the umbilical cord connecting Cus D'Amato to Mike Tyson was finally severed. Jim Jacobs had been an extension of the fabled trainer. Now the young champion was on his own for the first time. Just when the man-child had reached the top of his profession, just when he had scaled the summit of Mt. Olympus, the gods suddenly deserted him. He had proven himself in the boxing ring and he was the champion of the world. Now the gods seemed determined to test his mettle as a man. It would turn out to be a long and torturous journey. After Jacobs' funeral, Tyson tried to pick up the pieces, but family problems only added to his despair. His wife, Robin Givens, who had promised to bring peace of mind to his life, brought turmoil instead. With her mother, Ruth Roper, and the professional agitator, Don King, Givens lashed out at manager Bill Cayton, accusing him of mishandling Mike's financial affairs. The two women demanded that Cayton provide them with a complete accounting of Mike's finances. Soon after, they sought to cancel Mike's managerial contract with the elderly advisor.

As the weeks passed, the accusations from the Roper-King group increased until everyone in the Tyson-Roper family was embroiled in the dispute. The newspapers, TV networks, and pulp magazines had a field day, reporting on all aspects of the Tysons' private lives. The headlines that leaped from the newsstands were generally uncomplimentary to the motives of Robin and her mother. The two women were vilified as gold diggers—and worse. At one point, one week before the Spinks fight, photographs of Mike and Robin appeared on dozen or more magazines, including such popular non-sports magazines as *Time, Life,* and *People Weekly*. In the Bible, Samson was bewitched by a single woman, Delilah. Mike Tyson had inherited three Delilahs. Their names were Ruth, Robin, and Stephanie. The champ took the adverse publicity extremely hard, becoming very defensive and protective of his family. He cut short several interviews when the questioning infringed on his private life. Boxing experts feared the out-of-the-ring distractions might affect the champ's performance against Michael Spinks. The odds on the fight reflected this uncertainty, falling from 7–1 to 3½–1

Michael Spinks working the heavy bag (courtesy Paul Antonelli).

by fight time. In spite of all the notoriety surrounding his new family and his managerial problems, the kid from Catskill still had to prepare himself to meet the "People's Champion," Michael Spinks, in the richest match in boxing history, an estimated $80 million.

The super fight was labeled "Once and for All" by promoters Don King and Donald Trump, and the ticket prices reflected the popularity of the confrontation. Ringside seats went for the staggering sum of $1,500, while the cheap seats sold for a lofty $100. Needless to say, the cheap seats were sold out within an hour of being put on sale. Many of the $1,500 seats were purchased by the gambling casinos, who distributed them to their favored high rollers to entice them back to the gaming tables. Other ringside seats were handed out to popular celebrities in order to create a Hollywood-style atmosphere around the gala event. The diehard boxing fan was forced to pay at least $300 to witness the extravaganza in person. Preparations for the fight went surprisingly smoothly considering Mike's personal situation. His legal and managerial problems kept the champ in California longer than expected, and he arrived in Catskill two weeks late. When he finally did report to the Cus D'Amato Gym, he was a bloated 242 pounds. Kevin Rooney had only six weeks to melt away the fat and get the heavyweight king razor sharp for the toughest fight of his life, a seemingly impossible task. Insiders predicted that Mike would enter the ring at something over 222 pounds, the heaviest of his career. But Tyson and Rooney had other ideas.

The two D'Amato protégés fooled the experts. Tyson showed the public what it means to be a champion. Once inside the confines of Cus's gym, "Iron Mike" was back in his own element—where he was king. Blocking out all his outside problems, the Brooklyn native drove himself as never before, putting everything he had into his gym programs and his spar-

The Tyson-Spinks press conference (courtesy Paul Antonelli).

ring sessions. He gave himself body and soul to his tyrannical trainer, Kevin Rooney, and vowed to adhere to Rooney's stringent conditioning program. Nothing was left to chance. Mike did his usual three rounds on the slip bag daily as Rooney monitored the action. "The purpose of the slip bag is to get a fighter movin' his head, to get him in the habit of movin' his head correctly. You have to try to be elusive. As long as a fighter's tryna be elusive, he's gonna be all right. That's what I emphasize. That's what we've got over everybody else." Tyson stood in the path of the slip bag, bobbing and weaving to avoid the sand-filled cylinder as it completed its pendulum route, back and forth, back and forth. He bobbed and weaved as the bag passed, then ducked under the return pass and quickly sidestepped to his left, out of the path of the bag. Jumping back into the swing line once more, the champ spit out a series of jabs while dodging the teardrop-shaped bag, then executed a side-to-side maneuver as if facing an actual opponent. Moving over to the heavy bag, the kid from Catskill received more instructions from his trainer, who noted, "I work on his form on the heavy bag. I tell him, 'You're not movin' enough 'cause you gotta move at least three times. You throw a straight punch, you move three times. You throw a hook, you move twice.'"[15]

At the pre-fight press conference, Bill Cayton dedicated the match to his deceased partner, Jim Jacobs. "This is really Jimmy's fight. He often talked to me about tracing champions and how titles should be won and lost in the ring. Tyson holds all three belts but boxing historians claim Spinks is the real champion because he took the title from Larry Holmes, who was in a direct line of succession from John L. Sullivan." The "People's Champion," Michael Spinks, appeared apprehensive about the confrontation. Obviously nervous, the St. Louis fighter tried to mask his feelings by putting on an act, grabbing the microphone and screaming in fear, "I don't want to go. I don't want to go." On the serious side, Spinks admitted, "It'll be a nervous fight for me. But this is one that must happen. I think the public wants it." The most confident person in the room was the undisputed heavyweight champion, who promised, "I don't know how to lose and I can assure you this fight will not go the distance. There's nobody on this planet who can beat me."[16]

Two days before the fight, the combatants journeyed to the Trump Plaza for the official weigh-in. Mike Tyson astounded everyone by coming in at 218 pounds, only six pounds more than the challenger. Speaking with perfect tunnel vision, Mike Tyson exuded supreme confidence about the upcoming encounter. "My objective is to knock him out and to win in spectacular fashion. People that believe it's going to be the fight of the century are going to be disappointed. It won't go the distance." The fight itself almost took a back seat to the glitzy sideshow that had been arranged by King and Trump. The evening was a major media event, an extravaganza unequalled in the history of Atlantic City. In addition to the magazine coverage and daily newspaper articles, the three principal television networks carried live reports from the fight capital on their morning shows, *Today* on NBC, *CBS Morning News*, and ABC's *Good Morning America*. Thirteen hundred press credentials were issued to reporters from over 40 countries, and hundreds more were denied. Gambling casinos anticipated record takes as the three-day weekend was expected to gross $80 million at the gaming tables.

The celebrity list grew daily with more than 40 superstars from the worlds of business, politics, sports, and entertainment planning to attend the Hollywood-like affair. Big names included Jack Nicholson, Jesse Jackson, Frank Sinatra, Malcolm Forbes, Walter Payton, and Bjorn Borg. Mike Tyson appeared more relaxed as the big hour neared. As he had said more than once, "Fightin's the easy part. I enjoy that." By 7:30 on fight night, the Convention

Center resembled an Academy Awards celebration. Crowds of excited people-watchers gathered outside the great arena to catch a glimpse of their idols. Celebrities arrived in a steady stream of stretch limousines. The men, in their usual formal tuxedos, looked like so many penguins, but the women alighted from their carriages in a variety of glamorous designer creations that brought whistles and cheers from the male spectators and oohs and ahs from the envious ladies present. Spotlights raked the Boardwalk and flashbulbs popped endlessly as the parade of celebrities made their way into the great hall. The Boardwalk buzzed with activity as a circus atmosphere pervaded the seaside resort. Souvenirs of the fight sold like hotcakes. Gold-laden professional athletes strutted their affluence like brilliantly colored peacocks, and every first class pickpocket east of the Mississippi roamed the promenade with visions of a record nightly take dancing in his head.

The champion nervously paced his dressing room in anticipation of the long-awaited battle. As dangerous as Tyson was, Butch Lewis played into his hands even more by throwing a temper tantrum in Spinks' dressing room. First he complained that his representative was not present to witness the taping of Tyson's hands. Then he announced that Spinks would not enter the Convention Center first, but would wait for Tyson to go. The delay dragged on for almost 30 minutes while Tyson fumed. Even the casual fan could have told Butch Lewis that it was suicide to antagonize Tyson prior to a match. Just ask Mitch Green, Marvis Frazier, Lou Duva, or Tyrell Biggs about that. Further, history showed that, when Mike Tyson was mad at the fighter's manager, he took the fighter out quick. When "Smokin' Joe" Frazier made derogatory remarks about his boxing ability, the champ disposed of son Marvis in just 30 seconds. On the other hand, when the champion was angry at the fighter himself, he extended the fight in order to punish his opponent before putting him away. He pummeled Tyrell Biggs for seven rounds before knocking out the former Olympic champion. He disliked Mitch Green even more, so he carried the tough heavyweight for ten agonizing rounds, determined not to inflict the final coup de grace on the Bronx braggart. As Tyson explained, "If Green wants out, he'll have to quit. I'm not gonna go for a knockout." Based on these facts and Butch Lewis' poorly timed theatrics, Michael Spinks might have expected a short night in the trenches.

Michael Buffer brought the Convention Center crowd to a fever pitch with his long-awaited announcement, "Ladies and gentlemen, let's get ready to rumble!" As referee Frank Cappuccino brought the two fighters together, the champion oozed confidence and determination, while the challenger appeared apprehensive, almost resigned to his fate. Mike Tyson danced out quickly when the bell sounded, throwing a flurry of lefts and rights to the body and head of Spinks, who moved along the ropes and escaped. Spinks tried to catch the aggressive champion with a sneaky right hand as the champ moved in, but the punch fell short of its mark. Another right failed to connect as the two fighters mixed it up. Spinks seemed demoralized as Tyson chased him around the ring. The young champion was more elusive than Spinks thought he would be. Mike Tyson was aggressive and active, but he always fought under control. He practiced what Cus D'Amato preached, "It's always better when you can hit him and he can't hit you." Two hard rights to the head preceded a Tyson barrage that drove a confused Spinks along the ropes. A bone-jarring uppercut found Spinks' jaw, stunning the St. Louis fighter, who went into a crouch and covered up, trying to forestall the inevitable. A crunching right hand just below the heart dropped Spinks to one knee at the 1:02 mark. It took Tyson just three seconds to finish the job once the fight resumed. As the combatants approached each other, Spinks let fly a right hand, then ducked into Tyson just as the champion threw a vicious right uppercut. The punch caught Spinks on the right side of the head, knocking him straight back to the canvas. His head bounced off the floor with a sickening thud; his legs twitching convulsively in an eerie dance of distress. Cappuccino leaned over the fallen fighter and began the count. The dazed challenger attempted to rise, but as he got to his hands and knees, he slumped forward across the bottom strand of ropes. It was officially a one minute 31-second knockout, the fourth shortest in heavyweight history. Tyson was across the ring quickly to console his defeated opponent.[17]

With the electrifying knockout of Michael Spinks, young Mike Tyson had completed a dizzying attack on the heavyweight ranks—eight title fights in just 19 months, including seven against heavyweight champions or former champions. He found the heavyweight division in chaos. He left it in a shambles. At the tender age of 22 he was proclaimed "The People's Champion."

Epilogue

The Mike Tyson of the Cus D'Amato, Jim Jacobs, Bill Cayton, and Kevin Rooney era was the real Mike Tyson, and he may have been the greatest heavyweight boxing champion of all time. His 35–0 record, his explosive knockouts, many of them in the first round, and the complete domination of his opponents, where he won 109 of 120 rounds fought, produced 35 fights that lasted less than three rounds on average. The Catskill slugger was ring smart, the sport's most powerful puncher, and a superior defensive fighter as well. He was well spoken and polite to everyone, even during press conferences and interviews. He refused to get dragged into verbal confrontations with opposing boxers or their managers, instead letting his fists do the talking. And he was always concerned for the health of his opponent, frequently rushing across the ring to hug him at the end of the fight and to thank him for his effort.

Mike Tyson continued to fight for another 17 years after leaving his manager, Bill Cayton, for Don King following the Spinks fight, but he was never again the same man. His life inside the ring and outside the ring spiraled out of control, degenerating into a violent, vulgar spectacle that left him disgraced and broke. He lost all his titles to Buster Douglas in February 1990, and spent three years in prison for rape before staging a comeback in 1995. After four tune-up fights, including a victorious WBA Heavyweight Championship bout against Bruce Seldon, he met Evander Holyfield in Las Vegas on November 9, 1996, losing his WBA title on an 11th-round TKO. He was disqualified in the rematch with Holyfield when he bit the champion's ear, lost a title fight to Lennox Lewis five years later, and retired from the ring after knockout losses to two nondescript fighters. His last fight was a six-round TKO loss at the hands of Kevin McBride in the MCI Center in Washington, D.C., on June 11, 2005. He was 39 years old.

Tyson's final career record was 50–6–2 with 44 knockouts. He was elected to the International Boxing Hall of Fame on June 12, 2011, and is generally regarded as one of the greatest fighters of all time. Certainly the self-proclaimed "Baddest Man on the Planet" engineered the most brutal and exciting period in the history of professional boxing as he ran off 35 consecutive victories up to and including the Michael Spinks fight. His fights lasted just under three rounds, with 88 percent of his victories coming by way of a knockout, half of them electrifying first-round executions.

Mike Tyson's record for his first 35 fights compares favorably with the top heavyweight champions, as shown in the appendix. His record is on par with that of George Foreman, who was also a devastating puncher, but in Tyson's case, his 35 matches included seven with world champions or former world champions, while Foreman's record did not include any world class boxers.

Appendix

The Complete Amateur and Professional Boxing Record to June 27, 1988

Amateur Career

Year	Date	Tournament or Location	Opponent	Result
1981	May 17	N.Y. Junior Olympics, Saratoga	None	W
	May 23	Catskill, NY	John Shea	KO1
	June 13	N.Y. Regionals, Jr. Olympics, New York City, Semi-Finals	Tom French	KO1
	June 14	N.Y. Regionals, finals, New York City	Ira Turner	KO2
	June 24	Jr. Olympics, National Championships Colorado Springs, CO, Quarter Finals	Jesus Esparza	KO1
	June 25	National Championships, Semi-Finals	Randy Wesley	KO1
	June 27	National Championships, Finals	Joe Cortez	KO1
	?	?	Anthony Burnett	L3
	?	?	Rick Melton	W3
	October 29	East Greenbush, NY	Andy Robitelli	W3
1982	?	N.Y. Regionals, Jr. Olympics, Syracuse	None	W
	August 23	Jr. Olympics, National Championships, Colorado Springs, Quarter-Finals	Jonathan Littles	KO2
	Augist 24	National Championships, Semi-Finals	Don Cozad	KO1
	August 26	National Championships, Finals	Kelton Brown	KO1
	December 10	?	Al Evans	TKO by 3
1983	February 12	Western Mass. Golden Gloves, Holyoke	Jimmy Johnson	KO1
	February 15	New England Golden Gloves, Semi-Finals, Lowell, MA	Jim Brisson	KO1
	February 15	New England Golden Gloves, Finals	Jim Rayburn	Wdef
	March 5	N.Y. State Regionals, Finals, Ithaca	None	W
	March 22	National Golden Gloves Championships, Albuquerque, NM	Ron Williams	KO1
	March 23	National Golden Gloves, Albuquerque, NM	Andrew Stokes	KO3
	March 24	National Golden Gloves, Quarter-Finals	Mike Bradwell	KO3
	March 25	National Golden Gloves, Semi-Finals	Warren Thompson	W3
	March 26	National Golden Gloves, Finals	Craig Payne	L3
	May 21	Bronx, New York City	Bill Sammo	KO3
	August 13	Ohio State Fair, National Championships ?, Semi-Finals	Jerry Goff	KO2
	August 14	?, Finals	Hugh Copeland	KO1

231

Year	Date	Tournament or Location	Opponent	Result
	August 19	U.S. Junior Amateur Boxing Championships, Colorado Springs, CO, Semi-Finals	Dave Yonko	KO1
	August 20	U.S. Jr. Amateur Championships, Finals	Mark Scott	KO1
	September 17	U.S. vs. West Germany, Lake Placid, NY	Peter Geier	KO1
	October 7	Adirondack Regionals, Golden Gloves, Schenectady, NY	None	W
	October 27	New England-New York Olympic Regionals Lake Placid, NY	None	W
	November 8	Amateur Boxing Federation National Championships, Colorado Springs, CO	Kommel Odom	LDQ2
1984	February 18	Adirondack Golden Gloves, Queensburgh, NY, Finals	None	W
	April 4	N.Y. State Golden Gloves Finals	Mark Pettinato	KO1
	April 17	National Golden Gloves, St. Louis, MO	Roger Peppel	KO1
	April 18	Natl. Golden Gloves, St. Louis, MO	Derrick Isaman	KO1
	April 19	Natl. Golden Gloves, Quarter-Finals, St. Louis, MO	John Williams	KO1
	April 20	Natl. Golden Gloves, Semi-Finals, St. Louis, MO	Richard Johnson	KO3
	April 21	Natl. Golden Gloves, Finals, St. Louis, MO	Jonathan Littles	KO1
	May 29	P.A.L. Tournament, Niagara Falls, NY Quarterfinals	Jeff Thompson	KO3
		(Tyson withdrew from the tournament with an injured shoulder.)		
	June 7	U.S. Olympic Boxing Trials, Fort Worth, TX, Quarter-Finals	Avery Rawls	W3
	June 9	Olympic Boxing Trials, Semi-Finals	Henry Milligan	KO2
	June 10	Olympic Boxing Trials, Finals	Henry Tillman	L3
	June 29	U.S. Olympic Elimination, Colorado Springs, CO, Finals	Olin Alexander	KO1
	July 6	Olympic Boxoff, Las Vegas, NV, Finals	Henry Tillman	L3
	August 17	Empire State Games, Syracuse, NY Semi Finals	Ian Berkely	W3
	August 18	Empire State Games, Finals	Winston Bent	KO3
	August 25	Junior National Championships, Lake Placid, NY, Finals	Kelton Brown	KO1
	October 19	International Tammer Tournament, Helsinki, Finland, Quarter-Finals	None	W
	October 20	Intl. Tammer Tournament, Semi-Finals	I. Szegora (Hungary)	W3
	October 21	Intl. Tammer Tournament, Finals	H. Brock (Sweden)	W3

Mike Tyson's Amateur Record

Year	Wins	Losses	KO's	KO's Round One
1981	9	1	6	5
1982	5	0	4	2
1983	16	2	11	7
1984	17	2	11	7
Totals	**46**	**5**	**32**	**21**

Honors

1981 Junior Olympic National Champion
1982 Junior Olympic National Champion

1983 U.S. Junior National Boxing Champion
1984 National Golden Gloves Champion
Voted Most Outstanding Boxer in the Tournament
Junior National Champion
Voted Most Outstanding Boxer in the Tournament

Professional Record Through June 27, 1988

Year	Date	Location	Opponent	Result
1985	March 6	Albany, NY	Hector Mercedes	KO1
	April 10	Albany, NY	Trent Singleton	KO1
	May 23	Albany, NY	Don Halpin	KO4
	June 20	Atlantic City, NJ	Ricardo Spain	KO1
	July 11	Atlantic City, NJ	John Alderson	KO2
	July 19	Poughkeepsie, NY	Larry Sims	KO3
	August 15	Atlantic City, NJ	Lorenzo Canady	KO1
	September 5	Atlantic City, NJ	Mike "Jack" Johnson	KO1
	October 9	Atlantic City, NJ	Donnie Long	KO1
	October 25	Atlantic City, NJ	Robert Colay	KO1
	November 1	Latham, NY	Sterling Benjamin	KO1
	November 13	Houston, TX	Eddie Richardson	KO1
	November 22	Latham, NY	Conroy Nelson	KO2
	December 6	New York, NY	Sammy Scaff	KO1
	December 27	Latham, NY	Mark Young	KO1

1985 Totals

Fights	15
Wins	15
Losses	0
Knockouts	15

Year	Date	Location	Opponent	Result
1986	January 10	Albany, NY	Dave Jaco	KO1
	January 24	Atlantic City, NJ	Mike Jameson	KO5
	February 16	Troy, NY	Jesse Ferguson	DQ6
	March 10	Uniondale, NY	Steve Zouski	KO3
	May 3	Glens Falls, NY	James "Quick" Tillis	W10
	May 20	New York City	Mitch "Blood" Green	W10
	June 13	New York City	Reggie Gross	KO1
	June 28	Troy, NY	William Hosea	KO1
	July 11	Swan Lake, NY	Lorenzo Boyd	KO2
	July 26	Glens Falls, NY	Marvis Frazier	KO1
	August 17	Atlantic City, NJ	Jose Ribalta	KO10
	September 6	Las Vegas, NV	Alfonzo Ratliff	KO2
	November 22	Las Vegas, NV	Trevor Berbick	KO2

(Won WBC Heavyweight Title)

1986 Totals

Fights	13
Wins	13
Losses	0
Knockouts	11

Year	Date	Location	Opponent	Result
1987	March 7	Las Vegas, NV	James Smith	W12
	(Retained WBC title and won WBA Heavyweight Title)			
	May 30	Las Vegas, NV	Pinklon Thomas	KO6
	(Retained WBC and WBA Titles)			
	Aug 1	Las Vegas, NV	Tony Tucker	W12
	(Retained WBC and WBA Titles and won IBF Heavyweight Title)			
	October 16	Atlantic City, NJ	Tyrell Biggs	KO7
	(Retained WBC, WBA, and IBF Titles)			

1987 Totals

Fights	4
Wins	4
Losses	0
Knockouts	2

Year	Date	Location	Opponent	Result
1988	January 22	Atlantic City, NJ	Larry Holmes	KO4
	(Retained WBC, WBA, and IBF Heavyweight Titles)			
	March 21	Tokyo, Japan	Tony Tubbs	KO2
	(Retained WBC, WBA, and IBF Heavyweight Titles)			
	June 27	Atlantic City, NJ	Michael Spinks	KO1
	(Retained WBC, WBA, and IBF Titles and won "The Ring" Heavyweight Title.)			

1988 Totals (to June 27)

Fights	3
Wins	3
Losses	0
Knockouts	3

Complete Professional Record to June 27, 1988

Fights	35
Wins	35
Losses	0
Knockouts	31
First-Round Knockouts	16
Total Rounds Fought	120
Rounds Won	109
Rounds Lost	11

Average Length of Fight: 8 minutes, 36 seconds.

Mike Tyson vs. Boxing's Greatest Heavyweight Champions Over Their First 35 Fights

Name	Fights	W.	L.	KO's	% KO's	1st Round KO's	Avg. Time of Fight, Minutes
Dempsey	35	32	3	19	54	7	13.3
Louis	35	34	1	29	83	7	13.9
Marciano	35	35	0	30	86	10	10.3
Ali	35	34	1	28	80	2	15.4
Holmes	35	35	0	26	74	3	15.3
Tyson	35	35	0	31	89	15	8.6
Foreman	35	35	0	32	91	10	8.0

Chapter Notes

Chapter 1

1. *NYTimes.com*, May 21, 2002.
2. *Wikiquote.org*, January 1, 2012.
3. Clinton Mollett, *Eastsideboxing.com*, January 1, 2012.
4. Michelle, Dolores, and Grace Rattley, interview with the author, August 11, 1988.
5. *The Oprah Winfrey Show*, October 12, 2009.
6. Clinton Mollett, *Eastsideboxing.com*, January 1, 2012.
7. Bill Heller, *Capital Region Magazine*, February 1986, 42.
8. *Wikiquote.org*, January 1, 2012.
9. Ibid.
10. Clinton Mollett, *Eastsideboxing.com*, January 1, 2012.
11. Peter Heller, *Bad Intentions: The Mike Tyson Story* (New York: New American Library, 1989), 14.
12. Ibid.
13. Bill Heller, *Capital Region Magazine*, February 1986, 42.
14. Peter Heller, *Bad Intentions*, 15.
15. Bill Heller, *Capital Region Magazine*, February 1986, 42.
16. Ibid.
17. *Catskill Daily Mail*, 1980.
18. William Plummer, *People Weekly*, July 15, 1985, 78.
19. Ibid.

Chapter 2

1. William Plummer, *People Weekly*, 80.
2. Ibid.
3. Cus D'Amato tape, Sept. 13, 1985.
4. Ibid.
5. Ibid.
6. Roger Sala, interview with the author, September 1985.
7. Ibid.
8. Cus D'Amato tape, Sept. 13, 1985.
9. Ibid.
10. Ibid.
11. Ibid.
12. Ibid.
13. Ibid.
14. Ibid.
15. Ibid.
16. Peter Heller, *In This Corner* (London: Robson Books, 1973), 417.

Chapter 3

1. Teddy Atlas and Peter Alson, *Atlas* (New York: HarperCollins, 2006), 70.
2. Michael Marton, *Watch Me Now*, TV documentary, 1983.
3. Ibid.
4. Ibid.
5. Cus D'Amato tape, 1985.
6. Ibid.
7. *Watch Me Now*, 1983.
8. Ibid.
9. Cus D'Amato tape, 1985.
10. Ibid.
11. John Chetti, interview with the author, August 1986.
12. Cus D'Amato tape, 1985.
13. Atlas and Alson, 81.
14. Cus D'Amato tape, 1985.
15. Dick Stickles, interview with the author, August 1986.
16. *Catskill Daily Mail*, May 19, 1981.
17. *Watch Me Now*, 1983.
18. *Catskill Daily Mail*, May 1981.
19. *Watch Me Now*, 1983.
20. *Catskill Daily Mail*, March 6, 1985.
21. John Chetti, interview with the author, August 1986.
22. *Catskill Daily Mail*, May 1981.

Chapter 4

1. *Watch Me Now*, 1983.
2. Ibid.
3. Ibid.
4. Ibid.
5. Ibid.
6. Ibid.
7. John Chetti, interview with the author, August 1986.

8. *Catskill Daily Mail*, May 1982.
9. *Catskill Daily Mail*, August 1982.
10. Ibid.
11. *Watch Me Now*, 1983.
12. Ibid.
13. Ibid.
14. Ibid.
15. *Catskill Daily Mail*, June 27, 1982.
16. *Watch Me Now*, 1983.
17. Ibid.
18. John Chetti, interview with the author.
19. *Catskill Daily Mail*, November 22, 1982.
20. Ibid.
21. *Catskill Daily Mail*, November 25, 1982.
22. *Catskill Daily Mail*, November 1982.
23. Atlas and Alson, 104.
24. *Catskill Daily Mail*, December 10, 1982.

Chapter 5

1. *Watch Me Now*, 1983.
2. Ibid.
3. *Catskill Daily Mail*, February 14, 1983.
4. *Catskill Daily Mail*, February 16, 1983.
5. *Catskill Daily Mail*, March 26, 1983.
6. Mike Murphy, interview with the author, 1986.
7. Jim Murphy, interview with the author, 1986.
8. Bill Heller, *Capital Region*, February 1986, 43.
9. *Catskill Daily Mail*, May 23, 1983.
10. Jack Dempsey with Barbara Piatelli Dempsey, *Dempsey* (New York: Harper & Row, 1977), 204.
11. *Catskill Daily Mail*, August 14, 1983.
12. *Catskill Daily Mail*, August 19, 1983.
13. *Catskill Daily Mail*, August 22, 1983.
14. *Catskill Daily Mail*, September 15, 1983.
15. *Catskill Daily Mail*, September 20, 1983.
16. *Catskill Daily Mail*, October 22, 1983.
17. *Catskill Daily Mail*, November 8, 1983.
18. *Catskill Daily Mail*, November 9, 1983.
19. William Plummer, *People Weekly*, July 15, 1985, 78.
20. Cus D'Amato tape, 1985.

Chapter 6

1. Michael Marley, *Boxing Scene*, 51–54.
2. *Watch Me Now*, 1983.
3. *Catskill Daily Mail*, February 16, 1984.
4. *Watch Me Now*, 1983.
5. *Catskill Daily Mail*, April 4, 1984.
6. Ibid.
7. Ibid.
8. *Catskill Daily Mail*, May 29, 1984.
9. *Catskill Daily Mail*, June 1984.
10. *Catskill Daily Mail*, July 6, 1984.
11. *Catskill Daily Mail*, August 18, 1984.
12. *Catskill Daily Mail*, August 27, 1984.
13. *Catskill Daily Mail*, October 2, 1984.
14. *Catskill Daily Mail*, October 12, 1984.
15. *Catskill Daily Mail*, October 1984.
16. *Catskill Daily Mail*, November 29, 1984.
17. *Catskill Daily Mail*, December 4, 1984.
18. *Catskill Daily Mail*, December 28, 1984.

Chapter 7

1. *Boxing Scene*, December 1986, 51–54.
2. John Turek, interview with the author, August 1986.
3. *Catskill Daily Mail*, February 19, 1985.
4. *Catskill Daily Mail*, February 28, 1985.
5. Eric Bottjer, *The Ring Extra*, 1996, 6.
6. *People Weekly*, July 15, 1985, 77.
7. *Catskill Daily Mail*, March 7, 1985.
8. Cus D'Amato tape, September 13, 1985.
9. Author on site, May 23, 1985.
10. John Chetti, interview with the author, August 1986.
11. *People Weekly*, July 15, 1985, 78.
12. *Catskill Daily Mail*, May 26, 1985.
13. *Catskill Daily Mail*, June 22, 1985.
14. *Catskill Daily Mail*, July 12, 1985.
15. HBO, July 12, 1985.
16. *Catskill Daily Mail*, July 16, 1985.
17. *The Greene County News*, July 1985.
18. Cus D'Amato tape, September 13, 1985.
19. Paul Post, *Catskill Daily Mail*, October 10, 1985.
20. *Sports Illustrated*, January 6, 1986.
21. *Catskill Daily Mail*, November 2, 1985.
22. *Catskill Daily Mail*, November 5, 1985.
23. *The Greene County News*, November 14, 1985, 6A.
24. *Sports Illustrated*, January 6, 1986.
25. Paul Post, *Catskill Daily Mail*, November 1985.
26. *Catskill Daily Mail*, November 23, 1985.
27. *KO*, 1986.
28. *Sports Illustrated*, January 6, 1986.
29. Bryant Gumbel, *Today Show*, NBC, December 1985.
30. Jeff Ryan, *KO*, July 1986, 39.

Chapter 8

1. *Author on site*, January 11, 1986.
2. Roy Johnson, *Penthouse*, December 1986, 204.
3. *Catskill Daily Mail*, January 27, 1986.
4. Jeff Ryan, *World Boxing*, December 1986.
5. *Author on site*, February 16, 1986.
6. ABC Sports, February 16, 1986
7. Bill White, meeting with the author, April 2, 1987.
8. Paul Post, *Catskill Daily Mail*, March 11, 1986.
9. Jay Kimiecik, *Times Herald-Record*, Middletown, N.Y., May 8, 1986.
10. Robert Smith, *Catskill Daily Mail*, May 3, 1986.
11. HBO, May 19, 1986.
12. HBO, May 20, 1986.
13. *Mike Tyson, the Inside Story*, 1995.

14. Robert Smith, *Catskill Daily Mail*, June 4, 1986.
15. *The Ring*, September 1986.
16. Robert Smith, *Catskill Daily Mail*, June 16, 1986.
17. WNYT, CH-13 News, Albany, N.Y., June 28, 1986.
18. UPI, June 28, 1986.

Chapter 9

1. Robert Smith, *Catskill Daily Mail*, July 23, 1986.
2. *Times Herald-Record*, Middletown, N.Y., July 25, 1986.
3. Tim Layden, *Albany Times Union*, July 26, 1986.
4. Terry Egan, *Middletown Sunday Record*, July 27, 1986.
5. Gene Levy, *Sunday Times Union*, Albany, N.Y. July 27, 1986.
6. Terry Egan, *Sunday Record Sports*, Middletown, N.Y. July 27, 1986.
7. Gene Levy, *Albany Times Union*, August 17, 1986.
8. Peter Richmond, *Times Herald-Record*, Middletown, N.Y., August 18, 1986.
9. Tim Wilkins, *Albany Times Union*, September 4, 1986.
10. HBO, September 4, 1986.
11. HBO, September 6, 1986.
12. Bill Lyon, *Albany Times Union*, September 9, 1986.
13. UPI, September 8, 1986.
14. Ken Cohen, *Middletown Record*, September 1986.
15. AP, September 18, 1986.
16. Robert C. Smith, *Catskill Daily Mail*, October 1, 1986.
17. *Albany Times Union*, October 1986.
18. Bill White, *Catskill Daily Mail*, October 17, 1986.
19. *The Joan Rivers Show*, Los Angeles, November 5, 1986.
20. *Catskill Daily Mail*, November 8, 1986.
21. Raymond Pignone, *Catskill Daily Mail*, November 18, 1986.
22. UPI, November 19, 1986.
23. Bill White III, *Catskill Daily Mail*, November 24, 1986.
24. HBO, November 22, 1986.
25. Ibid.

Chapter 10

1. HBO, January 1987.
2. William H. White III, *Catskill Daily Mail*, February 3, 1987.
3. Ibid.
4. HBO, February 1987.
5. William H. White III, *Catskill Daily Mail*, February 6, 1987.
6. *Catskill Daily Mail*, March 5, 1987.
7. *Catskill Daily Mail*, March 9, 1987.
8. Ibid.
9. *Catskill Daily Mail*, March 12, 1987.
10. Paul Antonelli, *Catskill Daily Mail*, May 29, 1987.
11. Ibid.
12. Ed Schuyler, AP, June 1, 1987.
13. Paul Antonelli, *Catskill Daily Mail*, June 1, 1987.
14. *Catskill Daily Mail*, June 16, 1987.
15. UPI, June 1, 1987.
16. UPI, July 1987.
17. WNYT, CH-13, Albany, N.Y.
18. William H. White III, *Catskill Daily Mail*, July 10, 1987.
19. Ibid.
20. Tim Dahlberg, AP, July 1987.
21. UPI, July 31, 1987.
22. Ron Borges, *Boston Globe*, August 3, 1987.
23. UPI, August 1, 1987.
24. UPI, Ibid.
25. William H. White III, *Catskill Daily Mail*, July 10, 1987.
26. William H. White III, *Catskill Daily Mail*, September 15, 1987.
27. William H. White III, *Catskill Daily Mail*, October 9, 1987.
28. *Catskill Daily Mail*, October 5, 1987.
29. *Catskill Daily Mail*, October 16, 1987.
30. HBO, October 16, 1987.

Chapter 11

1. UPI, October 19, 1987.
2. Ibid.
3. *Brown on Boxing* (Knob Noster, MO: Crown Books, 1987).
4. Paul Antonelli and William White III, *Catskill Daily Mail*, December 2, 1987.
5. HBO, January 22, 1988.
6. Paul Antonelli, *Catskill Daily Mail*, December 16, 1987.
7. HBO, January 22, 1988.
8. Ibid.
9. Paul Antonelli, *Catskill Daily Mail*, January 25, 1988.
10. Ibid.
11. *Catskill Daily Mail*, February 9, 1988.
12. HBO, February 18, 1988.
13. Paul Antonelli, *Catskill Daily Mail*, March 21, 1988.
14. Tim Layden, *Albany Times Union*, March 24, 1988.
15. HBO, May 12, 1988.
16. Paul Antonelli, *Catskill Daily Mail*, March 31, 1988.
17. *Author on site*, January 27, 1988.

Bibliography

Atlas, Teddy. Correspondence with the author, 1986.

Atlas, Teddy, and Peter Alson. *Atlas*. New York: HarperCollins, 2006.

Berger, Phil. *Blood Season*. New York: Harper Paperbacks, 1989.

Berger, Phil. "Tyson, at Age 19, Rushes to Fulfill D'Amato's Vision." *New York Times*, February 2, 1985.

Boxing Scene. Palisades, N.Y.: Tiger Press, 1985–1988.

Brown on Boxing. Knob Noster, MO: Crown Books, 1987.

Catskill Daily Mail. Catskill, N.Y., 1980–1988.

Chetti, John. Interview with the author, August 1986.

D'Amato, Cus. Tape recording of presentation to a marketing group in Albany, N.Y., September 13, 1985.

Dempsey, Jack, with Barbara Piatelli Dempsey. *Dempsey*. New York: Harper & Row, 1977.

ESPN, 1985–1988.

The Greene County News. The Catskill Daily Mail, Inc.

Heller, Bill. "The Future Heavyweight Champion of the World." *Capital Region Magazine*, February 1986.

Heller, Peter. *Bad Intentions*. New York: New American Library, 1989.

Heller, Peter. *In This Corner*. London: Robson Books, 1973.

Hoey, Lori. Conversation with the author, August 12, 1986.

Illingworth, Montieth. *Mike Tyson: Money, Myth, and Betrayal*. New York: Carol Publishing Group, 1991.

"Iron-in-the-Hall." *Manilatimes.com*, June 7, 2011.

Johnson, Roy S. "Tyson's Time." *Penthouse*, December 1986.

KO, TV Sports, Inc., Rockville Centre, N.Y., 1985–1988.

Layden, Joe. *The Last Great Fight*. New York: St. Martin's, 2007.

Marley, Michael. "Mike Tyson's Secret Ally, A Hypnotist." *Boxing Scene*, December 1986.

Marton, Michael. *Watch Me Now*. TV Documentary, 1983.

Mike Tyson–A Portrait of the People's Champion. Don King Productions, Inc., Mike Tyson Productions, Inc., in association with The Guber-Peters Company, 1989.

Mike Tyson: The Inside Story. The Big Fights, Inc., 1995.

Mollett, Clinton. *Eastsideboxing.com*, January 1, 2012.

Murphy, Mike. Interview with the author, August 1986.

Nack, William. "Ready to Soar to the Very Top." *Sports Illustrated*, January 6, 1986.

The Oprah Winfrey Show. "The Life of Mike Tyson." October 12, 2009.

Plummer, William. "Cus D'Amato." *People Weekly*, July 15, 1985.

Rattley, Michelle, and Dolores Rattley, and Grace Rattley. Interview with the author, August 11, 1988.

The Ring. The Ring Publishing Corp., New York, 1985–1988.

The Ring Extra. The Ring Publishing Corp., New York, 1995–1996.

Ryan, Jeff. *KO*, July 1986.

Ryan, Jeff. *World Boxing*, December 1986.

Sala, Roger. Interview with the author, September 1985.

Smith, Gary. "Tyson the Timid, Tyson the Terrible." *Sports Illustrated*, March 21, 1988.

Stickles, Dick. Interview with the author, August 1986.

Times Herald-Record, Middletown, N.Y., 1985–1988.

Torres, Jose. *Fire & Fear: The Inside Story of Mike Tyson*. New York: Warner, 1989.

Turek, John. Interview with the author, August 1986.

Tyson, Mike, and Larry Sloman. *Mike Tyson: The Undisputed Truth*. New York: Blue Rider Press, 2013.

Tyson, Mike. *Wikiquote.org*, January 1, 2012.

"Tyson Remains an Object of Frustration." *NYTimes.com*, May 21, 2012.

White, Bill. Meeting with the author, April 2, 1987.

World Boxing, 1985–1988.

Index

ABC-TV 113, 131, 136, 140, 198
Adirondack Regional Golden Gloves Tournament 59, 73
Adirondack Regional Junior Olympic Boxing Tournament 52
Albany-Colonie Yankees 199
Albany Convention Center 102, 103, 107, 110
Albany Patroons 186
Albany Times Union 173
Alderson, John 114, 115, 233
Aleman, Alberto 184
Alexander, Olin 82, 86, 87, 232
Alexander the Great 29
Ali, Bashiru 194
Ali, Muhammad 23, 26, 30, 46, 47, 50, 113, 144, 177, 179, 195, 219, 234
Alumni Hall, DePaul University 215
Amateur Boxing Federation National Championships 73, 74
Anderson, Denise *see* Denise Tyson
Anderson, Roger 4
Angie 59, 78
Anthony, Tony 112, 119
Antonelli, Paul 149, 203, 216, 218, 221–223, 225, 226
Apollo Boxing Club 50, 70
Arguello, Alexis 51, 52, 60, 105
Armstrong, Henry 31, 64, 216
Armstrong, Tyrone 92, 101, 117, 188
Arum, Bob 60, 112–114, 163, 171
Astaire, Fred 169
Atlantic City Convention Center 196, 202, 208, 211, 215, 220, 227, 228
Atlas, Elaine 62, 89
Atlas, Nicole Marie 62
Atlas, Teddy 25–30, 32, 34, 36, 38, 40–45, 47–58, 60–62, 65
Atlas, Teddy, III 62

"The Babe Ruth of Handball" 33
Baez, Pablo 41
Balboa, Rocky 140
Ball Four 197
Baranski, Matt 11, 91, 103, 104, 129, 145, 162, 178, 188–190, 204, 210, 211, 217
Barr, Ernie 101
Barrett, Mike 195

Barry, Referee 71
Barrymore, John 171
Bates, Otis 108
Battle, Rudy 166–168
Beach Club condominium 215
Becker, Boris 114, 115
Becker, Ira 126
Bells Coffee Shop 187
Benitez, Wilfred 34, 51, 71, 173
Benjamin, Sterling 121, 122, 233
Bent, Winston 90, 232
Berbick, Trevor 38, 46, 135, 151, 158, 164, 165, 170–183, 200, 213, 219, 224, 233
Berkley, Ian 90, 232
Beverly Hilton Hotel 175
Bey, David 191, 193, 212
Bible 224
Big Egg *see* Korakuen Stadium
Big Fights, Inc. 140, 143, 163, 186, 208
Biggs, Tyrell 73, 74, 80, 84, 87, 114, 117, 120, 123, 144, 158, 164, 165, 184, 191, 193, 194, 207–214, 218, 228, 234
Birkle, Heinz 73
Blake, Joe 38, 39
Bonet, Lisa 184, 195
Bordick, Lee 38
Borg, Bjorn 227
Boston College 99, 100
Boston Globe 140
Bouton, Jim 197, 198
Boxing of the Americas Gym 125, 165
Boxing Writers of America 185
Boyd, Lorenzo 152, 154–156, 233
Bradwell, Mike 68, 231
Bramble, Livingstone 173
Breen, Kevin 116
Breland, Mark 89
Bright, Jay 26, 30, 45, 58, 123
Brisson, Jimmy 67, 231
Bristol Park 7
British Commonwealth Boxing Champion 92, 196
Broad, James 117, 126, 174, 175, 189, 205, 206, 217
Brock, Hakan 94, 232
Brown, Jim 92
Brown, Kelton 56, 57, 90, 91, 231, 232
Brown, "Panama Al" 31

Brown, Phil "Bazooka" 74, 131
Bruno, Frank 71, 72, 117, 135, 143, 144, 157, 158, 174, 194–196
Buffer, Michael 228
Burgess, Dion 152, 154, 159, 187, 189
Burke, Mike 66
Burnett, Anthony 42, 43, 231
Burns, Tommy 96

Caesar, Julius 29
Caesar's Palace 75, 107, 199
California Golden Gloves Champion 132
Camacho, Hector, "Macho" 152, 153, 179
Canady, Lorenzo 117, 233
Cappuccino, Frank 115, 119, 203, 228, 229
Carbo, Frankie 12, 15, 16, 19, 20
Carew, Rod 117
Carmack, Cody 152, 158
Carnera, Primo 96
Casares, Jonathon 205, 208
Catskill Boxing Club 11, 23, 28, 32, 38, 39, 44, 47, 52, 54, 59, 62, 95, 100, 103, 108, 186, 197
Catskill Boy's Club 27, 32
Catskill Daily Mail 43, 58, 119, 139, 148, 154, 159, 186, 188
Catskill High School 53, 70, 84, 100, 140, 187
Catskill Middle School 27, 38
Catskill Village Board of Trustees 176
Cayton, Bill 33, 34, 96, 100, 115, 128, 131, 134, 135, 147, 151, 152, 163, 164, 173, 183, 186, 187, 190, 191, 195, 196, 200, 209, 216, 219–222, 224, 227, 230
CBS 95
CBS Morning News 227
Cervantes, Antonio 71
Challenger space shuttle 131
The Champion 126
Chance, Dean 147
Channel 10 News, Albany, N.Y. *see* WTEN
Chavez, Julio Cesar 185
Chetti, Chris 45, 52
Chetti, John 34, 35, 39, 44, 45, 47, 52, 62, 69, 144
Chicago Bears 92
Cicero, Marcus Tullius 211

239

Clark, Jimmy 81, 97
Clay, Cassius 113
Clements, Father George 215, 221
Coetzie, Gerrie 144
Cohen, Mike 115
Colay, Robert 120, 233
Coleman, Ernestine 43
Community Theatre 52, 70
Connors, Jimmy 114
Continental Basketball Association 186
Cooke, Sam 178, 211
Cooney, "Gentleman Gerry" 38, 39, 69, 112, 125, 135, 158, 164, 165, 171, 173, 185, 191, 196, 202, 203, 207, 208
Cooper, Bert 152, 153, 194
Copeland, Hugh 72, 231
Corbett, "Gentleman Jim" 26
Cortez, Joe 42, 132, 134, 161, 162, 219, 231
Cosby, Bill 184, 196
Costen, Miss Vivien 18
Cotton Bowl 99, 100
Coulter, Tom 69, 73
Coutineri, Meghan 215
Cozad, Don 53–55, 231
Crawley, Terry 60, 61
Creed, Apollo 140
Crossgates Mall 95, 111, 158, 172
Cubas, Lou de 165
Cumberland Hospital 3
Cummings, Floyd "Jumbo" 46
Cuomo, Mario, Governor 97
Curran, Kevin 114
Cus D'Amato Gym 173, 174, 186, 198, 226

D'Amato, Anna 22
D'Amato, Constantine, "Cus" 11–34, 36–40, 42–45, 47–51, 55, 58, 59, 61, 62, 64–66, 68–75, 78–81, 83–97, 99, 100–114, 116, 118–128, 131, 134, 135, 143, 144, 152, 159, 162–165, 169, 172, 178, 180, 182, 183, 187, 197, 201, 207, 219, 224, 228, 230
D'Amato, Damiano 12
D'Amato, Elizabeth 12
D'Amato, Jerry 123
D'Amato, Rocco 22
Damiani, Fransesco 164, 194
Darrow, Clarence 13
David Letterman Show 149, 184
Davis, Anthony 152, 154, 155, 159, 187, 189
Davis, Kenny 101
DeLeon, Carlos 96, 101, 117
Delilah 224
Dempsey, Jack 20, 71, 91, 102, 178, 234
Detroit Tigers 169
De Wit, Willie 89, 120, 124
DiMaggio, Joe 208
Dokes, Michael 11, 39
Don King and Mike Tyson Productions 198
Douglas, James, "Buster" 190, 191, 202, 230

Douglas, Kirk 179
Dundee, Angelo 44, 180, 200
Duran, Roberto 51, 75, 76
Duva, Lou 208, 210, 212, 214, 217, 228
Dynamic Duo Productions 164, 168, 174, 190

Einstein, Albert 13
Elks Club 59
Empire State Convention Center 199
Empire State Games 36, 90, 232
Empire State Plaza 129
Enok 165
Epps, Melvin 149, 209, 210
Esparza, Jesse 41, 231
ESPN 114, 124, 137, 139
European Amateur Heavyweight title 72, 90–92, 94, 97, 232
European Heavyweight Champion 135, 158
Evangelista, Alfredo 39
Evans, Al, "Chico" 62, 63, 74, 231
Evans, Mike 165
Ewald, Camille 22, 25, 27, 28, 30, 31, 38, 43, 45, 50, 55, 58, 65, 75, 90, 95, 99, 108, 112, 123, 125, 205, 221, 224
Ewald house 26, 37, 57, 70, 100, 143, 154, 172, 199

Felt Forum 126, 127
Ferguson, Jesse, "Thunder" 112, 124, 134, 136–140, 189, 233
Fields, Alan 185
Fink, Stanley 142
Finkel, Shelly 191, 220
Firestone, Roy 188
Fitzsimmons, Bob 96
Flutie, Doug 99, 100
Forbes, Malcolm 227
Ford, Dr. Jock 162
Foreman, George 96, 144, 147, 190, 191, 203, 220, 230, 234
Foxx, Jimmie 169
Franco, Jim 187
Frazier, Marvis 117, 141, 145, 152, 156–164, 206, 210, 217, 228, 233
Frazier, "Smokin Joe" 46, 125, 157–159, 161–163, 191, 203, 228
French, Tom 40, 231
Frog Hollow 12, 14, 15
Frost, Stephen 163

Gandhi, Indira 95
Gardner, John L. 39
Gehrig, Lou 169
Geier, Peter 73, 232
George Foreman Youth and Recreation Center 191
Gillison, Edward 3
Gilmore Stadium 64
Givens, Robin 195–197, 199, 204, 209, 221, 224
Gleason's Gym 62, 125, 126
Glens Falls Civic Center 121, 144, 145, 152, 156, 160–163
Goff, Jerry 72, 231

Golden Gloves *see* National Golden Gloves Tournament
Gonzalez, Paul 89
Gonzalez, Tabita 205, 208
Good Morning America 128, 227
Gooden, Dwight 157, 164
Gordon, S.T. 177
Gossett, Lou, Jr. 215
Grammercy Gym 14, 17, 29, 32, 148
Grand Hyatt Hotel, New York 207, 215
Grange, Red 71
Greatest Fights of the Century 34, 64
Greek Theatre 204, 208
Greeley, Horace 81
Green, Charlene 148
Green, Mitch, "Blood" 147–151, 153, 174, 184, 210, 228, 233
Greenberg, Hank 169
Greenberg, Ross 135, 136, 140
Greene County Correctional Facility 116
Gretzky, Wayne 97
Gross, Reggie 152, 153, 233
Grossingers 71, 195
Gumbel, Bryant 127, 194
Gustavus I, King 94
Gutkowski, Bob 164

Hadley, Odell 223
Hagler, "Marvelous Marvin" 75, 76, 107, 108, 199, 200, 202
Halpin, Don 108–111
Halpin, Dr. John 37, 78, 100, 159, 233
Ham, Billy 38, 39
Hamsho, Mustafa 71
Handelman, Dr. Bruce 174
Harris, Roy, "Cut and Shoot" 20
Harris, Tracy 44
Hartman, David 128
Harvard University 196
Hearns, Thomas, "The Hit Man" 41, 44, 107, 108, 179
Henderson, Ricky 164
Hilton Hotel, Las Vegas 168, 170–173, 176, 178, 182–184, 188, 190, 193, 200–202, 204, 206
Hoey, Lori 165
Hogan, Frank 20
Hogan, Hulk 214
Holloway, Rory 172, 186
Holman, Oscar 188, 190, 205, 206
Holmes, Larry 39, 63, 69, 89, 91, 97, 98, 108, 109, 114, 116, 119, 135, 158, 164, 165, 173, 177, 179, 195, 203, 214, 215, 217–219, 224, 227, 234
Holy Angels Church, Chicago, IL 215, 221
Holyfield, Evander 194, 200, 203, 230
Holyoke Boys Club 66
Home Box Office (HBO) 135, 136, 140, 147, 150, 168, 171, 173, 179, 184, 185, 190, 193, 198, 200, 203
Home Box Office (HBO) Unification Series 135, 144, 158, 164,

168, 170, 173, 174, 185, 190, 196, 202, 206
Honda, Akahiko 219, 220
Hope, Maurice 71
Hopkinson Playground 5
Hosea, William 152–154, 233
Hostetter, Charlie 203
Houston Boxing Association 131, 132
Houston Cougars 99, 100
Howard, Kevin 199
Hubbell, Carl 157
Hujtyn, Nadia 52, 70
Hull, Charlie 151
Hurricane Charlie 166
Hussein, Muhammad 91, 92
Hussing, Peter 72, 73

IBC (International Boxing Council) 15–21, 80, 109, 117, 121
IBF (International Boxing Federation) 109, 135, 141, 158, 168, 173, 178, 179, 184, 185, 190, 196, 200, 202, 203, 206, 207, 234
Iovenella, Ron 74
Irving, Washington 23
Isaman, Derrick 81, 232

Jackson, Jesse 227
Jackson, Tommy, "Hurricane" 19, 20
Jackson, Tyrone 39
Jaco, Dave 129, 130, 233
Jacobs, Jim 22, 26, 33, 34, 64, 95, 96, 100, 102, 104, 112, 114, 117, 120, 123, 124, 128, 131, 134, 135, 140, 147, 152, 153, 163, 164, 173, 181–183, 186, 187, 190, 191, 193–195, 200, 204, 207–210, 214, 219–222, 224, 227, 230
Jacobs, Lorraine 224
Jameson, "Irish Mike" 71, 131–134, 165, 173–175, 187–191, 233
Jenkins, Marvin 51
Joan Rivers Show 175, 184
Joe Louis Award 108
Johannson, Ingemar 20, 94, 162, 163
John Paul II, Pope 154
Johnny Tocco's Gym 174, 175, 188–190, 200, 206
Johnson, Bill 78, 79
Johnson, David, "Big Foot" 125
Johnson, Jack 177, 216, 233
Johnson, Jimmy 67, 231
Johnson, Michael, "Jack" 118
Johnson, Richard 82, 232
Johnson, Roy S. 131
Johnstown Juvenile Center 9
Jones, Bobby 71
Jordan, Don 20
Jordan, Michael, "Air" 196, 221
Junior Amateur Boxing Championships 67, 72, 73, 90, 91, 232
Junior Middleweight title 71
Junior Olympic Champion 195
Junior Olympic Elimination Tournament 38
Junior Olympic Regionals 39
Junior Olympics National Championships 38, 40–42, 53–58, 61, 66, 84, 90, 231
Junior Welterweight title 71

Kalule, Ayub 41
Kanaan, Tony 7
Kennedy, John F. 21
Kennedy Airport 221
Khomeinin, Ayatollah 220
Kim, Duk Koo 60
King, Carl 171
King, Don 122, 135, 140, 147, 148, 150, 171, 173, 174, 187, 190, 191, 193, 207, 208, 210, 216, 220, 224, 226, 227, 230
Kipling, Rudyard 210
Kirakosian, Maral 208
Kirkpatrick, Jimmy 3
Knickerbocker Brewery 12
Knight, Ray 164
Koch, Edward, Mayor 152
Konishiki, Sally 222
Korakuen Hall 222
Korakuen Stadium, Tokyo, Japan 219, 223

L.A. Lakers 186
Lafleur, Guy 97
LaMotta, Jake 114
Lampley, Jim 223
Lane, C.D., "Larry" 142
Lane, Mills 181, 206
Latham Circle Mall 172
Latham Coliseum 120, 121, 124, 125, 128
Lee, Bob 173
Lendl, Ivan 114
Leonard, Benny 50
Leonard, "Sugar Ray" 31, 34, 41, 44, 50, 166, 170, 199, 200, 202
Lewis, Butch 135, 171, 173, 174, 185, 190, 191, 202, 203, 207, 214, 220, 228
Lewis, Lennox 230
Life magazine 186, 224
Liston, Sonny 21
Littles, Jonathon 53, 82, 231, 232
Lloyd, Chris Evert 114
Lobianco, Johnny 153
London, Brian 20
Long, Donnie 119, 120, 233
Lost Battalion Hall 40
Lott, Steve 145, 178, 188, 204, 205, 210, 216, 217, 224
Louis, Joe 16, 38, 53, 170, 195, 208, 210, 234
Lowe, Johnny 47, 49, 50, 58

Machaim, Marc 142
Madison Square Garden 21, 121, 125, 126, 147, 148, 152, 164, 184, 185
Maguire, Dick 53
Man O War 208
Mancini, Ray, "Boom Boom" 60, 63, 173
Mantle, Mickey 200
Marciano, Rocky 19, 31, 96, 129, 130, 134, 178, 208, 210, 234

Marion Correctional Institution 147
Maris, Roger 169
Mathews, Wallace 115
Maxim Joey 18
Mazer, Bill 149
McBride, Kevin 230
McCall, Oliver 209, 217
McCrory, Glenn 209, 210, *
McEnroe, John 114
McGirt, Buddy 199
MCI Center 230
Melton, Rick 43, 231
Mercado, Bernardo 177
Mercante, Arthur 142
Mercedes, Hector 102, 104–106, 233
Merchant, Larry 150, 166, 181, 213
Mid-Hudson Civic Center 116
"Mighty Joe Young" 101
Miller, Lorraine 102, 120, 121
Milligan, Henry 81, 82, 85, 232
Minicelli, Frankie 26, 30, 39, 44, 50–52, 58, 59, 71, 99
Mississippi Jets 186
Montreal Canadiens 97
Moore, Archie 19, 20, 106, 176, 179
Moore, Davey 40, 51, 105
Moore, Mane, "The Flame" 39, 40, 44, 49, 50
Morrell, Jackie 51
Most Outstanding Boxer Trophy 82, 90
Mount Bjelasnica 79
Mt. Sinai Hospital 120, 121, 144
Murkowski, Elfie 187
Murkowski, Werner 187
Murphy, Eddie 111, 196
Murphy, Jim 45, 69, 83
Murphy, Lee Roy 141
Murphy, Mike 45, 69, 83, 84
Murphy, Mrs. 69

Nack, William 31
Namath, Joe 79
Nance, Felix 38
Napoleon 29
Napp. Pat 42
Narita Airport, Tokyo 221, 222
Nassau Coliseum 141
Nassau Police Club 70
National Four Wall Handball 33
National Golden Gloves Tournament 36, 67, 68, 77, 79–82, 84, 96, 231, 232; 1984 90
National Hockey League (NHL) 97
National Police Athletic League Tournament 83, 84, 232
Navratilova, Martina 114
NBA All-Star Game 221
NBC Nightly News 128
Nelson, Battling 31, 216
Nelson, Conroy 124, 125, 233
Nevada State Supreme Court 196
New England Golden Gloves Tournament 67
New England–New York Olympic Regional Boxing Trials 74

New Jersey Athletic Commission 191
New Paltz Boxing Club 44
New York City 221
New York Daily News 208
New York Mets 164
New York Post 208
New York Rangers 148
New York State Boxing Commission 22, 103, 104
New York State Golden Gloves Tournament 81, 102
New York State Legislature 142, 143
New York Times 127
New York Yankees 117, 185
Newsday 115
Nicholson, Jack 179, 186, 227
Norris, James D., Jr. 16, 17, 19, 20, 109
Norris, James D., Sr. 16
North American Boxing Federation (NABF) 194
Norton, Ken 38, 74, 191

Ocasio, Oscar 203
Odom, Kommel 74, 232
O'Hare Airport 221
Ohio State Fair National Championships 72, 231
Ohio State University 100
Ohlmeyer Communications Co. 186
Oklahoma Sooners 100
Olivier, Lawrence, Sir 85
Olson, Carl, "Bobo" 21
Olympic Boxing Committee 80, 84
Olympic Box-offs, 1984 90, 232
Olympic Trials, 1984 80, 82, 83, 191, 194, 232
Orange Bowl 99, 100
Orlando, Tony 213
Ortiz, Luis 89

Padilla, Carlos 194
Page, Greg 127, 145, 153, 176, 177
Palomino, Carlos 71
Papenall, Don 44
Parade of the Roses *see* Rose Bowl Parade
Parkey, Rickey 200
Parsley, De Len 106, 107
Pastrano, Willie 21, 22, 29
Patterson, Bill 17
Patterson, Floyd 17–23, 34, 44, 95, 105, 123, 134, 162, 163, 169, 176, 178, 181
Patterson, Frank 17
Patti, Tom 30, 50, 91, 99, 123
Payne, Craig 68, 69, 74, 77, 231
Payton, Walter 92, 227
Pearl, Davey 169, 170
Peloke's Motel 165
Penthouse magazine 131
People Weekly 105, 224
Pep, Willie 106
Peppel, Roger 81, 232
Perez, Jose 35
Pettinato, Mark 81, 232
Pleasantville Recreation Center 216

Pledge, Bobby 39
Plummer, William 13
Post, Paul V. 22, 51, 109, 110, 122, 137, 141–143
Powell, John 59

Rademacher, Pete 20
Ramos, Judge Charles E. 221
Ramos, Jose 39
Rappaport, Dennis 202
Ratliff, Alfonso 168–170, 176, 233
Rattley, Dolores 5
Rattley, Grace 5
Rattley, Michelle 5
Rawls, Avery 85, 232
Rayburn, Jim 67, 231
Reagan, President Ronald 154, 220
Redman's Hall 27, 39, 45, 91, 97, 101, 114, 117
Reel Sports, Inc. 186
Renssalaer Polytechnic Institute (RPI) Field House 121, 135, 137, 152, 153
Resorts International Hotel 112, 114
Ribalta, Jose 164–168, 220, 233
Richardson, Eddie 123, 124, 233
Ring Magazine 127, 185
The Ringside 125
Rivera, Luis 137, 151
Robinson, Jackie 29
Robinson, Nate 101
Robinson, "Sugar Ray" 31, 34, 106
Robitelli, Andy 44, 231
Rocky 126
Rocky III 57
Rodriguez, Lucien 69
Romalla, Art 102
Roman, Jose, "King" 220
Rooney, Kevin 26, 28, 30, 32, 38–40, 44, 51, 52, 60, 61, 63, 65–74, 78, 80, 81, 84, 86–89, 91–94, 96, 97, 101–103, 105, 108, 113, 116, 118–121, 123, 125, 126, 129, 132, 137, 139, 142, 145–149, 151, 152, 154, 158, 159, 162, 163, 165–167, 170–175, 177–181, 186–195, 200, 201, 204–206, 208–210, 212, 213, 216, 217, 222, 224, 226, 227, 230
Roper, Ruth 195, 196, 224
Roper, Stephanie 195, 224
Rosario, Edwin, "Chapo" 152, 153, 173, 209
Rose Bowl 99, 100
Rose Bowl Parade 99
Russell, Bertrand 13
Ruth, Babe 71, 169, 172

St. Patrick's Roman Catholic Church 123
Sammo, Bill 70, 71, 231
Samson 224
Sands Hotel/Casino 203
Santemore, Walter 173, 175
Sarah Lawrence College 196
Scaff, Sammy 126, 127, 233
Schaeffer, Bill 208
Schultz, Dutch 12
Schwarzenegger, Arnold 95, 150, 198
Scott, Mark 72, 232

Scott, Richard 209
Seaver, Tom 117
17th Olympic Winter Games 78–79
Shanagher, Don 11, 50, 51, 103, 117
Shanagher, Pat 39
Shang, William 40
Shavers, Ernie 147, 174, 218
Shaw University 185
Shea, John 39, 231
Shoemaker, Willie 73
Simon, Mercea 177
Simpson, Dion 119
Sims, Jeff 165
Sims, Larry 116, 233
Sinatra, Frank 227
Singleton, John 96
Singleton, Trent 107, 233
Smith, Charles, "Tombstone" 141, 142, 144
Smith, James, "Bonecrusher" 144, 157, 166, 184–186, 188, 191–193, 195–198, 200, 201, 234
Smith, Rod 165
Snipes, Renaldo 74, 125, 153, 177, 218
Soto, Hector 39
Spain, Ricardo 113, 114, 233
Special Olympics 198
Spinks, Leon 39
Spinks, Michael 119, 158, 165, 168, 170, 173, 174, 184, 185, 190, 191, 196, 202, 203, 207, 208, 214, 215, 219, 220, 224–230, 234
Spofford Juvenile Center 8
Sports Extra, Channel 5, New York 149
Sports Illustrated 127, 131
Sports Look 188
Stallone, Sylvester 179
Stapleton International Airport 40
Steele, Richard 170, 193
Stenison, Marvin 97
Stevenson, Teofilo 80
Stevensville Country Club 152
Stewart, Bobby 9–11
Stickles, Dick 101, 140, 187
Stokes, Andrew 68, 231
Strawberry, Daryl 164
Strong, Bob 71
Sulaiman, Jose 63, 171
Sullivan, John L. 93, 210, 214, 215, 227
Sullivan, Tom 108, 114, 117
Summer Olympic Games: 1952 17, 18; 1984 67, 68, 73, 74, 77, 82–90, 98, 194
Super Bowl III 79
Sutherland, Murray 132
Sutton, Danny 193
Syracuse Carrier Dome 121
Szegora, Istvan 93, 94, 232

Tangstad, Stefan 135, 158, 168, 170
Tate, Frank 174
Tate, John 96, 124, 177
Teena Marie 13
Thomas, Pinklon 101, 114, 135, 169, 176, 177, 193, 194, 198–204, 234

Index

Thompson, Jeff 83, 232
Thompson, Warren 68, 231
Thurber, James 83
Thurman, Charles 102
Tiger, Dick 22
Tilden, Bill 71
Tillis, James, "Quick" 74, 142–147, 155, 159, 174, 191, 195, 196, 209, 217, 233
Tillman, Henry 72, 85–89, 98, 114, 152, 153, 194, 232
Time 186, 187, 224
Times Herald Record, Middletown, N. Y. 156
Times Square Boxing Club 125
Tita, Vasile 17, 18
Today on NBC 127, 194, 227
Tompkins, Barry 166, 169, 170
Top Rank, Inc. 171
Torres, Jose 21, 22, 29, 97, 123, 169, 178
Tosto, Danny 14
Tri City Promotions 102, 107, 112, 120
Trump, Donald 185, 191, 207–210, 220, 226, 227
Trump Hotel and Casino 114, 119, 131, 166, 191, 208, 209, 220
Trump Plaza, Atlantic City 185, 207, 208, 210
Tryon Division For Youth *see* Johnstown Juvenile Center
Tubbs, Tony 125, 131, 141, 158, 184, 194, 215, 220, 221, 223, 234
Tucker, Tony 174, 190, 191, 202, 204, 206, 207, 218, 234
Tunney, Gene 71
Turek, John 38, 101, 140, 187
Turn of the Century Fights, Inc. 34
Turner, Ira 40, 231
Tyson, Denise, "Nisee" 3, 4, 6, 7, 43

Tyson, Lorna (Smith) 3–5, 7–8, 43, 61, 65
Tyson, Michael Gerard (Mike) 1, 3–11, 25–45, 48–59, 61–75, 77–224, 226–230, 232, 234
Tyson, Rodney 3, 4, 7, 43

Ueno Zoo 222
United States Air Force Academy 40, 42, 53, 72, 74
United States Amateur Boxing Championships 62, 72, 92
University of Southern California (USC) 100

Valenzuela, Fernando 157
Vanderbilt, Gloria 126
Vanderbilt Hotel 5

Waldorf Astoria 199
Walker, Mickey 149
Wallau, Alex 137
Walters, Barbara 197
Washington Huskies 100
WBC Champion 176
Weaver, Mike 135
Weill, Al 19
Wembley Stadium 158
Wesley, Randy 41, 231
Western Massachusetts Golden Gloves Tournament 66
Whitaker, Pernell 89
White, Bill 186, 188
Whittaker, Lou 157
Wide World of Sports 156
Willard, Jess 96, 177
Williams, Carl, "The Truth" 70, 73, 108, 109, 112, 117, 134, 135, 145
Williams, Johnny 81, 232
Williams, Mike 175, 185, 186
Williams, Ron 68, 231

Williams, Ted 208
Wilson, Ken 132
Wiltwyck School For Boys 17
Wimbledon 114, 115
Winfield, Dave 152, 185
Winkle, Rip van 23
Witherspoon, Anthony 205, 206
Witherspoon, "Terrible Tim" 117, 125, 127, 131, 135, 144, 157, 158, 169, 184, 196, 200, 206, 220
Wolgast, Ad 31
World Boxing Association (WBA) 21, 63, 113, 135, 144, 158, 170, 172, 173, 178, 184–186, 191–197, 202, 206, 207, 220, 223, 230, 234
World Boxing Council (WBC) 63, 135, 141, 147, 151, 152, 154, 156, 158, 164, 168, 170–173, 176–179, 181, 183–187, 192, 193, 195, 200, 202, 206, 207, 233, 234
World Boxing Day 108
Wright, Garland 105
WTEN, CH-10, Albany N.Y. 104, 109, 118

Yankee Stadium 152, 164
Yeats, Barry 124
Yonko, Dave 72, 232
Young, Dick 208
Young, Gary 39, 40
Young, Greg 39, 59
Young, Jimmy 101, 108, 117, 144
Young, Kevin 39
Young, Mark 128, 233
Young, Rodney 39
Young Adult Institute (YAI) 197, 198
Young-Su 89

Zouski, Steve 141–143, 159, 191, 233